D1254207

The Path of the Righteous
Gentile Rescuers of Jews
During the Holocaust

The Path of the Righteous

Gentile Rescuers of Jews During the Holocaust

by
Mordecai Paldiel

Foreword by
Harold M. Schulweis

Afterword by
Abraham H. Foxman

KTAV Publishing House, Inc.
Hoboken, New Jersey 07030

in association with

The Jewish Foundation for Christian Rescuers / ADL
New York, New York 10017

Library of Congress Cataloging-in-Publication Data

Paldiel, Mordecai.
    The path of the righteous : gentile rescuers of Jews during the
Holocaust / by Mordecai Paldiel.
        p.   cm.
    Includes bibliographical references and index.
    ISBN 0-88125-376-6
    1. Righteous Gentiles in the Holocaust--Biography. I. Title.
D804.3P35   1992
940.53'18--dc20   92-34501
                                                               CIP

Manufactured in the United States of America

To Sigalit, Iris and Eli --
words of hope and inspiration

Contents

Foreword
The Moral Art of Memory

A fascinating tale told by Jorge Luis Borges in his *Funes the Memorious* is cited by Yosef Hayyim Yerushalmi in his *Zechor*. As a result of a fall from his horse at the age of 19, Ireneo Funes discovered that he could forget nothing, absolutely nothing. If you and I perceive three wine glasses on the table, Funes would see all the shoots, clusters, and grapes. ". . . in effect, Funes remembered not only every leaf of every tree of every wood but every one of the times he had perceived or imagined it."

* * *

Funes possessed an astounding retentiveness, but his gift of memory was hardly an unalloyed blessing. The scholar S.D. Luzzatto observed, "To remember much is not necessarily to be wise." Memory is not a camera indiscriminately recording everything. The art of memory is selective. Remembering the past, it has an eye on the future. Undifferentiated, memory may be a blessing or a curse, an ally of wisdom or of folly, a supporter of hope or despair.

We are mandated to remember; the Hebrew verb *zachar* appears no less than 169 times in the Bible. Before us is the mandate not to forget the Holocaust. But the question of our time is not whether to remember but what to remember and how to transmit our memory to our children and our children's children. "Only take heed to thyself, and keep thy soul diligently, lest thou forget the things which thine eyes have seen, and lest they depart from thy heart all the days of thy life: but make them known unto thy children and thy children's children" (Deuteronomy 4:9).

How shall we remind them of the Holocaust? My children were not even born during those fateful times. Still they must know the awesome truth. In Cicero's words, "Not to know what happened before you were born is to remain forever a child." It is irresponsible to raise a child who is fatally ignorant.

There are many reasons not to forget the Shoah (Holocaust). Memory is a warning, a protest, and an act of fidelity to the martyrs. More personally, I want my children to know the Holocaust so that they may better understand me, my fears, my anxieties, and, if you will, my hard-earned paranoia.

For me and my generation, the Holocaust remains the dominant psychic reality of our lives. Without knowledge of that reality, my offspring will have difficulty understanding my reactions to events that others seem to take in stride: my heightened sensitivity to the vandalizing of skinheads, the xenophobic rantings of rappers, the presentation of the Passion Play at Oberammergau, the rhetoric of David Duke and Louis Farakhan, the poisonous nativism of Jean-Marie Le Pen, the resurgence of the Fascist Ustashi movement in Croatia, the antisemitic stirrings of the People's Russian Christian Orthodox movement and the Pamyat.

To remember that past is painful. Perhaps it is to overcome our resistance to such memory that we are so often enjoined not to forget. To view, even on film, the charred skeletons, the mass graves, the excremental assault on the dignity of human begins is frightening and humiliating. To show it to our children's children is harder yet.

Every annual Yom Ha-Shoah commemoration brings new testimony of the previously forgotten: nightmares told by friends, congregants, survivors, and the children of survivors. A few years ago a psychiatrist, friend and congregant, shared with me his memories of Kristallnacht – the long, dark night of November 9, 1938, during which two hundred synagogues were destroyed, seven hundred Jewish businesses ransacked and burned, and twenty thousand Jewish men thrown into concentration camps. His father, a prominent physician in Frankfurt, was arrested by the Gestapo on Kristallnacht, dragged and thrown into a dark room, and seated before a large table. On the table were ten decapitated Jewish heads upon which the Nazis had placed ten skullcaps. They taunted him, "Here, Jude, is your minyan!" His memory is now mine. Shall I pass it on to my children?

At school assemblies annually memorializing the Holocaust, a short story by the Hebrew writer Hayim Hazaz, entitled "The Sermon" comes to mind. In the story Yudka, normally an inarticulate member of a kibbutz who rarely speaks on such occasions, startles everyone at the kibbutz meeting when he rises to declare, "I want to state that I am opposed to Jewish history." His stammering gives way to fury. "I would simply forbid teaching our children Jewish history. Why the devil teach them about our ancestors' shame? I would just say to them: boys from the day we were exiled from our land we've been a people without a history. Class dismissed. Go out and play football." There are times when I ask myself how wise it is to lay a stone upon the hearts of children, to crush their trust and hope with such morbidity. I am tempted to echo Yudka's "Go out and play football." And yet I know that we are morally mandated to keep that memory, though "the past weighs like a nightmare on the brain of the living" (Sartre).

More than the pedagogic question of how to transmit the Shoah to children troubles me. The memory of the Holocaust taunts my faith. So much of our tradition is based on the theological humanism drawn from the root belief reiterated in Genesis, "And God created the human being in His own image; in the image of God, male and female, created He them. God formed the human being and breathed into his nostrils the breath of life, and the human being became a living soul" (Genesis 1:27). It is the human being whom the psalmist declares to be "but a little lower than God." Characteristic of this religious humanism is the rabbinic interpretation of a verse in Deuteronomy that admonishes us not to allow a criminal to hang overnight because to do so is "a reproach unto God." Why is it considered a reproach unto God? The rabbinic commentators answer through a stunning parable: A noble king had a twin brother who was caught committing a crime, sentenced to death, and hanged in the public square. When the people passed by the hanging corpse of the king's twin, they cried out, "See the king is dead." In this rabbinic metaphor, God and man are twins. To defame man is to disgrace God. Divinity and humanity are inextricably bound. When asked to explain the wretched condition of the world, Rabbi Aaron of Karlin declared, "Either God is God and we are not helping Him or God is not God and it is all our fault." In any event, the dignity, power, and responsibility of the human being in the tradition is central. Either as partner with God or alone in the world, the integrity of the human image must be preserved.

Yet staring at the tortured image of Holocaust history, the tradition of theistic humanism is shaken to its foundation. The evidence of the betrayal of allies, the merciless neutrality of churches and states, the predators and the passive onlookers grind faith in the divine image into the fine dust of homiletic fantasy. Neither the arguments of Kant nor of Feuerbach are as devastating to belief as the stark statistics of the Holocaust. One and one-half million children murdered because of their Jewishness; nine of every ten European rabbis killed; ninety percent of East European Jewry decimated; two out of every three Jews living in Europe murdered; one third of a people condemned to death.

The memory of the Shoah further exacerbates the painful dissonance between history and theology, between memory and faith. Observing the deformed image of man, who can sustain praise of the image-maker with a straight face? Who can speak of the human being as the crown of His creation? Menachem Mendel of Vitebsk once said, "All my life I have struggled in vain to know what man is. Now I know. Man is the language of God." After Auschwitz, what language are we to use?

My teacher Abraham Joshua Heschel wrote, "If you ask me how to begin teaching children the conception of God, I would tell you to begin by teaching the conception of human nature." I ask myself how, in the wake of the Holocaust, human nature is to be taught? Is the Holocaust anything but a baleful confirmation of the denigration of human nature, a dark ratification of the pessimism and cynicism found in Hobbes, Machiavelli, Nietzsche, and Freud? Is not this sorrowful judgment reflected in our literature, in the theater, in movies, and on television? The negative characterization of human nature finds voice in a statement by the playwright Tennessee Williams: "The only difference between man and the other beasts is that a man is a beast who knows that he will die. . . . the only honest man is an unabashed egoist. . . . the specific ends of life are sex and money, so the human comedy is an outrageous medley of lechery, alcoholism, homosexuality, blasphemy, greed, brutality, hatred, obscenity."

I confess that I am drawn to the phenomenon of altruism carefully documented by Mordecai Paldiel in this remarkable book on rescue behavior not for the sake of historiography, or sociology, or psychology alone. I am drawn to his documentation of moral heroism for the sake of morality and morale and the future of civilization. In this record, we are presented with another glimpse of history.

History is not our enemy, and Yudka's stand in opposition to history cannot and need not be ours. We need not counsel our children to escape history on the playing field. The history of evil need not be suppressed in order to serve my wishful thinking. History must not be bent to fit into hopeful theological convictions. The role of memory need not and should not be blurred to save ourselves from the terrible revelations of ugly truths.

But if memory bears a responsibility for the future, if it is more than an open camera, it may not ignore the moral and morale implications of its teachings. Here enters the spiritual and educative significance of the Jewish Foundation for Christian Rescuers and of Paldiel's definitive study.

In the rescue behavior of ordinary men and women, valuable historical data – long buried in anonymity – are a treasure of information that must be unearthed from incidental footnotes and raised into the body of the text. This growing body of empirical data must be integrated into an honest transmission of the past.

The options before us are not those of either Cassandra or Pollyanna. The choice is not between reality and illusion. The goodness of rescuers is not wishful thinking or desperate fantasy. Before us is a documented reality of rare and precious power. While the evidence of goodness cannot and should not be used to counterbalance the record of evil quantitatively, its qualitative goodness may enable us to walk more confidently through the valley of the shadow of death. The episodes of tens of thousands of non-Jews who risked life and limb to protect doomed people of another faith are as real as the fires of the crematoria. The fact of heroic benevolence is indispensable for the transmission of sacred memory.

Our quarrel is not with history. Our quarrel is with the abuse of history that transmogrifies the incomparable tragedy into a polarizing metaphysics. History should not be manipulated into a metaphysics of despair and cynicism. The evidence, collected and still being collected, of rescue behavior by tens of thousands of men and women, contradicts the Manichean metaphysics surreptitiously imposed upon history and destiny. I refer to the schismatic Weltanschauung that views the world as primordially fissured into "them" and "us." This fatalistic view of history interprets the horror of the Shoah as confirmation of a dogma of the eternal recurrence of hatred against Jews. The history of the Holocaust directed by this dichotomous metaphysics serves to immortalize the divisiveness between peoples. Consciously or not it visits the curses of the past onto the future. It filters down a pessimism that forecloses the possibilities of the future, and paralyzes the human will to repair. It robs the post-Holocaust generation of that singular virtue that Erik Erikson identified as indispensable for vitality: "basic trust"; not Pollyanna naivete, but "the favorable ratio of basic trust over basic distrust." This basic trust, in religious vocabulary, is called *emunah*, "faith." It brings no honor to the victims and martyrs of the Holocaust to distort the character of human nature so that any and every evidence of human decency and moral courage is a priori dismissed as so much homiletical cant. It is no honor to religion to see men and women turn to God not out of love but out of revulsion for His human creation.

Let there be no misunderstanding. Paldiel's presentations of the evidence of altruism in no way deny the terrifying capacity of human beings to hurt and torture innocents, to seek out scapegoats, to salve the angers and frustrations of the predators. But the evidence of human goodness, of moral courage by tens of thousands caught in the vise of life-and-death choices, helps puncture the monolithic bias against human nature – *homo homini lupus*, man is to man a wolf – that prejudice which led even John Stuart Mill to dismiss altruism as an "egoisme à deux, à trois, à quatre".

A word about numbers. On a quantitative scale, altruism weighs in light. But some things small in number are great in consequence. The goodness we recognize is not a matter of numbers nor even of grand acts. Goodness in the hell of the camps was as simple as a boiled potato, a piece of bread, a mashed strawberry given to a starving and forlorn fellow inmate. I think of Primo Levi's account of Lorenzo, the non-Jewish Italian civilian worker who brought him a piece of bread and the remainder of his ration every day for 6 months in the concentration camp. Levi writes, "I believe it was really due to Lorenzo that I am alive today; and not so much for his material aid, as for his having constantly reminded me by his presence, by his natural and plain manner of being good, that there still exists a just world outside our own, something and someone still pure and whole, not corrupt, not savage . . . something difficult to define, a remote possibility of good but for which it was worth surviving. Thanks to Lorenzo I managed not to forget that I myself was a man" (*Survival in Auschwitz*).

We and our children need to know the something and someone, the reality of good for which it is worth surviving and that reminds us that we are men and women. We and they need to know names and places and the flesh-and-blood farmers, priests, nuns, and soldiers, the believers and nonbelievers, the old and the young from every background in every land who made the impossible possible.

It is important that children know everything. Why should our children and our children's children know only and exclusively the betrayals and cruelty, and nothing of the secret pacts of goodness, of simple men and women who, in the prophet Isaiah's words, "turned themselves into hiding places from the wind and shelters from the tempests"? Children who are not to be denied exposure to the facts of sadism and villainous exploitation ought not to be deprived of the tears of joy from the tales of the decency of ordinary people who shielded the hunted with their bodies. Reading this book, we are reminded that there are no heroes without villains, no rescuers without the estranged.

It is immoral and foolish to extinguish the few rays of light lest they brighten the darkness of the cave. If anything, the moral heroism of the rescuing minority illuminates the desecration of the majority. There are no heroes without villains. There were villains. But there were heroes. The post-Holocaust generation must know of those moral heroes who through their lives gave the lie to the alibi that there was no alternative to passive complicity with the enemy.

The witness we possess is particularly important in our times. For everywhere on this globe–in Europe, in the Middle East, in our home neighborhoods–there are ominous signs of a growing parochialism, a xenophobic nativism whose justification of corporate selfishness resonates with the insular ethos of Sodom and Gomorrah: "Mine is mine and yours is yours."

We must not lose sight of the singular character of altruism that drives the efforts of the Jewish Foundation for Christian Rescuers. It is not only the recognition of goodness that sacrifices self-interest for others that demands our attention, but the uniquely transcendent morality of the rescuers who risked their selves for others beyond their church, beyond their people, beyond their co-religionists.

In an era of moral isolationism in which the ethics of universalism is derided, it is all the more important to recall how many rescuers saw in the victims of hatred they protected not a believer or disbeliever, not a partisan, not a Jew, but, as the rescuers have so repeatedly stated, a human being, a man, a woman, a child of God.

The behavior of the rescuers has something important to teach us to counter the growing insularity of our times. They teach us the need to define or redefine the biblical meaning of "neighbor." Who is the neighbor define or redefine the biblical meaning of "neighbor." Who is the neighbor I am to love, against whom I must not bear false witness, who I must not defraud, and before whose blood I must not stand idly by nor hate in my heart? The rescuers defined "my neighbor" with the lexicon of their bodies. "The neighbor is not confined to the four cubits within my religious or ethnic jurisdiction. The neighbor is not restricted by my color or my catechism, but embraces those who stand outside the circle of our own faith and fate." Goodness must be searched for. It enjoys a poor public relations. Goodness must be studied. It has too long been held in abeyance. Theologians have spent much energy wrestling with the whence of evil – *unde malum*. They must turn some of their attention to *unde bonum* –whence goodness. Goodness is no less a mystery than evil. In my tradition, God is said to declare, "I am God only when you are My witnesses. If you are not My witness, I am, as it were, not God." Our memory calls for dual testimony: "Remember the evil and do not forget the good." Memory is an ambiguous energy; wisely used it is a life-affirming art, a blessing for our civilization, a gift of hope for our children. Distorted, it favors malediction and death. The Jewish Foundation is proud to co-publish this comprehensive work of scholarship which uncovers the sacred spark buried in the hell of darkness.

Rabbi Harold M. Schulweis,
Founding Chairman of The Jewish Foundation
for Christian Rescuers/ADL

Author's Preface

As I stood before the audience at the cultural center in Annecy, situated on the charming lake that attracts thousands of visitors to this beautiful corner of southeastern France, and glanced at my family's rescuer, it seemed that a full circle had been drawn. At last I was able to bestow upon Father Simon Gallay the honor he deserved. A debt had been paid, a moral obligation requited, and another rescue story could now be added to the annals of humanitarianism.

It had all started on an autumn day in 1943.

My family had found a temporary refuge from Nazi persecution in a tranquil village in the Haute-Savoie region of southeastern France, which was under Italian occupation. However, when Italy surrendered to the Allies in September of 1943 and the Germans moved into the Italian zone, our brief respite came to an abrupt end. Hurriedly leaving for Grenoble, we thence continued to Evian, near the Swiss frontier, where we had been told to contact the priest at the local church.

As we alighted from the train at the Evian station, we saw German troops milling about on the platform. While my father and I and my five siblings waited at the station, my mother proceeded to the church. The priest listened to her story and without hesitation said he would help us escape to Switzerland. Greatly relieved of her fears, and touched by the priest's magnanimity, my mother abruptly removed her wedding ring and offered it as a gift for the church, but the priest refused to accept it. Instead he told my mother to bring the rest of us to the baptistry.

After we arrived and had eaten the meal he provided, he arranged for us to hide in an isolated house near the border. We remained there for several days until it was deemed safe to attempt a crossing. One evening we were taken to the border and guided through a double barbed-wire fence into Switzerland.

On the Swiss side we were apprehended by border guards. They could have returned us to France, but instead they took us to a detention camp. We remained there for a while but finally obtained permission to live in Geneva until the war's end.

Upon my nomination as director of the Department for the Righteous at Yad Vashem in 1982, I began to make inquiries about the anonymous priest. After a long search (with the help of friends and colleagues) I learned his name and found that he was living in Annecy, where he had settled upon his retirement.

In 1988, thanks to the testimony of my parents and several other people he had helped, Father Simon Gallay was recognized by Yad Vashem as one of the Righteous Among the Nations. On May 6, 1990, I arrived in Annecy from Jerusalem, and in a moving ceremony, attended by religious and lay dignitaries, awarded my benefactor the medal and certificate of honor of the Righteous Among the Nations.

Thus a moral obligation had been faithfully discharged and a man publicly lauded for having defied the Nazis, asserting his humanity and (in his own words) keeping faith with his priestly vocation.

In 1946, when the Anne Frank diary first came to light, the following appeared in a Dutch newspaper:

> That this girl could have been abducted and murdered proves to me that we have lost the fight against human bestiality. And for the same reason we shall lose it again, in whatever form inhumanity may reach out to us, if we are unable to put something positive in its place. The promise that we shall never forget or forgive is not enough. It is not even enough to keep that promise. Passive and negative rejection is too little, it is as nothing.[1]

Little did the journalist who wrote this suspect that Yad Vashem in Jerusalem, Israel's official national Holocaust commemoration institute, would create a program for honoring non-Jews who had risked their lives to save Jews. Up to now, over 10,000 persons have been recognized by Yad Vashem. Reports in our files indicate that many more would be eligible if the institute's evidentiary standards were less rigorous. In many cases, for instance, the people who were rescued are now dead, and thus it is impossible to satisfy the requirement that rescue accounts must be substantiated by the testimony of the rescued. The courageous deeds of these knights of the spirit are, I submit, the proper response that the Dutch journalist vainly sought in order to counter the bitter legacy left by the Nazi criminals. The moral rectitude shown by these courageous men and women represents a challenge to the view that might is right, as well as to

---

1. Jan Romein, in *Het Parool*, April 3, 1946, cited in D. Barnouw and C. Van der Stroum, eds., *The Diary of Anne Frank: The Critical Edition* (New York: Doubleday, 1989), p. 68.

the notion that human nature is inherently aggressive (pontificated by such luminaries of the intellect as Hobbes and Freud), ideas which tend to describe man at his worst.

The deeds of these righteous persons, as illustrated in this book, are proof that the fight for humanity has not been lost, that man's true essence resides neither in his physical strength nor in his vaunted egoistic drives, but in his spirituality and humanity. The stories of the Righteous Gentiles are an inspiring tool with which we can work toward a better and more humane world. To the furthering of this goal, this book is dedicated.

In the fires of war, in the flame, in the flare,
In the eye-blinding, searing glare,
My little lantern I carry high
To search, to search for true Man.

In the glare the light of my lantern burns dim,
In the fire-glow my eye cannot see,
How to look, to see, to discover, to know
When he stands there facing me?

Set a sign, O Lord, set a sign on his brow
That in heat, fire and burning, I may
Know the pure, the eternal spark
Of what I seek: true Man.

—Hannah Szenes
*Executed in 1944 while on a
rescue mission inside Hungary*

Introduction

The Holocaust has been called a "tremendum." This grave and solemn term underscores its almost unimaginable fearfulness and magnitude.

Inexplicable by any normal standard of human conduct, the Holocaust was both an immanent and a transcendental event. This enormous and unspeakable crime was conceived, designed, and presided over by mortal beings, born and raised in a nation that stood in the vanguard of the modern era's cultural, philosophical, and scientific achievements. The deed (or rather misdeed) actually happened, and was perpetrated right here on planet earth, before our very eyes.

At the same time, this monumental outrage and unforgivable crime, this "massive assault upon civilization," in the words of Franklin Littell, was an event so immensely mind-boggling that it seems to have been an intrusion from a different universe. Nothing in history remotely resembles the horrors of Auschwitz. In this sense, the Holocaust transcends the reality of human life as predicated by the civilized values of all societies— as though a satanic meteor had captured and convulsed the lives of perpetrators, victims, and bystanders alike during the years of the Nazi reign of terror.

The Holocaust is, and will remain, an affront to the accumulated values and ethics of the entire course of man's history. It challenges the moral foundations of our civilization and our fond belief that we humans are sensitive, caring creatures.

The outrages committed during the Holocaust by a supposedly civilized nation may lead many sensible people to despairingly concur with those who believe that evil is the supreme force in human life; that man, at his profoundest level, is but an incorrigible brute, bent on an uncontrollable rampage of destruction if not inhibited by the laws of society and religion.

In light of this, what follows may strike the reader as paradoxical. For it is the major premise of this book that goodness is an inherent human attribute and predisposition, common to all of us whatever our background and beliefs—and as potentially effective as evil. Goodness is present throughout our lives but is not accorded due measure because of society's proclivity to give priority to the constituents of evil: to aggressiveness, competitiveness, pride, honor, and self-conceit.

Even the Bible gives voice to this view, as we can see from its assertion that "the imagination of man's heart is evil from his youth" (Genesis 8:21). The emphasis on man's evil disposition and fallen state was intensified by the Essenes, and later by certain tendencies in Christianity. In the secular sphere it is exemplified by the Hobbesian claim that man is inherently aggressive and the Freudian belief that he is but "a savage beast to whom consideration towards his own kind is something alien." From this standpoint, the prime function of society and religion is to rein in man's savage inclination, to prevent him from wreaking chaos upon others and himself, in the process bringing about the destruction of civilized life.

But the Bible also teaches us that man is but a step lower than the angels (Psalms 8:6); and that *hesed*, the quality of gratuitous love, was one of the elements with which the world was created. Indeed, the person of God is on many occasions identified with this attribute. "Save us in thy *hesed*," and "in the abundance of thy *hesed* answer me," implores the psalmist (Psalms 31:17, 69:14).

This theme served as midrashic material for the Sages of the first and second centuries. In rabbinic Judaism, the interplay in each person between the evil inclination (*yetzer hara*) and the good inclination (*yetzer hatov*) was considered essential for a balanced life, with priority given to the good inclination through the practice of Torah laws and ethics.

Thus, the idea that man was capable of good and meritorious deeds, for their own sake and without consideration of the advantages obtained by performing them, gained credence in ancient teachings. Nonetheless, it was usurped and supplanted by a more somber and pessimistic philosophy which regarded man as his own worst enemy and not to be trusted, since his main desire was to give free rein to his ego, with catastrophic consequences to all and sundry.

With this negativist philosophy in the ascendancy, it is no wonder that helping others in times of stress, without egotistical motivation and as an act of pure benevolence, was generally ridiculed as naive and foolish. Personal biases and prejudices, coupled with societal pressures, inhibited (and still do) most people from exercising their natural human predisposition to help others. When affective influences (i.e., social and personal prejudices against the oppressed group) and fear of retribution are added to the low esteem for altruistic acts, it is perhaps no wonder that so few, relatively speaking, have ever been willing to confront and brush aside the dangers to themselves and assert their humanity by coming to the aid of those in need.

During the Holocaust, the two latter of these three factors were especially prominent: prejudice against the oppressed group in the form of antisemitism, which in many ways prepared the ground for the Final Solution, and fear of retribution by the Germans for the "grave offense" of helping a Jew survive the Nazi hell.

Insofar as antisemitism is concerned, the record is clear and one need not long dwell on it. The degree of anti-Jewish feeling in any given country may be debatable, and so may be the question of whether any particular outbreak is a more or less virulent display of this vile phenomenon, but it is not possible to deny the presence of antisemitism and its effect on people's behavior.

In general, in the countries of Eastern Europe, most people were not too displeased, to put it mildly, to see the Jews vanish from the landscape (with the Germans taking all the blame) and looked askance at efforts by their own countrymen to obstruct the Nazi death machine. Those who defied this deeply ingrained hatred were often subjected to ostracism and physical violence.

In Western Europe, anti-Jewish feelings were more sublimated and thus less immediately evident, yet helping Jews was not the most popular cause, and certainly not one that would earn the doer the rewards of public approbation and praise. Here, too, the forces militating against such behavior were equal to, if not stronger than, those favoring it.

The second inhibiting factor was fear of retribution. The Germans made no secret of their determination to rid the European continent of all its Jewish inhabitants. The conquered populations were warned in no uncertain terms of the dire consequences for anyone who tried to thwart the effort to make Europe *Judenrein*.

On the Nazi scale of values, helping a Jew was a capital offense as serious as committing an act of treason against the Third Reich. The penalty for helping a Jew to elude a Nazi roundup was either the death penalty or incarceration in a concentration camp. The helper's family would suffer also, and might well incur the same punishment. Every means was used to make the public aware of this. Consider, for example, the following proclamation by Dr. Ludwig Fischer, the German district governor of Warsaw, on November 10, 1941:

> *Concerning the Death Penalty for Illegally Leaving Jewish Residential Districts*...Any Jew who illegally leaves the designated residential district will be punished by death. Anyone who deliberately offers refuge to such Jews or who aids them in any other manner (i.e., offering a night's lodging, food, or by taking them into vehicles of any kind, etc.) will be subject to the same punishment. Judgment will be rendered by a Special Court in Warsaw. I forcefully draw the attention of the entire population of the Warsaw District to this new decree, as henceforth it will be applied with the utmost severity.[1]

1. Yad Vashem Archives.

This warning, issued in German and Polish, was posted in public places throughout Warsaw at a time when many Jews were already in hiding in various parts of the Aryan (i.e., non-Jewish) section of the city.

The threat of retribution, not only to oneself, which for some individuals might have been bearable, but to one's family and loved ones, was probably enough to prevent most people from defying the Nazis. Life under the German occupation was precarious enough; it may well have seemed the height of foolishness to jeopardize it still further. When antisemitism and the social disinclination against radical altruism are added on, it is perhaps no surprise that very few were willing to champion the cause of humanity.

In any case, the Nazi death machine was so well oiled and efficiently operated that, given Germany's military might, the rescue of the overwhelming majority of the Jews of Europe would probably only have been possible if there had been a massive intervention by the Allies (e.g., by bombing the death facilities and the railroad tracks leading to the camps). Since nothing of the sort was forthcoming, the only rescue undertakings to occur were isolated efforts by fearless men and women operating either alone or in small clandestine groups. They could at best save but a relative handful.

No exact figures are available on the number of Jews saved through the help of individual non-Jews, but the total runs in the tens of thousands. In France, for instance, up to 200,000 Jews (two-thirds of French Jewry) were able to survive, many of them thanks to help provided by non-Jews. The approximate comparable figures for some other European countries are: Belgium, 26,000 (45 percent); the Netherlands, 16,000 (11 percent; an additional 6,000 in hiding were betrayed or discovered and arrested); Italy, 35,000 (80 percent); Denmark, 7,200 (90 percent); Norway, 1,000 (50 percent); Germany and Austria, 3,000 to 5,000 (2 percent); Poland, 25,000 to 40,000 (up to 1.5 percent); Hungary, over 200,000 (26 percent; a great part of this due to the superhuman efforts of Raoul Wallenberg and fellow colleague diplomats).

Only a fraction of the Jews in Nazi-occupied Europe were saved. And yet the fact that thousands of non-Jews, in every country of occupied Europe and despite the most oppressive circumstances, voluntarily endangered themselves to save Jews is a heartening phenomenon. It leaves the door open for the hope that the cause of humanity is not entirely lost.

The tiny band of courageous men and women who risked all to save Jewish victims from the Nazis had no ulterior motives. They stood up for decency when Germany's power was at its height and there was no way of divining the war's outcome or duration. In most instances they did what they did alone, or almost alone, without reward or encouragement. They acted, as they themselves have explained, because they felt that it was their religious duty or because it seemed the "natural" thing to do. Some of them have said that they would have been ashamed of themselves as human beings if they had not intervened.

Yad Vashem in Jerusalem, established by law in 1953 for the purpose of commemorating the victims of the Holocaust, has from its inception seen as one of its primary tasks the obligation to honor non-Jews who made it possible for Jews to survive—the Righteous Among the Nations, or "Righteous Gentiles" in popular parlance.

The program for honoring the Righteous Among the Nations was launched in 1962 with the dedication of the Garden of the Righteous by the then Minister of Foreign Affairs, Mrs. Golda Meir. That year a permanent committee for designating those qualified as Righteous Gentiles was set up, composed of over a dozen members and headed by a Supreme Court judge. The committee includes people from various public bodies, professions, and walks of life, almost all of them survivors of the Holocaust. Its duty is to meticulously study all applications for recognition, based on evidence provided by survivors and other relevant bona fide documentation, and to decide upon whom to bestow the honorific title of Righteous Among the Nations.

In order to arrive, as much as possible, at a fair evaluation of a rescuer's contribution to the saving of Jewish lives, the committee takes into consideration all the circumstances relating to the rescue, as well as the rescuer's motivations and the personal risks involved.

The criteria for admission to this unique international hall of fame include the following:

1. The rescuer extended aid to a Jew or Jews in danger of being killed or sent to a concentration camp, thus ensuring their survival.

2. The rescuer was fully aware that by doing this he was risking his own life, freedom, and safety.

3. The rescuer did not exact any material reward or compensation at the time of the rescue, and did not require any promise of compensation, either oral or in writing, as a condition for the aid he was giving.

4. The rescuer's role was not passive (e.g., failing to turn in a Jewish fugitive) but active; he acted on his own initiative, was directly involved and personally responsible, and in effect "caused" a rescue that would not otherwise have taken place.

5. The act of rescue or aid can be authenticated by evidence provided by the rescued persons or by other eyewitnesses and, whenever possible, by relevant bona-fide documentation (e.g., German court records for those tried on the charge of harboring or extending aid to Jews).

The committee also examines the following elements in the rescue story: (1) how the original contact was made between rescuer and rescued; (2) the nature of the aid extended; (3) the rescuer's motivations insofar as they are ascertainable (e.g., friendship, altruism, religious belief, humanitarian considerations, etc.); (4) whether any material compensation was paid in return for the aid extended, and if so, in what amounts; (5) the dangers and risks faced by the rescuer at the time; (6) the age of the persons submitting evidence; (7) relations between rescuer and rescued during the period of aid; (8) other relevent data and pertinent documentation shedding light on the authenticity and uniqueness of each rescue story.

In general, when the data on hand clearly demonstrate that a non-Jewish person, without obtaining any tangible benefits, risked his (or her) life, freedom, or safety in order to save one or several Jews from the threat of death or of deportation to a death camp, he (or she) is eligible for the title of Righteous Among the Nations. This applies even if the rescuer is dead, since the title can be given posthumously.

A person designated as one of the Righteous Among the Nations is awarded a specially minted medal bearing his name and a certificate of honor; and his name is inscribed in the Garden of the Righteous.

Those recognized so far as Righteous Among the Nations come from all walks of life. Among them are clerics and lay persons; intellectuals and illiterates; farmers and laborers side by side with white-collar workers; professionals, civil servants, and men in uniform as well as housewives, domestics, and the unemployed. They cover, indeed, the whole gamut of social and economic classes; more from the lower economic classes in Eastern Europe (probably because they comprised the majority of the population there) and a greater proportion from the the middle classes in Central and Western Europe.

One of the surprising discoveries about the rescuers is that the vast majority were not, so to speak, saints or hermits removed from the ebb and flow of the daily struggle for existence within their societies. They were ordinary people from many different fields and social backgrounds, fully integrated in their communities. Furthermore, they themselves view their deeds as anything but extraordinary, holding them to have been just a natural outcome of a moral imperative that was binding on them and should be on everyone else.

Yad Vashem's effort to identify and honor the Righteous Among the Nations is significant for several reasons.

1. By documenting the presence of rescuers in every occupied country, it proves that helping was possible. The excuse that the Nazi terror brought about some kind of moral paralysis is belied by thousands of incidents in which non-Jews helped Jews survive the Final Solution.

2. It shows that totalitarian regimes can and should be opposed—that resistance is always possible, not only by organized groups but by individuals acting on their own.

3. By publicizing the noble deeds of the Righteous Gentiles, it consecrates the principle of the sanctity of life, reminding us that life is an inviolable right and that the death of even one innocent is a moral challenge to the rest of mankind. Hence, the motto on the Righteous

medallion, borrowed from the Talmud: "Whosoever preserves one life is as though he has preserved the entire world."

4. Finally, it encourages us to emulate the deeds of the Righteous by showing that most of them were not saints or professional do-gooders, and had not been carefully trained in tolerance and nurtured with love, care, and understanding. To the contrary, they were, by and large, quite ordinary people, some of them bearing less graceful marks and influences from their tender years, and their prewar lives hardly suggested that they would ever have endangered themselves for the sake of others.

In their recent study of altruism during the Holocaust, Samuel and Florence Oliner divide human responses to the needs of others into two categories, the ethics of equity and the ethics of care. Despite the sociological terminology, the two categories are very similar to the behavioral modes that the Jewish tradition designates as righteousness (*zedek*) and gratuitous love (*hesed*).

The ethics of equity implies a pattern of social behavior based on the principle of reciprocity and on a contractual view of social relationships. It emphasizes rationality (reason and thought) rather than emotionality (feelings and subjective reactions) and calls for the fair application of accepted norms and procedures; for the values of honesty, truth, and respect; and for giving each person what he is entitled to on the basis of social and religious norms and accepted standards of behavior.

In contrast, the ethics of care seeks the welfare of others as a good in and of itself, without regard for legalistic questions, and whether or not what one does for someone else is fair in terms of the benefits accrued by both parties. It is a willingness to give more than is received; a behavioral pattern of benevolence and kindness, of action out of concern, and it focuses totally on the other person. The ethics of care holds that helping others is not merely desirable but obligatory, and that every means of doing so is justified, even if it violates the law or accepted norms.

According to the Oliners, those who rescued Jews during the Holocaust had integrated the values of care, while those who did not were moved by the values of equity. Care compelled action; it meant assuming personal responsibility, and people motivated by this value tended to have a universalist view of ethical obligation. They saw Jews not simply as Jews but as human beings with the same rights as any other human being.[1]

The accounts presented in this book demonstrate that the ethics of care was, and is, even more powerful than students of altruism are prepared to admit (if not throughout an individual's life, then at least during certain pivotal moments), and that it affects people of virtually every background and experience. They show, as well, that altruism is unquestionably in a class of its own as a human predisposition, although it may

---

1. S. Oliner, *The Altruistic Personality*, ch. 8.

manifest itself in many different ways, depending on the circumstances, as was the case with the Righteous Gentiles of the Holocaust period.

Most of the non-Jews who helped Jews during the Holocaust were suddenly drawn into helping without previously having done much that in scope, risk, or sheer magnanimity remotely resembled what they were doing now. In many instances these acts of heroic benevolence, carried out at such great risks to the rescuers and their families, stood alone as the only out-of-the-ordinary element in what was otherwise a completely uneventful life. Yet at the same time, because such acts were often just what was needed, in the particular circumstances, to make it possible for one or several Jews to survive, they illustrate the truth of the rabbinic saying, first recorded many centuries ago, that "one gains immortality through a single deed."

Each of the following chapters is devoted to a different country during World War II, but the format throughout is the same: a brief historical sketch followed by a selection of rescue accounts based on information in the Yad Vashem archives and on other relevant sources when appropriate. The parenthetical numbers following the various rescue accounts indicate the Yad Vashem files from which material is drawn.

In telling these stories, I have tried to emphasize the humanity of these largely unknown knights of altruism. Their names, unfortunately, are nowhere near as well known as those of the perpetrators of the Holocaust, but their deeds will serve as an inspiration for generations to come. That is the promise and the hope that led me to write this book. To these champions of love for others, it is dedicated.

France

The Historical Record

On October 3, 1940, hardly four months after France's abject defeat at the hands of the Germans, the newly formed French government, established in Vichy, promulgated racial laws which affected all Jews in both the German-occupied and the unoccupied (so-called "free") zone of the country. What is striking about the Statute on the Jews is that it was enacted without German instigation and that it initially went further and was more inclusive than Nazi ordinances and plans for French Jews at the time. Thus, under French law, it sufficed for a person to have only two Jewish grandparents—as against the Nazi-required three Jewish grandparents in the occupied zone—to be excluded from an influential position in a wide range of professions and his relegation to an inferior position in French society.

This was followed in the succeeding months with additional restrictive measures: liquidation of Jewish-owned property, forced registration of Jews, and the imposition of a "J" on all Jewish-held identity cards. A special bureaucratic machinery, the Commissariat of Jewish Affairs, was established to supervise this vast operation of reimposing on a national scale the disabilities from which French Jews had suffered before the dawn of the modern era.

Reversing its prewar tradition of tolerance toward minority groups, the new semi-independent French government that rose in the aftermath of the French defeat decided, on its own initiative, to bear down strongly on the over 300,000 Jews of France, approximately half of whom resided in the southern, mostly unoccupied zone and the other half in the northern, occupied zone (the overwhelming majority of them in the Paris region).

9

One immediate tangible effect of the new policy was the rounding up of thousands of foreign Jews and their incarceration in over thirty internment camps—ineffaceable blemishes dotting the French countryside and a reminder to all and sundry of the seriousness of the Vichy-sponsored antisemitism. During 1940–42, even before the start of the deportation to the gas chambers in Poland, some 3,000 Jews died in these camps as a result of mistreatment, malnutrition, and unsanitary conditions.

Later, in collusion with Vichy authorities, the Germans initiated the forcible roundup of Jews in the Paris region on July 16, 1942. Some 9,000 French police were involved in this operation, which netted some 12,800 persons (including 3,900 children). The Germans had expected twice that number, but the lukewarm attitude of the authorities and forewarnings by policemen and neighbors made it possible for thousands to escape and seek temporary refuge in time, during this massive manhunt for Jews in the Paris region. That same year, Vichy delivered 15,000 stateless and foreign Jews to German hands. All told, some 75,000 Jews were deported to their deaths in death camps established on Polish soil before the war was over, most passing through the dreaded Drancy internment camp outside Paris.

Viewed from a different perspective, over two-thirds of French Jews eluded both the Nazi and Vichy authorities and survived, many of these thanks to the help of Frenchmen from all walks of life. Once the deportations began in earnest in the occupied zone, Vichy authorities were anxious that stateless Jews, already incarcerated in internment camps in the south, be taken first and that children be made to accompany their parents, with the Germans naturally obliging. As Hilberg notes: "there were moments when the [Vichy] regime forgot itself and hit the Jews more strongly than German coercion could have compelled."[1] By offering foreign Jews as bait to the Nazis, Vichy hoped to still the appetite of the Nazis and thus save the native French Jews, who constituted a minority among French Jews. In the end, French collaboration only whetted the ravenous appetite of the Nazis.

The relatively "low" figure of 75,000 Jews deported (compared to other countries under Nazi rule and influence) is due to several factors, but also to the unenthusiastic attitude of lower-level French officials to implement the anti-Jewish measures of their superiors. If public opinion had remained passive on the anti-Jewish measures, during the early period of the occupation, it was now jolted from its slumber after witnessing the events of the summer of 1942.

The German edict of May 1942 for the obligatory wearing of the Yellow Star by all Jews in the occupied zone already provoked open resistance.

1. R. Hilberg, *The Destruction of the Jews*, p. 389.

Captured Nazi documents report the great discontent among the populace caused by this regulation. "Even antisemites condemn this measure," laments one Nazi report. German authorities decided to exact punitive measures on those brandishing yellow flowers, yellow handkerchiefs, or bits of papers with the inscription *"pour le sémite"* (ridiculing the Prussian military decoration *"pour le mérite"*) and other signs signifying sympathy with Jews and open contempt of the Yellow Star ordinance. Some twenty such offenders were incarcerated in Drancy, a group which included persons from all walks of life (baker, architect, student, electrician, official, secretary, merchant, and housewife). They were set free only months later, in September 1942.

Many ordinary citizens were repelled by the ghastly scenes of Jews being forcibly loaded into cattle cars and delivered to the Germans for an unknown destination. Police agents began to show an increased reluctance to carry out forcible roundups of Jews and many warned Jews of anticipated raids, thus affording them a chance to seek avenues of escape.

The role of the prefect (head of a province, known in France as a *departement*) was especially crucial in deciding the fate of the Jews in his region. The prefects had been accorded discretionary powers on the internment of Jews or their assignment to forced residence as well as on carrying out the registration of Jews in their area of jurisdiction. Some issued travel permits, enabling Jews to move about, and overlooked the presence of unregistered Jews in their district as well as others in hiding. Some prefects actually lent a hand in the escape of Jews, such as Bendetti of Montpellier, who paid with his life for his role in helping Jews escape arrest.

Lower-level administrators in the prefectures also frustrated the regime's efforts in this regard. Other officials in the Vichy administration dealing with refugees, such as Gilbert Lesage and Rene Nodot, concocted various schemes in order to make it possible for Jews to safely flee the country. This reluctance of Vichy secondary and lower-level officialdom to become stooges in the deportation of Jews (as contrasted with their earlier acquiescence in the application of restrictive measures against Jews) and the concomitant shortage of German manpower were largely responsible for the success of Jews in eluding their captors and finding refuge within the ever more sympathetic French population.

Of major importance in shaping public opinion was the position of the Catholic Church in France. In the early days of the Vichy regime, many Catholic prelates embraced the new spirit radiating from Vichy which had with one stroke abolished previous legislation directed against religious institutions and had expanded Catholic privileges in many fields. "Pétain is France and France is Pétain," Cardinal Gerlier of Lyon, the primate of France, had triumphantly declared in November 1940. The Catholic hierarchy passed over in silence the series of discriminatory decrees against the Jewish population, beginning in October 1940. None protested.

This reticence by the Catholic prelates changed dramatically in the summer of 1942. The forceful deportations of men, women, and children, with no regard to their age or state of health, was viewed as a significant departure from what had previously been considered as the more humane anti-Jewish discriminatory laws. The historians Marrus and Paxton note in this regard: "For the first time since the founding of Marshal Pétain's regime, significant numbers of moderate or conventional French people who had accepted the regime as a matter of course, or supported it enthusiastically, were deeply offended by something it had done. For the first time, voices of open opposition arose from establishment figures in positions of power. Those raised within the Catholic hierarchy had by far the most impact, in view of the Church's previous solid support for Vichy and all its works."[2]

The episcopal document which, because of its author and content, dominated the new church opposition to Vichy anti-Jewish measures in this overwhelming Catholic country was the celebrated pastoral letter of Jules-Gérard Saliège, archbishop of Toulouse, disseminated in his diocese on August 30, 1942. It reads:

> There is a Christian morality, there is a human morality that imposes duties and recognizes rights. These duties and rights refer to the nature of man. They come from God. One may violate them. No mortal being is capable of suppressing them. That children, that women, fathers and mothers be treated like cattle, that members of a family be separated from one another and dispatched to an unknown destination, it has been reserved for our own time to see such a sad spectacle. Why does the right of sanctuary no longer exist in our churches? . . . The Jews are real men and women. Not everything is permitted against these men and women; against these fathers and mothers. They are part of the human species. They are our brothers, like so many others. (197)

This pastoral letter by the partly paralyzed bishop of Toulouse, a man of great character and public popularity, spread like wildfire throughout southwestern France and was read in the majority of the churches in the diocese of Toulouse; it was carried from hand to hand, and sold clandestinely in Catholic bookstores.

Hiding children in religious institutions became the principal form by which Catholic clerics helped Jews elude their pursuers. Such homes also served as transit points for persons fleeing toward the Swiss border, with Lyon, Grenoble, and Annemasse serving as principal links on the chain of that freedom trail. These activities necessitated the issuing of countless baptismal certificates and various assortments of identity papers under assumed names. A certain Mgr. Pezeril from the Paris region is reported to have issued hundreds of such baptismals. For many of these Catholic

2. M. Marrus, *Vichy France and the Jews*, p. 270.

clerics, Saliège's forceful letter of August 1942 gave impetus and ecclesiastical backing to what they themselves felt to be the right course of action, of thwarting evil designs on innocent and helpless persons.

A no-less denunciatory statement was issued by the National Council of the Reformed Church of France, under the leadership of Pastor Marc Boegner, on September 22, 1942, which included the following forceful words:

> The Reformed Church cannot remain silent in face of the sufferings of thousands of human beings who have received asylum on our soil. A Christian church would have lost its soul and its reason for existence if it did not uphold the divine law above all human contingencies. And this divine law does not permit that families created by God be broken up, children separated from mothers, the right of asylum and its compassion remain unrecognized, the respect for the human person transgressed, and persons without defense consigned to a tragic fate.[3]

Soon CIMADE, the chief Protestant refugee welfare organization, which had earlier been involved in ameliorating the condition of Jews in various internment camps, now undertook to facilitate their refuge in private homes and their clandestine escape into Switzerland. As we shall later note, the mostly Protestants of the Le Chambon region operated as one group, under the spiritual guidance of André Trocmé, in the rescue of thousands of Jews.

Other non-Jewish organizations that lent a hand in the rescue of Jews included the Quakers, Unitarians, the YMCA, the Swiss Red Cross, and the American Friends Service Committee, which all coordinated their activities with Jewish organizations such as the OSE, ORT, and the American Joint Distribution Committee (the Joint, for short). The Quakers were especially prominent in the internment camps, where they were allowed to enter freely (some actually took up residence therein) and provide needed provisions for those already slated for deportation. To streamline the activities of these organizations, a coordinating committee was set up in Nimes (known as the Nimes Committee) with the American Donald Lowrie as chairman.

The principal Jewish organization dealing with safeguarding the children was the OSE (Oeuvre de Secours aux Enfants), which operated as an official organ of the UGIF (Union Général des Israélites en France), the government-recognized sole Jewish representative organization. The OSE gradually assumed a clandestine character as the persecution of Jews intensified, and it then organized a vast network which, with the help of the non-Jewish organizations mentioned earlier, found permanent hiding places for children with friendly families or facilitated their transfer

3. E. Fabre, *Les Clandestins de Dieu*, p. 25.

to Switzerland in specially organized convoys. Georges Garel, one of the principal operatives in this vast operation, secured the active assistance of Monsignor Saliège in Toulouse, who made it possible for dozens of children to be surreptitiously admitted into religious homes for the duration of the war. Aided by a reliable staff of Jewish and non-Jewish social workers and dedicated children escorts, headed by Mrs. André Salomon of the OSE, hundreds of children were sheltered in adoptive homes, mostly on farms.

All told, it is estimated that some 7,000 Jewish children were hidden in private homes and religious institutions. The fact that very few sheltering families were betrayed to the authorities is a noteworthy testament to the friendly disposition of Frenchmen of all walks of life. Maintaining thousands of children in hiding places in private homes was no mean task. As Donald Lowrie, the American head of the Nîmes Committee until late 1942, notes, first Christian parents had to decide to take upon themselves and their own children the risk of taking in a Jewish child, and Laval had proclaimed that hiding a Jew was an act of treason. Then a child had to be selected who more or less naturally fitted into a given family picture. If he was to be presented as a member of this family, he had to be of the right age and, if possible, the right complexion. The youngster selected had to be brought surreptitiously over long distances to his sheltering family and taught a new name and biographical data. Friendly shopkeepers sometimes provided extra food when no ration cards were available for the new addition to the family, and sympathetic officials in the local prefecture turned their eyes away from a too-close inspection of falsely fabricated new identity cards provided by clandestine organizations. In short, whatever one's feelings were toward Jews, the idea of causing harm to innocent children was such a reprehensible idea that it kept most Frenchmen from betraying the children's presence to the local authorities—who themselves, to a large extent, preferred not to be apprised of the children's presence in their district.[4]

For a brief nine-month interlude, the safest place for Jews in France was the region composed of the eight departments in southeastern France, east of the Rhone river, under occupation by the Italian army (an ally of Nazi Germany) from January to September 1943. Before the war, this area, especially the city of Nice, counted some 15,000 to 20,000 Jews. In 1943, this figure had swelled to over 30,000. The Italians put the Vichy authorities on notice that no roundup of Jews would be tolerated in the Italian zone of occupation.

This liberal Italian policy allowed Jews to live in total security, and Jewish social organizations were given full sway in expanding their welfare operations. Refugees were directed to special reception centers, some even guarded by the carabinieri (Italian gendarmerie) with orders to forbid

4. D.A. Lowrie, *The Hunted Children*, p. 237.

access to these centers to French Vichy police. Alexandre Angeli, prefect of Lyon, lamented on "the promised land" for Jews on the east bank of the Rhone.

After Italy's capitulation to the Allies on November 8, 1943, the Nazis swept into the Italian zone and, assisted by French collaborators, instituted a reign of terror and a systematic roundup of Jews which, according to the historian Poliakov, "exceeded in its hideousness and cruelty anything known until then, at least in western Europe."[5] Disregarding even the protests of Vichy authorities, the Germans rounded up thousands of French-naturalized Jews (until then not touched) as well as foreign Jews, who where all transported, via Drancy, to Auschwitz. Many Jews found refuge in friendly homes; others succeeded in crossing the Alps into Italy (though now under German occupation as well), where they hoped somehow to find refuge with the largely friendly Italian population, or fled north in a desperate race to cross into Switzerland.

With the Germans in full control of France and Italy, and in consideration of the physical difficulties in crossing the forbidden Pyrenean heights into Spain, Switzerland became in late 1943 the most tempting goal for fleeing Jews. Geopolitical factors created conditions in which a great proportion of Jews found themselves seeking hiding places in the southeastern part of the country—the Le Chambon, Lyon, and Grenoble regions; from there it was a relatively easy reach to the Swiss border. Until September 1943, the French-Swiss border was policed largely either by French gendarmes or Italian caribinieri and both could be expected not to too rigorously control all the secret crossing points on the border. The attitude of the Swiss border guards was of greater concern to the refugees. Many, upon apprehension inside Swiss territory, were forced back to the French side of the border and subsequently apprehended by the Vichy police, who proceeded to intern them.

With everything said and done on the attitude of French officials and the public at large on the deportation of Jews, the record shows that over two-thirds of the over 300,000 Jewish inhabitants of France survived. A major credit for this feat is undoubtedly due to the role of Frenchmen of all walks of life, who thwarted German and Vichy nefarious designs in this regard and made it possible for most Jews to elude their captors.

We now pass to individual rescue stories in France.

Where Rescuer and Rescued Knew Each Other

Many rescues involved people who previously knew each other, either as friends or as business acquaintances. The Epstein family lived on the third floor of a Compiègne apartment building; Henri and Suzanne Ribouleau resided one floor beneath them. When the police came to the

5. L. Poliakov, *Jews under the Italian Occupation*, p. 43.

Epsteins on July 19, 1942, they were allowed to contact the Ribouleaus, who willingly consented to look after the Epsteins' two children Rachel and Leon (aged nine and four respectively). Mrs. Epstein assured the Ribouleaus that the police wanted to take them in only for a brief interrogation. That was the last time the children saw their parents, who were transported to one of the death camps in Poland. The two children were welcomed into the Ribouleau family of four (including two sons). The Epstein children, who moved to the United States after the war, wrote of "eternal love for them which we have been trying to convey to them ever since we were young children . . . [to our] Mama and Papa." (1227)

Similarly for Angèle Marseille and her daughter Suzanne lived in a Paris apartment building where they met the four members of the Tzesselsky family who were Jewish. On March 19, 1943, Suzanne learned that the Tzesselskys were about to be arrested. She insisted that they all spend the night in her mother's apartment. Thus they eluded the police who came to fetch them late that evening. It was clear that the Tzesselskys could not remain in their apartment, for the police were sure to come looking for them again. Suzanne and her mother decided to take the parents to hide in their apartment; they remained hidden with Suzanne and her mother for eighteen months unbeknownst to all the other tenants. The two children were sheltered with another family; they were later moved to another place under assumed identities. Suzanne visited the children regularly; these visits involved long trips by train and a seven- or eight-hour walk to a lone village where she introduced herself as a relative of the "orphaned" children. The Tzesselsky family was reunited at the end of the war. The Marseilles, members of the Antoiniste Church, a theosophical religion which emphasizes the divine-spiritual attributes of the individual, refused any monetary compensation for their charitable deed. "Without them, we should not have been citizens of Israel but perhaps a bit of ash on Mount Zion [where ashes of the victims who were burnt in the crematoria are preserved]," Paulette Tzesselky states in her deposition. (525)

Elsewhere in the Paris region, when the gendarmes came to arrest Mrs. Mindler on July 16, 1942, she hurriedly phoned her friend Marie Fricker, who immediately came over with her husband Georges, a house painter. In response to the emotional pleading of Mrs. Mindler, the police consented to free her two children Joseph, age seven and Sarah, age nine, to the care of the Frickers. Mrs Mindler was eventually taken to Auschwitz, where she perished. Their father, who was taken to Auschwitz earlier, survived and returned to claim the children. (2594)

The parents of Denis Erner, born in 1939, befriended Blanche and Jean Péraud. Jean Péraud was an official in a lumber company in

Angoulême. Denis's father, who was of Polish origin, was arrested by Vichy authorities on July 14, 1941, and handed over to the Germans. Denis's mother, fearing she would also be arrested, asked Blanche Péraud to take Denis under her care; she willingly agreed. The Pérauds kept him for the duration of the war, overcoming many incidents, including one denunciation and a search of their home. Three months after his father's disappearance, Denis's mother was taken away, never to be seen again. Before boarding the train taking her and other Jews to Drancy, she arranged to have a letter mailed to Blanche Péraud, expressing her appreciation and thanking Blanche for her hospitality to Denis. She also asked Blanche to look after her daughter, who had been turned over to the care of a different person. Both children survived. (1293)

Elsa Fischer and her family of German origin, lived in southern France. They had fled to Nice after the Germans took over the city from the Italians in September 1943. The Germans had begun a large-scale roundup of thousands of Jews who were stranded there, so it was necessary to find a secure hiding place.

Fortunately for the Fischers, they had previously befriended Louis Mauro (who was the owner of a housewares store) and his wife Angèle, who lived in the nearby town of Pont St. Jean-Cap Ferrat. At first, Mauro hid the four members of the Fischer family in a nearby empty house, where they stayed for half a year. An expert plumber, Louis Mauro installed electricity, allowing the Fischers to prepare their own meals with provisions that he supplied and paid for. As it became too dangerous to prolong their stay there, Mauro transferred them to St. Roman de Bellet, one hour's drive from Nice, where they were sheltered in an unused flat until the area was liberated on August 28, 1944.

"We were one of the few lucky families, of the thousands of Jews in Nice, to be saved," observes Mariette, Elsa Fischer's daughter. "Mr. and Mrs. Mauro risked their lives to save us, for had anyone suspected that he was hiding Jews, he would certainly have been denounced and deported." After the war, the Fischers learned that Mauro had saved two other Jewish families, who were also in jeopardy of deportation. "Hence twelve Jews owe their lives to Mr. and Mrs. Mauro," Mariette concludes her deposition. (783)

Meetings Arranged through Third Parties

Fleeing Jews sometimes met their rescuers through third parties. One of the principal mediators between rescuers and rescued was the OSE, a Jewish organization that cared for parentless and abandoned children in its own institutions. When this was no longer possible, the OSE dispersed the children to compassionate non-Jewish families and institutions. It continued to look after the children, making sure they were well provided for until they could be retrieved from their adoptive homes to be reunited with their own families.

Alice Ferrières

One such generous person was Alice Ferrières, a mathematics teacher in the town of Muret (Puy de Dôme), near Clermont-Ferrand. Beginning in the summer of 1943, when the OSE-sponsored children's center at Beaulieu-sur-Dordogne was closed by the Germans, Miss Ferrières supervised the hiding of dozens of Jewish girls in the girls college in which she taught. The girls were registered as Protestant refugees; they were ostensibly fleeing from the large cities which were under bombardment by Allied planes. When the Germans intensified their search for partisans in the town's vicinity in the spring of 1944, Alice Ferrières hid the girls with cooperating peasants so that they might avoid falling into German hands. At this time the Germans were losing the war; they sometimes shot suspected Jews on the spot rather than bother with time-consuming transportation to the death camps in distant Poland. When France was liberated in August 1944, the girls were returned to the OSE. Alice Ferrières went back to teaching mathematics. "She made sure that we each lighted the Sabbath candles, and observed the holidays and religious traditions," Solange Factor recalls, adding: "Without her help during the war years, it is possible I would not have survived (my mother was deported in 1943). . . . Love of fellow man was the value dearest to her. Being single, she was able to devote herself freely to her noble deeds." (83)

Louise Demaison

Louise Demaison was one of many persons who willingly collaborated with the OSE. Her home in Solignac, near Limoges, was a clearing center for many Jewish children en route for placement with local peasants. One such child was eight-year old Henry Kessel, who had been born in Vienna. His parents had recently been deported to the death camps. Louise learned of Henry's poor health when an OSE courier brought him to her home. She decided not to send Henry to the peasants with whom she had made arrangements for him to stay, because the peasant's family had reportedly been infected with tuberculosis. Instead she asked her newly married daughter Eliane Traband whether she would shelter the boy in her home. Eliane and her husband, André (a school teacher), readily agreed, and the boy remained with them for two years. Because he spoke broken French, Henry was passed off as a refugee child from Alsace. Local inhabitants suspected Henry's Jewish origins, but no one dared betray the secret, not even a childhood friend of Mrs. Traband, who was a member of the pro-Nazi French Milice. The Trabands, who were devout Catholics, made every attempt to remind the boy of his Jewish heritage. "In fact," notes Henry

Kessel, "having found out that the *Shema Yisrael* was a holy Jewish prayer (which I vaguely remembered), they made sure that I recited it every night." With the country's liberation, the Trabands immediately contacted Henry's elder sister, who had been hidden in an orphanage, and brother and sister were happily reunited. While Henry was living with the Trabands, they took care not only of his basic needs but also of his education and his medical and dental care. "They encouraged him to read books, to collect stamps, to draw and paint," notes Clara, Henry's sister, adding: "And at the same time, she kept reminding him of his Jewish religion and his links with the Jewish people. They did all this out of the goodness of their hearts, out of human decency, without asking or receiving any remuneration." (814)

Father Raymond Vancourt

The story related by Irene Kahn is particularly touching. She was born in Mannheim, Germany, in 1921, and left for France in 1934 to join her aunt's family in Lille, close to the Belgian border. When a non-Jewish friend learned that Irene was on the Gestapo arrest list in September 1942, she led Irene through the dark and blacked-out streets of Lille to the residence of Abbé Raymond Vancourt, a priest and teacher, who shared a home with his niece, Raymonde Lombard. The house was adjacent to La Clinique St. Cathérine, where Father Vancourt officiated as chaplain for both the sisters and the patients.

Father Vancourt was a professor of theology and philosophy at two Catholic colleges in Lille. He valued Irene's language skills, and had her translate chapters of N. Hartmann's *Grundzüge einer Metaphysik den Erkenntnis* from German into French; the translation was subsequently published in 1945. She also did various household chores.

Irene was assigned the master bedroom for her private quarters. Although she was not permitted to leave the premises, she circulated freely within the expansive house complex. "All was open and available to me as if I were already a member of the family. I never opened the door to anyone ringing the bell; I never went to a window while the curtains were drawn open. The seasons came and went. . . . At night, I often lay in bed hearing the sound of boots coming nearer. . . stopping—my heart would stop, and they would stomp the sidewalk again, and my heart would race ahead of my breath, while I was lying in a cold sweat. . . A few times the bell would ring. M. l'Abbé would go to the door: it was sometimes German soldiers, and politely he would direct them away from the house, towering over them, determined, sure of himself, and probably praying with every fiber of his being. . . , but he would never let me know."

The Ehrlich family of four, cousins to Irene, were also sheltered in Father Vancourt's house for a six-month period. Eliane Ehrlich, then a frightened eleven-year-old girl, remembers the fear that gripped her as she and her family of refugee Jews spent long hours in the clinic's air-raid shelter, together with German soldiers, seeking protection from Allied bombings. After the war, Eliane, the wife of a rabbi in Metz, stated in her deposition: "Not only did he not take advantage of the situation to try converting us or simply draw us away from Judaism, but it was he who insisted that we act as though we were in our own homes, and that my father don his phylacteries as customary and that we celebrate the Sabbath and holidays." Eliane's brother, Claude-Chaim, who later became a philosophy professor, adds, "Words are insufficient to evaluate the humanity of Abbé Vancourt and Mme. Lombard. It is quite impossible to describe their nobility of the spirit. . . . Without their aid, there is no doubt that we would have been all deported—my parents, myself and my sister." Irene Kahn concluded her deposition with the prayer, "May the world and God know of their deeds" (909)

Fernande Leboucher

Fernande Leboucher was the principal associate in Marseille of one of the most remarkable of the rescuers, Father Marie-Benoît (of whom we shall learn more at the end of this chapter). Fernande was a fashion designer turned rescuer of Jewish lives. She rented an apartment, nicknamed "the dovecote," because the windows opening on the terrace enabled her charges to escape over the roofs in the event of police raids. Countless Jews were dispatched to her by Father Benoît from his Capuchin monastery for safekeeping in her home or transfer to other secure hiding places. He also sent her to the Rivesaltes detention camp to deliver false identities to Jewish detainees—in 1941 it was still possible to gain freedom. As a cover, she organized fashion shows. One such show, on November 24, 1941, was a great success. It featured a silver satin hat carrying an embroidery reproduction of Millet's painting "The Angelus." The danger of discovery of her rescue activites kept mounting. During one Gestapo raid, a group of ten Jews hiding in Leboucher's rooftop apartment was almost discovered. In June 1943, the Germans fully searched "the dovecote," but all they found was a jumble of ribbons, lace, and designs. Luckily, no one was hiding there at the time. The Gestapo was dumbfounded. They couldn't believe the person they sought—Father Marie-Benoît's secretive associate—was a young fashion designer. "I showed them my latest creations and how with a twist of the hand I could cut and drape and have a new design. They left convinced. But I shook for some time afterwards." She continued furtively distributing false identities to camp internees, a mission assigned to her by Father Marie-Benoît. After an especially dangerous mission to the Gurs camp, she was urged by an acquaintance, an official in the Marseille prefecture, to leave the city immediately or face arrest. She left for Paris, where she remained for the duration of the occupation. Years later, Father Marie-Benoît wrote to her:

"We were together in struggle. I am the immediate day-to-day witness of your courage and heroism." Asking her to accompany him to Jerusalem to plant two trees at Yad Vashem, Father Marie-Benoît added: "This will be the crowning of our common action, our confident and affectionate gesture in favor of this people who had to struggle against immense evils and which we fervently wish peace and prosperity." (791)

Random Encounters

Lucien and Agnes Bertrand

At times, rescuer and rescued first encountered each other at the time the desperate, fleeing Jew needed immediate assistance to survive.

Such was the case of Paula Tattman, who was living untroubled in the southern French town of Lagrasse, after luckily being released from the Gurs detention camp. She was restricted to the town, forbidden to work, and all her documents bore the distinguishing letter *J* (for "Jew") in red, but she was not harmed. A Jewish committee in Carcassonne supported her.

In May 1944, when she learned of an impending raid by the Germans on Jews in hiding, Paula appealed for help but found no response. In despair, she sought out the wife of the chief of police, whose son had been taken away to forced labor in Germany. Paula hoped this woman's feelings about the Germans' actions would lead her to show sympathy and perhaps assist her in her predicament. The police chief assured Paula that he would disclaim any knowledge of her presence in town, as well as that of the Jewish man staying with her; but he declined to provide further assistance. The village doctor told her he was prepared to help her but not her Jewish companion Martin. Helping two persons would be too risky, he said, "absolutely impossible."

Paula then suddenly recalled that Lucien Bertrand, owner of the local bakery, made periodic rounds to his clients in surrounding villages to deliver bread. She decided to seek his aid in locating a friendly peasant who might be willing to hide both her and Martin, perhaps in one of the isolated wine presses common in the region.

When she entered the bakery, she met Agnes Bertrand and told her the purpose of her visit. Agnes promised to discuss the matter with her husband Lucien, and suggested that Paula return in two hours. "Those two hours seemed like eternity," Paula recalls. "What if Monsieur Bertrand said no?" When she returned to receive Lucien's response, which she felt would probably seal her fate for better or worse, he said: "My wife told me everything. We have discussed this matter and we realize your danger. If you cannot find shelter elsewhere, we have a room in our house, right above the baking oven. It is rather hot there, but we will bring you water to sprinkle the floor." She was to stay completely indoors, would be fed daily, and her presence would not even be disclosed to the Bertrands' three daughters.

Paula, overwhelmed with emotion, broke down and wept, then thanked her benefactors. Recovering her composure, she asked whether she could bring an additional person. "I am not alone," she pleaded. "I have had a Jewish man hidden in my house for the past eight months. I cannot leave him alone." The Bertrands agreed to hide him as well. Agnes added, "We don't want any money from you. . . , not now and not later. If we can help save you, it will be our reward."

So Paula and her friend Martin were hidden for three crucial months in a room above the bakery oven. Paula was told to sprinkle water on the hot floor to reduce the heat when the oven was in use. The Bertrand children soon suspected something strange was happening in the storage room above the oven. After discussing the matter with Paula, the Bertrands decided to divulge the secret to their three daughters. The girls responded by tearfully embracing Paula and Martin. Lucien sighed, "Our task has become much easier, now that the children are part of it."

When the Gestapo learned that a local resistance chief was reported to have visited Bertrand's bakery, they threatened a thorough search of the premises. It was decided to move Paula and Martin to a different hiding place. Soon thereafter, in August 1944, the Allies landed in southen France and all were safe and sound. "I never experienced so much warmth and goodness," recalls Paula. "We were overwhelmed with so much affection. This went on for three months—it was to have been a few days." (235)

Hélène and René Bindel

Michel Deutscher, a refugee from Germany, had arrived in France on the eve of World War II. He enlisted in the army, was taken prisoner by the Germans, and spent five years in a POW camp. Returning to liberated Paris in April 1945, he learned that his wife Claire and their son Guy (born 1936) had been miraculously saved by people they had not known.

Claire's brother, Simon Dankowitz, owned a metallurgic firm with a non-Jewish partner in Paris. When the Germans decreed that Jews must relinquish ownership of their businesses (the so-called aryanization policy), Simon ostensibly sold his rights to his partner, in whom he had great confidence. Simon was then rounded up and deported. Simon had earlier urged Claire that if she were ever in need, she was to contact his former partner, who, he was sure, would extend aid. When Simon was sent to Auschwitz, never to return, he managed to slip a note in the mail reminding his sister to contact his former partner. When Claire feared she would be rounded up for deportation, she and her son Guy immediately went to see her brother's business associate to seek his help. To her great chagrin, the man, evidently overcome with fear, declined to help her.

Claire's son relates what then ensued. "This only possible recourse having been exhausted, my mother knew very well that sooner or later we were fated to be deported. Leaving the director's office in tears, she was stopped by the latter's secretary, Madame Hélène Bindel. Through the half-open door, she had overheard the whole conversation. She, whom we did not personally know, spontaneously offered us her help and immediately undertook to have us hidden."

Mother and son were first sheltered for a few days in Hélène's small two-room apartment, which she shared with her husband René and their ten-year-old son. Then, for two weeks, they were housed in René's mother-in-law's home. Finally, they moved in with Hélène's aunt Clotilde Pava, who lived in a sixth-floor garret apartment on Rue Lafayette. Claire stayed there for two years. Guy was enrolled in a Vincennes boarding school under a new identity. In May 1944, as the Germans stepped up their searches for hidden Jews, René Bindel thought it best for Claire and Guy to leave Paris. They were taken to Montreuil-aux-Lions (Aisne), where the two remained hidden until France was liberated.

Claire's husband was surprised by and grateful for his family's rescue by persons previously unknown to them. He writes, "Even after the war, we remained so close one to another that it would be no exaggeration to state that Hélène and René Bindel substituted for the grandparents our children lost in the Holocaust. For my wife and myself, they had become much closer than a family." (2203)

Help by the Clergy, Religious Institutions and Organizations

Some members of the clergy were heavily involved in the forging and acquisition of false credentials. False baptismal certificates were, of course, helpful instruments for obtaining other valuable identifications.

Abbé Albert Gau

Abbé Albert Gau was a priest in Carcassone, close to the Spanish border. He was very active in various Catholic youth movements and served, in addition, as chaplain in the high school of his hometown. Then one day in 1942, an energetic young Jewish woman presented herself before him with a request. Would he help her in her search for temporary shelter for Jewish youngsters with local families and in obtaining the necessary false identities which they needed until such time as they would be taken across the Pyrenees and into Spain? "She was a young and courageous girl by the name of Nicole Bloch. I could not say no," recalls Abbé Gau. And without much ado, he immersed himself in this new type of clandestine work, which was eventually to lead to his being placed on the Gestapo wanted list. In Nicole's own words: "He welcomed me enthusiastically and beyond anything that I could hope."

Nicole and her future husband, René Klein, both very active in the OSE and the Sixth (a clandestine Jewish organization), began to send to Abbé Gau Jewish children who with his help were then dispersed to various religious institutions and families. "Each day, or almost, I received Jews, particularly youth. I had to open a restaurant in order to feed them. . . . I also had to fabricate great quantities of false identity and ration cards. I even gave each Jew a baptismal certificate, under the sole condition that he not undergo baptism." Lest we forget, these are the words of a devout Catholic priest. Pierre Marie Puech, archbishop of Carcassonne, states: "The abbé transformed the large house of the [Catholic] youth movement into a reception center for all Jews arriving there."

It did not take long for the French police to suspect the true nature of the goings and comings in Gau's youth center. They staged a sudden raid, but luckily there were no Jews present at the time. The police searched the premises and did not find the incriminating false identity cards and official seals. Finally, out of respect for the sanctity of the religious home, they stopped short of ransacking the premises and abruptly departed.

The Germans showed no such compunctions. When they occupied that part of France, Abbé Gau was counseled to flee and go underground. "I could write a great novel," the Abbé reminisces, "but often a tragic novel, for reality surpasses one's imagination." However, whatever he did for the helpless Jews, it came to him "naturally."

Addressing an audience that honored him at Yad Vashem, in 1987, he stated: "I turn to you, people of God, and I dare say, you have nothing to offer to this pagan world but your faithfulness and the word of God and the long history not yet over of your martyrdom. A people that is said to be domineering [perhaps an allusion to De Gaulle's derogatory remarks in 1967] but which, is at one and the same time, fragile and strong, to the point of being able to outlive all other peoples; a people always singled out because it inconveniences other moribund peoples and empty souls; a people which is horrified at the spilling of blood and upon whom, for twenty centuries, the blood of its children has flowed. Continue on your road lined with obstacles. Don't leave us, for without you, our compass would lose its direction. People of Jesus, I love you . . . We love you." (3444)

Father Jacques Bunel

No less touching is the story of Father Jacques (Lucien Bunel by birth), a Carmelite priest who, from 1940 to 1944, was the head of the Petit College des Carmes in Avon (Seine-et-Marne), a Catholic school for boys. Deeply conscientious and religious, he decided to give shelter to three Jewish students and a renowned Jewish botanist, Professor Lucien Weil, who had been excluded by Vichy laws from teaching at the university. Denounced and betrayed to the Gestapo, he was arrested on January 15, 1944, together with his Jewish wards. The latter were taken to Auschwitz, where they perished. Father Jacques was interned in several concentration camps in Germany.

On June 2, 1945, four weeks after the liberation of Gusen camp, Father Jacques expired from exhaustion. His body was brought home for burial at Avon, in a ceremony attended among others by Rabbi Kaplan, representing Rabbi Julien Weill, the chief rabbi of France. Eulogizing Father Jacques, Rabbi Kaplan said: "Thus we have seen cruelty pushed to its extreme horror and benevolence carried to its highest degree of nobility and beauty." This tragic episode inspired Louis Malle, a former pupil at the college, to create the widely acclaimed film *Au Revoir les Enfants*, named from Father Jacques' parting words to the children, recalling the self-sacrificing humanism of this priest who perished for trying to save Jewish lives. (3099)

Monsignor Pierre-Marie Théas and Marie Rose Gineste

On August 26, 1942, Monsignor Pierre-Marie Théas, archbishop of Montauban, following in the footsteps of Monsignor Saliège of Toulouse, issued a pastoral letter condemning the deportation of Jews that was under way in the unoccupied zone. "I give voice to the outraged protest of Christian conscience, and I proclaim that all men, Aryans or non-Aryans, are brothers, because created by the same God; that all men, whatever their race or religion, have the right to be respected by individuals and by states. Hence, the recent antisemitic measures are an affront to human dignity and a violation of the most sacred rights of the individual and the family."

Théas then asked Marie Rose Gineste, an activist in Catholic social work, to see to it that his pastoral letter was duplicated and read in all of the diocese's churches on the following Sunday, August 30, 1942. "It is with great enthusiasm that I accepted this mission," Gineste recalls. She counseled the Monsignor not to have the letter sent through the post office, for the Vichy authorities would surely censor it. "I proposed to him to go myself by bike, to deliver it to all priests, and all parishes of the diocese."

With no time to lose, Gineste left early the following morning on her bike to visit the parishes of the Tarn and Garonne district. "It was a lengthy outing which I had to accomplish with my bike." A modern Paul Revere on bicycle, she rode through dozens of towns and villages: Bressols, Labastide et Pierre, Reynes, Villebrumier, Varennes, Orgueil, Nolic, Campsas, Savennes, Finhan ("where the good priest Hebrard offered me a fresh drink with biscuits"), Beaumont-de-Lomagne, Lavit, . . . and so on, for two days, morning to dusk.

"Thus all parishes of the Montauban diocese were in possession of the letter of protestation of Msgr. Théas which was read [from the pulpit] on Sunday, August 30, 1942, during all masses and in all the churches of Tarn and Garonne (with the exception of the Ardus parish, whose priest

was known to be a Vichy collaborator)." The echo of Théas's pronounce-
ment, following the one of Saliège a week earlier, shook the halls of the
Vichy establishment, and marked a turning point in the Catholic Church's
attitude toward Pétain's government. It signaled all Frenchmen to go forth
and protect Jews from deportation.

Impressed by her singular devotion to this cause, Théas charged Mrs.
Gineste with lending a hand in sheltering children and adult Jews in
various religious institutions in the region and in the fabrication of false
identities. "Until October 1943, I procured false papers and ration cards
through comrades in the resistance," Gineste states. "But from that date
on, we equipped ourselves: false seals turned over to Msgr. Théas and
others by my Jewish friends, René Klein, Nicole Bloch [of whom we learned
earlier in this chapter], and others." Vital ration cards were seized from
government warehouses and offices or freely delivered to her by sympathetic government officials (such as the 500 ration-stamp sheets dutifully
delivered to her each month by the head of the local ration cards
department, with the connivance of the vice-mayor).

Mrs. Gineste later explained her motivations: "My commitment, my
deeds, were never motivated by hatred. I believe I never felt hatred toward
anyone. All my deeds, from the first to the last day, were done out of my
Christian belief. Since my childhood youth it has dominated and oriented
my entire life—before the war, during the war, during the occupation and
afterwards. . . until this day, . . . in my various and numerous deeds, and
all the days of my life." (3256)

Monsignor Pierre-Marie Théas at Yad Vashem (1970). Courtesy of Yad Vashem.

Pastor André and Magda Trocmé

French Protestants were keenly aware of the constraints on religious freedom in a predominantly Catholic environment. Since the days of the Reformation, the Huguenots in France had borne the brunt of persecution. In their search for protection, they chose the Massif Central, a mountainous region in southern France, as a place of refuge. Here, they hoped, the combination of geographical conditions and distance from the country's main economic, political, and cultural centers would afford them relative security to practice their religion undisturbed. It is, therefore, not surprising that French Protestants, mindful of their own history, were very sensitive to the plight of the Jews. Protestants were thus to be found at the forefront of rescue activities on their behalf.

One of the leading spirits in these efforts was Pastor André Trocmé of Le Chambon-sur-Lignon, who, with the help of his wife Magda, initiated and oversaw a vast operation sheltering thousands of Jewish refugees in this mountainous Protestant region. Refuge here was a first step toward escape to Spain in the south or to the more accessible Switzerland in the east. The Trocmés were helped by other Protestant organizations and by many Catholic clergy who undertook the arduous and audacious mission of spiriting Jewish refugees across the Swiss frontier.

In the words of one who benefited from the Trocmés' generosity, the pastor was "the charismatic leader of Le Chambon," and his wife the "motor." Anny Latour of the Jewish resistance movement in France testifies, "Not a month passed that I did not address myself to him, to his colleagues or his community in order to hide Jews in danger of detection by the German police. During all these tragic years, Pastor Trocmé always acknowledged our call for help. He responded with enthusiasm, although he well realized that his activities on our behalf jeopardized not only his life, but those of his wife, children, and members of his community."

Magda Trocmé was in truth the grand organizer of this vast operation in which Jewish adults and children were housed in various public institutes and children's homes (such as the Collège Cévénol, La Guespy, "Tante Soly," Les Grillons, Maison des Roches) or with local townsmen and peasants for various periods of time. With the help of other associates, such as Pastor Edouard Theis, director of the Collège Cévénol, they were taken on dangerous treks, through French towns and villages to the Swiss border. They used assumed names, though many of them had originated in Germany and spoke hardly any French or spoke it with a heavy and easily discernible accent. They were then smuggled across the border and into the waiting hands of other Protestant suporters on the Swiss side (the Swiss authorities were not generally cooperative and could not always be relied on). Pastor Theis made several such journeys and, during the last months of the occupation, was on the Gestapo's wanted list.

Prewar picture of Maison des Roches, Le Chambon-sur-Lignon, France, where Jewish youngsters were sheltered during the war. Courtesy of Yad Vashem.

Plaque in Le Chambon-sur-Lignon recalling the community's role during the war. Courtesy of Yad Vashem.

Daniel Trocmé, a cousin of André Trocmé, head of the Maison des Roches children's home at Le Chambon, suffered martyrdom in the cause of rescuing Jews. He had been called away from his religious studies elsewhere by André Trocmé to supervise the Les Grillons children's home, which was almost totally composed of Jewish children, as well as the Maison des Roches.

Betrayed by a German army chaplain, who, like many other German military personnel, was staying at a military convalescent home in Le Chambon, Daniel Trocmé was arrested on June 29, 1943 and taken to Moulins for interrogation by the Gestapo. He readily admitted his role in sheltering Jewish children. Asked to respond to the charges levelled against him, Daniel stated, "I defend the weak." He was sent to Buchenwald concentration camp, where he perished in April 1944.

André Trocmé, overcome with grief, wrote the following to Daniel's parents: "The burden of Daniel's death weighs upon me, and yet I feel a religious inspiration when faced with his example. Many people will have died in this war for other causes than the false ideals of war, pride, hatred, conquest—for something even greater than liberty—for love. . . . I should prefer a premature death like Daniel's for my loved ones, rather than the slightest disgrace or cowardice . . . Daniel represents to me a witness, a martyr for the true purpose of the Gospels. He was a victim of the forces of evil. . . . I should like a photo of him, extracts of his letters, anything to inspire and help me in the struggle which begins anew, and which shall continue until God assumes His reign and enters His kingdom." Suzanne Heim, who as a young girl was helped by Daniel Trocmé, writes of his devotion to the cause of the Jewish children and his efforts to mitigate the pain of separation from parents and the anxiety stemming from the uncertainties of each day: "In his devotion to us, he was like a river which never fails. . . . His blessed activities will forever remain etched in the depths of my heart."

At one point Pastor André Trocmé was asked by the authorities to give them a list of the Jews in town who were living under assumed names. He replied, "Even if I had such a list, I would not pass it on to you. These people have come here seeking aid and protection. I am their pastor, their shepherd. The shepherd does not betray the sheep in his keeping." During another confrontation with the authorities, André Trocmé responded, "I don't know what a Jew is. I only know human beings."

The full story of Le Chambon and its environs, of how a whole region defied Vichy and the German authorities and saved thousands of Jews, has yet to be told. Also to be disclosed are the names of the hundreds who made up the "silent majority" in this Protestant community who felt they simply did what was expected of them, nothing more—and who prefer to maintain their anonymity. "Things had to be done, that's all, and we happened to be there to do them," explained an unpretentious Le Chambon resident to a visiting author who was preparing a study of this fascinating episode. "Helping these people was the most natural thing in the world . . . . Well, maybe it was unreasonable. But you know, I had to do it anyway." (612, 1037, and 2066)

Pastor Idebert Exbrayat

Idebert Exbrayat was a minister of the Reformed (Calvinist) Church in Rodez (Aveyron), in the so-called Free Zone. In 1942, the parsonage of his church became a base for helping hundreds of Jews in various ways during the remaining two years of Nazi rule. It all began one evening in 1942, when the pastor and his wife were awakened by several knocks on their door in the little country village of Rodez. To their astonishment, a rabbi, his wife, and their seven children stood before them—all fleeing the Gestapo and seeking temporary shelter. Years later, Pastor Exbrayat explained his state of mind on that summer evening: "I was thirty when all this happened. As a Calvinist, I understood the meaning of persecution. . . That is why I understood the persecution of the Jews and opened my door to the rabbi."

Exbrayat thereupon joined an eight-member Jewish underground network and offered them his rectory for their nocturnal meetings. Richard Levy, a Jewish refugee, recalls being hidden by the pastor in a small cabin in the woods, which the Calvinists used for their bimonthly gatherings. Denise Steinberg relates how she first stayed in Exbrayat's home, and was then taken to friendly parishioners at nearby Figeat, where she remained hidden for one year. While there, she was regularly visited by Exbrayat at two-week intervals, to bring her provisions and make sure everything was in order.

As the number of Jews seeking help increased, Exbrayat solicited help from his parishioners. Volunteers came from about seventy villages and hamlets. Exbrayat had a friend in the prefecture who alerted him to planned raids on Jews in his region. "It was dangerous work," the pastor recalls. "Of our group, four of the Jews were killed outright by the Germans; two were captured and deported. I was never afraid to die, but I was afraid to be tortured lest I reveal the names of my colleagues."

Among those hidden by Exbrayat was Henri Lévy-Bruhl, a noted law professor at the Sorbonne University. Former Prime Minister Paul Ramadier had confided Lévy-Bruhl and his family to the pastor's care. He sheltered them for two years.

When Yad Vashem announced that Pastor Exbrayat had been elected one of the Righteous Among the Nations, he expressed his appreciation to the Jewish people "for having given us the Law of Moses, the example of the prophets, the Bible and Christ. And for having sacrificed itself to bring hope to the world." Regarding his personal role in the rescue of so many Jews, Exbrayat was modest and self-effacing, as were the other Righteous.

"What we did for our Jewish brothers and sisters during the Nazi period—was frankly very little. . . . May God's peace be upon you. Shalom." In her testimony, Denise Steinberg speaks of Exbrayat's "great simplicity" and his "comforting smile," adding: "He is a saint and a brother—a person I shall never cease to praise." (1672)

Denise Bergon

Many children and adults found shelter in various religious institutions and various children's camps. The Pensionnat Nôtre-Dame de Massip, at Capdenac (Aveyron), was one such institution. Under the direction of Sister Denise Bergon, this rustic summer camp for Catholic children was transformed into a house of refuge for Jewish children and some adults.

It all began when Georges Garel, a leading figure in the Jewish underground, met Monsignor Saliège of Toulouse in September 1942 and asked for his help in sheltering Jewish children. Instructions were relayed to Bishop Louis de Courrèges d'Ustou, Saliège's immediate aide, and he in turn enlisted the services of Denise Bergon, a young nurse of thirty. She is described by her former charges as level-headed when making decisions, kind and devoted, and possessing the unusual quality of being able to calm, comfort, and instill in the frightened Jewish children, who had recently been separated from their parents under painful circumstances, a measure of security and self-confidence simply by her presence.

In all, some sixty-five children and eleven adult Jews passed through the doors of the pensionnat from the end of 1942 until May 1944, when a denunciation forced all to quickly abandon the place and find shelter at prearranged homes of friendly families or with their own families who were hidden elsewhere. Whenever she felt it necessary for the child's welfare, Denise Bergon would take the child to his or her parents and then stay overnight with them to comfort parents and child alike. She herself fetched the children from various locations, to bring them to Massip. Only the three top staff persons, Louise Thèbes, Marguerite Roque (the housekeeper), and Denise Bergon, knew the child's true identity. To the others, they were refugees from Lorraine, thus explaining the children's German-accented French pronunciation. To better dissimulate their origin, the children were made to attend services, but no attempts were made to expose them to the Catholic faith. Monsignor Saliège personally ordered Denise Bergon to stay clear of proselytism. "You will have to lie," he instructed her, "do so whenever you feel it is necessary. I grant you in advance all my absolutions."

Denise Bergon, however, needed no counseling for her motherly affection toward the children. "For us," she recalls, "who were familiar with their dramatic stories, they had simply become our children, and we had committed ourselves to suffer everything so as to return them safely to their families." The children reciprocated in kind. "We were more or less disturbed children and adults," states Annie Bach, "far from our families, who for the most part had been deported. However, we had Mme. Bergon, her smile and warmth, to console us." Helene Oberman, another of Bergon's former charges, writes, "We have cherished in our heart our love and appreciation for the one who, disregarding her young age, ambition and safety, gathered and saved many human lives." (1807)

Elizabeta Skobtsova

One of the most inspiring, though tragic, stories of altruism is that of a Russian-born nun of aristocratic parentage whom cicumstances placed in Paris when France came under Nazi rule.

Elizabeta Skobtsova was born in Riga, Latvia (at that time part of Russia), to a father who was chief prosecutor for the tsarist government in that city. In her youth she wrote poetry; one of her works, "Scythian Shards," was well-known in St. Petersburg literary circles. During the Russian Revolution, she joined the Socialist Revolutionary party, but when the Bolsheviks gained the upper hand, she left for Anapa on the Black Sea coast. There she married and bore two children to an anti-Bolshevik officer. The vicissitudes of the Russian Civil War caused them to flee. They eventually settled in France. Established in Paris, Elizabeta, after the death of her four-year-old daughter, decided to become a nun in the Russian Orthodox Church. In 1932 she took her vows and adopted the name of Maria.

Until the outbreak of the war, she coordinated welfare activities on behalf of Russian emigrés in France. This led to the opening of a dormitory and free kitchen for Russian exiles and of a convalescent home outside Paris. Her church purchased a building in Paris, on Rue de Lourmel, which soon became the nerve center of her extensive activities. Her immediate aide was Father Dmitri Klepinin, also a refugee from Russia.

With the onset of the persecution of Jews in France by the Germans, she decided that her Christian belief required her to come to the aid of Jews in whatever way possible. As a first step, she made the free kitchen available to them, then arranged temporary shelter for some. Father Klepinin, ever at her side, issued—unbeknownst to his superiors—false baptismal certificates for those needing new identities. During the fateful days of July 1942, when thousands of Parisian Jews were rounded up in the *Vélodrome d'Hiver*, in conditions of indescribable suffering, Mother Maria succeeded in penetrating the sports stadium and, with the connivance of bribed garbage collectors, smuggled out several children in tall narrow garbage bins. That same month, stunned by the German edict requiring Jews to wear the yellow star, she penned the following poem:

Israel —
Two triangles, a star,
The shield of King David, our forefather.
This is election, not offense.
The great path and not an evil.
Once more is a term fulfilled,
Once more roars the trumpet of the end;
And the fate of a great people
Once more is by the prophet proclaimed.
Thou art persecuted again, O Israel,
But what can human ill will mean to thee,
Who have heard the thunder from Sinai?

Unrelenting in her charitable zeal, she continued her work on behalf of Jews in spite of ominous warnings that she was being closely watched by the Gestapo. She simply could not relent, she confided to friends. She kept a diary, writing late at night after a full day of activities. The following passage gives testimony of her state of mind: "There is one moment when you start burning with love and you have the inner desire to throw yourself at the feet of some other human being. This one moment is enough. Immediately you know that instead of losing your life, it is being given back to you twofold."

On February 8, 1943 she and Father Klepinin were arrested. She readily admitted to the charge of helping Jews elude Nazi roundups. When Klepinin was brought in for interrogation, Hoffmann, the Gestapo agent decided at first on a conciliatory approach; it backfired, as the following dialogue testifies:

Hoffmann: If we release you, will you give an undertaking never again to aid Jews?
Klepinin: I can say no such thing. I am a Christian and must act as I must.
[*Hoffmann strikes Klepinin across his face.*]
Hoffmann: Jew lover! How dare you talk of helping those swine as being a Christian duty!
[*Klepinin recovers his balance. He raises the cross from his cassock and faces Hoffmann.*]
Klepinin: Do you know this Jew?

Klepinin received an additional blow which landed him on the floor. He and Mother Maria were taken to Compiègne. Klepinin was then transferred to Buchenwald concentration camp and from there to Dora camp, where he died from pneumonia on February 11, 1944. Mother Maria was taken to the notorious Ravensbrück women's concentration camp, north of Berlin. On March 31, 1945, days before the camp's liberation, her strength failed her and she was committed to the gas chamber.

Years earlier, Mother Maria wrote, "At the Last Judgment, I will not be asked whether I satisfactorily practiced asceticism, or how many genuflections I have made before the divine altar. I will be asked whether I fed the hungry, clothed the naked, visited the sick and the prisoner in his jail. That is all that will be asked." (3078)

Refuge in Lay Institutions

Marguerite Soubeyran

Nonreligious institutions also served as a haven for fleeing Jews. The story of how Alice Ferrières hid children in the school where she taught mathematics is reported earlier in this chapter. There are other similar stories.

Marguerite Soubeyran was the headmistress of the Beauvallon school in Dieulefit (Drôme). There, some forty Jewish children, mostly boys, were sheltered. The atmosphere prevailing in the school is succinctly stated by one of its former beneficiaries: "Once you arrived at Beauvallon, one was no longer a Jew, a German, neither a refugee nor a hunted person. One existed there as a human being."

Helmuth Meyer, born in Germany in 1926, was one of the fortunate Jewish boys placed in Mrs. Soubeyran's care by the OSE. On August 26, 1942, Vichy gendarmes from Chabreuil staged a sudden raid on the school compound. The Jewish children had been sent on vacation to various farms. Marguerite Soubeyran and her two codirectors, Simone Mounier and Catherine Krafft, tried to warn the peasants about the raid. Unfortunately, the family where Helmuth and two others boys wee staying failed to receive the notice in time, and they were apprehended.

Upon learning of the children's arrest, Soubeyran left to inquire as to their whereabouts. At Crest (Drôme), she learned that the children had been dispatched to Vénissieux camp outside Lyon, from which they were to be sent to an unknown fate in Poland. Continuing to Lyon, Marguerite interceded with Christian and Jewish organizations and succeeded in liberating the boys. They were immediately provided with false identities and taken back to Beauvallon.

Henceforth, they would no longer stay overnight in the school but in distant caves, and they would not show themselves at school until they were informed by prearranged signals that all was safe. They were instructed how to flee to the hills at a moment's notice and were cautioned to avoid all contacts with the local population. This fear and insecurity that marked the daily life of the boys lasted until France's liberation—but they survived, thanks to the devotion of Marguerite Soubeyran and her two principal aides. Dozens of other Jewish children and adults also found refuge in homes of Dieulefit residents. (493)

Suzanne Babut

Suzanne Babut, widow of a French Protestant pastor, gave dozens of Jews temporary refuge in the boarding house which she owned in Montpellier. As many as twenty Jews stayed there at a time, some of them for extended periods. To make room for as many fleeing Jews as possible, Suzanne Babut stopped leasing rooms to non-Jews. It seems that the underground helped to defray the costs. Her high reputation and the respect she was held in among the city's inhabitants minimized the chances of denunciation to the Germans, although the boarding home was located fairly close to the local Gestapo building and the French police.

Learning of Yad Vashem's decision to recognize her as one of the Righteous Among the Nations in 1976, she said that Yad Vashem's announcement "has confounded me, for I deserve no decoration. Besides, I am against decorations. However, I do not accept your medal as a decoration but as a sign of the friendship which penetrates my heart. . . Please, I beg of you, do not arrange an official ceremony for the awarding of this medal. One deserves no credit for doing what one's heart and conscience dictate. One need not be thanked for this: even less to glorify in them. Hence, I say: 'thank you'. . . simply thanks, with all the admiration and friendship that I bear toward your people." (1045)

* * *

Jews in Cannes, on the French Riviera, were not molested when the town was under Italian occupation. The situation changed drastically when Italy surrendered to the Allies in September 1943. The Germans swarmed into the former Italian zone and a savage hunt for Jews began.

Alban and Germaine Fort

Alban and Germaine Fort had been prominent in the French scout movement. In 1935, they founded in Cannes the *Rayon de Soleil*, a family-style, privately supported center for homeless children. This was one of many such homes founded in France in the years between the wars. The founders of these homes wished to ameliorate the condition of parentless children (orphans or unwanted and neglected children) who had been placed in state-operated child-welfare homes. Behind the comforting walls of the Rayon del Soleil, Jewish children were sheltered by the Forts during the most dangerous phase of street and home manhunts conducted by the Germans in the Cannes region in late 1943.

Julien Engel was one of those sheltered by the Forts. His parents had been deported to Auschwitz, never to return. Julien and his brother Georges were referred to the *Rayon de Soleil* through the good offices of the

Nice archdiocese. They remained there for three full years, after which they joined distant relatives in the United States.

At the *Rayon de Soleil* Julien and Georges found themselves among forty to sixty children, a quarter of whom were abandoned infants waiting for adoption. Since arrivals and departures occurred with some frequency, the movement of Jewish children as such was not out of character with the pattern of life at the *Rayon de Soleil*. At all times, there were eight to fifteen Jewish children in the home, located in the hills directly overlooking Cannes.

In this almost pastoral setting, Jewish children were made to forget the horrors just minutes away from the home. "Though we were no more than two or three miles from the center of Cannes," notes Julien, "the physical isolation of the Villa Clementine [where the home was housed], its relative self-sufficiency and particularly the inward-centered ambiance set by Alban and Germaine Fort, enabled us all to lead almost a life apart, buffered from the brutal realities of the world outside." This was at a time when arrests and disappearances of Jews were a daily occurrence in nearby Cannes. "Paradoxically, these were happy years for us, at a time when so many others in Europe lived in sorrow and suffering."

The "extraordinary courage, generosity, and strength of character (of the Forts) have left an indelible mark on us," says Julien, now a citizen of the United States. Serge Cymerman, another of those fortunate Jewish children, states in his testimony, "This French Catholic couple went to extreme lengths to allow me to finish my elementary school studies in the home itself. . . . Thus, at the risk of their own lives, the Forts saved many Jews, including the undersigned." (3133)

Sister Anne-Marie Llobet and Marcel Billières

Joseph Beigeldrut, of Polish origin, was securely settled in Lille, where he served as secretary to a rabbi. When the war began, Joseph served in the French armed forces. He was taken prisoner by the Germans but managed to escape and cross the demarcation line separating the two parts of divided France. In Tarbes, he found employment in a leather-manufacturing firm. On November 2, 1943, on his way to work, he was told that the Gestapo was waiting for him there.

Joseph later wrote, "From that moment, I was a hunted person." However, with the help of Maurice Trelut, mayor of Tarbes, he was referred to Sister Anne-Marie Llobet, who was interim director of the Mixte Hospital (as well as Mother Superior of the Sisters of Charity). At the hospital, Joseph found other hidden Jews. Nachma Brauner, who had succeeded in fleeing from the Beaunes La Rolande detention camp, was also welcomed in the hospital by Sister Llobet, first as a patient, then as a male nurse. "There I saw other hidden Jews in the form of nurse assistants or patients," Brauner reports.

Suddenly a new Vichy-appointed director was announced. "We were all overcome with great concern," Joseph Beigeldrut recalls. "If he was pro-German and a collaborator, then we were all lost." Marcel Billières, son of the Toulouse mayor, they soon found out, was of the same moral caliber as Sister Llobet. As Joseph relates, "He called me to his office, and learning that I was an escaped prisoner of war and a former secretary to Rabbi Berman of Lille (alas, he too was deported), he appointed me secretary in his own office. Thus, I, a man hunted by the Gestapo . . . a tracked person, there I was, typing correspondence while the director attended to the Germans who regularly visited the hospital in search of wounded partisans or of hiding and sick Jews."

Some twenty Jews continued to be lodged in the hospital, many of them officially listed as deaf or mentally deficient patients. The parents of Irene Cywiakowski occupied a bathroom transformed into a bedroom at night and a dining room and kitchen during the day. Mother and father were kept busy doing various hospital chores. For Irene and her brother, the OSE arranged a hiding place in a children's home in nearby Chabannes. Their parents, who remained at Tarbes, visited them occasionally. When the Gestapo raided the home they were whisked off in time for an emotional rendezvous with their parents at Tarbes. They were then sent to a religious institute, where they stayed until the end of the war.

When France was liberated, it was discovered that the German military command at Tarbes had placed Marcel Billières on the Gestapo "black list," to be arrested forthwith. After the war, he was elected mayor of Tarbes. "Without Marcel Billières," Mrs. Beigeldrut wrote after her husband's passing in 1985, "my husband would have died by deportation: I would never have had children and grandchildren who surround me today. Mr. Billières saved the life of my husband, of my children and grandchildren. He saved a fragment of Israel." (3315)

Help by Public Officials & Law Enforcement Agents

The possibility of a Jew's surviving the massive manhunts was to a large degree dependent on the readiness of non-Jews in various public positions to help him elude those who pursued him and also on the availability of forged credentials with which a hunted person could move about under an assumed non-Jewish identity. New identity papers were indispensable for most Jews wishing to survive the war by passing as non-Jews. There were a considerable number of French people prepared to help in this regard.

Edmond Dauphin

Edmond Dauphin, secretary general of the important Indre prefecture, with offices in Chateauroux, was ready to lend his great authority and influence to help prevent Jewish children from being deported to distant concentration camps. When, in August 1942, children began to be rounded up for the ostensible purpose of "family reunions" (in reality, to accompany their parents to the death camps), Dr. Gaston Levy (medical supervisor of the children's homes set up by the OSE in the occupied zone) knew he had to find a quick way to save the many children in the heretofore protected homes. They had to be swiftly hidden. Levy decided to sound out the local French authorities at Chateauroux in the hope of enlisting their support. It is important to note that whatever the French thought about the expulsion of adult Jews, the very idea of deporting innocent children was revolting to most of them.

"It is there [Chateauroux] that I met a man of great kindheartedness," Dr. Levy testifies. It was Dauphin. "Without hesitating, he summoned to his office the social welfare staff of his department. After informing them of the existence of my clandestine centers in three villages of the province, he told them: 'If the Germans should want one day to lay their hands on these children, you must assert that they are French children under the care of the social welfare department.'" He then gave orders that false credentials be issued for these children so as not to compromise their adoptive families.

Elevated in late 1942 to the post of secretary-general of the regional prefecture of Limoges (with supervision of several departments), Dauphin continued aiding in ways and means to prevent the children's center from turning into a death-trap. "Thanks to him," Levy emphasizes, "houses could be requisitioned for [ostensibly] non-Jewish projects, permitting us to disperse the children in family placements, in convents, and foremost in dispatching them on secret convoys outside France, toward Switzerland and toward Spain."

"Personally, I probably owe my life and that of my family to Mr. Dauphin," Levy remarked at the end of his deposition. In the spring of 1944 Dauphin alerted Levy that he was about to be arrested. He was thus able to flee to Switzerland with his family. (1234)

Jeanette Maurier

Jeanette Maurier, a clerk in the Annecy prefecture (Haute Savoie), issued false identity and ration cards to many Jews in the area who were waiting for an opportune moment to cross the Swiss border. In addition, she found temporary shelter for them with her friends in the resistance and warned them of impending raids. Georges Sandberger, who, with his family, benefited from Miss Maurier's generosity, notes that in Jewish circles she was known as a reliable person for aid in arranging for refugees to cross the Swiss border, because of her contacts with the right people. In September 1943, she found a hiding place for the children of Rabbi

Henri Schilli until the country's liberation. Years later, Miss Maurier, now Brousse, had this to say about her motivations: "Our first duty consists in overcoming our self-centeredness—to inconvenience oneself, to deprive oneself—when one of our human brethren is in danger, whoever he may be, from wherever he may come. This, in order to try creating a more just and brotherly world, where the privilege of life would no longer remain an empty word." To this day, Jeannette Brousse is active in her region in furthering a better understanding between Jews and Christians and in disseminating the story of the Righteous Among the Nations. (804)

Camille Ernst

Public officials often played an important role in the rescue of Jews by making new credentials available. Help by officials extended to other areas as well. Camille Ernst occupied the post of secretary general of Hérault province in Béziers. This office gave him responsibility for the local police. When the anti-Jewish laws went into effect in 1941, Ernst told a delegation of Jews, which included Rabbi Schilli, that if he could show that the Jews in his area were not living at government expense, he would not have to implement the new racial measures. The delegation understood that Enrst had just requested their assistance by making their presence in his district inconspicuous. Then in 1942 he constantly forewarned them of anticipated raids, thus giving them ample time to take preventive countermeasures. As a result of Ernst's assistance, the Hérault region had the smallest percentage of arrests of Jews of any regions in the non-occupied zone, according to Georges Ehrlich, a close acquaintance of Mr. Ernst. When the Germans occupied the southern zone in November 1942, Ernst commissioned Ehrlich to open a reception center for refugee Jews in Millau, in the relatively safer Aveyron district. "Thanks to the letters of reference given to me by Mr. Camille Ernst to the attention of various authorities, a significant number of women, men, and children were thus able to be sheltered and dispersed in the whole region, and were less exposed to persecution," notes Mr. Ehrlich.

Indicted for gross inefficiency in the pursuit of the anti-Jewish laws, Ernst was removed to Marseille. His underground activities there led to his deportation to Dachau concentration camp. He fortunately survived and later went on to fill important government posts until his retirement as director general of the Ministry of Interior. "Thanks to Mr. Ernst, we were able to save hundreds of Jews [in the Montpellier region]. . . . Not once did this noble person ask for compensation or gifts of whatever sort," stated Raymond Heyman, a Jewish social worker involved in the rescue operation. "On the contrary, at times he succeeded in extracting government funds for these persecuted persons."

After rekindling the eternal flame at Yad Vashem's Hall of Remembrance in 1972, Camille Ernst said humbly: "The righteous are really not only those who did their human obligation, but also those who died in the 'Night and Fog' period." (709)

Edouard Vigneron and Pierre Marie

Lower-ranking officials were also of great help and many times made the difference between life and death for Jews. In the city of Nancy, in the occupied zone, Edouard Vigneron and his assistant Pierre Marie were at their desk in the regional police commissariat. Vigneron was in charge of the foreign residents of the city. This included most local Jews, who were foreign nationals. In July 1942 there was to be a major roundup of Parisian Jews. Vigneron received a dispatch which stated that some 400 of the Jews of Nancy were soon to be rounded up by the Gestapo in one surprise swoop. Vigneron was troubled. He decided to take his aide, Marie, into his confidence. With the help of Marie and the other employees of his department, Vigneron immediately set out to warn all Jews (both foreigners and French citizens) to take precautionary measures and temporarily quit the area. All were provided with false identity cards to tide them over the emergency.

Fourteen-year-old Leon Herzberg was one of the fortunate Jews. As he left the high school building the morning of July 16, he was met by Pierre Marie, who placed in his hands a pack of newly fabricated identity cards for Leon's whole family. "He waited until I had tucked them in my school knapsack, then left," Leon recalls. "The meeting had hardly lasted two minutes, and I had with me two false ID's, but ostensibly in order, for my mother and grandmother."

When the Nazis launched their raid at dawn on July 19, 1942, only nineteen Jews were netted. The others had mysteriously disappeared and were in hiding. Vigneron was suspected of complicity in the disappearance of the city's Jews. He was arrested twice but survived the occupation. (2268)

Camille and Denise Mathieu

Camille Mathieu was a guard at the notorious Drancy transit camp, outside Paris. There, a group of Parisian Jewish men who were incarcerated on August 20, 1941, were waiting for their fate to be decided by the German authorities. The wives of the imprisoned men sought ways to establish contact with their husbands, to learn of their state of health and nourishment needs. Mrs. Herzberg and several other wives of the imprisoned men rented a hotel room in the vicinity and sought ways to approach the camp's fence. After several days of planning, they decided to draw near the fence at dawn.

As they approached, they were discovered by a militiaman from his observation post. It was Camille Mathieu. He cautioned them not to proceed further, as he was under strict orders to keep people away from the fence. Frightened at first, the women, Mrs. Herzberg, Mrs. Aidjenbaum, and Mrs. Fuks, regained their composure and pleaded their cause. After a brief silence, the guard responded by instructing them to note down their addresses on a slip of paper which they were to haphazardly drop on the ground. He promised to visit them in a few days time, when his period of leave was up. "I must truly say that we did not really believe in this promised visit," Mrs. Herzberg relates, "but ten days later, Mrs. Fuks came running home to inform me that the militiaman and his wife were at this very moment at her home and that we could through them deliver provisions and letters. . . . From this moment, for us, hope replaced desperation."

This first step led Mathieu to devise plans to have the three men liberated by placing them on the list of the very sick who needed immediate hospitalization. If this were to fail, he was prepared to lead them out through the sewer of the brick building which served as internment camp. But, luckily, they were released. Had Camille done nothing more, he would already have deserved praise and admiration. But he went far beyond. He and his wife decided to take these three families under their personal care. The Aidjenbaums were helped to cross the demarcation line into the Free Zone. Mr. and Mrs. Fuks were hidden with Camille's mother at Lignière (Aube) in the occupied zone, where they remained hidden until France was liberated—a full three years. Mrs. Herzberg was helped to cross into the unoccupied zone with her two daughters and then to join Mr. Hertzberg in Grenoble, where he had gone earlier. Denise Mathieu visited them there, bringing along new false credentials to replace those the Herzbergs had received earlier ("too obviously false"). Camille Mathieu was dismissed from his post, no doubt because his superiors felt that he could no longer be expected to faithfully carry out instructions.

There was never any talk of monetary compensation for his help. "The question never arose," Mrs. Herzberg emphatically notes. "The Mathieus are upright persons and what they did had no price. . . . They would not have understood it." "We would have been incapable [of paying them, if it had been demanded]," Mrs. Fuks adds. "As a tailor, I had on me only limited resources when tragedy struck us. . . . If we were able to last all this time [three years] at Lignieres, it is due to the generosity of our friends, Mr. and Mrs. Mathieu, who treated us as members of their own family." After the war, they remained in close touch. "They are for us more than a family," notes Mrs. Fuks, "sincere friends, on whose devotion we can count in all circumstances." Mrs. Herzberg adds to this: "At all times, we cannot but bless them for everything they did in such a natural way, to help us escape a fate that, without them, awaited us. *We were not alone* [Mrs. Herzberg's emphasis]. Can you realize what this meant for us?" (1098)

On the Move and Across Frontiers

Transferring Jewish children to safer locations within the country was, of course, of great concern to the OSE organization. The need for safe refuges for children was especially great because many of the Vichy authorities, conscious of public opinion, could not bring themselves to deport children to unknown destinations together with their parents. They consequently consented to set the children free. It thus became imperative to find permanent, or at least temporary, shelters for the children before the authorities changed their policy. Many non-Jewish escorters were enlisted in this urgent task and they acquitted themselves with selfless devotion in this dangerous mission.

Renée (Pauline) Gaudefroy

One of these was Renée ("Pauline") Gaudefroy, a young nurse and social worker by profession, who was asked by the Garel section of the OSE to place children with friendly families in the regions of Haute Vienne, Creuse, and Corrèze. She would provide the children with false identities and escort them on dangerous train journeys to their new homes. She was not beyond exerting pressure to have the children admitted for safekeeping; the directors of a children's home in La Souterraine near Limoges at first prevaricated, but then succumbed to Pauline's threats to have them denounced to the underground.

In June 1944, she was arrested by the notorious PPF (French Gestapo) in Limoges and severely tortured. Slipping out a back window that same evening, she escaped and hid for a while. Then all traces of her were lost. She was last seen in Dournazac on June 27th. Her fate will perhaps never be known for sure. Dr. Tuvi Salomon, who met her in 1943 when he was an OSE operative, describes her as "always quiet, smiling and unassuming, in her nurse's uniform. . . . Her moral behavior and modesty aroused the respect of her charges, who felt peaceful and confident in her presence. We all held her in great admiration: this young woman who shared our sufferings without being constrained to do so."

After the war, the OSE commemorated her memory by naming a new children's home outside Paris "Pauline Gaudefroy Home—OSE." She truly deserved this honor, for as many as 150 children owe their lives to her. (1038)

Dr. Rita Breton

The Paris metropolitan area was where the largest number of Jews congregated of any city. Hence, the task of spiriting the children out to distant farm and country localities, or even secure suburban dwellings, was the more compelling. There were always good people, such as Rita

Dr. Rita Breton, center, *at Yad Vashem (1987) with Dr. Mordecai Paldiel and Mr. Morgenstern,* right, *whom she saved during the war. Courtesy of Yad Vashem.*

Breton, who were willing to bear the burden. Dr. Breton, who was a physician in general practice, led some 200 Jewish children to adoptive homes in Normandy, without the host families being told at first—and sometimes at all—of the children's true origins. She was able to accomplish this with the complicity of Henriette Duchemin, who was the mayor's secretary and a schoolteacher in the village of La Chapelle du Bois, near Evreux.

Among her many responsibilities, Dr. Breton saw to it that new identity papers, ration cards, and other credentials were provided for this large group of children. She visited the host families to distribute money to defray the costs of the children's upkeep, monies which were made available by the American Joint Distribution Committee, via the OSE. "I did this with all my heart," emphasizes Dr. Breton, "In the midst of the general indifference, I heard the cries of women and children during the July 16, 1942 roundups, this new St. Bartholomew [a reference to the St. Bartholomew's Day massacre of French Huguenots on August 24, 1572] . . . . I could not accept this, and that is why I acted."

On October 19, 1943, Dr. Breton took Henri Morgenstern, an eight-year-old child born in Paris, and his brother from the OSE center to her apartment, where they spent the evening. Their father had just been picked up in a raid, and his fate was unknown. The following morning Dr. Breton took the Morgenstern children to La Chapelle du Bois to hide with a family. Dr. Breton provided a separate proper hiding place elsewhere for the children's mother, who was five months pregnant. Mrs. Morgenstern later gave birth to a girl. Leon Erder, another young refugee boy, was taken to St. Pierre des Bois, near Mans.

After the war, the no less arduous task of collecting the children from various places and reuniting them with their parents or relatives began— for those who were fortunate enough to return from the concentration camps or places of hiding. The terrors of those days caused Dr. Breton to want to forget this sad period. "I did everything to forget; to forget in order to continue living," she writes in a 1981 letter to Henri Morgenstern. (2290)

Suzanne Spaak

Suzanne Spaak was the daughter of a noted banker and sister-in-law of Paul-Henri Spaak, who later became the foreign minister of Belgium. She was affiliated with a nondenominational underground organization based in Paris and decided to concentrate her efforts on saving Jewish children. In this endeavor, she was helped by a select group of trusted aides (Jews and non-Jews alike, such as Dr. Fred and Denise Milhaud and Marcelle Guillemot). "We were not very optimistic regarding the capabilities of our new collaborator," relates B. Aronson, one of her colleagues in this mission, "but how great was our mistake. Suzanne Spaak belonged to the category of idealists for whom their private lives and personal needs cease to exist the moment a great idea comes to possess their soul and heart." Aronson's moving eyewitness account has been confirmed by others: When she came to us, she told us: "tell me what I must do; it is all the same for me to do this or that work, from the moment that I want to serve in the struggle against Nazism."

> And what did she not do! She pounded on doors of priests and demanded that they take a stand in the face of persecutions. She went to see judges and writers, reminding them of their sacred obligation to do something; she traversed the length and breadth of Paris to find a hospital to shelter sick Jews who were in hiding under a false name. Her apartment became the headquarters where representatives of different resistance movements met. During a 24-hour period, university professors, workers, priests, Jews, social workers, communists, and Gaullists passed through it. However, there was a special type of activity which was closest to her heart and to which she dedicated herself with a special enthusiasm: the rescue of Jewish children.
>
> Suzanne Spaak was the mother of two children, who had never known want and worry, in contrast to Jewish children. She was a happy mother to happy children but this happiness no longer fulfilled her when

she found herself for the first time facing the tragedy of Jewish children. From this moment on, she considered aiding Jewish children a most sacrosanct obligation. There were no obstacles and dangers which could stop her.

She furnished hundreds of children with false papers and provided them ration cards. In the city and countryside she located for them hundreds of families willing to give them shelter, thus saving them from the grip of the Gestapo. . . . Danger hovered over the heads of children at UGIF [Association of French Jews, the sole Jewish representative body recognized by the authorities]. . . . Hundreds of Jewish families, risking their lives, assaulted the UGIF offices demanding the return of their children. . . . When she learned of the danger facing these children, she (who as an Aryan was not even permitted entrance to UGIF premises) presented herself before these leaders and demanded that the UGIF centers be vacated of Jewish children and placed in secure hands. . . . Within twenty hours, over sixty children were hidden and the immediate danger was over, but they had to be fed and clothed and looked after.

Suzette Spaak took this upon herself. She led an admirable group of men and women . . . who helped her. . . , among them Countess de la Bourdonnais, Pastor Vergara, Mrs. Brasseur, and others. In a few days, the children were fully provided for. . . All the children she saved are alive and enjoy freedom, but Suzanne Spaak is no longer there.

She was arrested by the Gestapo in October 1943 and was kept incarcerated for a almost a year. On August 12, 1944, days before the liberation of Paris, she was executed. "We could not believe the news," states B. Aronson in his 1945 deposition, "but then, who could doubt the barbarism of the Nazis?" After the war, many of her former charges, now orphaned, were grouped in an institution in which one classroom bears her name. Such was the measure of this singularly outstanding woman. (62)

Marie Junker

When the war began, Marie Junker was a nanny in Belfort for the Blums, a Jewish family with three children. When war clouds threatened Europe during the Munich crisis in 1938 Marcel Blum, a reserve officer in the French army, was called up. Mrs. Blum asked Marie what she planned to do in the event of war. Would she pack and return to her native Switzerland or stay with the Blums? Marie said she needed a day to consider the matter before responding. The following day, she told Mrs. Blum in simple terms: "I am staying with you and will follow you!" Mrs. Blum embraced her (this "saint," as she calls her), not yet suspecting what in lay in store for both in the years ahead.

When the Germans occupied France in 1940, the Blums, like countless other Jews, fled to the relative security of the southern Free Zone. They arrived at Béziers, where many Jews were subsequently interned in the nearby camp of Agde. There, Marie Junker helped with easing the plight of the camp inmates. Dr. Gaston Lévy, the OSE-appointed doctor for the internees of the camp, must have been impressed with her personality and character, for Marie Junker became one of the principal couriers for Dr. Lévy and his colleagues, Dr. Hélène Schrotter-Légla and her husband Dr. Arthur Schrotter, in working to save Jewish children who were released from the camps.

Marie scoured the countryside to search for hiding places among families. She also looked after adult Jews released from the camps and daily visited two elderly women in hiding. "She exerted herself to uphold, physically and spiritually, the many children who lived in deplorable conditions," notes Dr. Lévy. When Dr. Schrotter had to go into hiding (because she was a Polish national, she was on the threatened deportation list) and had to separate from her infant son for his own security, Marie Junker (who in the meantime had followed the Blum family to St. Benoit du Sault) proposed to have the child registered as her out-of-wedlock son. She stoutly insisted to the Swiss consulate personnel in Lyon that the child was hers, and she somehow induced the hesitant and stolid Swiss officials to have the child registered on her passport.

Marie's name was brought to the attention of Georges Garel and Andrée Salomon, the heads of the OSE branch dealing with finding shelters and escape routes for thousands of Jewish children, and they entrusted her with a group of eighteen children to be led under her guidance on a long journey toward the Swiss border, and then across it. Reporting on the success of one such mission, she notes nonchalantly: "We arrived safely at Annemasse but were prevented from leaving the city at the train station. The children remained that evening in town, and the following day, I took with me a part of this group to cross the border with them. We arranged them with families in Geneva. Then they were taken to Basel."

She continued in her humanitarian cause, declining the offers of friends to remain in the serene atmosphere of her native homeland upon the conclusion of a mission. Instead she returned to the dangers of occupied France and the town of St. Bernard de Sault to undertake a new mission and look after the persons closest to her—the Blum family. "Do you recall," Marie Junker wrote to Mrs. Blum in 1961, "how once, upon my return from Switzerland, we went together to the Rivesaltes camp to distribute clothes that I had brought with me?" Such was the dedication of this woman.

Not satisfied with her commitments to the Blums and the OSE, Marie Junker also helped the French underground in various ways: caring for resistance personnel in hiding, organizing a nurse's course for the wives of resistance operatives, and thanks to her knowledge of German, persuading German soldiers who were searching for partisans to leave the town of St. Benoit and then calming the frightened population, who feared a repetition of the Oradour massacre in their hometown. The local St. Benoit du Sault and St. Martin de la Place muncipalities issued certificates verifying these facts. In all this, Marie Junker escaped detection and suffered no harm to her person. She was indeed a remarkably capable nanny! (527)

Rolande Birgy

Crossing the Swiss and Spanish frontiers was an enticing goal for many Jews in France seeking sanctuary from further persecution. In time, it became a necessity. Desperate to escape death at the hands of the Germans, Jews were willing to brave inclement weather, the forbidden mountains of the Pyrenees and the Alps, the dangers of detection, the possibility of being betrayed by dishonest smugglers, arrest by German and French border police, and—perhaps their worst nightmare—being driven back into France by Swiss border guards who were ordered to refuse fleeing Jews entry into Switzerland. To have even a minimum chance of successfully crossing the border, help was needed from non-Jews who were willing to risk their own lives.

One such remarkable "ferry-person" was Rolande Birgy. Affiliated with JOC (a Catholic youth movement), she was active in guiding Jews across the Swiss border in early 1944. At that time the Nazis intensified their search for Jews in hiding and applied brutal measures heretofore used only in the occupied countries of Eastern Europe. Rolande Birgy volunteered to lead group after group of Jewish refugees toward the Swiss border at the Annemasse-St. Julien crossing points. Emanuel Racine of the Jewish underground was in charge of this vast clandestine operation. He testifies that she accompanied hundreds of children and adults (including Racine's wife Sara and daughter Cécile). He describes her as instilled with exceptional courage, fearlessness, and devotion to serve a cause which she considered a "divine mission." "Hundreds of rescued persons owe her their lives," he states.

Among those she helped were Jacques Pulver and his family. Coming to their aid when they feared arrest by the Gestapo, Rolande took charge of them at St. Julien en Genevois, not far from the border, where they were temporarily hidden by a priest. She then crossed the border with them somewhere near Bossey. Jacques Pulver relates how it actually took place. "She accompanied us, as though we were on an excursion, alongside a frontier road, and then suddenly raised the barbed wire and made everyone cross. We had hardly crossed when a German patrol car appeared, and she barely managed to flee with the pushcart we had brought along for transporting our twin daughters (aged three years). A second too late, she would have fallen into the hands of the Germans." (2613)

Helga Holbek and Alice Resch

The American Quakers had established a good reputation in Europe since the days of World War I, when they freely helped many dislocated refugees—friend or foe—with food, clothing, moral uplift, and comfort. In the early 1940s, the Vichy government authorized them to enter the detention camps in southern France in order to pursue their charitable work. Their relative freedom of movement gave them a unique opportunity to help Jews smuggled out of the camps and eventually to help spirit them across the Swiss border. They acquitted themselves bravely and honorably in carrying out this task.

Two such Quaker volunteer workers were Helga Holbek and Alice Resch from Norway. They worked in close coordination with OSE personnel. Children were separated from their parents and taken to children's homes outside the camps. They were then taken to either the Spanish or the topographically more accessible Swiss border, where children and guides made a desperate rush to freedom. With the children safely tucked away in Switzerland, the two women returned to France and to the hazards and perils of additional missions. "She never said no to the missions we assigned her," remarks Ruth Lambert, an OSE worker, about Alice Resch. "In these missions, nothing was legal; one played for the highest stakes, the sole goal being to save Jewish children."

Martin Eckstein was one of the Jewish boys saved. Born in Weinheim, Germany, he and his entire family were removed from their homes by the Gestapo in October 1940 and sent together with all Jews from the Baden and Wurtemberg regions, across the French border. The French authorities, smarting from their defeat earlier that year, dared not protest the German action too loudly. The French already had a significant problem dealing with refugees; they simply incarcerated this new group at Gurs camp, which was located at the foot of the Pyrenees.

In the spring of 1941, in a joint OSE-Quaker operation, Martin was released and taken with forty other children to the orphanage at Aspet, where he stayed until February 1943. Alice Resch then brought him to Toulouse, and with a false Swedish passport in hand, began the long journey, with other children, toward the Swiss border. The children were told that if questioned on the train, they should reply that they were going on an outing to the Alps (they were appropriately provided with ice skates).

After they arrived safely in Annemasse, Alice, with the help of a Red Cross woman, rehearsed the bold crossing four times. Everything went through as scheduled, but it almost ended in disaster. The plan was to attempt the crossing at noon, when the French and Swiss custom officials would each be savoring their lunch break inside their guard posts. As Alice Resch relates: "We arrived at the spot where we had to separate and send the children off alone on an adventure. I hid behind a house; my heart was beating. . . . My God, there are three [boys] returning by running." The boys had been discovered by two custom officials who had stepped outside their shed to continue their conversation. Ordered to halt, three boys fled back to the French side. Martin, the fourth boy in the group, after hesitating for a split-second, made off toward the Swiss side. The custom guards decided not go give chase. "I am the sole survivor of my family," writes Martin Eckstein, now in the United States. "Miss Resch saved my life."

Kolos Vary and his wife, two adult beneficiaries of Alice and Helga's help, were not that fortunate in their crossing attempt. They had met and befriended each other inside the Gurs camp. One day, after a forced deportation of Jews from the camp, Helga Holbek confided to Kolos Vary: "I did not close an eye and have not slept for months. The humming of truck engines loaded with Jews, young and old, the harrowing cries of children torn from their parents; the desperate wailing of mothers bidding farewell to their little ones, have brought me to desperation. And I have also thought about you. You must leave, Kolos, you must leave this place."

With the help of French Red Cross representatives in the camp, they were able to obtain temporary exit passes. Outside, about a mile and a quarter down the road, Helga impatiently waited for them in a car with two French priests who provided them with false identities. They hurriedly left for Toulouse and then to the Swiss border which they crossed successfully. Arriving in Geneva, Helga exclaimed, "You are saved! You are in Switzerland!"

However, much to their dismay, they were arrested the following morning and driven back into France, where they were apprehended, tried, and incarcerated in an Annecy jail.

Helga doubled back to France and pleaded with the authorities not to have her charges returned to Gurs. They were, instead, assigned to a work labor unit from which, with Helga's aid, they succeeded in escaping and once again crossed into Switzerland; Helga was waiting there to welcome them. "This is how, thanks to this extraordinary woman, we are still alive," Kolos Vary wrote after the war. "Her humanity and her unequaled devotion saved us."

"How often, during all these years," Alice Resch wrote in 1980 from Copenhagen to one of her former charges at Aspet, now in Israel, "have I wondered what had become of my children from Aspet. . . . You were all so young then and surely do not remember much from that period. How lovely to hear that both you and Carl are doing so well. And also your brother Manfred. You ask if I remember you? I should say I do! I remember all my children from Aspet! You see, it was my very first experience of such a close contact with children, and so many! To me, the memory of that month I spent with you in the Pyrenees is very precious."

Menachem-Heinz Mayer, the recipient of Helga's long letter, was part of a group of children led across the Swiss border in March 1944 by Alice Resch. "I recall clearly her modesty on a task accomplished," recalls Ruth Lambert, an OSE leader at the Gurs camp. "A mission accomplished, she was soon available for other undertakings, all dangerous—for everything was dangerous for anyone trying to be even a bit human, regardless of [the helped person's] religion and nationality." Helga and Alice stood up to the test and preserved their humanity. (2142)

Pastor Roland de Pury

Arriving safely on the Franco-Swiss border meant traversing hundreds of miles, by train or bus, through an occupied country. The behavior of the French gendarmes was generally unpredictable. They occasionally examined identity papers and even interrogated those who took part in this "Underground Express" heading for the border. Relay stations were, of course, of cardinal importance, to rest, shore up strength, and map out the next stages. One such stopover was the home of Pastor Roland de Pury in Lyon. A Swiss citizen, he had studied under the noted theologian Karl Barth and came to Lyon in 1938 to assume a minister's post at the church on Rue Lanterne. He was one of the first to preach disobedience to the Vichy state.

On July 10, 1940, weeks after the French surrender to Germany, when most Frenchmen, including the Catholic hierarchy and even some Protestants, were rallying behind the aged World War I hero Marshal Philippe Pétain (who now shifted his country away from its democratic tradition), De Pury preached the following ringing sermon: "Better a dead France than one sold, defeated then robbed. One may weep over a dead France, but a France which betrays what the persecuted place in her, a France which has sold its soul and renounced its mission . . . this would no longer be France. Already people are no longer asking whether this was a just war; they regret having participated in it because they lost it. As if defeat removed the righteous nature of a struggle. As if success were the yardstick of truth. I admonish you, by the mercy God who has given you life, to offer your bodies, that is, your lives, your freedom, your time, your family, your goods, your work, as a living sacrifice."

True to his words, Pastor de Pury became involved in clandestine activities, assuming a link between CIMADE militants in France and Switzerland. His Swiss nationality facilitated his travels to Geneva, where he joined church leaders like Vissert Hooft and Adolf Freudenberg in pleading with the Swiss government to open its border to fleeing Jews. His house and church in Lyon were made available to all trustworthy "*passeurs*" and fleeing Jews from the internment camps in the south of France (Gurs, Rivesaltes, Noë, Récébédou) or for those arriving from the nearby Le Chambon area. His colleagues in this joint effort included Mireille Philip, Georges Casalis, and the distinguished CIMADE scout headmistress Madeleine Barot, as well as Catholic clergymen and lay workers.

An eyewitness who visited de Pury's house relates meeting Jews of all ages and professions from Germany, Austria, Hungary, Holland. "They were fed and sheltered with a total disinterest by de Pury's family, which charged itself with organizing their secret departure to Switzerland." Roland de Pury would accompany them to the frontier, and at times, would guide them as well into Switzerland. Rella Gottlieb, an employee of the *Union Générale des Israélites de France* (UGIF), a German-controlled Jewish umbrella organization, referred many Jewish children to the pastor's attention. "The number of Jewish children which she confided in the hands of the pastor, who hid them in France or sent them off toward Switzerland, increased day by day," remarks Anny Latour, who knew Mrs. Gottlieb from her underground work during the occupation and received from her the details of her work with de Pury.

On May 30, 1943, the Gestapo made a sudden irruption in de Pury's office. The eighty-six people there at the time, including Mrs. Gottlieb, were all deported. Only one returned. De Pury was thrown in jail and was awaiting interrogation by the Gestapo of his clandestine links when Germany and Switzerland decided on an exchange of spies or undesirable citizens held by both countries. On October 28, 1943, Roland de Pury, a Swiss citizen, was taken with other prisoners to Bregenz and released into Swiss hands. A stroke of good fortune had spared his life. (1066)

The Fathers of École St. François in Ville-la-Grand

Most of those who assisted Jews in crossing the border managed to elude the Germans and survive the war. Some were apprehended and paid with their lives. One of these was Father Louis Adrien Favre of the École St. François ("Juvenat"), a Catholic seminary located in the village of Ville-la-Grand. The advantage of this seminary as a crossing point was its location right on the border. The school's garden ended on one side of a wall which formed the frontier at this point. Crossings could be attempted, especially after the German border guards had passed within feet of the school and made a forty-five-degree turn alongside the garden wall, placing them out of sight for a few minutes. During this precious moment, a run could be made to the wall and with the help of a ladder quickly cross over to the Swiss side. The priests at the school estimate that hundreds were able to escape this way, the majority of them Jews.

The decision to become involved in this risky business was taken by Father Pierre Frontin, the school's head. "We formed a team of four or five instructors and brothers committed to saving the greatest number of persons possible who had asked us to help them cross—and save them." The prinicpal actors in this collegial effort were the Brothers Louis Favre, Gilbert Pernoud, Raymond Boccard, and François Favrat.

Boccard, the school's gardener, had a room under the roof which dominated the wall forming the border. "From there, one sees very far," Boccard relates, "thus I was able to observe easily the arrival of patrols. At

A former Jewish beneficiary, far left, *visits the Juvenat seminary in Ville-la-Grand, France, and two of its staff,* (2nd and 3rd from left), *immediately after the war. The fence behind them stands right on the border and is the one through which hundreds of Jews escaped with the help of the seminary's faculty. Courtesy of Yad Vashem.*

a favorable moment, when the German border guards, who scrupulously followed all the curves of the wall bordering on the frontier, could no longer see what was happening in our area, I gave the signal from my window by raising my hat. The fugitives had two minutes and thirty seconds time to make the crossing. One, therefore, had to hurry."

Boccard recalls feeding and sheltering hundreds of refugees in between crossings. Many were driven back by the Swiss, "We then sheltered these refugees for several hours or over night," recalls Boccard, "and it fell upon me to accompany them to the Annemasse train station, or to a certain coffee shop in Ambilly owned by underground sympathizers. On the way, I would tell these unfortunate persons to look natural so that they would be taken for the parents of pupils and therefore avoid drawing attention to themselves."

Of the hundreds thus helped, ninety percent were Jewish, according to Father Frontin's estimate. Among these were Alice Muller and her family, who were led across the border by Father Pernoud, at a point near the school. "My husband passed first; Father Pernoud handed him our daughters and I passed last," Alice recalls precisely. The Swiss border guards arrested them and took them to Geneva. They were then interned at the Bout-du-Monde camp. They were fortunate, they were not driven back into France, as so many others had been.

On September 12, 1942, David Wagner and his wife arrived at Ville-la-Grand, where they were welcomed "with open arms" by Father Favre. "He had the shining countenance of a saint," David recalls. "His eyes abounded with goodness. He told me, 'Oh, my son, how lucky that you are here already.' One had the feeling that this was a man ready to sacrifice himself to save other humans." Father Favre instructed them on the technicalities of the border crossing. "I crossed the barbed wire at midnight, and I ran for about 650 feet." Apprehended by the Swiss, David and his wife underwent a few anguished moments until the Swiss called their superiors to clear their entry into the country, already previously arranged.

Father Favre was less fortunate. Betrayed to the Gestapo, he and his colleagues were arrested on February 4, 1944. Father Favrat was released after a few days. Father Frontin was interned for five months. Louis Favre underwent brutal torture and was executed near Annecy on July 14, 1944. The seminary was subsequently shut down and all its residents expelled. (193, 3558, and 3601)

Jean Deffaugt

Annemasse was a town of some 8,000 inhabitants situated on the Swiss border. It was the place where most clandestine roads leading to the Swiss border met. The reputation of the town was not confined to its proximity to the frontier but also derived from the character of its inhabitants. This had much to do with the town's Vichy-appointed mayor, Jean Deffaugt. A mayor's comportment toward the refugees who surreptitiously passed through his town could well make the difference between the success or failure of their escape. It is not known why Deffaugt chose to throw in his lot with the refugees even though it meant disobedience to the Germans. He states that as a World War I veteran, he remained faithful to Marshal Pétain (whose portrait hung above his desk) throughout the occupation despite vociferous recriminations by members of the resistance, to which he also belonged.

His services to the persecuted began when he visited some refugees who had been caught by the Germans and incarcerated in an annex of the Pax hotel. There they had to withstand brutal interrogation by the Gestapo. Duffaugt collected food, medicaments, and blankets, which he carried to the Gestapo prison and personally delivered to the prisoners. The Gestapo jail register speaks amply on the makeup of the "criminals" languishing in that jail and their eventual fate, for example, "Folio 642:32 children, ages 2 1/2-18, caught trying to flee to Switzerland—sent to Drancy. Folio 127: Mila Racine, arrested 21.10.1943—sent to Drancy." Mila, the sister of Emmanuel Racine (whom we met in the Rolande Birgy story) had been arrested at Annecy leading a group of children. She left the following verses etched on her cell door: "For a friend who passes, and one day occupies this cell, remember: always keep your faith and smile, whatever happens." She was conveyed to the Ravensbrück women's camp, where she perished.

Anne-Marie (also known as Marianne) Cohn was arrested on June 4, 1944, leading a group of twenty-seven children to the Swiss border. The children had been carefully rehearsed to present themselves under their new adopted false names if stopped. Once across the border, they were to quickly fetch their credentials bearing their true name from the linings of their clothes and display them to the Swiss guards in the hope of being

Emmanuel Racine, on the steps of city hall in August 1944, thanking Mayor Jean Deffaugt, of Annemasse for his role in the rescue of several dozen Jewish children. Courtesy of Yad Vashem.

Memorial to Jean Deffaugt, in *Jean and Mrs. Deffaugt at Yad Vashem*
Annemasse, France, where he was *(1968). Courtesy of Yad Vashem.*
mayor during the war years. Courtesy
of Yad Vashem.

allowed entrance into the country (a government ruling exempted unac-
companied children from being driven back across the border). But they
had all been arrested and were now threatened with deportation. At this
stage, Deffaugt decided to intervene with Mayer, the local Gestapo chief,
on the children's behalf. "The trains are still moving," he told Mayer, "don't
you need them for bringing in reinforcements [he was speaking just after
the Allied landings on the beaches of Normandy] and not for transporting
children to camps?"

This was not the first time Deffaugt had pleaded with the Gestapo on
behalf of imprisoned Jews. As he later reminisced: "I do not believe those
who say they never knew fear. I was afraid, I admit. I never mounted the
Gestapo stairway without making the sign of the cross or murmuring a
prayer." (He once told an underground contact person that if he were ever
seen being taken away by the Gestapo, the resistance should try to shoot
him. He feared he would not be able to withstand the brutal interrogation
and would betray them under torture.) On this occasion, the Gestapo
agreed to release those under the age of eleven into Deffaugt's hands
provided that he make the following commitment, "I, the undersigned,

Jean Deffaugt, mayor of Annemasse, acknowledge receiving from Inspector Mayer, chief of the Security Service, eleven children of Jewish faith, whom I pledge to return at the first order." Deffaugt quickly placed them in the good hands of Father Duret, who hid them in nearby Bonne-sur-Menoge until the Allied liberation in the following weeks. However, the remaining sixteen children were kept imprisoned with their guide Marianne Cohen and made to do kitchen duties for German officers at their headquarters in the Hôtel de France.

A plan was hatched for Marianne's escape, but she would have none of it, she told Deffaugt, since she was convinced that the Germans would react by taking revenge on the children. On the night of July 7, 1944, she and four French underground men were taken to a nearby forest and shot together. In her cell she had written the following defiant poem: "Tomorrow I will betray, not today. Tear out my nails today, I will not betray. You don't know how long I can hold out, But I know. You are five rough hands with rings. You have hobnailed boots on your feet. . . . Today, I have nothing to say. Tomorrow, I will betray." She was not yet twenty years at the time of her death.

With the liberation of Annemasse by the U.S. Army the following month, all the children were collected by Deffaugt and turned over to Jewish organizations. "As a believing Christian, I always undertook to help and protect all those stricken with calamity, without distinction," Deffaugt said of himself after the war, his motto having been "Justice, love, happiness, and righteousness." Concerning his initiation into rescue activities, he stated, "It is only the first step that counts." The rest, we may add, comes naturally. (178)

* * *

We conclude this chapter with the stories of three unique individuals whose deeds place them in a class by themselves: the Capuchin monk Father Marie-Benoît, the Portuguese diplomat Aristides de Sousa Mendes, and the physician Adelaide Hautval. Their initiation into rescue activities took place on French soil but also extended beyond it.

Father Marie-Benoît

One of the most celebrated rescue stories to come out of the Holocaust is linked with the name of a French Capuchin monk, whose exploits on behalf of Jews can only be termed herculean and spectacular. In the summer of 1942, Father Marie-Benoît (born Pierre Péteul) was a resident monk in the Capuchin monastery at Marseille. There he witnessed the sad spectacle of thousands of non-French Jewish refugees being rounded up by Vichy authorities and handed over to the Germans for deportation to unknown destinations. Father Marie-Benoît's reaction to this travesty of basic human rights was swift and, so to speak, volcanic. As he stated at the time, "The law [under which Jews are imprisoned] is immoral, and one is not permitted to ignore such laws, but must actively resist them. There is no doubt in my mind that this is such a law, and such a time."

The Capuchin monastery at 51 Rue Croix de Régnier was transformed into the nerve center of a widespread rescue network; operating this network involved working with frontier smugglers (*passeurs*) and coordinating activities with various Christian and Jewish religious organizations. A printing press in the monastery's basement turned out numerous false baptismal certificates, documents needed by fleeing Jews in order to procure other vital documents.

With the German occupation of Vichy France in November 1942, the routes of escape into Switzerland and Spain were temporarily sealed. The nearby Italian zone of occupation now became the principal destination for escaping Jews. Journeying to Nice, Father Marie-Benoît coordinated plans with local Jewish organizations. He also met with General Guido Lospinoso, the Italian commissioner of Jewish Affairs (sent to Nice by Mussolini at the behest of the Germans, for the express purpose of initiating measures against Jews), and convinced him that the rescue, rather than the transfer to German hands (Lospinoso's original instructions), of some 30,000 Jews in Nice and environs was the divine order of the day. Marie-Benoît was promised that there would be no interference from the Italian occupation authorities.

Not satisfied with this commitment, and harboring presentiments as to the ultimate fate of the Jews in Nice, Marie-Benoît continued to Rome and, in an audience with Pope Pius XII on July 16, 1943, outlined a plan (with the blessings of Commissioner Lospinoso) for transferring the 30,000 Jews in Nice to northern Italy to prevent their falling into German hands. This plan was later elaborated to include their shipment to former military camps in North Africa, now in Allied hands. The new Italian government of Marshal Badoglio (Mussolini having been deposed by the Grand Fascist Council on July 25, 1943) was prepared to provide ships for this giant undertaking, and ways were found to funnel funds from Jewish organizations abroad. However, the Italian armistice on September 8, 1943, sooner than originally anticipated, and the immediate German occupation of northern Italy and the Italian zone in France foiled this plan.

Father Marie-Benoît now moved his activities to Rome. To be able to deal effectively with the onerous task of providing food, shelter, and new identities to thousands of Jewish refugees in Rome and elsewhere in Italy, he was elected a board member of DELASEM, the central Jewish welfare organization of Italy, and when its Jewish president, Settimio Sorani, was arrested by the Germans, Marie-Benoît was elected president and chaired the organization's meetings inside the Capuchin College (across the street from a notorious Gestapo prison). He escaped several attempts by the Gestapo to have him arrested as his fame spread among Jews and non-

Chief Rabbi Jacob Kaplan embracing Father Marie-Benoît during the presentation of the Legion of Honor by the French government (1984). Left, Israeli ambassador Ovadiah Sofer. Courtesy of Yad Vashem.

Jews, who dubbed him "Father of the Jews." His zeal, stamina, and devotion in the cause of Jews knew no bounds. He extracted "letters of protection" and other important documents from the Swiss, Romanian, Hungarian, and Spanish legations. With these documents thousands of Jews, under assumed names, were able to circulate freely in Rome. Father Marie-Benoît acquired a large batch of ration cards from the Rome police, ostensibly on behalf of non-Jewish homeless refugees stranded in the capital city.

After Rome's liberation in June 1944, Father Marie-Benoît was hailed by the Jewish community at an official synagogue ceremony. With the war over and the Jews safe, he returned to his ecclesiastical duties. France awarded him various military decorations; Israel, through Yad Vashem, the title of Righteous Among the Nations, in response to which he addressed the following letter:

> What I did for the Jewish people, what I did to merit being called Father of the Jews was but an infinitesimal contribution to what ought to have been done in order to prevent this horrible slaughter, unprecedented and satanic, of some six million Jews, which will undoubtedly remain the foulest stain in all of human history, a shame affecting all who participated or who allowed it to happen. They wanted to exterminate the Jewish people. But the Jewish people will not be exterminated. By divine decree, the Jewish people is determined to fulfill its divine providential goals, for its own good, and finally for the good of all humanity.

Untold thousands of Jews owe their lives to this self-effacing Capuchin monk, the epitome of the Good Samaritan. (201)

Aristides de Sousa Mendes

Aristides de Sousa Mendes was the son of a Portuguese supreme court justice. A professional diplomat, in May 1940 he was his country's consul general in Bordeaux. That month, with the German breakthrough in the Ardennes and the collapse of the Anglo-French front in northern France, the number of refugees fleeing the battle zone to the relative security of the south increased significantly. The majority sought entry to Spain, then to Lisbon in Portugal; from there they hoped to continue to different lands by ship.

In order to cross the Spanish frontier, the refugees needed a Portuguese entry or transit visa. However, on May 10, 1940, when the German invasion of the Low Countries and France began, the Portuguese government banned the further passage of refugees through its territory. The government also instructed its consular representatives in France not to issue visas to escaping refugees, and in particular not to Jews.

All passage of refugees across the Spanish border came to a sudden halt, creating a congestion of refugees in Bordeaux, the major French city closest to the Spanish frontier, where some 30,000 refugees—a third of them Jews—found themselves stranded. For lack of proper facilities close to 10,000 refugees settled down in and around the city's main square, many of them near the great synagogue, others, in front of the Portuguese legation. Thus they passed several sleepless nights. Rabbi Haim Kruger was among them, having arrived in Bordeaux from Brussels.

This was the grim background for the chance encounter between Mendes, out on one of his nocturnal fact-finding tours of the city, and Rabbi Kruger as he was preparing to spend another night on the streets. Rabbi Kruger relates that Mendes, touched by the rabbi's plight, invited him to the Portuguese legation, whose facilities he then placed at the rabbi's disposal.

That night Rabbi Kruger described the travails of his Jewish co-religionists: "If we should be trapped here, I don't know what will happen to us." He implored Mendes to grant entry visas to the stranded Jews outside. After some reflection, Mendes replied that he was prepared to issue entry visas for the rabbi and his family but could not, without his government's assent, extend this to other Jewish refugees. The rabbi, however, would not be placated.

After further soul-searching, Mendes announced that he had reversed his previous decision and was prepared to grant entry visas to anyone seeking them. Meanwhile a large crowd had gathered outside the Portuguese legation; Mendes asked the rabbi's help in lining up the people with passports at the ready. "I sat with him a full day without food and sleep and helped him stamp thousands of passports with Portuguese visas," the rabbi relates, adding, "He did not eat or sleep until late at night. And during this short time he issued several thousand visas until the enemy approached Bordeaux and we were forced to flee to Spain."

According to another account, Mendes's volte-face occurred immediately after he had seen his government's renewed instructions concerning refugees. Mendes was particularly upset that the Jews were singled out for visa denial. His reaction to this, as reported by his nephew Cesar Mendes, came in a speech to his staff. "My government has denied all applications for visas to any refugees. But I cannot allow these people to die. Many are

Aristides de Sousa Mendes at the wedding of his daughter Isabel in 1936, together with several of his other children. Courtesy of Yad Vashem.

Jews and our constitution says that the religion, or the politics, of a foreigner shall not be used to deny him refuge in Portugal. I have decided to follow this principle. I am going to issue a visa to anyone who asks for it—regardless of whether or not he can pay." Then, turning in the direction of his wife, he continued: "I know that Mrs. de Sousa Mendes agrees with me. Even if I am dismissed, I can only act as a Christian, as my conscience tells me."

Word of the consul's magnanimity had already spread like wildfire throughout the city, as Jews and others who had reasons to fear the Nazis sought his solicitude. To accommodate this huge influx of refugees, Mendes threw his home open to them. Cesar Mendes relates seeing people of all ages, including pregnant women and sick people, sitting on the floor and leaning against the walls outside the consulate. "They had waited for days and nights on the street. . . . They neither ate nor drank for fear of losing their place in the line. . . . They did not wash themselves . . . They did not change their clothes and they did not shave. . . . My uncle got ill, was exhausted, and had to lie down." Moise Alias, a witness to, and recipient of, Mendes's charity gives voice to the feelings of many: "It seems to me that it was due to divine intervention that such a person was to be found at the right time in the right place."

The reaction of the Portuguese government was not long in coming. Upon learning of Mendes's insubordination, it ordered his immediate recall. Two official emissaries were dispatched from Lisbon to accompany the recalcitrant consul home. On the way to the Spanish border, the party stopped in Bayonne, a city which came under the jurisdiction of the Bordeaux consulate. There, the local consul, heeding his government's instructions rather than those of Mendes, his immediate superior in Bordeaux, was refusing visa requests by petitioning Jews.

When Mendes learned of this, he remonstrated with the Bayonne vice-consul. According to an eyewitness report, Mendes asked the vice-consul, "Why don't you help these people?" The latter retorted, "I have received instructions from Lisbon not to grant any visas, especially to Jews. I am carrying out my superior's instructions." Enraged, Mendes countered, "I have not yet been removed from my position. I am still your superior."

With these words he walked over to the vice-consul's desk and gathered up the necessary seals and rubber stamps for the visas. No one could stop him, not even the two emissaries from Lisbon. Then, summoning the vice-consul, Mendes ordered him, "Go and tell these people [outside] to come to the chancellery . . . I am going to give them visas." These visas were unique documents that had never been issued before—slips of paper bearing the consulate's seal and the following inscription: "The Portuguese government requests the Spanish government the courtesy of allowing the bearer to pass freely through Spain. He is a refugee from the European conflict en route to Portugal." Mendes spent a full day in the Bayonne legation issuing such visas.

The following morning, Mendes and his entourage proceeded to the Spanish frontier. Arriving at the town of Biarritz, Mendes was surprised to discover that the Spanish authorities, evidently on cue from Portugal to Spanish officials, had closed the border to all refugees producing Portuguese visas issued in Bordeaux. Rabbi Kruger, who was present, relates what ensued, "As we were standing and imploring the border police, the consul appeared and told us to wait a while as he wanted to talk to them. After an hour or two he personally opened the frontier gate and all who presented a visa issued by him were allowed through. From there we boarded a train going straight to Lisbon." Another account has Mendes taking the refugees to a different frontier post on the assumption that the Spanish government had not bothered to relay its new instructions to the border authorities other than in the Biarritz area, where the refugees were concentrated. In this, Mendes proved to be right.

Upon his return to Lisbon, the government, fuming at Mendes's insubordination, summarily dismissed him from the Ministry of Foreign Affairs and suspended all his retirement and severance benefits. Mendes appealed directly to the government, but to no avail. Burdened with the onerous task of feeding a large family including thirteen children, and with no other means of support at his disposal, Mendes sank into poverty. As his situation worsened, he sold his ancient family estate in Cabanas de Viriato. HIAS, a U.S.-based Jewish welfare organization, did what it could to mitigate his suffering, and two of his children were helped to relocate and start new lives in the United States. In 1954, he died, forgotten, heartbroken, and impoverished (his wife had died earlier, in 1948). In 1966 he was posthumously honored as a Righteous Gentile by Yad Vashem.

Mendes constantly mentioned his religious beliefs as the mainspring of his actions. In one conversation, he said: "My desire is to be with God against man, rather than with man against God." After his dismissal, he told Rabbi Kruger (whom he met briefly for a third time in Lisbon), "If thousands of Jews can suffer because of one Catholic [i.e., Hitler], then surely it is permitted for one Catholic to suffer for so many Jews." He added: "I could not have acted otherwise, and I therefore accept all that has befallen me with love."

Bowing to pressure by the Mendes children and by various organizations in the United States, the Portuguese National Assembly decided, in 1987, to award Mendes a full posthumous rehabilitation. That same year, the Israeli government's commemorative citizenship was awarded him and presented to his family in a public ceremony. (264)

Dr. Adelaide Hautval

Dr. Adelaide Hautval was born in 1906 into a French Protestant family. She studied medicine in Strasbourg, and after her qualification worked in several psychiatric wards in France and Switzerland. In April 1942, on a trip to her mother's funeral, she was arrested trying to cross the demarcation line separating the two zones of France without a permit. Awaiting her trial in Bourges prison, she vehemently protested to the Gestapo against the harsh treatment of Jewish prisoners who were incarcerated there. The reply she received was, "As you wish to defend them, you will follow their fate."

She was eventually sent to Auschwitz with a convoy of Jewish women; she arrived in January 1943. She reportedly bore a sign, stitched on her overcoat, with the inscription: "A friend of the Jews." At Auschwitz, she helped hide a group of women, afflicted with typhus, on the top landing of her barrack and looked after them as best as she could. She was then asked by Dr. Eduard Wirths (the garrison doctor and an S.S. officer) whether she wished to practice gynecology. Curious to have a firsthand view of the sterilization experiments which she had learned were being practiced in Block 10, she accepted Dr. Wirths's offer. In this barrack, she soon discovered, Dr. Wirths was in charge of a team of doctors (Schumann, Clauberg, and Dering) who used women as guinea pigs, removing their ovaries either surgically or by means of radiation. These experiments were part of a large-scale plan, since sterilization was meant to be applied to all half- and quarter-Jews who would be left alive after all full-blooded Jews had been eliminated. The tests on both male and female reproductive organs were for the purpose of determining the dose that would automatically produce sterility.

Adelaide Hautval told Dr. Wirths that she was completely opposed to these experiments. Wirths was surprised that she would object to a program whose ultimate purpose was the preservation of a superior race. As she testified in London, 1964, in the Dering vs. Uris trial, Wirths "talked to me about the Jewish Question, and I answered that we had no right to dispose of the life and destiny of others." She reported in her testimony that Wirths then asked her, "Cannot you see that these people are different from you? I answered him that there were several other people different from me, starting with him." From that time, she refused to participate in any experiments in Auschwitz. Dr. Mengele was also involved in these experiments. She feared retribution but was not punished. She told a colleague: "The Germans will not allow people who know what is happening here to get in touch with the outside world, so the only thing that is left to us is to behave, for the rest of the short time that remains to us, as human beings."

After her confrontation with Dr. Wirths, she was advised to stay out of sight for several weeks. She continued practicing medicine in the nearby Birkenau camp as well as she could until August 1944, when she was transferred to the Ravensbrück women's camp. She survived and was liberated in April 1945.

At the London trial, in 1964, she refuted Dr. Dering's claim that it was futile to refuse obeying orders in Auschwitz, which for a physician meant performing experiments of whatever sort when so ordered by the camp medical authorities. According to Dering, "to refuse would be sabotage.

That meant only one thing in the camp"; he said that in Auschwitz "all law, normal, human, and God's law were finished." Adelaide Hautval, by contrast, in support of the testimonies of several of her former colleagues at Auschwitz, maintained that S.S. orders to remove women's ovaries could be bypassed in such ways as to avoid punishment. Justice Lawton in his summing up of the evidence to the jury described Dr. Hautval as "perhaps one of the most impressive and courageous women who had ever given evidence in the courts of this country [England]." Her reply to Dr. Wirths, he continued, would live in the jury's memory for many years.

Years later, recalling the years of the Holocaust, Dr. Hautval had this to say, "This unspeakable horror could have been avoided. If only this organized contempt of humanity, this megalomaniac insanity, had been confronted by a civilized world—lucid, courageous, and determined to safeguard its primary values." On a visit to Israel in 1966, she stated, "The return of the people of Israel to their own country is an accomplishment concerning not only itself but the world at large. It has been ardently awaited by non-Jews. Israel has always played a gestative, fermentative role, due to which it was hated or respected. Its mission in the world continues. May Israel remain faithful to it. The entire history of the Jewish people demonstrates the primacy of spiritual forces. Hence, its undertaking cannot but be successful." (100)

Dr. Adelaide Hautval, who refused to participate in Nazi medical experiments, at Yad Vashem (1966). Courtesy of Yad Vashem.

Belgium

Help by Many Segments of the Population

Germany invaded and conquered Belgium in May 1940. While the army laid down its arms, the government moved to London, where it continued to defy the legitimacy of Belgium's surrender by King Leopold. The Germans on their part, not willing to repeat the mistakes of the excesses inflicted on the population during World War I, decided on a relatively lenient occupation policy. The country was granted autonomy on internal matters and allowed to govern itself according to the laws in force. A military administration was superimposed to deal with overall security matters but with little interference in local administrative affairs. In contrast to occupied Holland, the heads of the various governmental ministries remained in Belgian hands.

On the Jewish issue, however, the Germans would brook no interference in the grand design to rid the continent of all Jews.

Notwithstanding this outward show of leniency, government and civic authorities, as well as educational institutions, reacted vigorously in late 1940 when the Germans moved to enforce anti-Jewish measures. Judicial and academic heads vehemently protested the attempt to introduce discriminatory regulations in their areas of activity. In May 1942, Jean Hérinckx, on behalf of all mayors of the Brussels metropolitan region, protested in a letter to the military government the imposition of the yellow star edict on all Jews. Similarly, the head of the Catholic church, Cardinal Van Roey, made no secret of his displeasure at the racial measures and interceded with the authorities on behalf of Jews. Thus, in Belgium as early as late 1940, there began a subtle but concerted effort by the heads of the conquered but still functioning administration to frustrate German anti-Jewish designs, the only effort of its kind in all of German-occupied countries.

There were some 90,000 Jews residing in the country at the start of the invasion. Most fled to France during the early days of the war. Of these, over a half returned when the dust had settled in the summer of 1940. It is estimated that some 60,000 Jews remained in the country in 1942 when the Final Solution went into high gear. Half of these were deported to the death camps, and the other half—close to 30,000—were saved, most by going into hiding in religious and secular institutions or with helpful families.

In mid-1942, as German intentions vis-à-vis the Jewish population became more menacing, a Jewish-led organization was set up to stream-line rescue activities in coordination with public institutions and private individuals willing to help—the Jewish Defense Committee (CDJ). As distinct from the Association of Belgian Jews (AJB), an organ created by the Germans to serve their nefarious purposes, the CDJ was a clandestine organization, the principal purpose of which was to alert Jews on the necessity to seek shelter for themselves and their children. It succeeded in enlisting the support of a whole range of organizations and individuals representing a gamut of the Belgian population from all walks of life.

The role of the church in this predominantly Catholic country was of especial importance in this endeavor. With the primate of Belgium, Cardinal Van Roey, himself taking a personal interest in the rescue of Jews, churchmen were encouraged to help find shelter for Jewish children in various religious institutions, taking note of the cardinal's instruction not to exert any overt or subtle pressure to attempt converting children of a tender age who had been entrusted to their care. This was of course in line with traditional Catholic thinking that children forcibly separated from their parents could not be converted without their parents' consent.

Noteworthy among clergy who helped was Monsignor Kerkhofs, bishop of Liège (whose feats are described as "legendary"), who urged all clerics in his diocese to rescue Jews in spite of the attendant dangers to themselves, and himself referring fleeing Jews to various institutions, such as Rabbi Lepkifker, who under the name of M. l'Abbé Boty was hidden in a monastery at Banneux. Other clerics of note include Abbé Joseph André of Namur, who actually represented the CDJ in that city and was responsible for dispersing hundreds of Jewish children in the surrounding region, as well as Father Bruno (Henri Reyndeers) from Louvain, who rescued over 300 children, by pleading and cajoling families to accept these distraught youngsters, and by persuading financial institutions to subsidize the upkeep of host families—all this while the Gestapo was on his trail.

Members of the clergy were not beyond utilizing various ruses in order to save their wards. Thus, when danger threatened the Jewish children at a convent in Anderlecht (Brussels), Sister Claire d'Assisse interceded with the underground to forcefully free the children before the Gestapo came to round them up, then innocently complained to the police of the unlawful intrusion by masked men on hallowed grounds. In the meantime, the children were safe and secure.

Protestant religious heads also helped, such as M. Noel of the *Notre Maison* children home in Uccle (Brussels), where over twenty Jewish children and two adults were sheltered.

Among secular organizations that lent a willing hand, the role of the National Children's Society (ONE), a public children's welfare organization, headed by the energetic Yvonne Névejean, is especially noteworthy. Some 4,000 Jewish children were spirited out of Antwerp and Brussels Jewish homes and, via the ONE network of children homes, dispersed far and wide among cooperating families. The Gestapo suspected Névejean's involvement but was never able to produce indisputable incriminating evidence to that effect.

Other welfare organizations included the Winter Fund (*Secours d'Hiver*), which provided various necessities for the upkeep of Jews in hiding. In the medical field, doctors such as Mrs. Hendrickx-Duchaine admitted children for hospitalization for various fictitious ailments, some of whom were placed in infectious diseases wards where they were safe, as the Germans (ever terrified at the prospect of themselves contracting infectious diseases) avoided inspecting these wards. Banks and other financial institutions advanced loans against real or fictitious promissory notes to help defray the cost of this major undertaking. Funds were also forthcoming from the Belgian government-in-exile, whereas the Jewish people, through the Joint Distribution Committee, made funds available clandestinely from its offices in Geneva, Switzerland.

With the exception of the Antwerp municipality, major cities refused to lend a hand in enforcing anti-Jewish measures, and devised bureaucratic entanglements tending to complicate and frustrate the implementation of such discriminatory regulations. While the Rexist collaborationist movement was vociferous in its pro-Nazi sentiments, the population on the whole was generally either well disposed toward rescue activities or not willing to frustrate these efforts. But denunciations there were, and many Jews and their non-Jewish benefactors were, as a result, apprehended and carted off to concentration camps, where many failed to return upon the war's end.

Compared with other countries under occupation, Belgium stands out for the civic responsibility displayed by the secular and religious leadership with regard to the Jewish issue which, to a large extend, made it possible for close to half of the Jewish population to survive the ravages of the Holocaust. For this, one recent author qualifies Belgium as meriting the highest "crown of appreciation" for the rescue efforts of its Jews.

We now pass to typical rescue stories by individual Belgians.

Father Joseph André

One of the most illustrious of the rescuers of Jews in Belgium was Father Joseph André of Namur. Hundreds of Jews, mostly children, owe their lives to this modest and self-effacing man.

Father André's role in saving Jews began in 1942, when he learned that a Jewish acquaintance of his was threatened with deportation. Dr. Arthur Burak, an attorney who was a refugee from Germany, had been driven out of Antwerp to Limbourg province in late 1940, as were most of the other other German Jewish refugees in Antwerp. They were then allowed to relocate elsewhere, but not back in Antwerp. Arthur Burak chose Namur as his next haven, taking with him his wife, Bertha, and their sons, Norbert and Werner. He could not have chosen a better place. In Namur, he was fated to meet the man who was to become a legend to many Jewish survivors of the Holocaust, a man Burak terms "our great friend and benefactor . . . a noble priest."

Father André found a hiding place for Arthur and his family at the home of Victorine-Ghilaine Dupuis, a widow living with her three daughters. There they remained in the pantry for two years, until the country's liberation. Mrs. Dupuis braved the risk of discovery by the local *Waffen-SS Walonne*, a Belgian collaborationist paramilitary force, whose local offices were located on the building's ground floor. Other than the Dupuis family, none but Father André and a close associate knew of the presence of the Buraks.

One week after the Buraks were settled in the Dupuis home, cousins of Arthur's showed up at Father André's parish of St. Jean Baptiste in Namur. They too were seeking his solicitude and help. It is difficult to know just how Father André felt as he faced Arthur's cousins. He had helped a family he knew; now he was being asked to help people he did not know. In hindsight, it is evident that Father André's encounter with the Buraks led this unassuming priest to embark on a new and very risky venture—a mission to help as many Jews in distress as possible.

Making contact with the Committee for the Defense of Jews (CDJ), a clandestine Jewish organization searching for hiding places for fleeing Jews, Abbé André indicated that he was prepared to be of whatever help necessary, and to find sheltering places for any and all Jews who would henceforth be referred to him at his parish office, which was coincidentally, located across from the the Kommandantur, the German military headquarters in Namur. Father André was soon involved in an undertaking which took him to distant places in an effort to help Jews elude the Nazi death machine.

Father Joseph André, from Namur, Belgium, rekindling the eternal flame at Yad Vashem, during the ceremony in his honor, in 1968, and flanked by some of the former children whom he rescued. Courtesy of Yad Vashem.

Father Joseph André, from Namur, Belgium, flanked by Lieutenant (and Rabbi) Harold Saperstein, of the U.S. army, on the day the children he had sheltered during the war were turned over to the Jewish community (1945). Courtesy of Yad Vashem.

As Mr. Vishnie, of the Jewish underground group, relates, "I personally referred many people to Father André, and he always found hiding
places for them and arranged their rescue. . . . It was not even necessary
to knock on his door, for it was always open. No one ever passed through
it without ultimately finding a suitable arrangement. Moreover, he kept
tabs on all Jews whom he directed to secure shelters. Convinced that a
particular place had become unsuitable or the treatment given was not
good enough, he immediately took steps to have the Jews transferred to
a new location. His role was especially significant in the rescue of children.
I personally, and not only myself, passed over to his hands many children
and kept them in his house until he found for them secure places. . . . There
is no doubt in my mind that he is one of the most illustrious Righteous
Among the Nations—without equal in all Belgium."

Testimonies at Yad Vashem abound on Father André's dedication to
his new-found cause. Sara Weinberg relates how he came to fetch her
several times for a visit to her mother, hidden elsewhere, so as to mitigate
the mother's anguish. Dov Toporok, another protege, took ill while in
hiding, and had to undergo an operation. Father André personally
arranged his admittance into a hospital—under a false identity. Afterward,
he kept him in his parish until he had fully recovered. "I saw him
welcoming Jews in his home, mostly children. He even gave his bed to them
while he slept on the floor." "My home is your home," he once told Dov.

André inspired many others in the region to follow in his steps and help
Jews in distress, such as Charles Berhin, a widower and father of five
children, who gave shelter in his home to fleeing Jews. Or Dr. Fernand
Arnould, a neurologist at the St. Camille Hospital in Namur. There, he
lodged many fleeing Jews, some in the contagious diseases ward of the
hospital, thus minimizing the risk of search and discovery by the
authorities.

Father André's transformation from a life of study and contemplation
to one of incessant activity surprised his colleagues and mentors. He had
been considered a mystic and dreamer, too much of an introvert, and not
inured to the realities of life. But as one observer of André's life notes,
events sometimes metamorphose human beings, and Abbé André, tested
by a trial of harsh circumstances, was revealed to be "a man of action of
unsuspected strength." Traveling from place to place, he pleaded and
cajoled at monasteries, convents, and private homes for Jewish children
to be taken in. Many were moved to acquiesce by his self-effacing and
angelic demeanor. His fame eventually spread throughout the Namur
region and well beyond it, and it did not take too long for the Gestapo to
realize that Father André was frustrating its designs to have all the
country's Jews deported to the death camps. André eventually became a
marked man and had to go into hiding until the liberation of Namur by the
U.S. Army in September 1944.

Thereafter, he undertook the no less arduous task of collecting the
children from far and distant places and returning them to their parents,

if they were still alive, or to Jewish organizations prepared to take them. Accosting a Jewish military chaplain of the U.S. Army, Father André brought him to his parish in order for the rabbi to lead the assembled children in prayer. "You pray to your God in your religion," he told the children; "I pray to him in mine. Our prayers converge." Lieutenant Harold Saperstein, the rabbi in question, wrote home in 1945 of his impressions of "*Le Vicaire*", "He is a gentle, frail fellow—humble in demeanor, with a gentle handshake and a bashful smile. Yet he proved himself to be of the stuff which spiritual heroes are made of."

On October 1, 1945, all remaining Jewish children in Father André's care left his home. The previous day, Rabbi Saperstein had organized a farewell party to which the Catholic children of the parish were invited. Father André spoke on the universality of God and the brotherhood of man. Together with the rabbi, they were tossed in the air by the children, accompanied with shouts of "Hip, Hip, Hooray!" In Rabbi Saperstein's words, "For many of the kids it was the end of several years of an intimate and loving association with the Vicaire André. For him it was the close of what must certainly have been one of the strangest, most active and most spiritually enriching periods of his life."

As the children boarded the truck, André embraced each child and kissed it on the forehead. "He tried to smile and tears welled up in his eyes. Impulsively I put my arms around the little priest in his long black cloak on which he wore not a cross but a Magen David and kissed him on both cheeks. . . . I rode in the truck with them. As we rounded the corner they let out a great cheer for the priest, who had really been a father to them."

Visiting Israel in 1967, Father André was greeted and feted by dozens of his former charges. A rabbi welcomed him with these words: "Blessed is the father who merits a son like Father André." On a visit to the United States, he told Rabbi Saperstein, "I do not think we will see each other again in this world. But I know that in the world-to-come we will meet each other face-to-face." When he died in 1973, the pallbearers of his coffin included several of his former Jewish wards.

Reminiscing on Father André, a nun describes him as the symbol of one's "total denial of the self in the cause of others." A former colleague terms him "the incarnation of evangelical love." His mentor, Abbé Himmer, states that what surprised him most about Father André was the lack of any sign of apprehension in spite of the enormous danger. "I am, however, convinced that he objectively considered the possible consequences of all his acts, but his personal fate was of no importance to him. He saw himself as an instrument of Providence, and he committed himself fully to God's wishes." (486, 756, 964, 1217)

Sister Marie Leruth

At the La Providence orphanage in Verviers, near Antwerp, Belgium's second-largest city, with a prewar Jewish population of 55,000, Sister

Marie (Mathilde Leruth) was privy to the secret that many of the boys in her charge were of Jewish parentage. Sister Marie belonged to the Sisters of Charity of St. Vincent de Paul, and during the war she was responsible for the boys at the La Providence orphanage. Some of these children's parents had been deported to concentration camps; others were in hiding.

Sylvain Brachfeld, now a journalist, was one of the children in the orphanage. He recalls that Sister Marie constantly listened in on the children's conversations to make sure that the Jewish boys did not inadvertently give their identity away to the others. Since the Germans made periodic surprise visits to look for Jewish children, the Jewish boys had to attend church with the others, to avoid arousing suspicion, but were not required to take communion or participate in confession. Once, when a major check was expected, they were taken on an outing to a nearby shrine in order to remove them from the premises.

Brachfeld describes Sister Marie as "a marvel of love under circumstances which obliged her to risk her life and liberty every day." Sister Marie recalls children being brought to the orphanage without advance notice. "Sometimes a child would just come home from school to find his parents and brothers and sisters taken away. Neighbors would quickly bring these children to us before the Germans started checking."

After the war the Jewish children were all released to their families or to Jewish organizations. "Sister Marie never sought to hold on to them or to make them undergo baptism," Brachfeld notes. Nor did she ask and receive any payment for her devotion and the dangers she faced during the war.

Informed of her election to the Righteous Among the Nations title in 1968, Sister Marie, now mother superior of the St. Vincent Home in Tilleur, responded: "I deserve no honor for saving Jewish children during the war. In welcoming them and especially in loving them with all my heart, I only fulfilled my obligation as a woman and a Daughter of Charity. Their parents having been deported to Germany, it was only right that I give these dear little Jewish children the maternal care and, even more, the warm affection that they lacked."

At the Yad Vashem tree-planting ceremony, Sister Marie spoke of the ashes of the Holocaust victims deposited in the crypt in the Hall of Remembrance. "I think of all your martyrs; I think particularly of the parents and relatives of my brave Jewish children whom I, like so many others, was able to hide during the war. Alas! Nobody can ever replace a lost father and mother." Then, turning to one of her former charges, she continued: "May the hand outstretched toward Maurice, the youngest of the children put into my care and trust, be a token of all my love for your people." (132)

Father Bruno Reynders

Another Belgian who rescued hundreds of Jewish children and adults was Father Bruno (born Henri Reynders), a Benedictine monk. Before the war he taught theology, specializing in the patristic period. After his release from a prisoner-of-war camp in 1941 (where he served as a military chaplain), he returned to Belgium. From his base at the Mont César monastery near Louvain, and in conjunction with the CDJ, he presided over a vast operation which included the dispersion of hundreds of children in many places in the Liege region—in convents and other religious homes, as well as secular institutions and private families, as the situation warranted. His brother's house at Ixelles served as a transit point. Taking full responsibility for the children's safety he dealt with acquiring food ration cards, other necessities, false identities, and financial support for the host families. .

Bernard Rotmil recalls his first impression of the man, when, as a teenage boy, he was referred to him: "He had a spark in his eyes that was so special to him." Bernard was taken by Father Bruno to several places where conditions, however, were not too comfortable. After the war, Bernard found the following passage in Father Bruno's journal: "I recall Bernard's appetite as sixteen-year-old boy, and the difficulty I had in this regard since I paid for his upkeep at the place where he stayed in Louvain. One day, I dared tell him to try to control his appetite, and I recall his distraught face as he replied, 'But I am always hungry." I was completely disarmed and I did not cease reproaching myself for my intervention. But nourishment was at that time a difficult and expensive thing." Bernard was finally taken to a farmhouse where the food was plentiful, and there he remained until the end of the war.

Father Bruno's travels and the buzz of activity at the Mont César monastery (including the activities of his colleagues who were active in the underground) soon drew the attention of the Gestapo, which staged a raid on the place in January 1944. Luckily for Father Bruno, he was away at the time; nevertheless his superior urged him to go into hiding. Discarding his monk's habit, he continued to direct his rescue operations clandestinely from Louvain and Brussels until the country's liberation in September 1944. A witness recalls hearing him say during the war: "I am happy to have discovered a new ideal and a way to devote myself to its realization."

Zvika Ariav recalls Father Bruno's visit to the monastery where he and others were hidden. "He always found time to visit us once a week, to make sure we were well treated. He always appeared without warning—be it daytime, at night, in rain sunshine or snow; one felt always under his protective wings. . . . When he visited Israel in 1964, it was for me a great joy to be able to embrace him."

Esther Krygier, another of his child beneficiaries remembers him as "very gentle, very fatherly. . . . He would take us by the hand, and explain to us that where we were going we were not to say that we were Jewish . . . , not to trust even a fellow child, to keep all to ourselves. . . . He represented to me security and trust. . . . He was the only one who had the gift to remove this fear that we had. I don't know how to explain this."

When some sheltering families asked his permission to have the children converted, he replied, "We are responsible for the lives of these children, but their souls do not belong to us."

Immediately after the country's liberation, and for the next three months, he searched for parents to come and fetch the children under his care. Paul Silvers recalls the visit of Father Bruno to a Brussels synagogue in September 1944: "The rabbi had stopped the service and announced that Father Bruno had arrived to have a final look at the children before rejoining Belgian troops as a chaplain. The congregation gave him a tumultuous welcome. The children pressed his arms while the parents, in tears, covered him with words of thanks and blessings. It took some time before calm was restored in the synagogue and the service could resume. When I scanned my eyes to look for him, I did not see Father Bruno. He had quietly slipped away."

Father Bruno minimized his personal role in this superhuman undertaking. On a festive occasion after the war, he said, "Really, what did I do? I sought places, but seeking without finding is a sterile thing. The essential thing was to find, but that did not depend on me; it meant that a door had to open, the door to a home, the door to a heart. . . . Those who sheltered were, in most cases, those who were solicited. It is them that I represent here." Yvonne Jospa, one of the founders of the CDJ with whom Father Bruno cooperated, states that he personally made all payments for the children under his care. She adds that all the children under Father Bruno's care came through the war safe and sound.

In Israel to plant a tree at Yad Vashem, Father Bruno recalled his wartime activities. "Three hundred and sixteen Jewish souls passed through my hands, among them 200 children. I can't begin to tell you how many doors I knocked on. I literally wore myself out, but it was all worth it." Then, in a humorous vein, he added: "Maybe Almighty God will give me a break in the next world."

Learning of his passing in 1981, Sacha Hirschovitz exclaimed, "Father Bruno, for us you are not dead. Your lesson of dedication, of selflessness, of courage and love has not been in vain. We bear in our heart the path you have traced, and which will guide me till my last day."

In 1991, ten years after he died, friends and former recipients of his generosity gathered at Ottignies, Belgium, the place where he had lived the last years of his life, to dedicate a memorial, which reads: "Father Bruno Reynders, Benedictine (1903-1981). Hero of the Resistance. At the risk of his life saved some 400 Jews from Nazi barbarism. Israel has proclaimed him a Righteous Among the Nations, and in his memory a tree was planted at Yad Vashem, Jerusalem. May 21, 1991." (84)

Father Louis Célis and Father Hubert Célis

In 1949, a Tel Aviv engineer named Gershon Rabinowitz was on vacation with his family at Kibbutz Shefayim. There his daughter Nurit befriended Sonia Rotenberg, who proceeded to tell her how she and her family had been rescued in Belgium by two Catholic priests who were brothers. Rabinowitz, in turn, told the story to his cousin Eliezer Kaplan, who at the time was Israel's finance minister, and persuaded him to allocate enough money to make it possible for rescuer and rescued to be reunited. The following year, Father Louis Célis of Halmaal, Belgium, was brought to Israel. A moving story was then unfolded.

In September 1942, Monsignor Louis-Joseph Kerkhofs, of Liege, convened a group of priests during which he urged that they become involved in the rescue of Jews. In view of the expected dangers to such a commitment, he emphasized the significance of risking one's life so that others not unjustly lose theirs.

Returning from that fateful meeting to the village of Halmaal, near St. Trond, in Limbourg province, Father Celis did not suspect that his thinking on this issue was soon to be put to a severe test. For on that very day, a Jewish woman (a refugee from Germany who fearing deportation had fled from Brussels) stood before him, tears streaming down her checks, and begged him to help her save her family (husband, two sons, and two daughters). A decision had to be made immediately. In Father Celis's words: "I then gave my word of honor to Mrs. Rotenberg to help save her family and to sacrifice my life, if need be, in that endeavor. Thank God, I was able to remain faithful to my word. Now that I am able to witness the happy lives of this family, I thank the Lord for having given me the strength for this purpose." He then took the necessary steps to have the family safely secured: sixteen-year-old Regina and two-year-old Sonia were taken to Father Célis's father's house in St. Trond; Wolfgang (thirteen years old) and Sigmund (nine ears old), to the home of his brother, Father Hubert Célis, in the village of Gotem, 8 miles from Halmaal. The parents were hidden elsewhere.

Betrayed to the authorities by informers, the parents were deported to Auschwitz, where they perished. On October 29, 1942, the day of their arrest, Father Louis Célis, suspected of having had a hand in arranging their refuge in his region, was taken to police headquarters for questioning. During the ensuing interrogation, Father Célis decided to confront his Catholic-born German interrogator with a dose of Christian morality. "You're a Catholic. Have you forgotten that the blessed Mary was Jewish, and that Jesus was Jewish, and that he commanded us to love one another and help each other? Jesus told us, 'I have given you my own example in order for you to behave likewise.' You are a Catholic, yet you don't understand that a priest can never betray his calling!" The interrogator decided to release the brave priest but ordered that a watch be placed on his activities. On another occasion, Father Louis Célis hid a Jewish couple who had jumped a train on its way to Germany and had wandered aimlessly into the village looking for shelter.

On May 3, 1944 Father Célis was again taken in for questioning after Regina was discovered hiding in his father's house. Eighteen-year-old Regina was sent to Auschwitz, thence to Ravensbruck, but luckily survived the horrors of these hells on earth to return and personally thank the brave priest for his help. In the meantime, Father Célis, who had again managed to talk himself out of arrest, cared for his Jewish wards until the liberation of Belgium in September 1944. Prior to that, he and his brother were themselves forced to go into hiding, the Gestapo having decided to deal with both more severely.

Wolfgang Rotenberg notes that while the boys were in hiding, Father Hubert Célis took great care that they pursue their religious practices. Noting that they were not donning the obligatory phylacteries on Saturdays, Célis inquired with his ecclesiastical superiors and was then satisfied that this practice was not required on the Sabbath. Father Célis was quite emphatic on this point. "I never attempted to convert the Rotenberg children to Catholicism, but I constantly respected their religious feelings, for several reasons. First, I did not want to take advantage of the sad events [of that period] to bear influence on them. Second, because Mrs. Rotenberg had expressed her full confidence in me when I gave her my word of honor as a priest, in this regard. I had no right to abuse this trust but rather the duty to remain faithful to the promise of eventually returning these children to their parents or family in like manner as they were entrusted to me. It is for this reason that I desired they remain faithful to their religion and the obligations which their religion imposed. Third, because I foresaw that the children would be returned to their parents after the war and receive a Jewish education, and I prefer a good Jew to a bad Christian!"

The Rotenberg children eventually settled in the United States. The ties between the rescued family and the Célis brothers remained close in the ensuing years. In 1947, Father Hubert Célis led Regina to the canopy as she married Isaac Wolbrom. In 1965, he was present at their son's Bar Mitzvah celebration in a New York synagogue. On that occasion, Regina stated, "My children have no grandparents. I think it is only fitting that Father Hubert should be on hand for my son's Bar Mitzvah because he was the last to see my parents."

In 1949, writing to Rabinowitz in Israel, Father Louis Célis belittled his deeds during the war.

> And so, my very dear Mr. Rabinowitz, you insist on considering me a saint because I was unfortunately able to save only a few Jewish lives. But was this not an urgent and serious obligation of every person, Jew, Christian, or atheist, still worthy to be considered human? The only profound regret

that I must always bear with me is for my not having been able to provide
for the welfare of *all* Jews in distress in Belgium and elsewhere, without
any distinction whatsoever, and not having been able to hide them and
thus fully remove them from this bloody persecution which, let's admit
it, will forever remain an irremovable stain for the whole of Europe.

His brother Father Louis, reminiscing on his former charitable deeds,
notes:

I feel I have done but my duty. Irrespective of our different religious and
political beliefs, we are all children of the Good Lord, hence, brothers who
ought to love one another. This is precisely what Christ wished to tell us
when he asked us to love our neighbor. . . . I have never been the recipient
of so much gratitude as from these children, who gave to us so much more
than we gave them. These four children are ongoing proof of how much
they merited this aid.

Regina Wolbrom's attitude, expressed in nonphilosophical language,
is no less moving: "He kept us alive. We can never do enough for him."
(1777)

Antoine & Flore Abbeloos

In August 1942, Majlek Traksbetryger, a Jewish refugee from Poland,
decided to disobey the German summons to report to the Malines transit
camp for deportation to Poland and, instead, to go into hiding just outside
Brussels, the city where he resided with his wife Esther and three children.
He ordered a truck from the moving firm headed by Antoine and Flore
Abbeloos for August 17, to remove his household items to a flat in Genval,
some six miles south of Brussels, which had been secretly leased by
Traksbetryger to coincide with his unannounced disappearance from the
Brussels apartment he now occupied. However, when the landlord learned
that his new tenants were Jewish, he took fright, reneged on the lease and
refused access to the apartment to the Traksbetryger family. Not knowing
what to do next and unable to return to his his former residence,
Traksbetryger was at a complete loss. Many a Jew faced such crucial
moments during the tragic days of the Holocaust, which decided their fate
for good or bad on the spur of a moment. However, in this case, the truck
driver became a rescuer. While Traksbetryger wondered what next to do,
Antoine Abbeloos told him to place himself in his hands, promising that
he and his wife, Flore, "will do the utmost to help you." Thereupon, the
Traksbetryger family was taken back to Brussels and to the second-story
flat of an unfinished building Abbeloos owned in the Anderlecht suburb
of the city. The Traksbetryger family lived there for about a year; then they
were helped to move to several different locations to avert dangers to their
safety. Their three children were sheltered at the home of Mrs. Abbeloos's

mother. All survived, even Georgette, the sixteen-year-old daughter of Majlek and Esther Traksbetryger, who, disregarding her benefactors' instructions, slipped out one evening to visit the cinema where she was recognized, arrested by the Gestapo and carted off to the infamous Auschwitz concentration camp. Luckily, she survived, to be able to return and be reunited with the rest of her family, who continued to be looked after by the Abbelooses for a full two years.

It is not clear from the evidence on hand whether Traksbetryger was familiar with Antoine Abbeloos's previous record: the help he had extended to refugees from Nazi Germany and Fascist Italy in the 1930s, the role he played in personally driving one of his trucks through France to the Spanish border to convey material and goods for the International Brigade during the Spanish Civil War, his arrest by the Gestapo on June 22, 1941, the day of the German invasion of Russia, and his release five months thereafter from Breendocks prison, making it doubly risky for him to be involved in any further anti-Nazi activities. The extent of Antoine Abbeloos's involvement on behalf of persecuted Jews became known only after the war. His initial encounter with the "Jewish Question" was witnessing the refusal of the Genval landlord to allow a Jew access to a newly leased flat. From then until the liberation of Belgium, Antoine and Flore kept their trucks constantly on the move, to help Jews hiding in various parts of the Brussels metropolitan area. The Jews often had to relocate swiftly because they had been denounced and were threatened with imminent arrest. Antoine and Flore even broke open apartments that had been sealed by the authorities when the Jewish occupants were summoned to Malines; they took the risk in order to be able to quickly remove the furniture and transport it to the fleeing Jew's new hiding place. "Thus, we risked being arrested by the Germans for two full years, . . . but we loved repeating our deeds for the gratification it afforded us to release from [the Nazi] grip [the household items] they wanted to steal from the Jews." Denounced for these activities, Mrs. Abbeloos-Devos was arrested and interrogated by the Gestapo for ten days, then released for lack of evidence.

A measure of the scope of the Abbelooses' involvement in ferrying Jews and their goods from one secluded home to another in the Brussels region is the public honoring of Antoine and Flore by the Belgian Jewish Association soon after the war's end, in the presence of Queen Mother Elisabeth, on May 5, 1946. Additional tokens of Antoine's honest comportment and personal modesty are the following two episodes. During the period of his hiding at the Abbeloos house, Traksbetryger wished to turn a huge sum of money over to his benefactors for safekeeping. The Abelooses, however, insisted that this only be done in the presence of a notary, and so it was. Traksbetryger refers to his benefactor as his "lucky star." In a deposition, Antoine Abbeloos relates the help extended to a certain Bercelweg, adding that he had not wished to ask the former for a confirmation of the story, for Bercelweg might have interpreted such an approach soon after the war's end as suggesting that his erstwhile rescuer now expected a reward for services rendered during the war, and this would have been "completely out of the question for me." Hence he hesitated to make even a discreet approach to one of his former beneficiaries. (944)

Louisa Mercier

Louisa Mercier was the head of the personnel department in a Louvain manufacturing firm when, in October 1942, she was asked by a friend to give temporary shelter to Friedel and Charles-Raymond Wiener, seven and three years of age respectively. The children's parents, in Brussels, were being sought by the Gestapo. Louisa agreed to help, and two days later won over the head of the production department, who in turn arranged for Friedel to be taken to home of a Louvain couple, where she stayed until her benefactors' arrest on January 20, 1943. (Mr. Desoppe, who had given shelter to the Jewish child, survived the horrors of the Dachau concentration camp, only to succumb from exhaustion soon after his liberation in 1945.) Three-year-old Charles-Raymond was hidden with another family; Louisa Mercier defrayed the medication costs for the treatment of the child's severe measles infection.

Louisa Mercier was content with her modest contribution to the saving of innocent lives, not suspecting that more was to be asked of her. The elder Wieners (Natan and Charlotte) found it necessary to ask to be periodically sheltered in Louisa's home out of fear of the increasingly frequent Gestapo raids in search of Jews in the area in which the Wieners were hiding. Louisa's mother, Céline, and her sister, Esther, willingly acquiesced to Louisa's request in this regard. As the Wieners' situation continued to deteriorate, Louisa decided to find a more secure shelter for them. At first, she tried an institute for the mentally retarded at Corbeek-Lo, where, it was hoped, Mr. Wiener's bad Flemish pronunciation would not arouse suspicion. But too many Jews and other refugees of Nazi terror were already hidden there, and for security reasons the institute declined to accept additional persons. An arrangement was finally worked out with a certain family, with Louisa visiting the Wieners once every fifteen days to bring food and moral support, at times spending the weekend with them.

It seemed that all was in proper order and that no further worries were in store for Louisa when in January 1943, upon Desoppe's arrest, little Friedel needed a new shelter. After much effort, a place was found in a Catholic institute in faraway Chimay, southern Belgium, where over a dozen other Jewish children were being surreptitiously kept. Parents and children occasionally met at Louisa's home during quickly arranged secretive get-togethers. The Wiener children had barely been safely secured when Louisa was troubled with yet another burden. The home where the Wiener elders had been staying had been sold in April 1943, and all tenants, including the Wieners, were forced to vacate. This time Louisa got her mother's and sister's consent to welcome the destitute Jewish couple in their own home, where they stayed for over a year—until October 1944, a month after the country's liberation.

Completely dedicated to her charges, Louisa even refused to vacate her home in April 1944 to seek shelter from mounting Allied air raids unless a secure shelter could also be found for the Wieners. "We had decided that they would live with us or we stayed with them," Louisa emphasizes. "A discreet hospitality, indeed, for other than a rare few initiates no one knew, no one saw, not even the residents of the building. This silence, this discretion was our strength and security." Several times each month, Louisa traveled to Brussels to fetch additional ration coupons to feed her family and her guests, at the same time not forgetting to send packages (including clothing, underwear, shoes, toys, candies, and presents) to the Wiener children at Chimay. She even arranged Mrs. Wiener's hospitalization and operation at a local religious hospital when that was needed, subsidizing all the necessary costs. "Welcomed as guests and as friends— the first [in the household] to be cared for," was Louisa's own stated motto concerning the persons she had accidentally met during the war. Minimizing the dangers and travails involved with looking after four Jewish persons (in transgression of then existing regulations), on top of having to care for her mother (bereft of means) and sister, Louisa notes: "We hence spent together some very good moments for two years and we never regretted having embarked on this adventure which, thank God, ended well." Louisa Mercier belonged to a Belgian aristocratic family but was not at all wealthy and had to work to provide for herself and her charges.

Twenty-five years later, Louisa explained that her actions had been "a gesture of humanitarian brotherhood which appeared to be our obligation at the time and any good-hearted person would have done likewise. God gave us the strength to do our deeds, for which we thank Him, and those we saved have become dear friends to us. Those who go through certain tragic moments together are bound by indestructible ties."

In an even stronger religious vein, Louisa states in a letter to Yad Vashem, "In helping Jews during World War II, we simply did what we are told to do by our Gospel and the precepts of your prophets, who are ours as well. . . . . [Also,] to prove that loving one's neighbor, especially when he is in danger, is not an empty phrase for good-hearted people." At the end of her letter she wrote that the greatest possible reward is the "sweet thought of having helped to rescue a family." (487)

Georges and Marthe De Smet

In the fall of 1942, with the intensification of mass roundups of Jews, Rose Lerner came to the decision that her continued residence in Brussels was no longer secure. She and her husband, Morris, decided to place their three-year-old daughter Yvette into the caring hands of the convent Soeurs du Très St. Sauveur, located near their home. There Yvette joined some thirteen other Jewish children in hiding. Yvette's parents were free to seek shelter for themselves in a new location.

In May 1943, the Gestapo raided the convent after being tipped off that Jewish children were being kept there under assumed names. As none of the children were at school on that particular day, the Gestapo announced that they would return the following morning and asked the mother superior to have all the Jewish children prepared for departure. That evening, the mother superior contacted the underground, who immediately came and spirited the children out of the building to eventually disperse them among helpful families. Yvette Lerner recalls regretting having to part with Sister Claire, of whom she had become especially fond. After a ten-day temporary stay with a certain family, Yvette was dispatched to the home of Georges and Marthe De Smet, in Dilbeek, a rural suburb of Brussels. The De Smet family included four adult children (including two sons who had recently returned from an extended stay in a German prisoner-of-war camp). There, Yvette also met another Jewish girl in hiding, Régine Monk, who had been fetched from her Brussels home in August 1942 by Marthe. According to Régine, as told to her by her mother, after being seated on Marthe's knees, the latter exulted, "She already seems to know us, so we'll take her with us." The die had been cast, fortunately for Régine.

At the De Smets', Yvette, Régine, and another Jewish girl who was admitted later lived in total security until Belgium's liberation in September 1944 and were spared the horrors of the Holocaust. The children were thereafter returned to their natural parents, who had remained hidden in other parts of metropolitan Brussels.

Marthe De Smet is described as a deeply devout Catholic who sought to do good, loved children, and had an "enormous compassion for human suffering." Her husband, Georges (a chemist in the manufacture of food stuffs and sweeteners), is described similarly: a very religious person "of sterling character and deep compassion for all human beings." While the De Smets dutifully attended mass every morning, the Jewish children in their household were reminded of their true origins (on occasions, Marthe took them to prearranged secretive meetings with their parents), and the De Smets even went to great lengths to provide kosher meat for their wards. The adult De Smet children yielded their own portion of fresh milk to the youngsters in their midst. Marthe (called "Mamy" by the children) washed their laundry at an outside hand-operated water pump.

Yvette and Régine recall their stay at the De Smet house as a period of security and parental care and love. Marthe was confident that she would not be betrayed by neighbors and friends, who, it seemed, suspected the presence of small children in an otherwise household of adults. "This admirable family," notes Régine Monk, "hid and protected us without taking the smallest amount of money until the war's end and cared for us as she would her own children." Upon the return of Yvette to her parents, her father suggested financial compensation for the over one year nursing of their daughter at the risk of their own safety, whereupon Georges promptly replied, "We want only your friendship." He added that in the event that Yvette's parents' new life in America did not work out "the door in Dilbeek was always open to them." Rescuer and rescued remained on close terms in the ensuing years. In 1978, Yvette (now an attorney in the United States) visited the De Smets in the company of her husband and children, staying with them for ten days. "It was important to us that our children meet these wonderful people and deepen their understanding of what they did for us," Yvette stated. (1975)

Frans and Margueritte Lemmens

Frans and Margueritte Lemmens of Hoboken, an Antwerp neighborhood, were good acquaintances of the Jewish Walzer family. In mid-1942, Meir Walzer was dispatched to a labor camp, from which he never returned. Ethel, alone with three children and fearing worse things to come, arranged for her children to be sheltered by a certain family in return for monetary compensation. After despoiling Mrs. Walzer of her money, the family decided to put the children out on the street. At her wits' ends, Mrs. Walzer then turned to the Lemmens family, and they in turn agreed to care for her children (aged fourteen, twelve, and two). This was done in the nick of time, for soon thereafter Mrs. Walzer was carted off to a concentration camp, where she perished.

Marcella, Léon, and Oscar were now the responsibility of the Lemmenses alone; they had to bear the full burden of providing shelter for three Jewish children on top of rearing their own daughter. They did so for a full two years, and they did so successfully. Frans Lemmens was the owner of a barber shop built as an annex to his home. The clients were frequently coming and going, so care had to be taken that the sheltered children not show themselves in the living quarters during working hours for fear of being detected by customers on their way to the household bathroom. Frans also built a closet in the niche of a wall to serve as a temporary shelter in the event of an emergency when there would be no time to rush to the cellar. Rosa, the Lemmens's fourteen-year-old daughter was the only person, other than her parents, privy to the secret; she never divulged the presence of the three children who were sought by the Gestapo, not even to her close schoolmates.

Frans repeatedly reassured the frightened children, kept hidden for a two-year period in a back room of the home, with the words, "You are my children and you shall stay here—but do take care." He suggested such precautions as not approaching a window so that they would not to be noticed by passersby on the street. On one occasion, Lemmens stoutly denied the presence of Jews in his house to a suspicious local grocer, adding for good measure the threat that the underground would surely deal severely with the grocer in the event the Gestapo ever came to his home to investigate. The Lemmenses also arranged tutoring for the children so as to make up for time lost from school. For an additional year after the liberation of Belgium, the Walzer children stayed with the Lemmens family until proper arrangements had been made for their further upbringing amidst their people in Palestine.

Close to her death in 1976, Margueritte Lemmens asked to see, for the last time, one of her former wards. Marcella (now an adult) flew from Israel and rushed to her benefactress's bedside in time to embrace her. At this momentous occasion Mrs. Lemmens, clutching in her feeble hands the necklace sent to her earlier by Marcella, stated she had been confident that before departing this world she would be privileged to see for the last time one of the children she and her late husband had rescued. (378)

Leonard and Maria Duerink

"There are things in life, beautiful and moving, that remain indelibly etched in one's memory. They reside in a wider expanse than our usual feelings—where happiness and tragedy are its ultimate frontiers." Thus begins Helena Zick's account of her childhood experience as a refugee in the home of Leonard and Maria Duerink.

In early 1943, Helena and Miriam Zick and their parents, who had been constantly moving from one place to another, were in hiding somewhere in Brussels. Faced with the mounting fear of denunciation, the family decided in March of that year to split up: the two girls (aged four and three) would be sheltered in Temse (some 10 miles southwest of Antwerp) by Leonard Duerink, the brother of the Brussels couple with whom the Zick family was then staying; the parents would continue to attempt to hide in Brussels. Leonard Duerink, a former policeman and tramway conductor, was a sick man. Five months after the arrival of the two Jewish girls, he died at the age of fifty-one from a stomach ailment. A week thereafter, Helena and Miriam's parents were denounced to the Gestapo and were hauled off to a concentration camp to be consumed in the flames of the Holocaust. Before this tragic moment, the Zicks managed to visit their children secretively at the Duerinks home. There, they were allowed to see their children from a hidden attic annex, their presence not divulged to the children for their own safety lest they accidentally disclose their parents' visit to outsiders.

The burden of providing for her own three teenage daughters and, in addition, sheltering two Jewish girls as well now fell entirely on Maria Duerink's shoulders. To protect Helena and Miriam from denunciation, she shared the secret of the girls' true origin with none save the local priest.

To her daughters and visitors she explained that these supposedly Christian girls' parents had been taken to Germany for forced labor (a common phenomenon in those days) and therefore had no one to look after them. Some people suspected otherwise, but in Helena's words, "the gamble paid off."

At first, the two girls were sheltered in the attic to keep the echo of their weeping as faint and distant as possible from outsiders. Much later, as the Flemish language replaced the Yiddish which the girls had initially spoken, they were allowed to circulate freely in the household. False credentials were also acquired for them, and in 1944 they began attending the local school. Following the liberation of Belgium, Maria Duerink continued for an additional three years to devoutly care for the orphaned Jewish girls. Then in 1947, she was required to release them to an Antwerp Jewish orphanage. The parting was painful and is still etched in the girls' memory. "To this day, she keeps the calendar leaf on which that sad date appears," Helena notes. For two years thereafter, she visited the children on a biweekly basis, bringing with her various gifts and taking them home with her for short spells during holidays. On the eve of the girls' departure for a new life in Israel in 1949, Maria Duerink came for a final visit. As farewell presents she gave them an armband with the girls' names engraved thereon and some pictures of the girls' parents which the latter had left with her before they disappeared in the long night of the Holocaust.

Twenty-eight years passed, and in 1977 Helena (now known as Haya) returned for a reunion with her aged benefactress. "How surprised I was to find her with the same warm and loving disposition which I remember from my childhood," Haya noted. Maria gave her two precious mementos which she had kept over the years: the girls' baby teeth and a comb left by Haya's father for Maria to back-comb the girls' curls. Two years later, Maria and her late husband were added to Yad Vashem's roster of the Righteous Among the Nations. (1674)

Marie-Thérèse Delmez

In November 1938, Jack Hochberger, a Polish Jew residing in Berlin, was carted off with countless other Jews and dumped on the German-Polish border (an event that led to the assassination of a German legation official in Paris by an enraged Jewish youth, which in turn triggered the infamous *Kristallnacht* pogrom). Regina Hochberger, Jack's wife, felt the ground burning under her feet and those of her three children (Gisa and Adele, born 1923 and 1926 respectively, and the infant Isaac, born in July 1938). She managed to arrange for the eldest daughter to leave legally for Palestine through an arrangement with the Jewish Agency and for Adele and Isaac to be spirited out to Belgium through the good offices of the Red Cross. She then hurriedly left for Poland to join her stranded husband just before the war broke out in September 1939. The youthful Isaac was taken

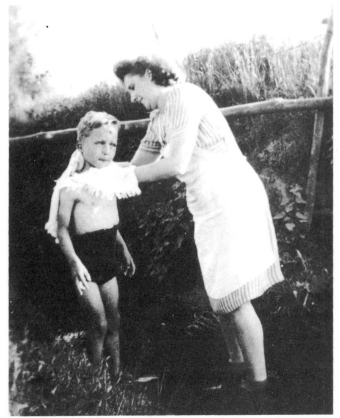

Marie-Therese Delmez, from Belgium, washing the young Yitzhaq, whom she sheltered in her home, in a wartime picture. Courtesy of Yad Vashem.

to Les Petites Abeilles, a Red Cross institute in Brussels. There, he was visited by his sister Adele, who was staying in a different institute in the city. The following year, when Belgium and France were occupied by Germany, Adele fled toward the Swiss border, but was apprehended by Swiss border guards and forced back into France. There, she was dispatched to Drancy camp and thence, in 1943, to Auschwitz, where she perished.

In the Les Petites Abeilles home, where Isaac continued to be cared for and protected, a nurse by the name of Marie-Thérèse Delmez became very attached to the little boy, whom she affectionately called Isi. When it was rumored that Les Petites Abeilles was about to be closed down, she took the child to her home village of Dion-le-Val. There, the four-year-old Isi was given a new name (Yves Berger) and integrated into the life of the village, which was off the beaten track.

The war years passed safely for Isi, and upon the liberation of Belgium, Marie-Thérèse began to correspond with Adele, in Haifa, with a view to establishing links with Isi's parents, who had been removed by the Russians into the interior of the country and were thus, luckily, spared the ravages of the Holocaust upon the German invasion in June 1941. Marie-Thérèse also succeeded in establishing Gisa's whereabouts until her deportation to Auschwitz and relayed the sad news to her sister. She assured Adele that Isi was well cared for and would continue to be so until his eventual reunion with his parents. Isi was now told about his true identity and the nature of his arrival at Marie-Thérèse's home. "Since the liberation," Marie-Thérèse wrote in a letter to the boy's parents (the Soviet embassy in Brussels served as intermediary), "Isi has been waiting for you. He constantly hopes to see you arrive, like the village war prisoners whose return is celebrated." In a return letter to their son, the Hochbergers wrote, "What good fortune to rediscover you a beautiful boy, alive, thank God, in a noble and honorable family who saved your life."

Finally in 1947, parents and son were reunited and Isi was sent off to Antwerp to a new life. The adjustment to being a Jewish child and to parents he hardly remembered was painful for Isi, and the scars of his forced separation from the woman who gave him love, warmth, and comfort for seven precious years were still to be felt for many years thereafter. In 1986, Marie-Thérèse Delmez and her husband came to visit Isaac in Israel, a married man with children of his own, at which occasion they visited Yad Vashem to share their rescue story with the institute's personnel and to record it for the benefit of future generations. (3542)

Henrik and Josephine Mans

In October 1942, Irena Freiman was in bed with a high fever in her father-in-law's home in Antwerp, newborn infant Esther lying next to her, when the Gestapo suddenly staged a raid. The entire family was rounded up. The Gestapo agent asked Irena for the baby's age. She responded that the infant was two weeks old. The agent decided to spare her. Thus, Irena was left alone with Esther in a hostile world. Most of her family was gone; her husband had already been deported. Through a sister-in-law, contact was made with Elisabeth Niys, who promised to help find a secure place for the forlorn Jewish mother and child. Elisabeth traveled to her sister, Josephine Mans, in the distant village of Herentout, and the latter agreed to help. Irena Freiman left her home stealthily, dressed as a Flemish country woman, and together with her infant and Elisabeth took the train to the village where Henrik and Josephine Mans resided.

Henrik Mans barely eked out a living as a coal miner to provide for his wife and thirteen-year-old daughter Maria. None told the neighbors of the presence of the Jewish mother and child. Irena and the baby stayed indoors during daylight hours and stepped out only at night for a fresh breath of air. They remained hidden there from November 1942 until April 1944. Elisabeth, Josephine's sister, often came to visit, riding hours on her bike in rain and cold. In Irena's words, "The attitude of these two families (Mans and Niys) toward us was as warm and friendly as if we had been kin, and it stemmed from compassion and pity toward us, and from their being honest and courageous people with a loving disposition toward others. They tried as best they could to make my stay pleasant and lighten my pain at the loss of my family, as well as to give me hope for better days to come."

In early 1944, Esther suddenly took ill. As her situation worsened, it was decided to risk disclosing her presence in the village by calling in a doctor, an old friend of the Mans family. Irena was hidden in the attic during his visit. The doctor came and left without asking questions about the child's identity, but from that time relations between the doctor and the Mans family turned cool, even hostile.

To make matters worse, a neighbor overheard Esther weeping and informed the authorities. On April 21, 1944, the Gestapo raided the Mans home. Henrik and Josephine were severely beaten, and Josephine was told to deliver the child immediately to a certain children's home in Antwerp. Henrik was deported to Buchenwald, Irena to Auschwitz. Henrik survived the brutal treatment at Buchenwald but returned home a broken man. A few years after the war, he died prematurely. The hope of somehow seeing her child again reinforced Irena's will to live. "I knew for certain that Elisabeth and Josephine would look after the child, for their love toward her was a true love from the depth of one's heart." Irena also notes that her survival in Auschwitz was due to her relatively short confinement there (only nine terrible months) and because "for a year and a half I had lived in a village and eaten my fill of bread and vegetables;" and moreover, she added, "my high spirits and joy at the development of my daughter" also enabled her to survive.

When she was liberated, Irena, down to half her previous weight, was in no condition to look after herself. Again Elisabeth and Josephine and their husbands came to the rescue. Irena returned to the Mans home to recuperate and regain strength. Esther was miraculously found in a children's home (somehow overlooked by the Germans). She was, however, in a shocking state—undernourished and terribly frightened. "Josephine nursed her for several weeks with love and dedication," Irena recalls.

Now in Israel, Irena stated in her deposition that all this was done for no ulterior motive, monetary or other. "These courageous people risked their lives and acted out of an inner moral command and sensitive heart and respect and love for others. Had they not believed in these human values, it is hard to visualize how they could have stood up to the daily difficulties for so long a time, swimming against the rising current of anti-Semitism and Jew-hatred surrounding them and the self-abasement by many before the Nazis and their collaborators in return for personal favors." (2971)

Émile and Marie Taquet

We conclude this chapter with the extraordinary story of the rescue of dozens of Jewish children by a team of teachers in a former manor which had been turned into a children's home.

In 1985, Pierre-René Delvaux of Namur wrote to Yad Vashem, asking whether the institute could help him locate some of the children sheltered during the war in a certain children's home in the Ardennes region of southeastern Belgium (Luxembourg province). Delvaux stated that many of the Jewish children had arrived there through the intercession of Father André of Namur and added: "I am retired for reasons of health and should like very much to locate them. Please understand that since the end of the war I have dreamed about them every day, for in a certain way they are my children." Thus, gradually unfolded one of the most remarkable rescue stories in Belgium.

Mr. Delvaux was a teacher in the Queen Elisabeth Home, located in Chateau du Faing in the remote village of Jamoigne-sur-Semois (5 miles east of Florenville), deep in the Ardennes forest. This home, owned by the Sisters of Charity of Besancon, was in 1941 transformed into a center for feeble children, under the patronage of the country's queen mother, and subsequently opened its doors to many fleeing Jewish children. Some seventy-five children, at least half of the total population, were Jewish, They had been brought there through Father André or Mrs. Névejean of the National Children's Society (ONE), both working closely with the CDJ. Funds came from the *Secours d'Hiver* and the overall administration of the home was located in Brussels, headed by Princess Jean de Mérode, representing Queen Elisabeth. After the war the children were returned to their parents or guardians, and all traces had been lost of their where-abouts. Now, forty-one years after the war's end. Delvaux was making a major effort to relocate at least some of his former charges.

Mainly as a result of announcements placed in the Jewish press, an increasing number of former residents of the Queen Elisabeth Home responded to the appeal. Pierre-René Delvaux wrote to each of them words of thanks and appreciation, suggesting the creation of an association of former residents of Jamoigne. He added, "I admit that since then I have cherished a permanent paternal feeling toward you and this feeling has never weakened for over forty-one years. This is the reason why I have never ceased searching for you. As both I and you bore false names, a fortunate coincidence of circumstances was necessary for me to be able to find you."

Within two years, the newly created association had traced forty of the Jewish children and fifteen of the non-Jewish instructors, among them (listed with their former *noms du guerre*): David Inowlocki (Merckx), Charles Berkenbaum (Bergenboom), Joseph Dawidowicz (Duez), Paul Schwarzbart (Exteen), Akiva Kaminsky (Charles Camée), and Abraham Kwiat (Albert Devos)—to mention a few.

The true heroes of this extraordinary rescue story are the home's director, Marie Taquet-Mertens, directly in charge of day-to-day events in the home, seconded by her husband, Major Emile Taquet, responsible for the home's administration in coordination with the main office in Brussels.

Akiva Kaminsky relates arriving at Jamoigne in 1943 after being spirited out of another children's home where he and other Jewish children wore the required yellow star. He was surprised at the amiable reception and the peaceful, friendly, and relaxed atmosphere at the Queen Elisabeth Home. He relates that Mrs. Taquet took care to make sure that Jewish children (required to attend church services in town so as not to arouse suspicion by their absence) would not be exposed to any form of conversion. Akiva emphatically states, "The period that I spent at Jamoigne was my childhood's best; . . . this especially so because I found there, for the first time that I can ever remember, a loving and caring home . . . which was to a large degree due to Mrs. Taquet, who evoked, as much as conditions allowed, warmth and love. . . . The instructors too were kindhearted; they knew how to instill in children at least the delusion of a warm home." Akiva also mentions, as do the others who submitted testimony, Mrs. Taquet's nightly rounds of the children in their beds, putting each to sleep with a reassuring kiss.

Jacques Funkleder (then known as Van Humbeek), another of Mrs. Taquet's charges, relates the first difficult days when he arrived at Jamoigne in 1943, an eight-year-old boy accustomed to the sheltering comfort of a mother. "But Mrs. Taquet's smile, as well as that of her husband 'the Major,' instilled confidence in us from the start, and we found so much warmth there that for us the manor became a vacation camp." He adds that daily activities consisted of studies and scouting in the nearby woods. Life was filled with songs, games, and gaiety.

But danger was lurking close, for the Gestapo went to great lengths to prevent Jewish children from escaping being rounded up and deported to the death camps. In September 1943, for instance, the Germans raided the home. The officer in charge asked Mrs. Taquet point-blank, "Are there any Jewish children here?" She replied, "Do you really think we would keep Jewish children here? It would be much too risky!" The Germans did not carry out a thorough search of the premises, and departed peacefully. On another occasion, the Jewish children were told to pack and prepare for a full month's outing to Olloy-sur Viroin. After the war, Jacques learned that, as the non-Jewish children had been released to their families for a month's duration, the continued stay of the Jewish children (with no families to visit) on the premises would have attracted undue attention and jeopardized their security. Hence, the then inexplicable long outing.

In October 1944, all children were dutifully released to their families, themselves hidden during the occupation years. Taken to Brussels on trucks provided by JOC (the Catholic youth movement), they were swept up in the arms of their families. The joy was "indescribable," Jacques recalls.

Forty-three years later, tens of Mrs. Taquet's former wards came to visit her in a nursing home in order to thank the now eighty-nine-year-old woman (still fully alert) for her wartime maternal care. A year later, she was awarded Israel's highest honor in a public ceremony, Yad Vashem's Righteous Among the Nations medal and certificate of honor.

While at Jamoigne, during the war years, the children dedicated special congratulatory messages to Mrs. Taquet on Mother's Day. These two messages are typical of them.

> *Dear Mother Taquet,*
> As today is Mother's Day, I have
> decided to thank you for all your good deeds and concern
> for us. You are for us a mother. Mother Taquet, please
> listen to a little tale. There was once a charming small
> country; very peaceful, where perfect happiness
> prevailed. Alas! This did not last long. A very
> terrible evil spirit came, to trouble this peaceful
> atmosphere. This terrible spirit was war! Very soon
> thereafter the country's children grew weaker;
> they were hungry and cold. Afflictions of every kind bore down
> on them. The children would still be very unhappy today had a
> good fairy not appeared and led all these to a
> magnificent palace where she now spoiled them and comforted
> them for their sufferings. Mother Taquet, you have
> certainly guessed who this kind fairy is. Yes, you are
> not mistaken. It is surely you. You saved us from
> disaster, danger, hunger, and cold! What would have
> happened to us if you hadn't come?
> *Albert Devos*
>
> *Dear Mother,*
> I write these few verses to you in
> honor of Mother's Day:
> To you whom we love so much, really more than a mother.
> For a long time, I have known that you love us tenderly,
> otherwise you would not have risked so much for us, the other small
> children.
> You tire yourself day and night to care for us.

> We wish with all our hearts that you will always know happiness,
> always have these children.
> Here then are the wishes of Jean-Jacques and Joseph, your dear children
> [family names still unidentified].

"What joy to evoke together such unusual memories that we have all lived through and that we shall never forget," Abraham Kwiat wrote in his deposition. It is hard to imagine how the word "joy" may be utilized to describe conditions against the setting of the Holocaust. Such is the measure of the humanity of a woman and her associates that remained etched in the minds of these young children. (3773)

The Netherlands

The Historical Data

The Dutch people were taken by surprise when on May 10, 1940 Germany invaded the Netherlands. It was generally taken for granted that the Germans would respect Dutch neutrality in the conflict which had broken out the previous September, as they had done during the First World War. Within a week of the German onslaught, Dutch resistance collapsed, after absorbing a particular brutal and devastating bombardment of Rotterdam which left many areas of the city in ruins.

In contrast to Belgium and France, where only a military occupation prevailed, the Germans imposed both military and civil control over the Dutch people. Five German general-commissioners were appointed as quasi-ministers to supervise five different departments of the Dutch administration, headed by a Reich High Commissioner, Dr. Seyss Inquart-Hart.

The choice of this man was no accident. Inquart-Hart, an Austrian, had helped engineer the collapse of independent Austria, which led to the country's incorporation into Greater Germany under the Anschluss of March 1938. It was now hoped that he would similarly ease Holland's outright annexation to Germany. Nazi scholars valued highly the race qualities of the Dutch. Hitler considered the Dutch a kindred Germanic tribe which as a result of historic developments had parted ways with its Nordic roots and set up a separate state. This was now to be corrected.

Overriding the objections of the Dutch Fascist leader Mussert that the country be allowed to evolve into a separate Nazi state, allied to Nazi Germany, Hitler decided that little Holland must be made to join the Reich as quickly as possible and the Dutch people converted to National Socialism. The Nazis therefore applied their racial policies with greater rigor in the Netherlands than in other occupied countries of western Europe, and the Dutch Jews were made to suffer the attendant consequeces with greater thoroughness than their brethren in Belgium and France.

In 1940, Holland counted some 140,000 Jews, who enjoyed a freedom rooted in the Dutch tradition of tolerance which had marked the country since it secured independence from Spain in the seventeenth century. There was little active antisemitism in prewar Holland, although many among the Dutch populace viewed with dismay the influx of Jewish refugees from Nazi Germany, and continued to regard Jews as different and a foreign element. But Dutch Jews felt "thoroughly at home in the Netherlands," in the words of the noted historian Dr. Louis de Jong, and assimilation was on the rise. The moderate success of the Dutch fascist party (N.S.B.) in the 1930s (which initially even admitted Jews into its ranks) did not dampen Jewish confidence in the future of the freedoms which they enjoyed. No one in his right mind could foresee that within three years of the German occupation, some 80 percent of Dutch Jews would disappear from the Dutch landscape, and perish in death camps in distant Poland.

Under Nazi rule, anti-Jewish measures followed one another in quick succession. In October 1940, the civil service was closed to Jews and all employees were required to fill out a statement specifying their "Aryan" origin. When the Germans moved against institutions of higher learning, protests erupted in several universities. At Leiden University, 1,700 out of a total 2,400 student body signed a declaration condemning all forms of discrimination. Professor Scholte of the Amsterdam University collected a similar petition signed by 209 members of the faculty (50 percent of the total). Notwithstanding this, on November 22, 1940 the heads of the universities were summoned to the Ministry of Education, where they were handed dismissal notices for Jewish faculty members on their staff. The secretary of the Leiden University refused to accept. Students at the Delft Technical Institute threatened a walk-out. Professor Cleveringa of Leijden University publicly condemned the anti-Jewish measure. The Germans reacted by shutting down the Leiden and Delft universities and arresting several of their faculty members. When church heads added their voices of protest to those of the university heads, the Nazi leaderhip realized that Holland's induction into National Socialism would take longer than originally anticipated.

When in early 1941 the Germans ordered the registration of all Jews at the offices of the Jewish Council (a Nazi-controlled umbrella organiza- tion which, as in other occupied countries, became a tool for a more effective application of anti-Jewish measures), the obedient Jews com- plied, little suspecting that this voluntary submittal of personal data would greatly facilitate their later roundup, based on records of this census, and their deportation. Then, in February 1941, violence erupted in the Jewish quarter of Amsterdam as a result of Jews defending themselves against attacks by members of the Dutch N.S.B. movement. Under orders from Himmler, head of the S.S., the Germans reacted vigorouly. On February 22, 1941, 425 Jewish youths were randomly picked up, brutally beaten, then shipped to Buchenwald and Mauthausen camps, where most perished that same year.

This brutal Nazi measure shook the Dutch people out of the benevolent complacency which had marked the period of German occupation until then. Initially inspired by the Communist underground, strikes broke out spontaneously among Amsterdam tramway workers; then embraced metal and shipyard workers in several adjacent cities. This strike was the first act of public resistance against the German occupation, not only in Holland but elsewhere in Nazi-occupied Europe, and it had been called in support of the Jews. Although they reacted forcefully, arresting many of the strike ringleaders, the Nazis had been taken completely by surprise at the Dutch making common cause with Jewish sufferings, and this led them to conclude that the pace of integration of the Netherlands into the Nazi empire would henceforth have to slow down. On the other hand, there was to be no let up in the "War Against the Jews."

Jewish firms were forcibly liquidated, and Jewish doctors and attorneys were prohibited from serving non-Jewish clients. Thousands of Jews were expelled from certain regions of the country and others inducted in work groups for forced labor under difficult physical conditions. Then came the start of the deportation in July 1942 which was to decimate Dutch Jews within a year and a half. The Dutch Theater in Amsterdam served as the main assembly point for the close to 80,000 Jews of that city (58 percent of total Dutch Jews), wherefrom men, women, and children were taken to the Westerbork transit camp (in the northeast Drente province), where they were joined by other Dutch Jews. From there the vast majority were sent to either Auschwitz or Sobibor death camps in Poland.

Of the 95,000 Jews who arrived at these two notorious camps, only 1,100 survived (of the 34,000 sent to Sobibor alone, only 19 survived). Of the total 107,000 deportation figure, approximately 5,000 (less than 5 percent) survived the horrors of the Holocaust.

Those who eluded Nazi roundups fell into several categories. Some 2,500 persons escaped to Belgium and France, thence to either Spain or Switzerland. Some committed suicide (the figures are not exact). Many of the thousands living in mixed marriage with non-Jewish spouses or qualified by a special German bureau as half- or a quarter-Jewish, were spared. Estimates for Jews in hiding are not precise. One reliable figure places the number at 25,000, a third of which were eventually discovered and dispatched to concentration camps. The remainder, some 16,000, remained successfully hidden with non-Jewish families.

There were many factors which contributed to the success of the Nazis in obliterating so many Jews in spite of the Dutch population's uncon-

cealed abhorrence of Nazi intentions in this regard. The German-super-
vised Dutch administration remained obedient to instructions received
from above without much regard to personal sensibilities regarding the
issue on hand. Thus, the Dutch railways (which employed 30,000
persons), dutifully transported Jews from the Westerbork camp to the
German border.

It has been argued that the stolid, lawabiding character of the Dutch
people and their concern with punctuality and precision, coupled with a
centuries-instilled tradition of trust toward persons in authority, did not
predispose them to acts of defiance, or even of half-hearted and sloppy
performance of orders from above. This, of course, played into Nazi hands.
Also, that in contrast to the Belgians and French, the Dutch were exempt
from the terrible experience of World War I and therefore lacked this
important yardstick by which to gauge German intentions and measures
over occupied populations. In addition, the Dutch resistance, which came
to birth immediately after the occupation, only flourished as a large-scale
movement in 1943, when most of Dutch Jews had already vanished into
the Nazi concentration camp world and could no longer be aided. Still, as
we shall learn, the Dutch resistance played a pivotal role in rescuing the
remnants of Dutch Jews which elected to go into hiding.

From the Jewish side as well, matters played into the hands of the
Germans. Those reporting for deportation had no knowledge of the fate
awaiting them in distant Poland. It was generally believed that it was less
dangerous to embark on this journey than to be dispatched to the
Mauthausen camp (which the Nazis threatened would befall those not
reporting for deportation) from which frightening reports had filtered back
on the fate of Jews incarcerated there. The general view among Jews (and
non-Jews alike) was that they were were to undergo harsh conditions in
either labor or agricultural camps in Eastern Europe, but with good
chances of survival, and with their families intact.

No one suspected wholesale killings immediately upon arrival at their
destination. Hence, Dutch Jews by and large preferred the rigors of an
unknown journey and an uncertain fate to an uncomfortable existence as
persons on the run, and necessitating, in some cases, the splitting up of
families and separating from one's own children. The dangers of going into
hiding were consequently exaggerated and the dangers of deportation
were psychologically underestimated.

It should also be pointed out that the Netherlands does not enjoy
favorable topographical features, such as forbidding mountainous regions
and inpenetrable stretches of forests, which could serve as natural
hideouts for people on the run. Holland's borders as well did not offer the
prospect of escape and safety across them. From all aides, the country was
surrounding by Nazi-controlled territories. The opportunies presented for
many French Jews to attempt flight to neutral Spain and Switzerland or
friendly (to the Jews) Italy were not available to Dutch Jews.

All these factors contributed to the high mortality rate of the Dutch Jewish population, one of the highest indeed of most Nazi-occupied countries.

These negative factors should, however, not blind us to the positive elements which militated in favor of Jews in hiding. First was the general public sympathy with the oppressed Jews as a result of the deep revulsion aroused by the inhumanity of the Nazi measures. Though Dutch feelings toward Jews were perhaps not always that clearcut, and granted that some were not at all friendly disposed toward Jews, there was a consensus that Jews as other human beings ought not to be deprived of their dignity and security. This was the rock upon which all previously pro-German sentiments were shattered. In July 1942, Reich commissioner Dr. Schmidt, defending the deportations, noted in dismay: "The Dutch look upon the entire [Jewish] problem through glasses of ridiculous humanitarianism."

The incapacity of the Germans to appreciate Dutch sensibilities in this regard lost them the support of this conquered people upon which they had placed such high hopes at the start of the occupation, although German policies in Holland were relatively milder in contrast to those applied in Eastern Europe. The persecution of Jews remained a constant irritant around which large-scale active resistance crystallized and caused a violent and emotional rejection of the occupying regime. There were even incidents of Dutch policemen resigning their posts rather than be personally involved in the roundup of Jews.

The churches too made no secret of their opposition to the anti-Jewish measures. The country was one-third Catholic and two-thirds Protestant. Some churches urged their members to practice civil disobedience rather than betray Jews in hiding. The Calvinist church, for instance, which upheld a more fundamentalist anti-Jewish theology, displayed an extraordinary amount of courage and dedication in the rescue of Jews. This church community, which represented only about 9 percent of the total population, was reponsible for the sheltering of at least one-fourth of all Jews in hiding.

The Calvinist case is a clear illustration of the strong anti-German feeling aroused as a result of the forcible deportation of Jews without regard to Dutch sensibilities, although the theological belief of preserving the Jews as God's chosen people also played an important role. The Calvinist spirit of self-reliance and sacrifice, as well as their highly developed sense of responsibility for one's fellow men, no doubt also were contributing factors for those who volunteered to help Jews.

In brief, it was not necessarily pro-Jewish feelings which motivated the religious-minded Dutch people but a deeply rooted belief in the sanctity of the individual person's right to life and security. Those thus motivated interpreted their help to Jews as a clear articulation of this belief.

Once Dutch objections to anti-Jewish measures had crystallized, the Dutch underground played a leading role in moving persons from one place to another, in the effort to find for them suitable hiding places and avoid detection and arrest. A special branch within the resistance (the L.O.), looked after the needs of the *onderduikers* (literally "divers"), who at first consisted principally of Jews, but later came to include tens of thousands of others who had reason to flee from Nazi arrest. The L.O. distributed false ration cards and subsistance allowances to families sheltering Jews. Special large-scale operations included the transfer of hundreds of children from the large cities, such as from the Creche in Amsterdam, to be dispersed among friendly familes in various parts of the country.

The dangers of detection were great. One survivor in a study of Dutch Jews under the occupation states: "There is, in fact, not a single Jewish survivor who went into hiding and did not have a narrow escape" (Presser, 389). Some persons were forced to move to over a dozen different places to keep them out of reach of the authorities. There were also those who agreed to hide Jews only in return for exorbitant amounts of payment, then showed their charges to the door when the money ran out. There were, in addition, elements within the underground who strenuously refused to lend a hand in this effort, but they were in the minority. And there was danger of betrayal by informers, those ideologically sympathetic with Nazism and those motivated by greed and ready to sell out anyone in return for ransom payment.

To encourage these, the Germans progressively raised monetary rewards for denouncing Jews in hiding: from 5 florins to eventually 40 florins per Jewish head. The Police Gazette (*Algemeen Politieblad*) regularly published lists of missing Jews sent in by various municipalities. In addition, special units of the Dutch police specialized in searching, collecting information, and identifying Jews, and were aided in this effort by various Nazi security units, such as the notorious Green Police. Dutch persons caught hiding Jews were generally carted off to Nazi concentration camps where some perished and most suffered permanent damage to their health.

With no woodlands or other favorable topographical features and hostile borders on all sides, coupled with the small size of the country and population (some 8 million) and the undampened Nazi zeal and determination in rounding up all Jews, it is perhaps surprising that 16,000 Jews were able to elude the Nazi dragnet. As the Dutch Jewish historian J. Melkman notes, this was made possible because thousands of Dutch people were enlisted in extending aid to their Jewish neighbors in defiance of the risk to themselves. When one adds to these considerations, the extensive period of the Germany occupation (five full years), as well as the harsh "hunger" winter of 1944/45, when people literally starved for lack of food, the commitment of those who continued to shelter Jews in their homes is all the more illustrious and praiseworthy.

Following, are noteworthy examples of rescue efforts by individual Dutch individuals and groups.

Random Encounters and Casual Acquaintances

We begin with several stories that are noteworthy because at the outset rescuers and survivors were either unacquainted or knew each other only casually and came together quite by chance.

Franciscus Molmans

Samuel Van Creveld was a retail butcher in Woerden, a town not far from Utrecht and about 19 miles south of Amsterdam. Late in 1942 he and his wife were ordered to report to the Vught transit camp for "resettlement" in Poland. After making arrangements for their three children to be cared for by friends, they closed the shop and began preparing for the journey.

Two days before their scheduled departure, Samuel was standing outside his house when Franciscus ("Frans") Molmans, a policeman, passed by on his way to work. As usual Molmans stopped for a chat. When Van Creveld told him about the deportation order, Molmans advised him to go into hiding. Realizing that Van Creveld had no idea how to go about it, Molmans went back home to discuss the situation with his wife. The two of them decided to take in the Van Crevelds for as long as necessary.

Molmans found it difficult to persuade Cecilia Van Creveld to accept the offer. She was afraid she and her husband would become an unwelcome burden and did not want to endanger the Molmans and their three children. Eventually she came around, however, and that night, under the cover of darkness, Molmans took Samuel and Cecilia home.

Although the Molmans house was quite small, the Van Crevelds had a room of their own; for safety's sake they had to remain in it for the next two and one-half years, until the liberation of Holland on May 5, 1945. Henriette Molmans, Frans's wife, became almost as much of a prisoner as the Van Crevelds. Fearful that an unexpected caller might discover them, she almost never left the house and eventually took to carrying a pistol in her brassiere to be used in the event of a German raid.

Of the three Molmans children, only the eldest, ten-year-old Annie, was privy to the secret, and she was responsible for keeping her two brothers away from the upstairs room and explaining the coughs, sneezes, and other noises that occasionally emanated from it. She visited the Van Crevelds every day and kept them supplied with crayons and other drawing materials to help pass the time. Henriette also made a point of finding chores to keep them busy, such as sewing, knitting, and cleaning vegetables, and as the months passed she and Cecilia Van Creveld became close friends—so much so, in fact, that Henriette named her fourth child Cecilia.

In the meantime, Frans Molmans had left the police force and was now employed in an office in Oudewater that distributed ration coupons. He also joined the underground and occasionally helped to hide young men who had been conscripted for labor in Germany. Before long the Germans put him under surveillance. They searched the house, but missed the hidden door to the room where the Van Crevelds were hiding, and once held him for several days of questioning at the Amersfoort police station, eventually releasing him for lack of evidence.

Two Jewish persons hiding in a closet, The Hague. Courtesy of Yad Vashem.

Jew climbing into a hiding place located above a toilet in The Hague (postwar picture).Courtesy of Yad Vashem.

In his deposition to Yad Vashem, Elly Van Creveld, the son of Samuel and Cecilia, wrote that Frans and Henriette Molmans were "two wonderful and brave people." And indeed they were, for at the height of the Nazi terror, as a result of a chance conversation, they undertook to save the lives of two fellow human beings whom they had only known casually. (941)

Jan Blok

Samuel Visser, the owner of a dry goods store in Utrecht, had a similar stroke of good luck. In May 1940, during the German invasion, Visser served in the Burgenwacht, a civilian volunteer force, while his wife fled to France. Reunited after Holland's surrender, they reopened their store and managed well enough until July 16, 1942, when a neighbor warned them that the city's Jews were about to be rounded up for deportation to Poland.

In anticipation of this day, Visser had arranged for himself and his wife to hide with a friend of a friend in the countryside outside Utrecht. The Vissers went to the man's farm as planned, but ten days later he had a change of heart and abruptly told them to leave.

The couple mounted their bikes and began peddling, but as Visser recalls, "We had nowhere to go." About 15 miles from the farm they asked for help at a religious nursing home but were refused. Continuing on their way, they stopped at the farm of Jan Blok in Ysselstein. "We told him we were Jews in need of a place to hide. He agreed immediately, saying that God had sent us to him."

The Vissers stayed with Blok and his wife until the liberation more than two years later, hiding in a recess under the kitchen cupboard when anyone dropped in, and staying in the cellar when friends were expected for longer visits. The Bloks kept their presence in the house a secret and freely provided them with food and all their other needs. "He never asked for any payment whatsoever," Samuel notes. "He wouldn't even accept gifts from us."

Jan Blok sold his own ration coupons to buy things for the Vissers. His wife was not too happy about having them in the house, and sometimes she and her husband argued about it. Whenever this happened the Vissers would offer to leave, but each time they did so Blok countered that he had taken them for the duration and had no intention of breaking his promise.

Despite these moments of stress, the Vissers and the Bloks have become good friends in the years since the war. (1605)

Albert and Wilhelmina Jansen

In September 1942, in the village of Holten, situated about equidistant between Apeldoorn and Enschede, Mrs. Abraham Pagrach told Wilhelmina Jansen, a casual acquaintance, that she and her husband expected to be deported before very long. Mrs. Jansen replied, "If you ever have to hide from the Germans, come to our place, and we'll take care of you."

That evening Mrs. Pagrach told her husband what Mrs. Jansen had said, concluding, "She is certainly willing to help us, but I don't think she and her husband understand the risk they would be taking." At that moment there was a knock at the door. It was Albert Jansen, who had come over to reiterate his wife's offer. "You are welcome to stay in our home," he

said, "and we will do everything we can to protect you and keep you alive."
The Pagrachs asked Jansen how much they would have to pay. "Just for
what you eat," he replied; "no more and no less." When he left he handed
them a key to his house, saying they would be welcome at any time.

Two months later, in November 1942, the time came. Abraham
Pagrach and his wife moved in with the Jansens, while Pagrach's parents,
having made their own arrangements, hid elsewhere. Around the middle
of 1943, however, the parents had to find a new refuge. Pagrach's father
asked the Jansens if he could join his son and daughter-in-law, and they
replied, "Where there's room for two, there's room for three." When
Pagrach's mother, soon afterward, made the same request through her
son, they replied, "Where there's room for three, there's room for four. Your
mother is welcome in our home."

The four Pagrachs occupied a sitting room and two bedrooms in the
Jansen house. Since it was located in the center of town, they never went
outside, even at night, but despite this precaution the situation was very
risky for the Jansens. They had to buy food for the Pagrachs on the black
market, and for several weeks, during which the Pagrachs hid in an alcove
off one of the bedrooms, they were required to billet German military
personnel. Albert Jansen was eventually conscripted for forced labor in
Germany, but in his absence Wilhelmina and her daughter continued to
look after the Pagrachs.

On April 8, 1945, Holten was liberated by Canadian troops and the
Pagrachs were able to step outside for the first time in more than two years.
After the war, Albert Jansen took up his former occupation as an
upholsterer and became active in local politics. He and Wilhelmina were
both awarded the Order of Orange-Nassau, Holland's highest civilian
decoration, and in 1973 Holten named a street in his honor.

Albert Jansen's death in 1972 left Abraham Pagrach convulsed with
grief. The Jansens, he wrote, "never boasted about what they had done and
never asked for any reward. They simply did what their hearts dictated and
persevered. . . . They knew us only superficially [but] felt they had to do
something to help the Jews during the war and thus they acted. We had
the good fortune to be the people they helped." (1816)

Laurens Mieloo

Laurens Mieloo, a window washer from the village of Loosduinen, was
at work at the home of Sam and Flora Jacobson in The Hague when they
received a registered letter telling them to report to the Westerbork transit
camp. He immediately told them that they could hide in his house
whenever they wanted to "dive" (Dutch slang for going underground).

Before deciding whether to accept the offer, Sam Jacobson asked
Mieloo how much he would charge to hide a certain non-Jew who was

wanted for sabotaging a factory. Mieloo replied that he was not interested in strangers or their money but was willing to help Sam and his wife. He made only one condition: that they not tell anyone, even their closest relatives, where they were going.

On August 18, 1942, the day they were due at Westerbork, Sam and Flora Jacobson said goodbye to their parents and friends, and, without telling anyone, went straight to Mieloo's house in Loosduinen. They remained there until May 5, 1945, when the country was liberated.

During their thousand-day sojourn with the Mieloos the Jacobsons were confined to a 6 by 9 foot cubicle in one room of the family's apartment. They had to keep away from the windows, since the Mieloo house, like all the others in the village, had no curtains, and this could not be changed because it would have attracted attention. The presence of a German living in the apartment on the floor below made it necessary for them to talk in whispers at all times and to move around on tiptoes.

In addition to the Jacobsons, Laurens Mieloo and his wife Anna also sometimes hid other Jews for short periods, either in their house or in a garage they owned in the center of the village. Two of them, a father and a son, were arrested by the German Green Police (so-called from the color of their uniforms) and under torture confessed that Mieloo had been hiding them.

When brought in for questioning, Mieloo pretended to be outraged by the charges against him, showering the father and son with such a medley of curses for falsely accusing him that he persuaded the police of his innocence. He somehow also managed to convince them that the father and son were so unreliable that it would not be worth questioning them any further.

Laurens and Anna Mieloo took care of the Jacobsons without help from the underground. "From the very beginning we had a good and friendly relationship with our hosts," Sam says. Anna did all the errands for the two of them, including a daily visit to the village's communal kitchen to fetch additional meals.

The Mieloos were always in danger, and their house was searched three times by German police looking for fugitives. Each time the Jacobsons hid in the cesspool behind the outhouse. Once they had to remain there for seven hours.

"There is really no way to repay these people for what they did for us," Flora wrote in her 1973 deposition. "In ordinary circumstances, we say that jumping in the water to save someone from drowning, or pulling someone out of a burning building, is an act of bravery. But who can adequately evaluate the deeds of a whole family whose feats of courage extended over two long years, with their lives constantly in danger, every day and every night, and without any gain or personal profit?" Especially, she adds, because both Mieloos worked hard and were very keen on their few hours of privacy and rest after an exhausting day. (855)

Piet Suuring

In the spring of 1941, Leofried Durlacher, who lived in Bennekom, a small town situated between Utrecht and Arnhem, regularly played tennis at the local resort hotel. There he got to know the hotel's owners, the Suurings, and their eighteen-year-old son Petrus (Piet).

Toward the end of the year, when the Nazis instituted a series of severe anti-Jewish decrees, the Suurings told Leo Durlacher that he and his family could count on their help if the need arose. Meanwhile, as the roundups in Amsterdam increased in scope, many Jews from the capital began fleeing to the countryside.

By this time Leo and Piet had become close friends. They often spent their days biking from farm to farm to find householders who would be willing to take in Jewish fugitives, either gratis or for a fee. In November 1942, after placing two Jewish boys, Leo was returning to town by himself when he was arrested by the Dutch police, who sent him to Westerbork, the huge transit camp where Jews from all over the country were assembled for "resettlement" in Poland.

Leo soon came down with scarlet fever and was transferred to a hospital in Groningen, where Piet often visited him even though it meant a journey of about 100 miles each way. In April 1943 Leo told Piet that he would soon be returned to Westerbork and then deported to Poland. There and then Piet decided to do whatever was necessary to save his friend.

That evening he phoned his father, who dropped everything and took the next train to Groningen, bringing along one of Leo's suits. The next day they slipped the suit into Leo's room during visiting hours. He quickly

Two men hiding above toilet, The Hague (postwar picture).Courtesy of Yad Vashem.

changed and the three of them left the hospital at the end of visiting hours without arousing any suspicion.

Their destination was the home of a friend of Piet's father about three miles away. Having spent the last three months in bed, Leo found it hard to keep up with his two companions, but with their help he made it. They spent the night at the friend's house and over the next week Leo was hidden with several other people in Groningen. Finally, when it seemed safe enough, he returned to Bennekom by train.

The Suurings met him at the station and took him by bicycle to their hotel. Soon afterwards his parents joined him there, and the three of them were provided with new papers by the Suurings' underground contacts. Over the next six months Leo realized that a number of the hotel's other guests were Jews in hiding; he and they often exchanged glances that spoke a thousand words but for understandable reasons never engaged in conversation with each other.

Toward the end of 1943 Leo and his parents were moved to a different location in Bennekom. Piet visited them regularly, bringing along food and letters from relatives in hiding and, in Leo's words, "pepping up our spirits, which, as you can well imagine, were sometimes quite low."

Thus, the courageous owners of a resort hotel and their son saved a young man and his parents whom at first they had only known through occasional meetings on a tennis court. (2483)

Tine Boeke

In 1939, Tine Boeke was a student nurse in a hospital in Zaandam. She had, of course, read about the Nazi persecution of the Jews, but when one of her patients, a recent escapee from Germany, told her about the situation there, she was shocked. "To hear such things from someone who had personally experienced them was so shattering that I resolved to do something about it."

Tine's opportunity was not long in coming. In mid-1940, soon after the German conquest of the Netherlands, a Nazi sympathizer was appointed head of the hospital. Outspokenly contemptuous of him, Tine had to find another position. She moved to Amsterdam and there joined the resistance, eventually organizing an underground ring, based in her own home, that specialized in preparing false papers and finding families to take in Jewish fugitives. Some of them lived with her for brief periods while she arranged permanent places for them.

Among the many people who survived the war thanks to Tine's help were the Van der Lijn-Nijman family—husband, wife, and two children, one six months old and the other five years. Another was Jacob Frankel, his wife, and his young daughter.

Frankel, an attorney, was referred to Tine by a colleague in August 1942. As Frankel reports in his deposition, he went to Tine's home and "she promised on the spot to find a place for my three and one-half year old daughter, and within a week she brought us the good news that she had a place for her. She did not tell us the address, in order to protect the adoptive family." For several days Tine went for walks with Ruth to win her confidence, and then, on September 1, 1942, she took her to her new guardians. She also found a place for the Frankels on a farm near the Belgian border, and before they went into hiding provided them with identity cards that had originally been issued to someone else, but had been retouched with their names, photos, and fingerprints by a professional forger in her circle.

Tine's most striking feat involved an elderly Jewish woman named Liesel Weiss, who had escaped from Germany in 1938 and was living with a Dutch family in Amsterdam when the war began. Mrs. Weiss had a serious heart condition, and Tine first became acquainted with her as a visiting nurse after she left Zaandam and moved to the capital. Home care was not enough, however, and around the middle of 1942 Mrs. Weiss was admitted to the Jewish Hospital in Amsterdam.

Not long after this Tine learned that the hospital's inmates were being deported. Putting a yellow star on her nurse's uniform, she entered the hospital and encountered a scene completely at odds with what one would expect in a place of healing. "There was a terrible commotion and everything was in chaos—German police shouting, patients and staff confused and upset."

Able to move about freely because of her uniform, Tine searched for Mrs. Weiss. "I found her all alone in a ward that was already completely empty, and I dragged her outside. She was hardly able to walk, so I hid her under a blanket in a small wheelbarrow."

Somehow Tine managed to get Mrs. Weiss home, and now began a desperate struggle to restore her failing health, which had been worsened by depression and stress. Although working full-time as a nurse and also busy with her underground activities, Tine devoted herself to caring for Mrs. Weiss. As a friend commented years later, "To this day I still can't imagine how, from the practical point of view, she managed to do it." Thanks to Tine's efforts, Mrs. Weiss steadily improved. She herself attributed her recovery to her "unshakable confidence" in Tine.

In August 1943 Tine Boeke was picked up by the police. Although released soon afterwards, she realized that she was under suspicion. Fearing that if she was arrested again Mrs. Weiss might be left on her own, Tine decided to find another place for her. Soon thereafter she moved her into a pension, where she lived safely for the duration of the war.

Tine's lot was not so fortunate. Arrested soon after this, she was taken to the transit camp at Vught, then to the concentration camp for women at Ravensbruck, and finally to Oranienburg-Sachsenhausen, where she was liberated on April 22, 1945.

Returning home weakened in body, due to a serious stomach ailment, but not in spirit, Tine immediately went to visit Mrs. Weiss. Discovering that the medical care at the pension was inadequate, she arranged for her to be hospitalized. After Mrs. Weiss recovered, Tine helped her to join her brother in Israel, where she lived out her remaining years. Tine and her husband, a professor of clinical psychology at the University of Groningen, visited her there several times before her death in 1958.

Still captivated by his memories of Tine more than forty years after the war, Jacob Frankel describes her as "a woman who radiates so much warmth that one cannot help falling in love with her." (2874)

Antoinette Taselaar-Ponsen

In 1934 Willem Prins began teaching a weekly course in business English at the secretarial school run by Mrs. Taselaar-Ponsen and her daughter Antoinette in Rotterdam. They asked him to stay on when the employment of Jews in non-Jewish firms was outlawed in 1941, but because it would have endangered all three of them he decided to resign.

About a year earlier Prins had gotten married, and now his wife's sister came to live with him and his wife. As more and more Dutch Jews began receiving deportation notices, he was at his wit's end. Finally, on August 7, 1942, he paid a visit to the Taselaars and asked their advice.

In Prins's words: "Mrs. Taselaar turned to her daughter, who in reply gently nodded yes, and then Mrs. Taselaar handed me a key with the words, 'Here is the key to our front door; come with your wife and sister-in-law tonight or tomorrow.'" A bit taken back by Mrs. Taselaar's unexpected generosity, Prins warned that if caught she and her daughter would go to prison and might even be executed. Besides, he added, he only had a few hundred guilders, hardly enough to pay for what might be a long stay in their home.

"I shall never forget her answer," Prins states in his deposition. "That you have almost no money is no objection at all, and we are not afraid to give shelter to the three of you, because helping people in distress is our human duty." Antoinette Taselaar was then thirty-two years of age; her mother considerably older.

It was decided that Willem, his wife Rebekka, and her sister Elizabeth would move into the Taselaars' home the next morning. They would occupy a room in the attic next to the Taselaar's bedroom. On the floor below was a living room and another room used for prayer and meditation by the Taselaars, and the secretarial school was located on the floor below that.

Initially the Taselaars refused to accept payment of any kind, although Prins's last employer, who had fired him in July 1942 on German orders, continued to pay him 150 florins a month, delivered regularly by a

Woman pulls strap to lift trapdoor above hiding place in closet, The Hague (postwar picture).Courtesy of Yad Vashem.

coworker, to help defray his expenses in the Taselaar household. After a while, pressed by Prins to let him share the costs, the Taselaars agreed to accept nominal sums toward the cost of electricity, gas, and food, but they refused anything for rent and heating, insisting that the only compensation they wanted was the "spiritual satisfaction of keeping three people out of the claws of the Nazis."

Life in the Taselaar house was quiet and uneventful. Willem spent most of his time reading, Rebekka and Elizabeth busied themselves with knitting, while downstairs students came and went without ever suspecting a thing. In October 1944, after an attack on a nearby police station, the Germans captured an underground member who was in possession of a list of persons in hiding. As a precaution, Willem, Rebekka, and Elizabeth were moved to another location, but they returned to the Taselaars' house on December 20th.

Mrs. Taselaar had died in their absence, so the full burden of caring for them now fell on Antoinette. Rotterdam was liberated on May 5, 1945, but because of the difficulty of finding apartments the three remained with her for another few months. Thus from August 1942 until August 1945, a full three years, an elderly woman and her daughter willingly placed their lives and careers in jeopardy in order to save three persons—two of them total strangers, one a former employee—solely for the "spiritual satisfaction" it gave them. (3443)

Pastor Gerardus and Dora Pontier

We end this section with a story that took place in Heerlen, the southernmost city of the Netherlands.

One day in 1942, Shlomo Zilber and his younger brother Hanan were walking along the street when a passing cyclist, noticing their yellow stars, stopped and approached them. Shlomo remembers him as a man of about fifty, blue eyed, with short-cut gray hair, very tall and heavily built. Greeting the two lads, he asked how they were faring during these trying times.

Shlomo responded by describing how his family could be sent to a concentration camp almost any day. "God knows what will happen to us," he concluded. To this the stranger replied, "They are doing a satanic deed, and it is terrible to hear about it." He closed his eyes for a minute as if in prayer, then told the boys that if they should ever need help, he would be ready to assist them. He gave them his name and address: Pastor Gerardus Jacobus Pontier of the Dutch Reformed Church in Heerlen.

A week later the Zilber family received the dreaded deportation notice. Shlomo was sent to Pontier's home to find out whether the pastor really meant what he had said. When the boy told him about the impending deportation, which was scheduled for August 25, 1942, Pontier assured him that he would help. "He exuded so much confidence and warmth," Shlomo recalls, "that I felt as if I were standing in the presence of a protector. To tell the truth, I was really waiting for him to do something for us."

After a moment Pontier went inside to get his wife, Dora. Then, standing side by side, with tears in their eyes, they told Shlomo that he and his parents would be welcome in their home. "Don't worry, my child," the pastor said, "we have made a decision, and God will protect us. Son of Israel, we are happy to give you any help. It is the duty of every Christian to help those in danger."

Over the next few days Pontier moved his two daughters into a neighbor's house and gave their room to the four Zilbers. About a year later, on November 6, 1943, Pontier was warned that the Germans were about to arrest him because of his underground activities. The Zilbers, learning this, offered to leave, but Pontier insisted that they stay on.

While this conversation was still in progress, a car screeched to a halt outside. Two Gestapo agents burst in, grabbed Pontier, and took him to the Scheveningen prison, where he was held for six months. In the days that followed Dora Pontier helped the Zilbers to find shelter elsewhere. Meanwhile, Pontier was released on May 17, 1944. His first concern was to see how his former proteges were faring.

"What a surprise and what a happy reunion. All of us thanked him, because if not for his sacrifice we would certainly not have been there to see the day of his release," Shlomo Zilber states.

Pontier related that the Gestapo had tried to wear him down through undernourishment and continuous interrogations. "They tried to break me spiritually. It was terrible. But God gave me strength, I prayed for hours."

Recalling the day of his arrest, he added: "What happened was a real miracle and undoubtedly God's work. When I saw one of the Nazis stop halfway up the stairs without going any farther [to the room where the Zilbers were staying], I seemed to see an angel standing there with a sword in his hand. This vision made me confident that God would protect you in every respect."

After the war, the Zilbers learned that Pastor Pontier had also helped four other Jewish adults and scores of Jewish children in conjunction with an underground network known as the N.V. group, which will be described below. (422)

Rescuers of Children

Jewish children and infants presented a very difficult problem. The parents were usually unwilling to part with their offspring; the rescuers had not only to persuade them but to find adoptive homes. Complicating all this was the constant possibility that the relocated youngsters might blurt out the truth about their origins, as well as the painful trauma suffered by children separated from their parents and made to take on new identities. (At the end of the war some of them went through the same trauma a second time when removed from their adoptive families and returned to their real parents.)

Pieter Linschoten and Catherine Rowe

Mozes and Sophia Bouwman were hiding in the home of Frederik and Hendrika Van Enck in Oldebroek, where Mozes, claiming to be an army officer on the run from the Germans, operated a photo lab in the Van Enck pharmacy. The Bouwmans' two young children were staying in the home of Hendrik and Jacoba Bley.

Until early 1944 life went on more or less uneventfully, except for an occasional German search, during which the Bouwmans hid in a church cellar. But then Sophia discovered that she was pregnant. What was to be done? Under normal circumstances, going to a hospital to have a baby was a routine matter. But for the Bouwmans (and for the Van Encks as well) the registration procedure might prove very dangerous. Help, however, was forthcoming.

In Utrecht, about 43 miles south of Oldebroek, Elizabeth Linschoten worked as a confidential clerk in Maison Carry Ltd., a firm belonging to Mozes' brother Isaac, who at that time was under arrest and about to be sent to Sobibor, where he perished. Isaac Bouwman's mother and aunt were hiding with Pieter Linschoten, Elizabeth's father, who was the head of De Stichting Volkswoningen, a municipal in-patient facility for drug addicts and alcoholics.

When Pieter Linschoten learned about Sophia Bouwman's predicament from Elizabeth, and was told by his other daughter, a secretary at Trip Ltd., that the manager of her office, Vivian Rowe, an English national born in the Netherlands, and his wife, Catherine, were eager to adopt a child, he soon hatched a plan. Sophia would have her baby at the De Stichting Institute and the Rowes would register it as their own child. They were to return the child to the Bouwmans at the end of the war, and no one except the Linschotens would know its true origin.

In accordance with the plan, Catherine Rowe told her friends and family that she was pregnant and began wearing maternity clothes. Sophia Bouwman came to Utrecht in July and spent the last few months of her pregnancy in the Linschoten house. When her labor began she was taken to the institute and there, attended by a doctor and nurses sworn to secrecy by Linschoten, gave birth to a boy on September 2, 1944. The child was named Albert Dirk in honor of the two men who had helped the Bouwmans find a home for their other two children.

The next evening, Pieter Linschoten put the baby in a bag, fastened it securely to his bike, and took it to the Rowe house. The following morning, September 4th, the Rowes joyfully announced the birth of a son, whom they named Thomas Franklin and officially registered at the municipality of Maartensdij, Utrecht province.

The Rowes took care of the child through the infamous "hunger winter" of 1944-45, selling many of their personal possessions in order to buy food for him. As Sophia Bouwman later wrote, "The real parents could not have done better." In May 1945, when the war ended, the Rowes dutifully returned the child to the Bouwmans. As an expression of gratitude, the Bouwmans added the name the Rowes had given him to his original name.

A certain amount of bureaucratic red tape now ensued, as it was necessary to re-register Thomas Franklin Rowe under his new name and in the names of his real parents. Once this was accomplished, the Bouwmans, together with their three children, returned to their prewar home in Haarlem. (2734, 2735, 2737)

Pastor Jelis and Francoise Van Creutzberg

The story of Daniel and Elisabeth Sanctcross resembles that of the Bouwmans in some ways. In 1943 they were hiding on the farm of Johannes and Petronella Korsten in the village of Beringen, Limburg province, after having escaped from Westerbork a year earlier. On September 11, Elisabeth gave birth to a son in the hospital at Naarden. She felt safe enough in the hospital but was worried about what would happen after her discharge. There was no way she and Daniel could keep the infant with them on the farm, because its crying would soon reveal their presence, endangering both them and the Korstens.

Noting Elisabeth's anxious state, her nurse, Pieta Vincentia Creutzberg, read aloud to her from the Bible. When Elisabeth revealed that she was Jewish and explained what was on her mind, Pieta slipped the baby out of the hospital and brought it to the home of her parents in Arnhem. Over the next sixteen months, until the liberation of northern Holland in February 1945, little Peter-Pinchas Sanctcross was cared for by Pastor Jelis Van Creutzberg and his wife, Francoise Nelly.

Meanwhile, Elisabeth had rejoined her husband on the Korsten farm. In the summer of 1944, the Germans announced a call-up of able-bodied men from Beringen for forced labor. Many of the area's menfolk fled rather than be sent to Germany, but Johannes Korsten decided not to follow suit, fearing that if he failed to report as ordered, the Gestapo would investigate, discover the two Jews hidden on his farm, and as a result arrest him and his family. While he was in Germany, Petronella, who was pregnant, took care of their five children and ran the farm by herself.

Allied troops moved into Limburg in September 1944. With their arrival the Sanctcrosses left the farm and went to Arnhem, where they met the Van Creutzbergs for the first time and were reunited with their child.

Daniel Sanctcross later wrote in his testimony that some ministers in Pastor Van Creutzberg's position might have been tempted to baptize Peter, but "on the contrary, he considered it a great joy and satisfaction to himself and his wife to return a Jewish child to its parents unharmed in order to preserve a child for the Jewish people." The Van Creutzbergs lost two sons in the war, one to the Germans, the other to the Japanese, and it may be that saving a helpless newborn provided them with some consolation. (967)

Gertruud Kruger

Isidor and Sarah Van der Wal of Groningen were two of the many thousands of Dutch Jews who ended up in Auschwitz. Their ordeal was made somewhat less onerous by their knowledge that the underground had arranged for a family in Friesland to take care of their daughter Henriette Myrna, born on September 11, 1942, about five weeks before they were deported. What they did not know, however, was that the host parents had a change of heart after a few days and asked to be relieved of the infant.

B. Amsing, an underground agent who specialized in finding refuges for Jews, took Henriette to the home of the Krüger family in Noorddijk, a village near Groningen. To explain the sudden presence of a sixth child in their household, the Krügers told their neighbors that Henriette was the illegitimate child of Gertruud, their eldest daughter.

Life now turned grim for Gertruud. The inhabitants of Noorddijk, moralistic Calvinists with no tolerance for scandal, treated her as a pariah. To further complicate things, her fiancé joined the Dutch Nazi Party. She wanted to end their relationship but continued seeing him from fear that breaking the engagement might make the police suspicious. In the end she took Henriette and fled to another village, remaining there until the end of the war.

In August 1945 the Van der Wals returned home and reclaimed their daughter. They subsequently emigrated to Israel, where Henriette is now a practicing physician. All of the Krügers, and especially Gertruud, had become very attached to Henriette during the three years she was with them, and they still regard her as a member of their family. (748)

Cornelia Blaauw

Gentile host families or individuals often adopted the Jewish children they had cared for during the war when it was learned that their natural parents were dead. In many instances, including the one that follows, the adoptive parents told the children about their origins and took steps to ensure that they were not be estranged from the Jewish people.

Cornelia Blaauw was the director of a nursery in Haarlem when the war began. From time to time she hid Jewish children, so naturally she agreed in May 1943 when her underground contact, Else Ortt (a Jewish woman whose real name was Aliza Heyman), asked her to take in Nico Visjager, a newborn infant whose parents were about to be deported. The Visjagers turned him over to Cornelia in high hopes that they would eventually be reunited, but as Jacoba Van Tricht, Cornelia's roommate and companion, wrote in her postwar deposition, "Alas, the name Sobibor is enough to tell you the outcome."

Three months later, in August, Cornelia and Jacoba went to Friesland on vacation, leaving Nico in a children's home in Haarlem whose director was a friend of theirs. While they were away the Germans conducted a search of the home. Since Nico's name was not on its official roster, they informed the director that they would return for him the next day.

Else Ortt telephoned Cornelia, who rushed back to Haarlem and went to the police station. She was Nico's mother, she told them, citing as proof a leave of absence she had taken around the time he was born, but, she explained, the birth had been at home, with Jacoba in attendance, and it had never been registered because the father was a German officer now on the eastern front and she had feared public condemnation for consorting with the enemy.

The police bought Cornelia's story. After rebuking her for the "inexcusable conduct" of carrying on a liaison with a German soldier, they issued the birth certificate that formalized Nico's status as her son.

When Nico's parents failed to return at the war's end, their closest surviving relatives petitioned the Jewish Supervision Board to let Cornelia adopt him. As soon as he was old enough she told him about his family background and arranged for him to have frequent contacts with other Jewish children.

Nico went on to become a psychologist. In 1966, when he was twenty-three, he wrote of Cornelia that she had not only saved his life but had given him a childhood and adolescence with as much care, warmth, and love as any child could expect from its own parents—and even more so. Jacoba, Cornelia's lifelong companion, wrote in her own statement, "We rejoiced at what was entrusted to us, and this joy has continued through all the years." (233)

Cornelia Los, the Groothand sisters,
Repke and Rieck Wieringa

"My noble rescuers refused to accept any award for doing what they regarded as their duty," says Rabbi Abraham Prins, formerly of Amsterdam and today an Israeli, in his 1971 petition to Yad Vashem. "However, they are now old and sick, and I have decided, against their wishes, to make sure that they receive the honors due them." Rabbi Prins goes on to tell how he and his family, including his infant daughter, were saved by four heroic Dutch women and a married couple.

When Rabbi Prins first met Cornelia Los and the three Groothand sisters, Johanna, Maria, and Hendrika, they were already well known for their rescue activities. All told, he says, they saved many dozens of youngsters, removing some from their homes literally on the eve of their parents' deportation and housing them with cooperative non-Jewish families. After hiding the children they continued to look out for their welfare, providing ration cards and other necessities to the host families, especially during the terrible winter of 1944-45, when food was very scarce. Rabbi Prins and his family of six survived the war only because these four courageous women hid them in an apartment in downtown Amsterdam and took care of them throughout the occupation.

The Groothand sisters were eventually betrayed to the Nazis. Johanna and Maria were sent to Ravensbruck, Hendrika and her husband to Dachau. When the camps were liberated the three women were still alive, but Hendrika's husband, unfortunately, had died. Rabbi Prins, who knew them well, notes in his statement that the sisters and Cornelia Los were not especially religious and "their rescue activities were based on purely humanitarian motivations." He adds: "They asked no payment of us during the two years [of our confinement] and refused to accept anything afterwards. . . . They performed wonders, and the Jewish people owes them a great debt for their unbounded dedication."

Betty Prins was only a year and a half old when the family went into hiding in 1943. Because keeping a baby cooped up in a small apartment would have endangered the others and impeded her normal development, arrangements were made to place her with a gentile family. On the scheduled day two of the Groothand sisters took Betty and the rabbi for a walk. After a while he slipped away and they brought the child to a safe house and then to the home of Repke and Rieck Wieringa in The Hague.

The Wieringas, a devout Protestant couple, had been married for seven years but were childless. They were very attentive to Betty during the two years she lived with them. During the "hunger" winter of 1944-45, when everything was in short supply, Rieck unraveled one of her own sweaters and used the wool to make one for Betty.

For security reasons, Rabbi Prins had never been told where his daughter was taken. In May 1945, when Amsterdam was liberated, he placed ads in several papers calling on whoever was caring for her to get in touch. Repke Wieringa saw the ad and the following Sunday, after a five-hour bike ride from The Hague, since public transportation had not yet been restored, went to see him.

"I lack the talent to describe this unforgettable meeting," Rabbi Prins recalls. "Verily, before us stood one of the Righteous Among the Nations." Several days later, Rabbi and Mrs. Prins went to see Betty at the Wieringa house and were introduced to Repke, who had taken care of her all this time. "She was like an angel in our eyes," he wrote.

At first Betty regarded her parents as total strangers. Over the next few weeks, during a series of visits, she became accustomed to them, and when the time was ripe, her departure from the Wieringa household was carefully orchestrated to spare her any trauma.

A year thereafter, a son was born to the Wieringas. They saw this as a reward from heaven for their kindness to Betty. Three more children followed in quick succession. One of them, a girl, was named Hetty (Betty's name while in hiding with them). In reciprocation, when Mrs. Prins gave birth to a son, he was given the same name as the Wieringa's oldest boy.

"Ever since the end of the war," Rabbi Prins wrote in 1972, "we have visited each other and maintained a friendly relationship, writing to each other regularly and keeping tabs on important events in the lives of both families." The Wieringas, he added, preferred that no fuss be made about them, protesting, "We only did what was required of us as human beings; please do not dwell on it any further." (716, 801)

The N.V. Group

The Creche, a day care center in a predominantly Jewish neighborhood of Amsterdam, was situated across the street from the Hollandse Schouwburg, a theater that became the main reception center for Amsterdam Jews who received deportation notices. On arrival at the theater, parents and children were separated, and the children were sent to the Creche to await transport to Westerbork. All told around 4,000 Jewish children passed through the Creche between 1942 and 1943. Most of them ended up in the death camps, but thanks to the efforts of Henriette Pimentel, the headmistress, aided by Walter Süskind, and Dr. Johan Van Hulst, the director of a nearby teachers' seminary, 1,000 of them were able to slip out and be hidden with adoptive families for the duration of the war.

An operation on so large a scale could only take place with the participation of dozens of volunteers. Some picked up children at the Creche and took them away by streetcar or other means. Others hid them in their homes until permanent accommodations could be arranged or took them from Amsterdam to the homes of host families as far away as Friesland in the north and Limburg in the south. And still others provided ration coupons and new identity papers, visited the children periodically to make sure they were well, and when necessary moved them to new homes.

Several underground cells were involved in this immense effort. Two were student groups, one in Utrecht and the other in Amsterdam. Another, headed by Jaap Musch and Joop Woortman, was sometimes referred to as the Limited (Ltd.) Group but is more often known as N.V. from the abbreviation for *Naamlose Vennootschap*, meaning "anonymous company," the Dutch counterpart term to the English "corporation."

Hester Van Lennep was one of the operation's couriers, escorting children from the Creche to their new homes and sometimes hiding them in her own place for a while. One day, she recalls, a bundle was left on her doorstep. "When I opened it, I saw a baby inside. Its diapers had not been changed. Its skin was covered with festering sores. It was an awful sight. I took it to my family doctor, De Groot. He never said a thing when I brought infants to him (I was single at the time), nor did he charge me."

Hetty Voute and Gisela Sohnlein belonged to one of the student groups. Gisela was responsible for the Utrecht-Amsterdam link. In addition she and Hetty had to visit Jewish parents and talk them into turning their children over to the group. Hetty Voute recalls: "We were young girls entering the homes of complete strangers. We never even mentioned our names, but the parents trustingly gave us their children (and we thanked them for their faith in us). We urged them to hide too, but in most cases they did not. They only cared about whether their children were safe!"

In a Yad Vashem deposition, a Jewish woman told how Gisela Sohnlein came for her. "May 23, 1943, a day that will live forever in my memory, was the day all four of us were to go into hiding. At 7:00 a.m. my father was called for and left the house. My sister left a short while later, to be escorted to her new address. When my mother's turn came, she had a hard time making up her mind. She would have to leave her youngest child—I was thirteen at the time—without knowing what my fate would be. It was difficult for her to decide what to do, but there was no alternative. So I had to wait alone, knowing, and hoping, that Gisela would not let me down. Later that afternoon, Gisela came and took me from Amsterdam to the home in Eindhoven where I spent the rest of the occupation years in hiding."

About a month later someone informed on Hetty Voute and Gisela Sohnlein, and the Gestapo arrested the two girls at the Utrecht railroad station on their return from taking several children to host households. Hetty relates: "The interrogations were terrible. At times, out of decency, they removed my eyeglasses before slapping me across the face. This in itself did not anger me. It was worse when they were polite, because then I found it harder to remain silent."

But silent she did remain, divulging nothing about the operation or her comrades. Hetty and Gisela were sent to the detention camp at Vught and then to the women's concentration camp at Ravensbruck in Germany. Both of them survived.

As was mentioned above, the rescue operation connected with the Creche also involved the N.V. group. The dominant figure and spiritual leader of N.V. was Jaap Musch, a laboratory worker, who was captured and tortured to death near the town of Ommen. Another of its dozen hardcore members, Joop Woortman, formerly the owner of a taxicab company, died in Bergen-Belsen. N.V. placed children with families in a dozen different rural localities, mainly in Limburg province, where the Vermeer house in Brunssum served as a waystation and temporary shelter. It also provided false credentials and ration coupons.

Anne Marie Van Verschuer, a student member of the N.V. group who is now a baroness, describes a typical mission with Woortman in the summer of 1943. The Creche, unlike the Hollandse Schouwburg, was unguarded. She would wait on the street while he went inside, picked up a group of children who had been readied for him, and held them just inside the entrance until the next streetcar stopped in front of the Creche, cutting off the view of the German guards across the street at the theater. Then, "in a split second, Jaap pushed the children out and I immediately hustled them aboard."

Depending on the arrangements the group had made, Anne Marie would either take the children to destinations in Amsterdam or go straight to the railroad station and board a train for the country. "I would be on the train all day, arriving around five in the afternoon, usually in Heerlen (Limburg province). Sometimes someone would be waiting for the children. Other times I myself would bring them to their new homes. I would ring at the address given me and hand over the child as if it were a package. It was a difficult thing to do, but there was no alternative. I was very young and had only one thought in mind: the children had to be saved."

Anne Marie visited the children from time to time to reassure them and allay their anxieties. "We did not always have enough hiding places. If you found a place willing to shelter a Jewish child, you took down the information. Let's say they ordered a child about four years old with dark eyes. You passed on the message and brought them the dark-eyed boy. The bright-eyed eight-year-old girl remained in the Creche. That's how it was." The biggest problem involved children with distinctly Jewish features. "Judith had such a face and we could not find a refuge for her." In the end Anne Marie Van Verschuer took her to her mother's house.

The care provided by the adoptive parents ran the gamut from cold indifference through sympathetic attentiveness to genuine concern and affection. Max, for instance, was only three years old when he was spirited out of the Creche and placed with the Micheels family in Heerlen. At the end of the war he was reunited with his natural parents. He later wrote of the Micheelses, "It wasn't just that they saved my life, but the fact that they did it and the way they did it made it possible for me to retain my faith in mankind despite everything that happened in the war."

Another youngster helped by the N.V. group was Hanoch Nenner, an escapee from Westerbork. He ultimately spent time in twenty different households. Most of his transfers were arranged and supervised by Jaap Musch, and he was nearby, able to see everything, when the Germans arrested Musch in Nijvendal.

Ten-year-old Ed Van Thijn was smuggled out of the Jewish Hospital in Amsterdam by the N.V. people, and thereafter, he says, "the organization took care of me." Altogether he stayed in eight different places in Limburg and ten in Overijssel province until November 1944, when he was picked up and sent to Westerbork, where he remained until the end of the war.

Rita Cohen was six when N.V. couriers took her to Limburg, where she stayed with several different "new uncles and aunts." She finally ended up in the home of Michael Mesicek, a miner, and his wife Maria. Only the Mesiceks and two of their four children knew the truth about Rita. As far as everyone else was concerned, she was an orphan from bombed-out Rotterdam.

The Mesicek household was warm and loving, and Rita remembers thinking, soon after her arrival there, that she would no longer be homesick. She became so attached to the Mesiceks that she asked to be baptized so that she could truly be one of them, but they categorically refused. "Only with your parents' permission," they replied.

Rita slept in the same bed as one of the Mesiceks' daughters, which added to her sense of belonging and security, and she attended the local school. Even so, she was never able to shed the sense of estrangement and alienation brought about by her abnormal existence, an emotional pattern that still affected her years later as an adult. "I could speak freely as long as I watched what I said, which I was very strict about. Even as a child of six, I was very conscious of the fact that if I ever revealed my real name or age or any facts about my past, the punishment would be death, for me and, as well, for those who so lovingly looked after me." When the war ended Rita was reunited with her parents and brother, who had also been hidden by friendly non-Jewish families.

Among those who worked with the N.V. group were Harmen and Sarah Bockma, whose farmhouse in Heerlen became one of the main stopping places for children being placed with families in Limburg province. Harmen, a miner, purposely inflicted an injury on one of his fingers so that he could go on sick leave and devote himself full time to N.V. activities.

With eight children of their own plus groups of Jewish transients always hiding in the house, the Bockmas were barely able to manage. Finally they had their eldest daughter, Rins, give up her job as a domestic to help them. "The situation at home was weird," one of their other daughters remembers. Because of the crowding the children were always coming down with something—whooping cough, scabies, lice, and when they did it was Rins who took care of them. "There were so many people in the house that we had to eat in shifts."

In the circumstances, the Bockmas were hardly in a position to entertain friends, and as a result they began to feel isolated. To add salt to their wounds, it was rumored in the district that Harmen Bockma, who spoke German and had gone to elementary school in Germany, was a member of the Dutch Nazi Party. Ironically, this story turned out to be a useful cover for some of his activities. Once, for instance, he was in the town of Terwinschen to check on some children he had taken there. When he learned that the Germans were planning to round up the local Jews, he entered the house where the children were living and, shouting in German, got them out and away just moments before the police arrived.

Another important N.V. waystation in Limburg was the home of Hannah Van der Voort in a village near Tienraij. Over 100 Jewish children passed through it, sent to "Aunt Hannah" mainly by a student group in Amsterdam. Denounced to the authorities, Hannah Van der Voort was arrested, tortured, and imprisoned. She survived but suffered permanent damage to her health which may have contributed to her untimely death.

Nico Dohmen, a Catholic student, was Aunt Hannah's right-hand man. He is credited with having saved 120 Jewish children. One of them,

Two Jews hiding in closet, The Hague (postwar picture).

Peter Kaufmann, was eighteen when he arrived at Tienraij and was placed with a local farm family. Older than most of the others, Peter was later able to give a good account of Nico's personality and activities.

"Day and night he worked to make placements with farmers who already had plenty of children of their own," Peter reports. Once he found a likely family, he would have a talk with the village priest, who in turn would persuade them to take in a Jewish child. From time to time Nico also served as a substitute father, dealing with bedwetting and other emotional problems experienced by some of the children.

Aaron, a youngster whom Nico placed with a family in Maastricht, told about Nico's frequent visits and pep talks. He also reported that Nico helped organize the escapes of Allied fliers who were shot down over Holland. Virginie, a child-care worker at the Creche, recalls that "he always talked with us and always had time for everyone."

Relating how Nico moved her from household to household until he found a suitable refuge for her, Virginie said, "I thank him from the bottom of heart for everything he did for us." Peter concluded his account by saying: "Any honor the Jewish people may bestow on Nico would be a minuscule compensation for what he gave the Jewish people during the years 1942–45."

Perhaps the final words in this section should be spoken by Hetty Voute and Gisela Sohnlein. After the war they were interviewed by a journalist. "I have nothing to say. . . . It simply had to be done," Hetty told him. Gisela added: "I have no idea how many children we saved. Perhaps a few hundred. But what difference does the number make when you think about what you were not able to do?"

Several years later, at a reception in their honor at Yad Vashem, Gisela said that she and Hetty had never regretted their work on behalf of Jewish children, even when they ended up in the hell of Ravensbruck. "On the contrary," she said, "unlike the Jewish women at Ravensbruck, who were there only because they were Jews, we were there for a reason, and we were proud of what we had done. We have always felt this way, and we deserve no special honor." (3853, 2083, 374, 966, 2878, 3276)

On the Move

Mobility was the name of the game for many Dutch Jews. Being ready to pack on a moment's notice and move from one hiding place to another often meant the difference between arrest and survival.

As an example, consider the Joosten family from Utrecht. Benjamin and Mietje Joosten initially found a refuge in the home of Abraham Pfaan, a railroad worker, and his wife Gerritje. The Pfaans were hiding several others Jews as well, and when one of them was arrested just outside the house, the Joostens decided to leave. They were taken in by Maria Kemper-Verschoor, a widow with three daughters who ran a boarding house and was already sheltering three of the Joostens' six children, Joost, Salko, and Rolf.

Mrs. Kemper-Verschoor died on December 28, 1943. Since her daughters were still minors, the court appointed a guardian for them. Known for his pro-Nazi sentiments, he wanted the girls to volunteer for work in Germany. They refused, however, and instead managed on their own in the family's house, continuing to shelter the Joostens until the end of the war.

When the Joostens first went into hiding, their youngest son, Benno-Arend, born in 1937, was taken in by Cornelius and Trijntje Roelofs in Apeldoorn, who thought he had been orphaned during the bombing of

Rotterdam. The Roelofs were both blind. Totally devoted to Benno, they refused to part with him when Trijntje's brother was arrested for his underground activities and there was reason to fear that he would reveal the child's true identity. Fortunately, this did not happen and Benno survived unscathed.

The Joostens' other two sons, Arend and Philips, also a member of the underground, were not so lucky. Both were arrested and sent to Auschwitz, where they perished.

After the war, Salko Joosten married Heintje Zeehandelaan. She too was a survivor, and at various times had been sheltered by three different Dutch families.

As the Joosten family's story illustrates, mobility and adaptability were indispensable ingredients spelling the difference between survival and doom—for the few lucky ones. (1895)

Here are two other stories that make the same point.

Arie and Eeke Verduijn and Others

Over a period of eighteen months, thirteen-year-old Ruth Winter passed through seven households. It all began in Eindhoven in April 1943, when Ruth's parents received their deportation notice.

Having fled to the Netherlands in 1935 from Germany, where Ruth's father, Dr. Karl Winter, had been a magistrate in Munich, the family knew the ways of the Nazis. Some while before the notice was received Dr. Winter had begun making arrangements for them to go into hiding. A farm family had agreed to take in him and his wife, and someone else had promised to hide Miriam, the older daughter, but there had not been enough time to find something for Ruth.

Through a friend, an engineer named Arie Verduijn got in touch with Dr. Winter. The following Friday, even though it was now against the law for non-Jews to enter Jewish homes, Verduijn visited the Winters. Placidly puffing his pipe, he sat down with the worried family and explained why he was there. A relative of his had told him about the Winters' predicament and he wanted to help by taking Ruth.

There wasn't much time and the Winters had to make up their minds quickly. They decided to accept Verduijn's offer. So Ruth packed a few belongings, grabbed her favorite doll, and followed this total stranger into the unknown.

Verduijn lived in the nearby city of Helmond with his pregnant wife Eeke and their three children. Miriam moved in with them and was treated like one of the family. In fact she still remembers how Eeke kissed her and the other children each night at bedtime.

The Verduijns kept in touch with the Winters, who dropped in for quick visits to Ruth every once in a while. Arie recalls one such visit in June 1943. Mrs. Winter had come unexpectedly from her place of hiding in De Peel, a marsh about 20 miles east of Helmond where many Jews were secretly living on farms. At the time the Germans were staging house-to-house searches for Jews and underground members, and when Arie looked out the window he was stunned to see Mrs. Winter approaching accompanied by the two daughters of a neighbor who was a member of the Dutch Nazi Party.

As it turned out, she had stopped them on the street and asked them to help her find the Verduijns' address. Arie was very concerned. What with her strong German accent, her foreign manners, and her unusual facial features, he reasoned, no one could have failed to realize that Mrs. Winter was a Jewish refugee from Germany. Surely the two girls would tell their father about her, and in short order the police would be on them. Something had to be done fast. Verduijn rushed over to one of his neighbors who was working in his garden. After a bit of small talk he explained the problem. The neighbor's face fell. "You want me to take in a Jewess? You must be kidding!"

Verduijn went on to another neighbor's house. "I'm not up to it right now, Arie," she said. In response he remonstrated: "Do you think Eeke is up to it? She's expecting in November and is already feeding three extra mouths. And by nine o'clock [curfew time] it will be too late." But the woman would not budge.

Returning home, Verduijn decided to leave everything in God's hands. He recalls murmuring a silent prayer: "O God, what do you want from us? Don't let them arrest us and make orphans of our children."

Eeke came over and took his hand. She whispered softly: "Remember what you were reading yesterday at dinner time about Elisha, when the Syrians came for him? How he prayed: 'O Lord, smite this people, I pray thee, with blindness'? He will smite His enemies again."

Nothing happened that night and the next day Verduijn found accommodations for Mrs. Winter at a boarding house run by two sisters, introducing her as a distant aunt from bombed-out Rotterdam. Three weeks later, when they were sure that the coast was clear, Mrs. Winter returned to the farm in De Peel.

Still wary of the Nazi neighbor and with Eeke's pregnancy entering the final stages, the Verduijns decided it was time for Ruth to move on as well. Arie arranged for her to stay with Siege and Cornelia Postuma in Helenaveen, a village in De Peel, where Siege worked for a peat-mining company.

Ruth moved in with the Postumas in June 1943. Most of the couple's eight children were already out on their own, but among those still at home was a girl her own age, Dinah, whose bed she shared. The Postumas treated her well, but the danger of hiding a Jew put too much stress on Siege, who was ill, so in October Ruth once again had to be transferred.

This time she was taken in by Bert and Louise Driessen in the village of Sevenum. Bert was a truck driver. Ruth helped Louise with various household chores and in the vegetable garden, and the Driessens registered her for a correspondence course in English under her assumed name, Ria Van der Veen.

Everything was going well, but then, in January 1944, the Dutch underground killed an S.S. man not far from where the Driessens lived. Fearing that the Germans would search all the houses in the vicinity, Ruth was hurriedly moved to the home of Pastor Engelbert Gommans in another part of town, where she stayed for four days and, thanks to arrangements made by the Gommanses, had a brief visit from her father.

Her next stopping place was the home of Piet and Anna Verhaag, the owners of a tavern and bowling alley in Sevenum. She was very happy there, but Anna was pregnant with her fourth child, and when it came time for her to deliver Ruth returned to Helenaveen, where she stayed with Victor and Wilhelmina Ulens on their small farm.

A number of other fugitives were also hiding at the Ulens place. Several were non-Jewish men who had been called up for forced labor in Germany. But wonder of wonders, one of them was Ruth's sister Miriam, who had been put out by her former host family when she developed a prolonged illness and was no longer able to work around the house, thus becoming a burden rather than an asset. The Ulens had taken her in and nursed her back to health.

In June 1944 Ruth moved in with the Verduijns in Helmond again, but in September, with the Allied armies steadily advancing and major fighting expected, she returned to the Ulens house in Helenaveen, where she felt it would be safer. For a while she also stayed in the village of Blerick with one of the Ulens' relatives, Aunt Mien, who was hiding several other people, including a Jewish child.

As the Allied forces drew closer, the Germans evacuated Blerick. Together with some other people from the village, Ruth and Miriam fled to Helenaveen, where they were again evacuated on September 28th. During a heavy British artillery bombardment they hid in an empty chicken coop.

On October 8th all the ablebodied men in the area were rounded up and sent to Germany for forced labor. With no one left but old people, women, and children, conditions became very difficult. Ruth and her sister decided to go to the Verhaags' house in Sevenum, where they unexpectedly ran into their parents, who were also on the move during this chaotic period. The Winters spent the last few days of the German occupation huddled in a cellar with British shells exploding overhead.

Finally, after an unusually heavy bombardment, British troops moved into Sevenum on November 22, 1944. In Ruth's own words: "Through a thick fog, we saw them marching by, with mine detectors leading the way. For the four of us it spelled the end of our period of hiding. We had managed to remain alive in this terrible time because of the help and self-sacrifice of all the persons named heretofore, and others, who risked their lives in order to save ours." (2411, 2487—91)

The De Zoete Family's Peregrinations

Around the end of 1940, Hendrik De Zoete, the head of the Municipal Pharmacy in Rotterdam, was fired because he was Jewish. He and his wife Sophia, a registered nurse, managed for a while, but by August 1942 they realized that it was time for them and their three daughters to "dive." In order to maximize the changes of survival, the five De Zoetes decided to go their own separate ways. By the war's end they had stayed with a total of thirteen families, all but three of whom were total strangers to them in 1942.

The oldest of the De Zoete children, Miriam, was eleven when she was placed in the care of Jan Van Gelder, the director of an art institute in The Hague (and after the war a professor of art history). Miriam lived there for about a year, and throughout her stay was tutored by Mrs. Nan Van Gelder to make up for the work she was missing in school.

In 1943, when Nan's father, a Jew by birth who was married to a non-Jew, had to move in with the Van Gelders to avoid deportation, Miriam was transferred to Haarlem, where she stayed in the boarding house run by Petronella Van Vliet, a divorcee with four children. She remained there until the liberation. Mrs. Van Vliet was also hiding two other Jewish children, a brother and sister, and after the war they were married to two of her children.

Judith De Zoete, who was ten when the family went into hiding, was taken in by Alida Wouters in Wassenaar. Alida, a widow with two children, one of whom was an invalid, treated Judith like a member of the family and even arranged for her to take piano lessons.

As the danger of police raids increased, Mrs. Wouters decided to hide Judith with a friend if it ever looked as if her place would be searched. Ironically, the one time she had to implement her contingency plan, the police descended on her friend's street and not on her own. Fortunately, they did not immediately take notice of the little girl sleeping in a corner of the woman's bed, and by the time they came back she had been awakened, dressed, and returned to the Wouters house.

Under the circumstances it might well have been dangerous for Judith to remain there, so she was moved to the farm of Cornelius and Prijna Heemskerk in Rijnsburg, South Holland province. The Heemskerks already had seven children, but they reasoned, "Where there are already so many kids, one more doesn't matter." Nonetheless, things were not always that simple. There was often not enough food, and when Judith came down with pneumonia proper medical treatment could not be obtained. Prijna nursed her through the illness, however, sleeping at her bedside, and Judith remained with the Heemskerks for the duration of the war.

Hadassah, the youngest of the De Zoete sisters, was nine in 1943. Mrs. Van Gelder, with whom Miriam lived for a year, arranged for her to be taken in by Franciscus and Petronella Lafontaine, the owners of a hardware factory in Wassenaar.

As it turned out, the Lafontaines were on the verge of a divorce. Because of the tension in their household, Hadassah was given over to Hendrika Dekkers in Rotterdam. Hendrika was the head of a nursing facility but also ran an employment agency for nurses in her home, and as a result there were always people coming and going. Since she was single, some of them became curious about the little girl living with her.

After six weeks Henrika decided to move Hadassah to the home of Hendrik and Jans Van der Leer, also in Rotterdam, where she stayed for about six months. During this period Henrika kept tabs on her welfare and occasionally took her on walks past the place where her parents were hiding, so that they could observe her secretly for a few precious moments.

In the interim Franciscus Lafontaine remarried, and at his request Hadassah was returned to his home, where she remained until the end of the war. No one other than Lafontaine ever knew her true origin, and his motives for sheltering a Jewish child are still unclear. Since his factory was producing war matériel for the Germans and he had to keep on good terms with them, it may be that hiding her was a kind of atonement. In any case, Henrik De Zoete describes Lafontaine as a good man who displayed fatherly concern for his daughter and protected her until she could safely rejoin her family. De Zoete and Lafontaine had not known each other before the war.

The parents Hendrik and Sophia De Zoete hid separately at first, but then moved in with Johann Leepel-Labotz, a teacher and family friend who lived in The Hague. About six weeks later, unfortunately, the Germans ordered all unmarried persons in Leepel's neighborhood to find other accommodations in order to make room for married couples evacuated, for military reasons, from areas along the coast. This unexpected develop-ment began a series of dislocations for the De Zoetes.

After living in several different places over the next six months, they met a Jewish woman in Rotterdam who was married to a non-Jewish Italian. She took them to Utrecht and introduced them to an underground agent who put them on a train for Ede in Gelderland province. There they were met and escorted to the home of Tjeerde Miedema, a furniture salesman, and his wife Antje. About three months later, the Germans captured the man who had brought them there. Afraid that he might break under torture, the De Zoetes decided to move on. They later learned that they had made the right decision, for the Miedemas and the other members of their cell were all arrested by the Gestapo and sent to Vught camp.

For the second time in less than a year the De Zoetes found themselves on the run. On April 22, 1943, the very day that the Germans ordered the deportation of Rotterdam's remaining Jews, they bumped into a prewar friend, a pharmacist named Jacques Wolf who was about to "dive." While they were in his apartment, Gerrit Brillenburg-Wurth, a minister of the Dutch Reformed Church, came to bid him farewell. Brillenburg said nothing when told that the De Zoetes had nowhere to go, but he returned the next day and announced that he had arranged for them to stay with Jacob Groeneveld, an elderly bookkeeper in his parish.

The De Zoetes lived with Groeneveld for about six months, but his house did not have a secure hiding place, and since the police were stepping up their searches, Pastor Brillenburg decided to move them to his church. He hid them in the building's attic, a place so cramped and dark that he intended it only as a temporary refuge, but as things worked out they remained there until the end of the war, which was still a year off.

Brillenburg took the sexton, Hendrik De Mars, into his confidence and discovered, to his surprise, that De Mars was hiding four other Jews in another part of the attic. In order to make an alcove large enough for all six of them, the two men laid some boards across the joists in the part of the attic above the church's organ. To get from one part of the attic to another it was necessary to crawl along a plank about 2 feet wide and 5 feet long.

Every day Gerrit Brillenburg and his wife, Gerda, secretly brought food to the six hidden Jews, carefully making their way into the attic through a trapdoor in the church storeroom. On their way out they removed the day's accumulated bodily wastes. When Brillenburg was under arrest for a while, De Mars took over these tasks.

It was particularly important to make sure that the six Jews were not in the part of the attic over the sanctuary during services, since even the slightest noise would have given away their presence and there might well have been an informer in the congregation. Whenever possible they were moved to the De Mars house before services began. One of the women was pregnant, and it was there that she delivered her baby, attended by Hendrika Dekkers, the nurse with whom Hadassah De Zoete had lived for a while.

During the final month of the occupation Hendrik De Mars was arrested and taken to the notorious Rotterdam prison known as the "Orange Hotel," where he was severely beaten. Anna was desperate with worry but in his absence took care of the six Jews in the attic, and after the war he returned safely home.

Hendrik and Sophia De Zoete and their daughters were spared the horrors of the Holocaust through the assistance of thirteen different families. What made these people undertake such tremendous risks to themselves and their loved ones? As at least a partial answer, Henrik De Zoete says that they were motivated by "Dutch humanitarianism and love for freedom . . . courage, love of fellow man, sentiments of righteousness, compassion, courage, tenacity . . . and an unshakable belief in Christianity and its ethics." (48)

The Religious Factor

As some of the preceding stories indicate, many Dutch rescuers of Jews were motivated by their religious beliefs. The following four accounts underscore this point.

Johannes Bogaard

Johannes Bogaard was a farmer in Nieuw Vennep, Haarlemmermeer, about 12 miles southwest of Amsterdam. Raised in the Calvinist tradition by a father who taught him to respect the people of the Bible, Johannes decided, toward the end of 1941, that his religious beliefs obliged him to do everything he could to help the Jews. According to Dr. L. de Jong of the Dutch War Documentation Institute, "One may say that from the moment he began his resistance work his life became a series of crises." Within a year there were about 300 Jews hidden in and around the Bogaard farm.

The Bogaard family's activities on behalf of Jews actually began with Johannes' father. A bearded patriarch who never left his home without his Bible, he was arrested by the Germans for publicly condemning their antisemitic program but after questioning was released as a religious fanatic of no consequence.

Not long after this Johannes—or Uncle Hannes, as he was affectionately known—began traveling to Amsterdam, Rotterdam, and other cities to seek out Jews in need of help. He hid the first few dozen in his chicken coop. As the number of Jews on the farm increased, he dispersed them to his brothers' farms and then to the farms of other Calvinist farmers in the area.

Before the war Johannes had never been anywhere outside the rural area where his farm was situated. His journeys to save Jews now brought him to Amsterdam and other big cities for the first time. In addition to finding Jews to hide, Johannes used his visits to the cities as opportunities to obtain money, ration cards, identity documents, mattresses and blankets, and all sorts of other necessities, persuading friends and even casual acquaintances to help. "No one who knew him was able to refuse him anything," recalls J. Hesseling, a textile merchant in Doorn, who supplied many of his wants.

An enterprise of such magnitude could not go long undetected, and in November 1942, the Dutch police raided the Bogaard farm, netting three Jews. Two more raids followed in the succeeding months, and several dozen other Jews were apprehended in the vicinity. When a policeman was killed in a confrontation with the Bogaard family, Johannes' father, son, and a brother were sent to a German concentration camp, where they reportedly perished.

Initially Johannes operated on his own, but by the end of 1943 he was able to link up with an underground organization, although he still conducted his rescue activities independently. His religious fervor was proverbial among the underground members who knew him. One of them, Johannes M. Snoek, says: "I felt that the man standing before me looked just as I would have imagined the prophet Amos."

After the war, asked why he had helped so many Jews, Bogaard replied with a biblical quotation, then added: "If more of my countrymen had seen with their own eyes, as I did, what was happening to the Jews, I'm sure they would have done more."

In the opinion of Dr. L. de Jong, Johannes Bogaard, working almost singlehandedly, saved more Jews than anyone else in the whole of the Netherlands. (28)

Gerrit Don and Michael Ruigrok

"God gave me the spiritual strength to help a good many Jews by hiding them with farmers and later in city homes. I was very happy to have the privilege of doing something for God's people." So says Gerrit Don in his 1975 deposition about his activities during the war.

Employed by a soap factory in Vlaardingen, Don was an underground agent who helped downed Allied pilots escape to England and hid several Jews when the Nazi roundups began. Among those he saved was Mrs. B. Kokernoot, then a girl of twelve in Rotterdam. In the spring of 1943, Don visited her parents and offered to arrange their escape. They put off making a decision but allowed him, a few days later, to take their daughter to stay with the Warnaar family near Vlaardingen. Unfortunately, by the time they too were ready to "dive" it was too late. They were deported to a concentration camp in Poland and died there.

Another of Don's rescues involved the Van Dijk family. On June 6, 1943, the three Van Dijks were brought by truck to his house, where they found three Jewish children already in hiding. The following afternoon, they were moved to the home of Michael Ruigrok, a coworker of Don's at the soap factory.

Ruigrok gave them a friendly welcome. "Look here," he said, "we are devout Catholics and you are observant Jews. Let us all remain faithful to our own religion." The Ruigroks had never met the Van Dijks before, but when asked they agreed to take in five relatives of Mrs. Van Dijk's, raising the number of Jews in their little house to eight. They turned the two bedrooms over to their guests and themselves slept in the attic. Whenever there was the possibility of a house search, the eight hid in the cellar.

Despite the inconvenience and the enormous danger, the Ruigroks asked no compensation and refused all offers of money except modest contributions for food. The Van Dijks, in turn, did all they could to keep from becoming a burden, and on several occasions Mr. Van Dijk accompanied Mrs. Ruigrok on trips to the countryside to buy fresh milk and vegetables from local farmers. The Dons also did what they could to help.

Wilhelmina Don, for instance, regularly came by to cut the children's hair, since it would have been dangerous to take them to the barber.

Thanks to the Ruigroks and the Dons, all eight Jews were safe and sound on the day of liberation in May 1945. Judah Van Dijk was five years old at the time. He writes: "For me what happened was important not just because eight lives were spared; of even greater importance is the fact that those yet to be born were also saved. Today, when I see my children growing up as proud Jews in their own free country, I know it is due in large measure to those brave and modest Dutch friends who risked their lives in order to fulfill what they considered a humanitarian obligation."

The Van Dijks were not the only beneficiaries of Gerrit Don's self-effacing decency. One of the others was a retarded Jewish child whom he and his wife took in when the parents were deported. The mother died in a concentration camp; the father survived, only to die soon after the war. Before his death he asked Don to continue taking care of the boy and Don agreed. "He is like a member of our family," the eighty-one-year-old Don wrote in 1975, "and our offspring will look after him when my wife and I have passed on."

In a letter to Yad Vashem, Don explained how he came to regard the saving of Jews as a personal mission. One day in 1943 he and his wife took two Jewish boys into their home. As was their practice, they opened the Bible at random, and Don found himself reading Psalm 41, "Blessed is he that considereth the poor: the Lord will deliver him in time of trouble. The Lord will preserve him and keep him alive; and he shall be blessed upon the earth: and thou wilt not deliver him unto the will of his enemies."

Don saw this passage as a sign of divine approval for their decision to hide the boys. "So then we knew," he said, "that what we were doing was in accordance with God's will, and we enjoyed the rest [that had to be done] during the whole period of the occupation, because we knew that we were only doing this work in order to please our Heavenly Father."

He concluded: "I am convinced that God has blessed us, and I apply to myself Artur Rubinstein's famous statement that he had found the world's happiest man and it was himself. I wrote to him that I have had a similar experience and consider myself no poorer than the richest man."

In a subsequent letter to Yad Vashem, written in 1977 when he was eighty-three, Gerrit Don said: "We are especially thankful that our God allowed us to help His children, the chosen people, during the occupation of Holland, and we are very happy to be able to say that by God's grace not one of the Jews under our care died through acts by the German soldiers." (979, 980)

Anton and Henriette Tellegen

Dr. Anton Tellegen and his wife, Henriette, lived in Zeist, where he was the head of the regional health department and an active member of the underground. Their house served as a transit point for untold numbers of Jews on their way to permanent hiding places.

Among the Jews the Tellegens helped was Margalit Derech, who moved in with them toward the end of 1943. One day Gestapo agents came to the house looking for Anton. He was not at home but Hannah Hemelberg, a Jewish refugee, happened to be there. Mrs. Tellegen introduced her as the local tailor, explaining that she had come to mend the children's clothes.

Paying no attention to Hannah, who began working on some garments that Henriette handed her, the Gestapo agents settled down to wait for Anton. After a while, Henriette excused herself and stepped outside to wait for Margalit, who was not home at the time.

Anton returned while she was gone and was promptly arrested. After a brief trial for his underground activities, he was executed. Though left with five fatherless children to care for, Henriette continued helping Jews in transit.

The Tellegens were devout Catholics. Margalit attended church with them on Sundays in order to keep up appearances, but Anton insisted that she recite the Sabbath prayers at home every Saturday, and in the evenings he and Henriette would read aloud a selection from the Old Testament for her sake. Ironically, it was due to this pious Catholic couple that Margalit first became consciously aware of the Judaic religious heritage. (103)

Jan Gort

Jan Gort was a teacher in the village of Buitenpost. He and Emma, his wife, belonged to the Dutch Reformed Church. Though they had two children of their own to care for, they also managed to hide two Jewish children during the war.

The Gorts took in young Joseph Hess in October 1942 and his sister, Rachel, in May 1943. Despite the difficulty of obtaining enough food for their own children, the Gorts never slackened in their determination to protect Joseph and Rachel. As Joseph wrote in his deposition, they felt it was a religious obligation "to protect God's people, the people of the book." On many occasions Emma had to bike long distances in order to get food—and because of wartime shortages the tires of her bike were overlaid with wood, which made the task of pedaling much more difficult.

In 1977 Jan and Emma Gort went to Jerusalem to plant a tree in the Garden of the Righteous at Yad Vashem. Just before the ceremony began, a small boy walked up to Gort, took his hand, and said, "Thank you." Visibly moved, Jan Gort told the audience that he and Emma thanked God for "making us rise above ourselves so that we dared say yes when we were asked to shelter Jewish countrymen."

He explained how they had found the inner strength they needed. "We kept in mind the words of Queen Esther when she went to King Ahasuerus: 'and if I perish, I perish.' And those of our Redeemer, who said: 'For whosoever will save his life shall lose it; and whosoever will lose his life for my sake shall find it.' And God did protect us. 'A thousand shall fall at thy side, and ten thousand at thy right hand; but it shall not come nigh thee.' Thus it is written in the psalm that was recited on the occasion of our marriage, Psalm 91." (1104)

Some Who Paid the Price

Many Dutch rescuers suffered physical harm when caught by the Nazis. A typical case was that of Sietze Romkes.

Sietze Romkes

Sietze and his wife, Hendrika, lived with their five children on a large vegetable farm in Nieuwe Wijk Dedemsvaart. In mid-1944 they took in young Abraham Hartog after he had to leave his previous hiding place. Later on they gave temporary shelter to several non-Jews who were fleeing from the police. One of them turned out to be a Nazi spy.

Early in the morning of December 2, 1944, while Abraham was fast asleep in the bed he shared with sixteen-year-old Johannes ("Joop") Romkes, the German Green Police raided the farmhouse. Awakened by the loud knocking on the front door, Abraham leaped out of bed and hid in a lower compartment of the cupboard that had been set aside for just such a contingency.

Meanwhile, the Germans began questioning the family. When Sietze denied hiding anyone he received several hard blows to the head, one of which caused him to lose the hearing in his left ear. The police then took Joop up to his bedroom. From his hiding place inside the cupboard Abraham listened as one of the Germans held a pistol to Joop's temple and said, "You have three seconds to tell us where the Jew-boy is." He slowly counted to three, whereupon Joop replied, in tears, that the Jew had set off for the southern part of the country, which had recently been liberated.

Convinced that he was telling the truth, the Germans gave up the search but arrested Sietze, taking him to the regional police station at Zwolle, about 18 miles away. As soon as they were out of sight, Henrika let Abraham out of the cupboard and told him how to get to the home of a family in nearby Ommerkanaal who would help him. Meanwhile, the police interrogated Sietze for five grueling days. In the end, however, they did not shoot him, as they had threatened, but dragged him from his cell to the front door and threw him out on the street.

After the liberation, when the Romkes learned that Abraham had lost his entire family, they took him in again and did everything they could to help him adjust. He stayed with them through the difficult early postwar years and now lives in Israel. (1377d)

Albert and Aaltje Zefat

In July 1942, Leo Kropveld and his parents fled when the Germans began rounding up the Jews in the town of Emmen in Drente province. In the ensuing confusion the twenty-one-year-old youth was separated from his parents. He hid in a cornfield until sunset, then headed for a nearby farm, where they allowed him to hide in the barn for the night. A few hours later his father turned up at the same farm and was also taken in. Leo was unable to sleep that night. "I remember just repeating the words 'I want to come through, I want to survive.' "

Three days later Leo left the farm and found shelter successively in the homes of a farmer, a laborer, a butcher, and a railroad worker. "Most of them were religious and regarded the Jews as God's chosen people. That was why they helped."

The railroad worker sent Leo to the chicken farm of Albert and Aaltje Zefat in the village of Valthe. Arriving there on foot at the break of dawn, Leo received a warm welcome and was hidden in one of the chicken coops. That evening he had dinner with the family and was introduced to the Zefats' three children—one boy and two handicapped girls.

Several days later the Zefats took Leo to a cabin deep in the nearby forest. There he discovered that they were already hiding several other Jews.

It had all begun a year earlier, on August 15, 1942, with Adolph From, a business acquaintance of Albert Zefat's. When From told Zefat he had received his Westerbork notice, Zefat responded: "You must not go there, for then the Germans will have you in their grip. I shall take care of you for as long as the war lasts."

Zefat hid Adolph on his farm, and before long other members of the From family had joined him, as well as members of the Jakobs, Bachrach, and Meiboom families. Altogether, Zefat now had eleven people hiding on his farm. This was much too dangerous, so he moved the group to a nearby wooded area where they built an underground hideout large enough for all of them and a shed in which to store food and other supplies. The addition of Leo Kropveld raised the group's size to twelve, and soon after his brother became the thirteenth member.

The group spent all of their time in the forest but had dinner at the farm each night. One day the thirteen were surprised to see Albert Zefat rushing toward their hideout in broad daylight. Almost out of breath from haste and anxiety, he explained that rumors had been spreading in the Valthe area about Jews in the forest and he was afraid that the police had been informed. It was necessary, he told them, to move to another part of the forest.

Naturally they did as he said, and once in the new locale they had to build another underground hideout and another shed. "That meant cutting down trees and digging out earth," Leo recalls. "And all the time,

Albert Zefat was there, cutting and digging and warning when we laughed too loudly. When the foundation was ready he brought the lumber and the roofing material." And when the hard day's work was done, he took everyone back to the farm for food and coffee.

On a July day in 1944 the German security police descended on the Zefat farm. As the thirteen in the forest later learned from Mrs. Zefat, the police wanted to know where they were hiding. When Albert refused to talk they beat him severely and then shot him in the head. She warned the group not to come to the house for dinner anymore but sent food to them through third parties and later persuaded several local families to take some of them in.

When the village of Valthe was liberated about a year after this tragic incident, all thirteen were alive and well. For Aaltje Zefat this was a moment of happiness, for it meant the fulfillment of the mission she and her dead husband had undertaken. "Aaltje Zefat never uttered a single reproach," Leo Kropveld tells us. "She accepted the death, as did her children. They had only one wish—that all of us would come through and thus that their father would not have given his life in vain."

As a symbolic expression of their gratitude, the thirteen survivors paid Aaltje Zefat's traveling expenses when she visited Israel in 1972 to plant a tree in her husband's memory in the Garden of the Righteous at Yad Vashem. (731)

In a Class by Themselves

The following stories do not fit into any of the other categories, but the humane sentiments they evoke are no less touching.

Franciscus and Hillegonda Snel

Shlomo Cohen, an Israeli army reservist, was killed in the Six-Day War. Nearly two decades later, his son, Uri, began going over his papers and discovered letters, an unfinished story, and other items pertaining to Shlomo's rescue by a Dutch family during World War II. Piecing everything together, and filling in the gaps with information provided by the Dutch family, Uri reconstructed his father's wartime rescue and in 1988 submitted a petition to Yad Vashem on their behalf. The story ran as follows:

Shlomo Cohen, known at that time as Sallo Cohen, was separated from his parents at the age of seven and over the next six months stayed with seven different families, each in turn rejecting him, also because he was a bedwetter. Meanwhile, Franciscus and Hillegonda Snel had just gotten married. When an underground agent who met them at a party asked whether they would be willing to take in a Jewish child, they said yes.

Arrangements were made, and little Sallo was turned over to Hillegonda at the railroad station. Apparently fearing another rejection, he immediately told her about his bedwetting problem, but she ignored his embarrassed whispers and took him home.

At the outset the Snels told no one about Sallo, not even their parents, and kept him hidden whenever visitors dropped in because they had no way of explaining his presence, especially since he had dark curly hair and did not resemble either of them. After a while it became evident that confinement indoors was affecting his health, so they bleached his hair and allowed him to play outside. The usual routine was for him to go to the park on his own and Hillegonda to follow a few minutes later. The two, pretending to be strangers, would strike up a casual acquaintance and then spend the day together.

At home Hillegonda tutored Sallo in reading, writing, and math to ensure that he would be at the proper grade level when he was able to go to school again. She and her husband were very fond of him, and when his parents failed to return after the liberation, they wanted to adopt him even though they had a child of their own by then.

On September 4, 1945, Sallo's older brother and another relative visited the Snels to confirm that the Cohens were dead. They were going to Israel and wanted to take Sallo with them. Though it was a painful separation on both sides, the Snels turned him over to his kin, but they urged that he be placed with a family and not in an institution, and his brother agreed.

Sallo returned to the Netherlands in 1960, at the age of twenty-four, to visit the Snels, and from then until his death he and they kept in touch by mail. After reconstructing the story, Uri Cohen visited them twice, and they came to Israel as well. "These are people who knew and know the meaning of love for one's fellow man and love for the Jewish people," he wrote in his deposition. "I know that my father planned to submit testimony on his World War II rescuers. As his death prevented him from fulfilling this strong wish, I see it as a personal obligation, as if it were his last will and testament to me, to finish the work he began." (2622)

Brother Bernardinus

Brother Bernardinus, who was known as Leonard Hendriks before he took holy orders, was a Roman Catholic monk. During the war he ran a reform school for juvenile delinquents at a monastery situated on the outskirts of Helden, not far from the German border.

In May 1943 the underground asked him to hide a seventeen-year-old Jewish boy from Amsterdam named Yehudah Pimentel. Bernardinus agreed and after coaching the youth on how to act so that he would fit in with the others, he assigned him a room in the delinquent wing of the monastery. In addition to coming on as tough, street-smart, and unruly, Yehudah had to attend Mass regularly, but no religious pressure was ever put on him.

During this trying period when he had to behave in a manner totally at variance with everything he had been taught before, Yehudah would never have managed without the constant encouragement and assistance of Brother Bernardinus. The monk, as it turned out, was also hiding Jews in other parts of the monastery while waiting for host households to become available. Among them Yehudah particularly recalls a youth who survived the war only to be killed in Los Angeles years later by a robber.

According to Yehudah, Brother Bernardinus "was known as a man whose word was gold, and a request from him was like a command." He was widely respected throughout the region, and not just by the Dutch. It once happened, for instance, that German soldiers hunting downed Allied pilots wanted to search the monastery. With complete aplomb, Bernardinus phoned their commander and demanded that he order them to leave. The officer complied.

Yehudah lived in the monastery until the end of the war and then went to Israel. Brother Bernardinus, he says, "was and remained a father to me. . . . We are still friends. . . . We correspond constantly. I have arranged two visits to Israel for him, one of them so he could attend my daughter's wedding." In 1983, on his eighty-fifth birthday, Brother Bernardinus was recognized by Yad Vashem as one of the Righteous Among the Nations. (2607)

Victor Kugler (Anne Frank Story)

Otto and Edith Frank, and their two daughters, Margot and Anne, escaped from Nazi Germany in the mid-thirties and began a new life in Amsterdam. In 1941, when Jews in German-occupied Holland were required to sell their businesses, Otto Frank transferred the two firms he owned to his trusted Dutch associates Jan Kleiman and Victor Kugler (Renamed Kraler in Anne Frank's diary).

The following year, when it became apparent that the Jews of Holland were in serious danger, Frank decided to go into hiding with his family. Aided by Kleiman and Kugler, and later by Miep Gies and Elisabeth Van Voskuijl as well, and working after business hours so as not to arouse suspicion, he furnished and equipped the upper two floors of the building at Prinsengracht 23 as a refuge. These two floors, located to the rear of the building, were separated by a staircase, which was closeted off by a false bookcase.

On July 5, 1942, when Margot received a summons to report to Westerbork, the Franks knew the time had come. The next morning they moved into the hideout, together with H. Van Daan, Mrs. Van Daan, and their son Peter. To give the impression that the Franks had left the country,

Victor Kugler took a farewell letter written by Otto Frank and mailed it to himself from a border town.

Over the twenty-five months that followed the Franks and the Van Daans, joined in November 1942 by an elderly dentist named Albert Dussel, never left their hiding place. As millions of people throughout the world know from Anne Frank's diary, or from the award-winning play and film based upon it, their life was difficult and often unbearable but had its joyous moments. The eight inmates of the upstairs hideout were utterly dependent on their four Dutch confederates, who provided them with food, reading matter, and everything else, including news and much-needed encouragement, sometimes inventing Allied victories in order to counteract spells of depression. Victor Kugler remembers bringing to Anne the latest magazine, although her mother frowned at this type of literature. "I remember Anne would always be waiting for me at the top of the hidden stairway, saying nothing but the the look in her eyes told me that she hoped I had remembered." Kugler recalls. To still Anne's unsatiable learning appetite, Kugler arranged to have her enrolled in a Latin correspondence course. "And she did quite well." Years later, Kugler still recalls her as "always inquisitive, sometimes melancholy."

Kugler probably did not suspect that Anne Frank was keeping a diary for the 25 months of her enforced confinement, in which she unfolded the story of life in seclusion for herself and the others, so eloquently recorded as to become known throughout the world under the title "The Diary of Anne Frank." The revelations of a young girl groping her way into womanhood in the most trying of circumstances have been shared in a score of foreign languages, made into a Broadway play and depicted in a major motion picture. In Anne's diary, Victor Kugler appears as "Mr. Kraler," Miep Gies - "Miep Van Santan", Elisabeth Van Wijk - "Elli Vossen", and Jan Kleiman - "Mr. Koophuis." In one passage, she mentions that Kugler's (Kraler's) responsibilities were "sometimes so much for him that he can hardly talk from pent-up nerves and strain."

On August 4, 1944, tragedy struck. Betrayed by an informer, the hiding place was raided by the police. The eight Jews were taken to Westerbork and then to Auschwitz and Bergen-Belsen. With the exception of Otto Frank, none of them survived. Anne died of dysentery in March 1945 just a few weeks before the liberation of the Bergn-Belsen camp.

Kugler and Kleiman were able to persuade the Germans that the two secretaries were innocent but were themselves sent to the Amersfoort concentration camp. Kleinman was released through the intercession of the Red Cross but Kugler did seven months at hard labor and was about to be deported to Germany when he escaped during an air raid, hiding with relatives in Hilversum until the end of the war.

Victor Kugler went back to work for Otto Frank when he reopened his business after the war, but the ongoing conflict between the Netherlands and Indonesia, formerly the Dutch East Indies, disrupted the supply of spices, and in 1948 he closed up shop. Opting to start a new life in Canada, Kugler settled in Montreal, where he was, at various times, an electrician, a bookkeeper, a photographer, and an insurance clerk.

In Israel in 1975 for a ceremony in his honor at Yad Vashem, Kugler broke into tears as he addressed the audience. "I tried to do what my conscience dictated," he said. "I tried to save the lives of my friends. And it is my greatest sorrow that I failed." When a reporter asked him about the many awards and honors he had received, he replied, "They were my friends. What else could I have done? . . . I don't understand what all the fuss is about."

When Victor Kugler died in 1981 at the age of eighty-one, an honor guard of Jews and Christians stood outside the funeral home in Toronto as his coffin was carried past. (706)

* * *

We end this chapter with the stories of four persons who carried out rescue operations on a grand scale.

Arnold Douwes

Arnold Douwes, the son of a pastor, was recruited for the underground by Johannes Post, a farmer and town councillor in the village of Nieuwlande, Drente province. Like Douwes, Post was a member of the Dutch Reformed Church. He had never had very much to do with Jews or Judaism, but when antisemitic measures were introduced, he threw himself body and soul into the effort to help Jews on the run, even at the expense of neglecting his farm and his eight children. Before long the Germans had put a price on his head, and in 1944, when they finally caught him, he was executed.

Already before Post's death, Douwes had taken over. Jews ordered to report to Westerbork were sent to him by the underground. He in turn, assisted by Max ("Nico") Leons, a Jew posing as a Protestant, scoured the countryside to find families to shelter them. In addition to finding places for them to stay, Douwes provided the fugitives with food, new identity papers, and financial support. Thanks to his efforts, virtually every household in Nieuwlande and the surrounding countryside—a total of several hundred Dutch families—took in at least one Jew.

Among the many Jews saved by Douwes was Lou Gans, who was left on his own in Amsterdam after his family was deported to Poland in the summer of 1943. "I sometimes slept in parks and playgrounds, sometimes in my parents' house," he writes. "The people in the neighborhood were too frightened to give me any practical help. Buying forged papers was impossible because I didn't have any money, and often I had to steal food from shops in order to keep myself alive. . . . Most of the Jews in Amsterdam

. . . were rounded up in big razzias, arrested, and via Westerbork, sent to Germany and Poland. The very few who escaped the Germans, if they had no money to go underground, just wandered aimlessly—bewildered, lonely, panic-stricken, with no funds, no idea where to go, where to hide, and how to solve their problems. The world seemed to be insane, with informers and murderers lying in wait at every streetcorner. People wanted nothing to do with the few remaining Jews. They turned their backs on you, sent you away, and kept their doors shut. We were alone in a hostile world."

At this low point Lou Gans met Piet Van den Akker, a colleague of his parents. Van den Akker turned him over to Arnold Douwes, who arranged for him to stay for a while with Jan Dekker, Nieuwlande's postman. Over the next several months he also lived with Hendrik Kikkert, a local farmer; Seine and Jans Otten, both of whom were teachers (Seine also occasionally disguised himself as a German soldier in order to steal ration books from the distribution office); Simon Dijk, a housepainter (his house had a workshop were counterfeit identity cards were printed); and Engel Bolwijn, a baker.

"Our task was not easy," writes Arnold Douwes. "The victims them-selves were the main problem. It was very difficult to convince them. Many did not wish to acknowledge the dangers facing them. . . . We had to resort to lies in order to get the parents to give us their children! . . . We told them stories about green pastures and similar fantasies. . . . When we told people 'one week,' it really meant until the liberation. When we said 'two days' we meant two years. . . . We used to contact people in Amsterdam and beg them to let their children go, assuring them that there were safe places waiting for them. There were really no such places. Our thinking was that we would somehow find suitable places the moment the children arrived. They had to be found and were indeed found: in homes, cellars, attics, or elsewhere."

Douwes personally met the children in Amsterdam or at the train station when they arrived in Drente. In Amsterdam he worked through an intermediary. "I usually met her near the concert hall. She handed me the addresses where I was to pick up children."

Haim Roet was sixteen when Douwes took him by train from Amsterdam to Zwolle in eastern Holland and then by bicycle to Dedenswaart. There Haim was reunited with his brother, but when he fell ill, after about a month in hiding, the local doctor refused to treat him. Douwes came to the rescue. He took Haim to a physician in Zwolle and after his recovery brought him back to Dedenswaart. A few months later, when the host family decided to turn Haim out, Douwes biked him 20 miles to another household in Nieuw Amsterdam.

According to Haim Roet, Douwes systematically traversed great stretches of the Dutch countryside on his bicycle, stopping at every house and farm to ask whether they would be willing to lodge a Jewish child. When the Green Police staged raids in the area, Douwes spent the night on his bike, transferring children from one location to another right under their noses.

"I well remember sitting on the back of Arnold's bike, riding the narrow lanes beside the canals that crisscrossed the area," relates Miriam Whartman. When she told Douwes that her host family in the village of Hollandse Veld was subtly trying to convert her, he immediately moved her to another household.

A glance at Douwes's secret diary gives us some idea of the scope and diversity of his activities:

> VdB [Mrs. Van den Bergh]: The house is full of Jews. One is leaving, thus making room for another one.
> D [Deeskers]: I promised him a girl but didn't keep my promise. [Instead, I brought him a boy.]
> vD [Van Dijk]: Found a place there.
> E [Ekelenburg]: He has room for a Jewish domestic. Very good. I'll bring him the woman, and he'll get three extra food coupons.
> H [Hoogeveen]: The woman staying there is on the verge of a mental breakdown; it seems we shall have to hospitalize her.
> K [Kikkert]: Told us that someone has informed on him; Hermann [i.e., Lou Gans] must be moved elsewhere at once.
> This morning, I got up early and visited at M[eus]. The hidden people there are all O.K.
> Slept over at N[ijwening]. Most people where I sleep over are taking care of Jews.
> At O[tten], it is already full up to the roof. There's no room for anyone else.
> S[choneville] stopped me on the road; the Gestapo is looking for me and I'd better be careful.

An operation of such magnitude could not go long undetected, so it is no surprise that Douwes was soon on the Gestapo's most wanted list. To avoid arrest he changed his appearance, sporting a moustache and wearing a hat and eyeglasses to hide his face as much as possible. "These accessories served their purpose so well that even my brother had to look twice before he recognized me," Douwes reminisces. Despite all his precautions, Douwes was arrested in January 1945. He was awaiting execution in the prison at Assen when the underground, in a daring eleventh-hour operation, rescued him.

According to Leons, his closest aide, Douwes was responsible for saving at least 500 Jews, including around 100 children. "He is one of the best and most righteous persons I have ever met. He dedicated himself fully to others, without concern for himself and his own affairs."

In his Yad Vashem deposition, Lou Gans wrote: "What can one say about Arnold Douwes? . . . He was one of the few. You met him, looked in his eyes, looked at his tight-lipped face; then you understood that no brute force in the whole world could make a man like him talk against his will. . . . He not only saved my life but enriched it!"

After the war, one of the people Douwes had rescued said to him, "Arnold, what would we have done without you?" He replied, "It was nothing." To which the survivor responded: "No, it was important; for God sent you to us." (56, 1148)

Pastor Bastiaan & Johanna Ader

Bastiaan Jan Ader was a pastor in Nieuw Beertha, province of Groningen, situated far from the main Jewish population centers in the southwestern part of the Netherlands. However, in the autumn of 1943, at the height of the Nazi terror campaign, he turned up at the Jewish Invalid Hospital in Amsterdam, 75 miles from his hometown, and told the director that he was willing to help any patient or staff member who was looking for a place to hide.

Some of the hospital's personnel did not trust Ader and doubted that anyone so young and innocent-looking had much chance of outsmarting the police. Afraid to offend him but equally afraid to accept his offer, they procrastinated as long as possible, but most of them changed their minds when all other avenues of escape were closed off.

One of Ader's earliest beneficiaries was Josephine H. Ganor. She first met him in the hospital's office on October 9, 1943. Later that same evening, as arranged, Ader waited for her and her friend at the home of a sculptor and then took the two of them to his parents' home in Groningen. Eight months later Josephine was transferred to a safer location, where she remained until the liberation.

Sali Seijffers, another of Ader's beneficiaries, tells in her deposition how she was stranded on an Amsterdam street after eluding a Nazi razzia by the skin of her teeth. "A pastor suddenly appeared like an angel (whom, at first, I frankly mistrusted) and took me and two other Jewish girls to a village in Leiden, South Holland, where a friendly family had already agreed to shelter us."

Ader's activities ranged far and wide across the Dutch countryside. He escorted Jews from Amsterdam to refuges in Utrecht, Zeist, Rotterdam, and points as far south as Limburg on the Belgian frontier and as far north as his hometown of Nieuw Beerta, where there were sometimes as many as a dozen Jews living in his house. As if all this were not dangerous enough, he occasionally burglarized government offices in order to obtain ration cards for his wards throughout the country.

Naturally Ader did not work alone. His network included Arie and Johanna Sparreboom, whose old-age home in Rotterdam, known as Emma House, served as a waystation for many of his charges in transit. Also included were Ader's brother-in-law Dirk Appels, a building contractor in Driebergen, and his daughter Nelly Margot.

Dirk was very active in the underground, and his home became a safe house for Jews on the move to other locations as well as a permanent haven for several of them. Nelly was only sixteen years old when she joined the underground in 1941. After graduating from high school she took a job at the post office, where she had access to a phone, something which proved very useful for Ader's operations. She also spent many hours biking around the countryside to bring food, money, and ration cards to Ader's wards.

Ader's associates in Limburg province included a miner and his wife, both Roman Catholics. The wife's son from a premarital affair agreed to participate in the rescue operation but insisted on being paid. Once he had the money he threw out the Jews he had agreed to shelter, then denounced his stepfather to the police. Based on the information he provided, his stepfather was arrested and sent to Bergen-Belsen, where he died from exhaustion soon after the camp was liberated. The mother never spoke to her son again, and at war's end he was imprisoned by the Dutch government.

Aided by his wife, Johanna, Ader was always on the lookout for new hiding places. He was sometimes rebuffed by people who were willing to put up resistance fighters and Allied pilots but not Jews. His reply would be: "So sorry: I deal only in Jews."

Ader could have remained in Nieuw Beerta, far off the beaten track. Instead, since the town had no Jews for him to help, he entered the lion's den of Amsterdam, seeking out Jews in need and offering his services. A devout Christian, he saw the rescuing of Jews as a divine mission, a means of fulfilling the commandment to love one's neighbor as oneself.

In November 1944, while he was in Haarlem trying to find a refuge for a Jewish girl, the Germans finally caught up with Pastor Ader. He was executed, and Johanna, then in the final months of pregnancy, was arrested for a short time. On her release, though burdened with two small children, she continued his work until the liberation of northern Holland in May 1945. Shortly after the war Jewish survivors raised the funds to build a church in his memory.

At the Yad Vashem ceremony in Bastiaan Jan Ader's honor, his widow stated: "I think of my husband as having been a disciple of Jesus Christ. I have continued his work in two parishes." Evoking her faith in the future, she stated: "Through all tribulations, God is great and is leading us to the holy future. Jews and Christians will experience this holy future together."

Recalling his calm, reassuring, benign face, a Jewish protege of Ader's said: "To write a few words about Pastor Ader is not a simple task. . . . Even a whole book would not suffice to detail all the good he did to save human lives—especially Jews—from the enemy. A man like him can only be described as not merely noble but saintly. I, Shlomo de Leeuw, hid with eighteen other people in his home from March 1944 till the end of the war, and I know and have heard of the danger to him and his life as a result of his activities. . . . We shall never forget Pastor Ader. Not ever!" (423, 223, 1159)

Pastor Leendert Overduin

Another minister, Pastor Leendert Overduin, set up a network in Enschede that managed to save about a quarter of the town's 1,400 Jews, placing them throughout the country but mainly in towns and villages in the northern province of Friesland. In addition to directing operations and supervising the work done by the members of his organization, Overduin regularly visited the Jews they placed to make sure they were well taken care of and to provide them with counterfeit identity cards and ration books.

Sarah Brommet, whose husband was a member of Enschede's Jewish Council (and therefore supposedly exempted from deportation), recalls how Pastor Overduin came by one night in December 1942 to warn them that they were on the list for the next roundup. Determined to save them, he took Sarah and her husband to the home of a family in Boekelo, province of South Holland, where they remained for the next year and a half, while his sister, Corrie Verduijn, temporarily took their son into her own house and then moved him to the home of Pastor Johannes Vijlsma in Leeuwarden, Friesland province.

Overduin made it his business to visit the Brommets as often as possible, bringing along ration cards, cigarettes, and most important of all, news of family and friends. Once, when Sarah was in the doldrums because she missed her young son, he made the long and sometimes dangerous trip to Friesland simply to bring her a recent photograph of the child.

"I cannot begin to explain what this meant to us," Sarah writes, "but I am giving all the details so that you will understand Overduin's thoughtfulness and the chances he took to visit us." Her words were seconded by Dr. Menko, another Jew helped by Overduin, who tells how he regularly checked in at their hiding place "to make sure it was well stocked with coal to keep us warm and with bags of potatoes for our food."

Pastor Overduin's activities eventually led to his arrest, and he remained in prison until the liberation. He has refused to accept any honors or commendations for his wartime activities, but the 350 Enschede Jews who survived because of him are living proof of his humanity and courage. (805)

* * *

We conclude with the story of a man whose impact on those who knew him has not diminished in the nearly five decades since his death. His story is linked with that of a group of young Zionist idealists who hoped to participate in the rebuilding of the Jewish homeland.

Joop Westerweel

The Dutch branch of Hechalutz, an organization that prepared young people for a life of pioneering and agricultural work in Palestine, had a training farm in Loosdrecht, near Utrecht. In July 1942, the sixty-odd trainees and instructors at the farm learned that they were slated for deportation to Westerbork within a few weeks. Menachem Pinkhof and Joachim ("Shushu") Simon, the group's leaders, desperately began seeking a means of escape.

From Miriam Pinkhof, one of the instructors, they learned about a man in Utrecht who was already hiding a Jewish couple in his home and might have useful underground contacts. His name—Joop Westerweel.

Born in Zutphen in 1899 to parents who belonged to the Darbyite Church, also known as the Plymouth Brethren, Westerweel had attended a denominational teachers' college for a while but then dropped out and completed his education through correspondence courses. In the process he formulated an idiosyncratic personal philosophy that combined elements of socialism and anarchism with his own version of evangelical Christianity.

Westerweel's first teaching job was in the Dutch East Indies, but he was soon in trouble for protesting the exploitation of the native population, and when he refused to report for compulsory military training he was expelled from the colony. On his return home he joined the faculty of a school that emphasized physical labor by the students as a means of molding character, and it was there, some while later, that he first came in contact with Jewish refugee children from Germany, among them Miriam Whartman, and learned about the plight of the Jews under Hitler.

In 1942, when Pinkhof and Simon turned to him for help, Westerweel was the principal of a Montessori school in Utrecht. He was, as well, a renowned nonconformist. As a pacifist opposed to military expenditures, he had long since stopped paying his taxes, and he refused to carry an identity card on the grounds that it was a violation of his right to privacy.

The meeting between Westerweel and the Loosdrecht group was a decisive turning point. He listened attentively as the youngsters told about their desire to help rebuild Palestine. Though opposed to nationalism in any form, he was impressed by their idealism and concluded that he had at last found a cause worthy of his fundamentalist piety, his faith in socialism, and his contempt for the Nazis.

Immediately swinging into action, Westerweel set in motion a far-ranging plan to temporarily hide the farm's staff and students with friendly gentile families and then move them to neutral Spain, where they would be safe from the Nazis and might even be able to go on to Palestine. To get to Spain meant traveling hundreds of miles across occupied Belgium and France. Under wartime conditions the journey was extremely dangerous, especially the border crossings, but things were a bit easier in France because the youngsters had papers supposedly identifying them as Dutch workers for the Todt Organization, the German construction firm that was building the coastal fortifications known as the Atlantic Wall. Once they reached the Spanish frontier local guides would take them across the Pyrenees Mountains.

Westerweel organized and personally directed virtually every aspect of this operation, aided by his wife Wilhelmina and about a dozen underground activists. Though he continued as principal of the Montessori school, every night, day off, weekend, and vacation was devoted to it, and he personally escorted most of the escapees all the way from the Netherlands to the Pyrenees.

One of them later recalled his parting words one freezing afternoon in 1944 high up in the mountains: "You are on the threshold of freedom. Soon you will arrive in the land of freedom and will fulfill your goal of building Eretz Israel as a homeland for the world's Jews. I wish each of you happiness and good luck, but do not forget your comrades who fell along the road and by sacrificing their lives paved the way for your journey to freedom. Build up your land and erect a memorial for them, immortalizing their memory. Remember Shushu [arrested by the Germans, he had committed suicide in prison] . . . and all the other comrades who gave their lives to rescue their comrades. Remember the world's suffering, and build your land in such a way that it justifies its existence by providing freedom for all its inhabitants and abandoning war."

Not long afterward, on March 11, 1944, Joop Westerweel was betrayed by an informer and apprehended by the Nazis at a Dutch-Belgian border-crossing point. Wilhelmina, pregnant with her fourth child, had already been arrested and had been sent to a camp. Brutally tortured, Westerweel refused to divulge the names of his associates. He was transferred to Vught and executed on August 11, 1944, just a few days after an abortive attempt to rescue him ended with the arrest of several more members of the Westerweel group.

Joop Westerweel, who was forty-five at the time of his death, drew his strength from his religious beliefs. The night he agreed to help the Loosdrecht group, he looked at the apprehensive faces of his newfound Jewish friends and said to them, quoting Jesus' words in Matthew 10:37, "He that loveth father or mother more than me is not worthy of me; and he that loveth son or daughter more than me is not worthy of me."

Writing long afterwards, one of Hechalutz members who was at the meeting observed: "With that statement, he put the whole undertaking on an exclusively moral pedestal. He made it clear to us that we were setting off along a new road in underground activities that would give new sense and meaning to the values of the past."

Westerweel never went anywhere without a Bible, and at tense moments he would read a favorite passage from the Sermon on the Mount, "Blessed are the poor in spirit, for theirs is the Kingdom of Heaven." It soon became evident that he saw himself as emulating Jesus, carrying his own cross in the footsteps of his Master. "One takes to the road with the cross on his back," he would say; another time he said, "You're wrong in thinking I am helping you because you are Jewish. Even if you were blacks or Hottentots, no matter what, I would help you in the name of justice, for you are in need."

A tree has been planted in memory of Joop Westerweel at Yad Vashem and a entire forest near Kibbutz Gal-Ed has been named after him. Those he saved have formed an organization to keep his memory alive and hold regular convocations in his honor. One of them has written: "The more the passage of time dims the darkness of the period which became the altar on which he gave his life, the stronger shines the nobility of his deeds." Another, Naftali Asher, wrote in 1975, "If the Department for the Righteous [at Yad Vashem] did not exist, we would have to create one in honor of this extraordinary man . . . who transformed his spiritual torment into deeds. . . . The written word can in no way do justice to our feelings about him."

In his solitary-confinement cell, awaiting execution, Joop Westerweel penned a farewell message. It reads in part: "There they are . . . all my comrades, standing side by side with me; together we have advanced along this road to confront the enemy. . . . Whether I die or live is now all the same to me. A great light has dawned within me, enriching me. It is time for silent thoughts. The night is dark and long. But I am fully aglow from the splendor within me." (32, 67)

Germany

Germany, the homeland of National Socialism (better known as Nazism), was quick to adopt a broad program of anti-Jewish measures after Hitler's advent to power on January 30, 1933. On April 1, 1933, the first large-scale anti-Jewish demonstration took place, in the the form of a boycott of Jewish-owned shops and offices. A week thereafter, the first of a series of laws were passed with the aim of completely removing Germany's 505,000 Jews from the economic, political, and social life of the country. The April 7, 1933 Law for the Re-Establishment of the Professional Civil Service adopted the term "non-Aryan" as a legal designation, and prohibited Jews from holding public office. All Jews were ordered removed from various professions: law, public administration, culture, media, and public health. This was soon followed by the Law Against Overcrowding of German Schools (April 25, 1933), for reducing the numbers of Jewish children in higher institutions to the proportion of Jews in the population (i.e., less than 1 percent), and by a series of additional legislative measures gradually restricting Jewish freedom of movement and employment possibilities. Jews were barred from train dining cars, resorts, and beaches. By November 1938 they were fully expelled from all German schools, and that year also saw the start of their forcible transfer from their homes to specially designated, crowded "Jewish houses." Jews were gradually also barred from having phones in their homes, and restricted from using public transportation other than those traveling to workplaces located at least 7 kilometers from their home. Finally, in April 1942, the marking of Jewish homes with a Star of David was made obligatory, thus making it easier to round them up for transportation to the death camps.

One of the most radical measures adopted was the Law for the Protection of German Blood and Honor of September 15, 1935, better known as the Nuremberg Laws, which provided a precise definition of Jews

147

by origin (race), religion, and family ties, and disenfranchised them to a large extent. It also added the stipulation that sexual contact between Jew and "Aryan" was to be considered as race defilement (*Rassenschande*) and strictly forbidden, thus prohibiting intermarriage between both sides. A new race was, paradoxically, created, consisting of the offspring of mixed marriages, better known as *Mischlinge*, which was to give no rest to Nazi racists for years to come. A first-degree *Mischling* was a person with two Jewish grandparents who did not belong to the Jewish religion and was not married to a Jewish person (a person with three Jewish grandparents was considered fully Jewish). A second degree *Mischling* was a person with only one Jewish grandparent. There were further categories for persons with even lesser degrees of Jewish parentage.

After a two-year respite (1936—37), anti-Jewish measures were vigorously renewed in 1938: adding of the middle name "Israel" on identifications for all Jewish men, and "Sara" for women; the marking of passports with a bold *J*; obligatory wearing of the Star of David on Jewish clothes (1941), and enforced sale of Jewish enterprises (known as "aryanization"). The violent smashing and burning of Jewish synagogues, shops, and homes on Kristallnacht (November 11, 1938) was followed with the imposition of a stiff collective fine of 1 billion marks on the impoverished Jewish community.

In 1933 the Jewish population of Germany numbered over 500,000 souls. An additional 200,000 were added in March 1938 with the annexation of Austria. Between 1933 and 1938 around 150,000 Jews emigrated. From the Kristallnacht pogrom on November 11, 1938, to the invasion of Poland on September 1, 1939, another 150,000 left the country, but once the war began emigration was no longer possible.

In November 1941, transports of Jews began leaving for ghettos and concentration camps in Poland. Those qualified as "prominent" or talented German Jews were first dispatched to the "model" camp at Theresienstadt, thence to Auschwitz, where most were gassed. Among these were included decorated Jewish war veterans, as well as disabled veterans. Initially an estimated 10,000 Jews employed in the vital armaments industry were also spared. After a massive roundup of Jews in Berlin in early 1943, the city was officially declared "clean of Jews" (*Judenrein*) on May 19, 1943. The authorities were, of course, fully aware that an unspecified number of Jews, estimated at close to 3,000, had not been netted, and were reduced to either roaming the alleys, parks, and train stations of Berlin or were receiving shelter in non-Jewish homes. Jews living illegally were sometimes referred to as "submarines"—*U-Boote*.

In summary, of the estimated remaining 260,000 Jews in the country (including Austria) at the start of 1941, over 90 percent were deported to the death camps. Those spared included many of the thousands of *Mischlinge* (whose final disposition the Nazi bureaucracy, after marathon discussions, failed to decide on) and some 28,000 Jewish spouses intermarried with non-Jewish Germans. However, after the foiled attempt on Hitler's life in July 1944, the regime began rounding up more of the *Mischlinge*, and they too sought shelter with non-Jews.

Help extended to Jews by individual non-Jews encompassed persons from many walks of life, including some of the clergy. The churches, though, failed to take a clear public stand on the Jewish issue, save in half-hearted attempts to rescue (or mitigate the sufferings of) converted Jews, those officially designated as "non-Aryan Christians." The Catholic Church, by signing a concordat with the Nazi regime soon after assuming power in 1933, precluded any potential Catholic institutional opposition to Hitler, and weakened Catholic opposition to the new regime (the ideology of which was profoundly anti-Christian). The same may be said for most Protestant churches, with the exception of the Confessing Church (a movement incorporating pastors from many churches), which took an outspoken stand against certain Nazi teachings at the Barmen Conference in 1934, but failed to take a similar stand on the Jewish issue. Individual churchmen from the Confessing Church, though, did make great personal sacrifices in helping to secure the safety at first of baptized Jews and later of the nonbaptized as well.

Clemens August von Galen, the prominent Catholic bishop of Münster, preached a sermon in August 1941 denouncing the Nazi euthanasia program (which forced an enraged Hitler to cancel it), but failed to speak out similarly on the deportation of Jews. Likewise for Cardinal Konrad von Preysing of Berlin, who regretted the killing of innocent persons without specifically referring to their religious or ethnic affiliation. Individual Catholic clergymen who stood up in the cause of Jews included Bernhard Lichtenberg, a priest at the St. Hedwig Cathedral, Berlin, who was arrested after being overheard praying for the "poor persecuted Jews," and was incarcerated in Dachau, where he perished. Worthy of note also is Dr. Gertrud Lückner of the Catholic Caritas Society, who helped baptized and nonbaptized Jews, and suffered imprisonment at the notorious Ravensbruck concentration camp, which she survived.

On the Protestant side, Evangelical Bishop Theophil Wurm of Württemberg originally spoke in indirect language, such as referring to the sufferings of the innocents, but in December 1943 (when there were hardly any Jews left in Germany), in a letter addressed to the government, he declared that "we Christians consider the policy of extermination of Jews to be a grave wrong," and saw the heavy Allied bombings of German cities as "a just retribution for what has been done to the Jews." Individual pastors helped Jews survive include, among others, Harold Poelchau, the prison chaplain at the Pölötzensee jail in Berlin, and Pastor Wendland. The Quakers and the Jehovah's Witnesses are the only churches which helped Jews in distress as church policy.

Rescuers of Jews included, of course, lay persons as well, and we shall presently relate some individual rescue stories by Germans (including

Austrians) from different walks of life, including army and civilian personnel in the occupied countries.

Dr. Hermann Maas

In Heidelberg, before the war, Prelate Dr. Hermann Maas, working with Pastor Heinrich Grüber in Berlin, helped many Jews emigrate to England. He affixed a mezuzah to the doorpost of his house so that Jews coming for help would know they were welcome. In 1942, because he spoke out so often against Nazi antisemitism, Maas was ordered to stop giving sermons, but he continued helping Jewish fugitives get to safety in Switzerland. In 1944, when he was sixty-seven, he was arrested and sent to a labor camp in occupied France. Despite his age he survived and after the liberation returned home.

Asked once by a rabbi to explain why he had always been so dedicated to Jewish causes, Dr. Maas replied: "I really don't know. All I can say is that the Almighty has led me down this road since my earliest youth." As far back as 1903, he explained, while a student in Basel, he had attended some of the sessions of the Sixth Zionist Congress, and all his life he had sought to keep faith with his grandmother's admonishment to him as a child: "You must always venerate the Jews, for they are the children of God's people."

After the war, Dr. Maas was one of the first Protestant leaders to argue that Christianity's long tradition of theological Jew-baiting had prepared the ground for Hitler. "The mystery of Israel," he wrote in 1968, "accompanies me day in, day out, now and forever. . . . The rhythm and vicissitudes of Israel's tragic history are embodied in that mysterious secret."

Earlier, in a letter to Yad Vashem, he asked not to be addressed with the salutation *Hochwürden* ("your reverence"). "To my Jewish friends," he wrote, "I only wish to be a Jewish brother." A Yad Vashem official who had escaped from the Warsaw ghetto responded: "I bow to you with a deep sense of awe." (74)

Pastor Erik Perwe and Pastor Erik Myrgren

As was mentioned above, close to 3,000 Jews managed to live through the war in Berlin, Germany's capital city and the seat of Nazi power. Some were helped by Pastor Erik Perwe of the Victoria Church in Wilmersdorf, often referred to as the Swedish Church.

Perwe arrived in Berlin in September 1942, sent there from Sweden by Archbishop Earling Eiden for the express purpose of saving Jews. Before leaving his homeland, Perwe wrote in his diary: "God calls, I must obey."

Aided by a devoted staff and a few German friends, and well provided with money for bribes, Pastor Perwe turned the church compound into a haven for Jewish fugitives. By paying off airline or railroad officials, he was able to arrange for many of them to go to Sweden. Often this was not possible, however, and in such cases he provided money, food, documents, and spiritual support for those who had to take up an underground existence as *U-Booten* ("submarines"), hiding throughout the Greater Berlin area in parks, train stations, bombed-out buildings, or even, at times, the homes of courageous sympathizers.

On November 29, 1944, Perwe was killed when the plane in which he was flying to Sweden for a brief visit crashed over the Baltic Sea. Rumor has it that the plane was sabotaged by the Gestapo because Perwe was not on church business, as he claimed, but on behalf of some German leaders who wanted to begin peace negotiations with the Allies. Whatever the truth of this may be, there is no doubt that Perwe's rescue operation might well have come to an end at this point, but fortunately a man of no less zeal and courage was waiting in the wings.

Several days before the fatal flight, a young minister named Erik Myrgren, the pastor of the Swedish Seamen's Church in the East Prussian port of Stutthof (now Sztutowo, Poland), had arrived in Berlin. For some time now his congregation had been virtually nonexistent, since the military situation was so dangerous that Swedish merchant vessels no longer called at Stutthof. When the church building was destroyed in an air raid, his superiors back home had decided there was no point in repairing it and recalled him for a new assignment.

At loose ends and eager for some useful work, Myrgren readily agreed when Perwe met him at the Berlin railroad station and asked him to take over during his absence. A week later, when news of Perwe's death arrived, it was evident that Myrgren would have to remain in Berlin as his permanent replacement, but he felt quite unequal to the task. "I was overcome by panic," he later wrote. "I knew so little about Perwe's work and practically nothing about his sub-rosa activities."

Over the next few nights, when darkness cloaked their movements, Perwe's "submarines" began coming to the church to pay their respects. Myrgren was haunted by the sight, and by what they told him. Some old, some young, they all had the worn, haggard look of hunted animals; no longer able to lean on the man who had been their only prop, they were gripped by despair.

A few weeks later, standing before the church altar while conducting Christmas services, Myrgren was reading aloud from the Book of Isaiah. As he recited the second verse of the ninth chapter, "The people that walked in darkness have seen a great light; they that dwell in the land of the shadow of death, upon them hath the light shined," everything suddenly fell into place for him. "It was as if the words had left the page and somehow entered the present reality. They had been changed into people I knew, events so terribly real. Everything was there: the sounds of war, the torture camps, the despair, the bloodshed, but also the beam of light, the hope of final victory, the love despite all."

Now fully committed to the task of carrying on Perwe's mission, Myrgren was like a new man. "Slowly, slowly, I myself became part of the machinery Perwe . . . had built up so carefully." For five hectic months, until Berlin's surrender on May 2, 1945, he devoted himself to helping some of the persecuted remnant of Berlin's once substantial Jewry.

During these final months of the war, as the Nazi regime convulsed in its death agony, the hunt for Jews intensified and the stream of people passing through the church increased. With the help of German transportation officials angling for better postwar treatment by the Allies, Myrgren got scores of Jews out of the country by sea via the port of Lübeck or by plane from Tempelhof Airport, the last such flight taking off on April 11, 1945.

Long after the war Myrgren told about some of his experiences. In particular he recalled an old man who had been a powerful magnate in the days before the Nazis came to power. The former VIP, weeping uncontrollably, had grasped Myrgren's hand, fallen to his knees, and abjectly pleaded for help. At that moment, Myrgren said, "I realized that he was innocent and I was guilty. . . . A burning hatred flared up within me against a system that could so deeply humiliate someone and so trample on an old man's dignity that he found it necessary to beg a young lad for his life, at his feet. It was terrible. But it was also good for me. It strengthened my resolve. It made me stronger and more mature."

In 1987, informed that Yad Vashem had designated him one of the Righteous Among the Nations, Myrgren responded: "I feel very humble, and surely I am not worthy of being honored with such an outstanding distinction. Whatever I did during my time in Berlin, I never felt there was anything special about it. On the contrary, I always felt that it was not enough. I simply tried, as best I could, to do what my sainted parents taught me: Help your fellow man, whatever he is and whatever he needs." (3546)

Dr. Elisabeth Abegg

Elisabeth Abegg was born and raised in Strassburg (now Strasbourg), where she met the legendary Albert Schweitzer as a girl. A history teacher by profession and a Quaker by religion, she moved to Berlin when Alsace-Lorraine was returned to France after World War I and there joined the faculty of the Luisen girls' school. In 1933, at the age of fifty, she was fired because of her anti-Nazi views.

In 1942, operating out of her apartment in the Tempelhof quarter, where she lived with her older sister and their bedridden eighty-six-year-old mother, Abegg became active in an escape network made up of Quaker friends, ministers of other denominations, and former students. Over the next three years, financing her activities by selling her jewelry and other valuables, she helped dozens of Jews in Berlin and other parts of Germany to avoid arrest and in some cases to cross the border into Switzerland. She also tutored Jewish children in her home to make up for their not being able to attend school and regularly crisscrossed Berlin by subway and elevated train to deliver documents, money, and food to Jews in hiding.

One of the people Abegg helped was Charlotte Herzfeld, a girl whose parents committed suicide on the eve of their deportation for "resettlement" in the east. "You were there—calm, serene, courageous," Charlotte wrote to Elisabeth Abegg years later; "perhaps one should add 'self-composed.' I regained trust, I sensed warmth, I felt safe. You reminded me of my mother's calmness, warmth and equanimity, under different circumstances."

Every Friday afternoon Jews who had been hiding all week in cellars, condemned buildings, and public parks throughout Berlin gathered at Elisabeth Abegg's apartment for a home-cooked meal and a bit of companionship. "It enabled us to forget that we no longer had the right to exist as human beings," recalls Liselotte, one of her wards.

Others whom Abegg helped describe her as the epitome of tolerance, compassion, and love for others, "able to see man's inner light even where many of us thought it dead and extinguished." Yitzhak Schwersentz says: "She encouraged us not to despair and to believe in a better future. . . . I always think of her as a guardian angel in the midst of that terrible hell. She acted, not for compensation, but out of love for the persecuted."

In 1957 a group of survivors published *And a Light Shined in the Darkness*, a book of testimonials in honor of Elisabeth Abegg's seventy-fifth birthday. One of them, by a woman named Hertha Blumenthal, says: "With Fraulein Dr. Abegg was revealed the truth that a life of love for one's fellow human beings, together with respect for others, is the most elevated and eternal value. . . . Her rectitude, straightforwardness, and endless love will always be the model . . . upon which I pattern my life and will come into play whenever anyone needs my help."

During the war Elisabeth Abegg told a friend that one of the greatest evils perpetrated by Nazism was the way it forced everyone, whether they wished to or not, to see the things that made people different—noticing that this one was Jewish, this one German, and so on. Under the pressure of the continuous Nazi propaganda, even those who hated Nazism could not help making such distinctions.

A further insight into what made her so willing to aid Jewish fugitives may be inferred from her response when a grateful couple thanked her for helping them: "We are indebted to you! We have so much to make up for!" (345)

Gerhard and Ilse Schwersensky

In 1941, fifteen-year-old Lorraine Jacoby, together with her fellow students at a Jewish boarding school, was drafted for forced labor at the

Blaupunkt Company's airplane assembly plant in Berlin. About a year later she slipped away in the hope of escaping to Switzerland. When the attempt failed she returned to Berlin, only to discover that all her friends had been sent to Auschwitz. Uncertain what to do, she turned to the members of a Quaker group that had helped the youngsters when they had first gone to work at the plant.

Lorraine's contacts referred her to two other Quakers, Gerhard and Ilse Schwersensky, a social worker and kindergarten teacher respectively, who often hid Jews on the run. She moved in with them and their three children, and was introduced to the neighbors as an out-of-towner who was in Berlin to take a secretarial course. The Schwersenskys were also taking care of Lottie, a former employee of Berlin's Jewish communal organization. She had lived with them for a while after receiving her deportation notice, and now they were supplying her with food and other necessities while she hid out elsewhere, spending her days in crowded parks and railroad stations, and sleeping in bombed-out buildings or the basements of office buildings.

Even in the bleakest days of the war, when Germany was victorious on every front, Gerhard and Ilse Schwersensky never doubted that good would triumph and Hitler would ultimately fall. "Their religious beliefs and fierce opposition to Hitler's regime sustained them," wrote Lorraine, adding that as Quakers they felt an obligation "to take a moral stand and do everything possible to defeat Nazism, being fully aware of the dangers facing them and their children."

In 1987, when she received Yad Vashem's Righteous award, Ilse Schwersensky, then seventy-seven years old, gave a no-nonsense explanation for her wartime heroism: "My mother always said, 'Pick up whatever God puts on your doorstep.'" (3201)

Karl and Eva Hermann

Dr. Karl Hermann was a physical chemist at the I. G. Farben complex in Mannheim. He and Eva, his wife, both of them Quakers, were outspoken pacifists and critics of the Nazi regime. In October 1940, when the Jews of Mannheim were deported to France, they publicly helped as many as they could with food, clothing, and money. After the city was declared *Judenrein* they took in a Jewish couple in need of a place to hide. They were also known to regularly violate the law against listening to BBC news broadcasts.

For a long time the authorities did nothing about all this because Hermann's work was vital to the war effort, but the couple were eventually arrested, and on July 9, 1943, they were tried before a special tribunal.

The trial record illustrates the German judiciary's subservience to the Nazi government. Acknowledging Hermann's reputation in the field of radiological structure research, the judges stated that his great devotion to science had made him unworldly and blinded him to the facts of life; as a result, he had focused on trivialities and abstractions, and had not come to grips with reality (i.e., the Jew as the enemy). Crippled by his failure to understand the Jewish threat and his reservations about Nazism, he had acted against the interests of the state. While he had not done so out of malice and had never intended to be an enemy of National Socialism, the court said, his behavior on the Jewish question showed that he was opposed to the movement on a central issue. By giving succor to a Jewish couple, he put himself in conflict with the state's attempt to solve the Jewish problem.

Because Hermann's contribution to the war effort was so important, the court handed down a "mild" sentence—eight years in prison for Karl and three years for Eva. Hermann was to spend his nights in his cell, but every morning would be taken to his laboratory at the Farben plant to continue his work. Karl and Eva Hermann served two years each, regaining their freedom when the war ended.

In 1976, when her husband was elevated to the ranks of the Righteous, Eva Hermann penned the following words: "I am fully conscious of the fact that my late husband and I did nothing special; we simply tried to remain human in the midst of inhumanity."

A year later, while in Israel to receive a medal and plant a tree in the Garden of the Righteous, she said: "How can I not hesitate before accepting? Are we sufficiently aware, against the background of the darkest chapter in German history, of how guilty we are for rescuing no more than a tiny droplet out of the endless sea of despair of that period? Righteous can therefore have no other meaning than the attempt, the obligation, to do what is right and to live humanly even during times of inhumanity." (970)

Erna Härtel

On the night of January 31, 1945, with the Red Army drawing ever closer, the S.S. guards at the labor camp near Stutthof, East Prussia, assembled the 10,000 Jewish inmates, among them a young woman named Frieda, and marched them off into the darkness. The night was bitter cold, and the thinly clothed, starving women were driven forward through the ice and snow, the guards shooting anyone who could not keep up with the column. "We left many corpses on the road," Frieda Kleinman recalls.

As they made their way toward the nearby Baltic shore, the prisoners were told that they were to be transferred by sea to camps out of the reach of the advancing Soviet forces, but when they got to the beach, they found out what was really in store for them. Group after group was made to lie down on the ice-covered shingle and then was sprayed with machine-gun fire from the surrounding cliffs. Flares lit up the sky to help the gunners see their victims.

Frieda felt two bullets pierce her legs. She fainted from the pain and did not come to until several hours later, when the ice-cold water of the incoming tide began to lap at her side. There was a deadly quiet all around, and dead bodies were drifting aimlessly among the chunks of floating ice.

Wrapped in some soaking-wet garments that she found on the beach and shivering from the cold, Frieda began walking. When she reached the nearby village of Moldinau, she knocked at the first door. A woman answered, and Frieda begged her for help.

Erna Härtel stared at the young woman, covered with filth and blood and dressed in rags. "Germans did this?" she said, tears running down her cheeks. "I heard shooting last night, but I never dreamed it was anything like this."

As Frieda recounts in her deposition, Erna Härtel "swept me into her home, hugging and comforting me. From that moment she cared for me like a mother." Erna removed Frieda's rags, washed her and combed the lice out of her hair, and dressed her wounds. She was about to put her to bed, but when Frieda saw the sparkling white sheet, she refused to get in and said she would sleep on the floor in a corner of the room. "When I said this," Frieda writes, "she began to weep like a child, took me in her arms, and put me in the bed. Then she said: 'Now you're a human being like everyone else. You'll stay here with me until the war is over.'"

Two and a half months later the Red Army moved into the area and Frieda was able to take up her life again. (243).

Loni and Albert Harder

Celina Manilewitz also survived the death march from Stutthof. She still remembers arriving at the beach ("great, steep cliffs sloping down to the sea"), the sound of machine-gun fire from all sides, then being struck with the butt of a rifle and reeling down into the ice-cold water. When she regained consciousness, "half in the water and half on a block of ice," the machine guns were still barking, the sky lit up by flares to illuminate the human targets. "All around, in that gray-green sea, corpses were afloat, half hanging on the blocks of ice. The wounded were moaning; some begged God to let them die."

When the shooting came to an end and the S.S. men left the area, Celina and two other women waded ashore and made their way to the village of Sorginau. They knocked at the door of a farmhouse and were admitted by a dour-looking German peasant. A week later, when he learned that the Russian advance had been stopped, he threw them out, then reported them to an S.S. unit quartered in the vicinity.

By the time the S.S. men arrived on the scene, however, the girls were gone. They had been taken in by Loni and Albert Harder, who lived nearby and had seen what happened. The Harders hid them in their pigsty until the coast was clear, then moved them into the house, where the girls were able to bathe, eat a hot meal, and then sleep.

Celina, who at twenty-three was the only surviving member of her family, remembers her thoughts at the moment: "It was almost too much. It was like a dream—having a proper bed again, for the first time, after so many years in a concentration camp. . . . Here in the midst of our enemies, the Germans, we three Polish girls—and Jewish, too—had suddenly found a mother."

Loni shaved the girls' lice-ridden hair and helped them to prepare a cover story: they were German refugees from Memel, now in Russian hands, and their heads had been shaved because they had contracted typhus. Celina and the others lived with Loni and Albert for the next two and a half months, until the arrival of the Red Army on April 14, 1945.

A difficult period now began for the Harders. Along with most of the other German civilians in East Prussia they were held in a Soviet internment camp while awaiting transfer to Germany, and there Albert Harder died. His last words to his wife were: "Any news of our girls?"

Celina finally located Loni in 1948, living on the outskirts of Berlin. Now it was her turn to help. She and her husband wanted to take Loni with them to Israel but she demurred, preferring to remain in her homeland.

Loni lived with Celina and her husband until their departure. "We only had the one room, and we were newlyweds," Celina writes, "but we put up the old lady nonetheless. You've no idea what she was like; goodness itself, an angel in human form. What she did for the three of us, out of sheer humanity, just couldn't be recompensed." (225)

Heinrich Aschoff and other Münsterland Farmers

"I know when it all began but I don't know how it will end," wrote Marga Spiegel years after the Holocaust, still unnerved by her experiences before and during the war.

Hitler had been in power several years and the Nazis' anti-Jewish program was in full swing when Marga's marriage to Siegmund, a Westphalian cattle dealer, took place. As a World War I veteran and a recipient of the Iron Cross, Siegmund for some time assumed that he and his loved ones would be exempted from the worst of the Nazi excesses.

The death of Marga's father in the concentration camp at Sachsenhausen in 1937, soon followed by her mother's death at the age of forty-nine, did not change Siegmund's thinking, but in November 1938, with a new sense of realism instilled by the Kristallnacht pogrom, he decided it was time to leave Germany. The war began, however, before he could make the necessary arrangements.

Forced to sell their business and their home in Ahlen, Siegmund and Marga and their infant daughter Kristin, born in 1938, were relocated to Dortmund, where they had to share a flat in the Jewish quarter with six other families. In 1941, when Siegmund was conscripted for compulsory labor, they moved from the flat to a dilapidated former army barracks assigned to his unit.

Worried by rumors about the impending "resettlement" of Germany's Jews in the east, Siegmund contacted some farmer friends to see whether they would help if he and his family received deportation orders. Several promised not to let him down, and in addition, whenever they could, began visiting at the barracks with gifts of food to supplement the meager rations allocated to Jews. One of them, Hubert Pentrop, who had a farm in Nordkirchen, gave Siegmund a grim warning: "If they want to send you to Poland, don't go. The news from there is no good. Come to me and I'll hide you."

In due course Siegmund received the dreaded deportation call-up, and on February 27, 1943, he, Marga, and Karin slipped out of the barracks and headed for the railroad station. On the way they removed the Star of David patches from their coats, but since throwing them away might have attracted attention, Marga stuffed them in her glove. At the station, as they boarded the train that would carry them away from Dortmund, they saw the town's remaining Jews waiting on the eastbound platform. "Not one of them came back," Marga writes. "Out of thirty-seven families, not a single one survived."

Aware that they would arouse more suspicion as a family than as individuals, Siegmund and Marga had decided to hide separately, even though they knew they might never see each other again. Marga and five-year-old Karin were to stay with Heinrich Aschoff on his farmstead in Hebern, and Siegmund, with another family in nearby Dolberg.

During a stopover at Werne, Marga telephoned the Aschoffs, fearful that they would not keep the promise they had made so many months earlier. She heaved a sigh of relief when Mrs. Aschoff replied that one of her daughters would be waiting for them when the train arrived.

Heinrich Aschoff, as Marga later wrote, was "a sincere, straightforward man, a typical Münsterland farmer," and his wife's heart "was overflowing with generosity and love." Despite the obvious risks, and even though they had never met Marga before, the Aschoffs took her and Karin into their home. Of the seven children in the household (an eighth was away in the army), only the two oldest daughters were told the truth about Marga. As far as everyone else was concerned, she was Mrs. Krone, the wife of a soldier at the front.

Things did not go as well for Siegmund. The farmer who had agreed to help him tried to live up to his promise, but circumstances had changed in the interim. His wife had died, two of his sons had been drafted, and his grown-up daughters were afraid to have a Jew on the premises. As a result, after about three weeks, he politely asked Siegmund to leave.

Recalling Hubert Pentrop's words back in Dortmund, Siegmund decided to approach him. Pentrop had six children and a seventh on the way, and Mrs. Pentrop, who was seriously ill, had been in the hospital for several months, but despite all this he willingly took Siegmund in. "You'll stay here for the time being," he said. "Then we'll decide what to do."

Because of Mrs. Pentrop's illness, Maria Südfeld, the daughter of a neighboring farmer, had moved in to lend a hand with the household chores. One evening, hearing footsteps from a supposedly empty upstairs room, Maria began to think that the place was haunted. She was so upset that Pentrop had to tell her the truth, but Maria promised not to betray the secret that he was hiding a Jew.

Siegmund stayed with the Pentrops for nine months but left when an apprentice farmhand accidentally saw him. He stayed at several other farms in the area for short periods; one family asked him to leave because the head of the household was becoming ill from anxiety caused by his presence.

On the day after Christmas in 1943, Siegmund finally found a safe refuge in the home of Heinrich Silkenbömer. Heinrich and his wife gave Siegmund an empty room belonging to one of their two sons, both of whom were in the army. They treated him with compassion and warmth, and even arranged for Marga to visit him from time to time.

Most of the German civilians who were staying on farms had fled the cities because of Allied air raids, and occasionally returned home for one reason or another. In order to avoid the questions that might have been asked if Marga never did so, the Aschoffs arranged for her and Karin sometimes to spend a few weeks with families in other towns. Among these were the Sickmanns. Marga often accompanied them to church while staying at their house. She still recalls how the priest, with a pained expression on his face, once said: "Look at my beard. It's turned prematurely gray because of my sins. If only more of our clergy and leaders had spoken out in time, if only they had protested against the heinous crime being perpetrated against our Jewish sisters and brothers, it might have helped."

Although Marga and Karin were usually not in any direct danger, they had one or two close calls. At the Aschoffs' fiftieth-anniversary party, for instance, Karin was performing a little dance, and all of a sudden a yellow patch with the Star of David fell out the glove Marga had given her. To this day Marga is not sure why she saved the patches when they left Dortmund; in a way they helped her to feel she was still Jewish. In any event, although none of the guests seemed to notice, she decided, for safety's sake, to move out for a while.

The Aschoffs arranged for Marga and Karin to stay with the Pentrops in Nordkirchen. One night in May 1944, tipped off by an informer, two policemen turned up there. Marga and Karin managed to escape but were at their wit's end. Where were they to go? After riding about on their bicycles for a while, they made their way to the Sickmann house, and there they stayed till the war's end a year later. Marga's feelings of despair and bitterness in those days often made her recall ("with painful intensity," she says) a verse of Goethe's that she had read at school:

> Who ne'er his bread in sorrow ate, Who ne'er the mournful midnight hours Weeping upon his bed has sate, He knows you not, ye Heavenly Powers.

Siegmund, Marga, and little Karin survived the Holocaust thanks to the courage and decency of the Aschoffs, the Pentrops, and the Sickmanns, unpretentious farm families when viewed from one perspective, but giants of the spirit from another. Because of their great humanity, they were all recognized by Yad Vashem in 1969 as Righteous Among the Nations. (463)

Maria Potesil

Maria Potesil's husband was captured by the Russians in 1915 and died in a POW camp, leaving her with two small children, Anna and Adolf. Twelve years later, at the age of thirty-three, the Viennese war widow adopted a third child, two-year-old Kurt, born out of wedlock to a mother who had died four weeks after giving birth. In 1931 she learned that Kurt's father had been a Jew by the name of Berko Berkowitsch.

With the Anschluss in March 1938, Austria became part of Nazi Germany. In the aftermath, Kurt's status now became a major issue. First the Vienna municipality informed Maria that she would no longer receive child-support payments because Kurt was half-Jewish. Next she had to transfer him from public school to a Jewish school. Then she had to sew the obligatory yellow patch on his clothing.

Maria complied with all of the regulations but refused to give Kurt up when this was urged upon her. The authorities took a dim view of the matter, however, and in the fall of 1942, the police pulled Kurt out of his bed one night and took him to a transit center for deportation to a concentration camp.

Maria was beside herself. She ran from government bureau to government bureau, desperately trying to find some way to save Kurt. At S.S. headquarters, the official in charge of Jewish affairs in Vienna, Obersturmführer Anton Brunner, angrily called her an "Aryan swine" and had her thrown out. Another officer, enraged at her concern about a Jewish child, hurled insults at her, followed by a chair.

Although the officials Maria consulted were hostile and contemptuous, they could not deny that Kurt was only half-Jewish and, as well, the legally adopted child of an Aryan. The standing this gave him eventually made it possible for Maria to obtain his release. By then, however, he was seriously ill, running a high fever and delirious, but back home she devotedly nursed him back to health.

Despite Maria's apparent victory, the authorities kept up the pressure. Maria was told that if she and Kurt remained together, they would have to live in the Jewish quarter and be subject to the curfew, rationing, and other restrictions imposed on Vienna's Jews.

Since periodic roundups were a frequent occurrence in the ghetto, Maria made a point of not letting Kurt out of her sight. She took him with her whenever she went shopping, and often would be stopped on the street by policemen who noticed that Kurt was wearing a yellow star and she wasn't. This anomaly seemed to indicate a variety of infractions: that she was a Jew trying to "pass," that she was a non-Jew illegally helping a Jew, and so on. But each time Maria would produce documents showing that she was Kurt's legal guardian and the police would let her go.

Kurt survived the Nazi era because of Maria's Potesil's bravery and persistence. She gave up the comfort of friends, was forced to live in want, and was subjected to indignities, insults, and the danger of physical harm—all to save the life of a single child.

A passage in the Midrash says: "Whosoever preserves one life is as though he has preserved the entire world" (Aboth de Rabbi Nathan, chap. 31). (1400)

Dorothea Neff

"The Lord gave me friends who were willing to stand by me when the need, the terrible need, occurred." So begins the testimony of Lilli Wolff, a retired dress designer from Cologne. In it she tells about her friendship with Dorothea Neff, who was "sent by God to help me overcome the Nazi terror, so that my life could be saved."

Dorothea Neff, born in Munich in 1903, was an actress. Lilli, then a young theatrical costumer, got to know her in Cologne in the years before the war, but their acquaintance was cut off when Dorothea moved to Vienna to accept a position at the prestigious Volkstheater. Their friendship was renewed in 1940, however, when Lilli, erroneously believing that Jews would be treated better in the former Austrian capital than in Germany proper, turned up at Dorothea's fashionable apartment on Annagasse in Vienna's Inner City and asked for help.

Dorothea was only too happy to see "Lillichen." As a Jew, Lilli had to register with the police and live in the city's Jewish quarter, where she didn't know a soul, but Dorothea found her a room with a family there. Jews were prohibited from leaving the quarter except for a few hours each day, but Dorothea often visited Lilli, bringing medicines and other necessities, and sometimes Lilli managed to visit Dorothea.

In October of 1941 Lilli received her deportation notice. Earlier that year, when they first realized that she might be sent east, Dorothea had gone to Berlin to see whether she could arrange for Lilli to be hidden there, but to no avail. Now, as the two of them sat in Dorothea's kitchen, sorting and weighing Lilli's possessions and packing the two suitcases she was allowed, Dorothea suddenly exclaimed: "You're not going anywhere! I'll hide you!"

Years later Dorothea described the thoughts that ran through her mind at that moment. "As I looked into Lilli's pale face, I was so overcome by compassion for this poor abandoned human being that I knew I couldn't let her go off to face the unknown." Driven by an inner voice that seemed to say, "You must not let this happen," Dorothea took Lilli's hand and made her stop packing, assuring her that everything would be all right.

For the next three years, Lilli lived secretly in a back room of Dorothea's apartment. Every night, Dorothea would rush home once the theater closed, her heart pounding as she turned the key and opened the door for fear something might have happened to Lillichen, but no one ever found out about her, even the guests Dorothea entertained after openings and on other occasions. During air raids, when the two women went to the shelter, Dorothea introduced her as a friend from bombed-out Cologne.

In February 1945 Lilli developed a lump in her breast and the danger of discovery loomed. Fortunately, however, Dorothea was able to get her into a hospital under a false name, and to add to their good luck, the lump

Israel ambassador Yissachar Ben-Yaacov presenting the Righteous award to Dorothea Neff in Vienna (1980). Courtesy of Yad Vashem.

proved to be a benign cyst. Just a few weeks later, in April, Vienna fell to the Red Army and Lilli was finally safe.

In 1980, at a ceremony in the Burgtheater before an audience that included scores of government officials and luminaries of the stage and screen, the Israeli ambassador to Austria awarded Dorothea Neff the Yad Vashem Righteous medal. In her acceptance speech, the now partly blind Dorothea said: "The greater the darkness of a period, the brighter is the light of a single candle."

Lilli, in the meantime, had moved to Dallas, Texas, where she resumed her career as a dress designer. In her Yad Vashem deposition she wrote: "God chose Dorothea Neff to save my life. . . . When she was born, the world became more bountiful, and part of that bounty was bestowed on me." She selected a quotation from the Bible to express the feeling of security Dorothea had given her during her years in hiding: "When thou passest through the waters, I will be with thee" (Isaiah 43:2). (1652)

Josef Meyer

Before the war Solomon Altmann was an attorney in Zloczow, a Galician town that became part of the Soviet Union when Hitler and Stalin partitioned Poland in 1939. Following its capture by the Germans on July 1, 1941, more than 3,000 of the town's 16,000 Jewish inhabitants were massacred and the usual repressive measures were put into effect.

Unable to practice his regular profession under the Nazis, Altmann became the manager of a large bakery. One day in December 1941 a German civilian official stopped in to inspect the place, introducing himself as Josef Meyer, director of the district department of agriculture and food procurement. Noting that Altmann spoke German, Meyer told him to get into his car, which was waiting outside. Altmann complied, expecting the worst.

To his surprise, the driver took them to Meyer's house. Inside, Meyer invited Altmann to sit down, something German officials never did when dealing with Jews. Altmann desperately tried to figure out what Meyer was up to. Meanwhile, Meyer gave him a searching look. "Tell me the truth," he said. "I want to know who was responsible for the pogrom last summer. It must have been the S.S., but I'd like to have that confirmed by you."

Certain by now that Meyer wanted to provoke him into saying something incriminating, Altmann did not answer. He had no way of knowing, of course, that on September 1, 1939, the day Germany invaded Poland, Meyer had been arrested by the Gestapo for making antiwar statements. He had been held for five weeks, but family and friends had wangled his release and a civilian job in the occupation administration.

As if to allay Altmann's misgivings, Meyer continued: "I am a believing Catholic and a strict and uncompromising opponent of this criminal regime. My last assignment was in Radom, where both Jews and Poles know me for my views. Please tell your friends—but cautiously—that within the purview of my duties I shall do everything I can to help."

Having said this, Meyer turned on the BBC's noontime news program from London. Altmann, still somewhat suspicious and aware that listening to enemy broadcasts was punishable by death, stood up and asked permission to leave. "Sit down and be quiet," Meyer replied. "Don't you want to know what the world is saying about us?" The two men listened to a report on the German army's latest setbacks in Russia, after which Meyer let Altmann go, embracing him as he left.

The next day, true to his word, Meyer began to act. Having learned from Altmann about the widespread starvation among the town's Jews, he doubled the number listed as productively employed so as to justify a commensurate increase in the ghetto's food allocation. Meyer personally made the necessary alterations in the bookkeeping ledgers, telling Altmann, "I know that this is against the law and punishable, but the end of saving human lives justifies the means; my conscience is perfectly clear."

Among other things, Altmann had suggested that a free kitchen be set up in the ghetto to feed several hundred people. The following month, by increasing the ghetto's food allocation still further, Meyer made it possible for the kitchen to start operating. From then on, the food it used was entered in the books under the names of fictitious business firms and army units.

In the spring of 1942, Altmann told Meyer that the Jews of Zloczow had been unable to get any cooking oil for Passover and therefore would be unable to prepare meals during the eight-day period. Meyer drove over to the district warehouse for edible oils and conducted an unannounced inspection. Examining one batch, he wrinkled his nostrils and shouted at the manager, "How dare you requisition such foul-smelling oil for Germans? Do you want to poison us! Get rid of it immediately. Better yet, sell it to the Jews!" The frightened manager did as ordered, and gave the oil to Altmann at a discount price in order to get it off the premises as quickly as possible.

Another of Meyer's projects was the establishment of a candy factory so as to increase by a few dozen the number of Jews registered as productive workers and thus exempt from liquidation. By smuggling in medicines and soap, he also saved the 1,000 Jewish inmates of a nearby labor camp when an epidemic of typhus broke out and the S.S. intended to exterminate them if it did not subside.

In January 1943 Meyer was arrested while in Lwow, the district capital. The Gestapo had been watching him for some time but had not been able to build a solid case, and when he managed to get through three days of interrogation without admitting anything, they let him go. On his return to Zloczow he told Altmann: "Don't worry, I'll still help, but we'll have to be even more careful."

Meanwhile, throughout 1942 the Nazis had been rounding up Jews from Zloczow and sending them to the death camps. The final liquidation of the Zloczow ghetto, where only 7,000 of the prewar population of 16,000 still remained alive, was scheduled for April 1943. In anticipation of this disaster, Meyer began making plans to help his closest Jewish friends escape.

With his connivance, the Strassler brothers, who ran the candy factory, tunneled out from the factory's cellar and dug an underground hideout large enough for thirty people under the town's market square. Once they were inside, Meyer provided them with food and other necessities. Every so often, at a prearranged time and place, a Pole who worked for him would deliver a new supply of provisions and a woman from the group would sneak out to pick it up.

The thirty Jews lived underneath the bustling market square for almost a year. The Germans suspected that there were people hiding in the area, but since the shelter was almost 20 feet underground, their dogs weren't able to detect anything, and the inmates' cooking smoke was vented into one of the town's sewers.

Although the Strassler group required a good deal of attention, Meyer did not neglect Altmann. First he got Mrs. Altmann a set of identity papers that would enable her to "pass," then drove her to Lwow and put her on a train for Warsaw, where friends had agreed to take care of her. Next, in exchange for a regular supply of food and other commodities, and a license to operate a tavern, he persuaded a local Pole to hide Altmann, Altmann's son, and Altmann's father in a bunker behind his barn. Using the same currency, Meyer found another Pole to hide his Jewish valet-handyman Joseph and Joseph's wife.

After the final *Aktion* in April, Zloczow and the surrounding region were officially *Judenrein*, but unknown to anyone except Josef Meyer, thirty Jews were still alive in a hideout underneath the market square and five more were hiding in two other locations. All of them were alive and well when the Red Army arrived in July 1944, although by then Meyer and the other officials of the occupation administration had been evacuated westward with the retreating Wehrmacht.

Rescuer and rescued met again, however, some in Germany immediately after the war, others when Meyer visited Israel in 1965 to be honored by Yad Vashem as one of the Righteous Among the Nations.

In a postwar deposition, Josef Meyer stated that as a Catholic he had reared his children to withstand the corrosive antisemitism of the Nazis and thus "to see the human being in the Jew." He added: "Everything I did for my charges at Radom and Zloczow, at a time when humanitarianism was torn asunder and even considered a crime, was done out of love for my fellow men, for that is morality's cardinal tenet."

Solomon Altmann wrote: "The fact that he saved our lives is certainly important. But the fact that Herr Meyer kept alive our belief in man is even more important." (157)

Eberhard Helmrich

Eberhard Helmrich, a major in the German army, was the commander of a large farm attached to the Hyrawka labor camp in Drohobycz, East Galicia. He had to meet food production quotas set by the army, but as long as he did so he had more or less a free hand in running the farm. Almost two-thirds of his 300 workers were Jews from the Drohobycz ghetto, and thanks to his kindness many of them were saved from arrest or the periodic roundups. On several occasions he hid Jews in his home, and he obtained the release of others by claiming they were needed for the farm's proper functioning.

When he learned that all the Jews in the region were to be liquidated, Helmrich was horrified. He and his wife, Donata, who happened to be visiting him from Berlin, came up with a plan to save at least some of them. At the time large numbers of Ukrainian and Polish girls were being sent to Germany to work as domestics. Helmrich, in Drohobycz, would provide

Michael Arnon, Israeli consul-general in New York, awarding the Righteous medal and Certificate of Honor to Eberhard Helmrich (1964). Courtesy of Yad Vashem.

the false credentials that would enable some of the local Jewish girls to go along, and Donata, in Berlin, would find jobs for them, making sure there were no real Poles or Ukrainians working in the houses where they were employed.

Altogether, the Helmrichs saved over a dozen girls. After the war, they were asked about their motivations. "We were fully aware of the risks and the conflict of responsibilities," they said, "but we decided that it would be better for our children to have dead parents than cowardly parents. From then on it was comparatively easy. We figured that once we saved two people we'd be even with Hitler if we were caught, and every person saved beyond that would put us one ahead."

Donata added: "I only did what I felt had to be done." (154)

Lieutenant Roman Petsche

In March 1944, when the Germans occupied Hungary, the city of Novi Sad, which had been part of Yugoslavia until 1941, came under their control. During the three years of the Hungarian rule the city's 4,000 Jews had been decimated. Now, it seemed, the curtain was to fall on the remnants of its Jewish community.

When the German troops moved in, Dr. Tibor, one of the local Jewish leaders, tried to escape to Hungary proper, but was caught at the border and never seen again. His wife, with their twin five-year-old daughters, Hava and Miriam, went to live with her sister. Several days later some German officers were assigned billets in the sister's house, among them Lieutenant Roman Erich Petsche.

On April 15th, learning that the city's remaining Jews were to be deported the next day, Petsche resolved to help his hosts. Aware that fast action was necessary, he immediately took the twins and their nursemaid to a convent in Budapest, 100 miles away, where he knew they would be safe, then returned to Novi Sad. He also made arrangements for Mrs. Tibor and her sister who were to be deported that same night, instructing them to jump off the deportation train as it slowed down for a switch not far from Vienna, then continue on foot to his house, where his wife was expecting them. After they left he took Mrs. Tibor's mother to hospital and thereafter visited her regularly to make sure she was all right.

Mrs. Tibor and her sister, afraid to jump from the train, ended up in Auschwitz, where Mrs. Tibor died. Her sister, however, survived, and after the war returned to Budapest for the twins. The three of them now live in Israel and remain in close contact with Roman Petsche. (2265)

Oskar Schindler

Oskar Schindler was an ethnic German born in Zwittau, Moravia (now Svitavy, Czechoslovakia), which as part of the Sudetenland was annexed by the Third Reich in October 1938. Toward the end of 1939 he arrived in Cracow and took over an enamelware factory and wholesale distributorship, situated in Zablocie, just outside the city, that had belonged to Jews before the German conquest of Poland the previous September.

Under Schindler's management, the enamelware firm manufactured pots and pans for the German army. Before long it had 900 employees, most of them Jews. In April 1943, when the Nazis liquidated the Cracow ghetto, transferring 6,000 able-bodied workers to the nearby Plaszów labor camp, Schindler persuaded the Armaments Administration to let him set up a branch camp on the factory grounds, arguing that this would increase productivity since the workers would not have to go back and forth to Plaszów each day. His real purpose, however, was to protect them from the exceedingly harsh conditions there.

As the Red Army moved into Poland, the Germans began relocating vital industries to safer areas. In October 1944, Schindler persuaded higher authorities to reestablish his now-defunct enamel plant in the Moravian town of Brünnlitz and transform it into a munitions plant, producing shell casings for the German army. In an operation unique in the annals of the Holocaust, he managed to take along virtually his entire Jewish labor force, many of whom were in fact too weak, ill, or old to be counted as productive workers and would have been killed if left behind. Close to 800 men were transferred to Brünnlitz by way of the Gross-Rosen concentration camp, while some 300 women were sent there via Auschwitz.

In Brünnlitz, as in Zablocie, Schindler treated his 1,100 Jews considerately and did everything he could to obtain adequate supplies of food and medicine for them. That winter, when he learned that a train from the Golszów concentration camp had been abandoned at nearby Zwittau, its cargo of Jews left to die in the bitter cold, he went there with some of his workers, broke open the locked doors of the ice-covered boxcars, and rescued the 100 skeletal men and women who were still alive. Under the supervision of his wife, Emilie, the survivors were nursed back to health. Those who died were buried in accordance with Jewish rites.

Oskar Schindler was always thoughtful and humane in his dealings with Jews, and thanks to his efforts most of the workers at his factories survived. One of them later wrote: "He was the first German since the beginning of the war whose presence did not terrify me."

What is most remarkable in this story is that Schindler, by his own admission, went to Poland only to enrich himself, hoping to exploit the cheap Jewish labor available there under Nazi rule. To the Jews who met him in Cracow in 1939, he seemed no different from any other German. Yet somehow he underwent a personal transformation, and in the end, undeterred even though several times arrested by the Gestapo, he rescued more Jews than any other German on record.

According to Schindler, his metamorphosis was sparked by the shocking immensity of the Final Solution. In his words: "I hated the brutality, the sadism, and the insanity of Nazism. I just couldn't stand by and see people destroyed. I did what I could, what I had to do, what my conscience told me I must do. That's all there is to it. Really, nothing more."

Nothing indeed! All told, 1,200 Jews owe their lives to this singular man. (20)

Imgard Wieth

Until June 1941, when Germany invaded the Soviet Union, Josef Podoszyn was the manager of the largest pharmacy in the East Galician city of Lwow. After the German conquest he was demoted to sales clerk. One day, toward the end of the year, he overheard another employee tell a woman customer that he could not sell her the medication she had asked for unless she brought in a proper prescription. Podoszyn waited for him to become busy with something else, then edged over and gave the woman the medicine she wanted. The woman returned several times thereafter, and Podoszyn always filled her orders without making undue inquiries.

The woman's name was Imgard Wieth, and she was a secretary from Germany working for the occupation administration. Initially she had no idea that Podoszyn was Jewish. When he was transferred to a pharmacy in the ghetto, however, she went to see him there. The S.S. had by this time begun rounding up the ghetto's residents for deportation to concentration camps, and she told him he could use her apartment if he ever needed someplace to hide.

Podoszyn responded by asking Wieth whether she would be willing instead to take in his wife, who at that moment was hiding in the cellar of the pharmacy. She replied that she would be more than willing, since now the thirteen-year-old Jewish girl who was already living with her would have a companion. She gave him her address and the next day returned for his wife.

Before the war, in his professional capacity, Podoszyn had become acquainted with priests of the Catholic Uniate Church and in fact had trained one of them in pharmacology. In May 1943, when the final liquidation of the Lvov ghetto began, he approached them for help.

His first request, that they hide his son, was immediately granted. The second, that they arrange for him to join a partisan band, was more complicated. The priests knew that many of the partisans were antisemites who would kill Podoszyn or any other Jew who turned up in their midst. They told him it would take a little while to make arrangements and procrastinated whenever he asked what progress they were making.

Meanwhile, Podoszyn joined his wife, thirteen-year-old Lily, and Cecilia Stern, Lily's mother, in Imgard Wieth's apartment. Imgard had first met Cecilia while she was working for the Germans as a tailor. When Cecilia's husband and son were killed, Imgard took Lily in, but for the time being Cecilia stayed in the ghetto with her aged parents. She moved in with the others after her father was shot by the Germans and her mother committed suicide.

Imgard Wieth's apartment was located in a prestigious building reserved for high-ranking officials, among them the commander of the Ukrainian militia and an S.S. officer who took a liking to Imgard and was in the habit of popping in unexpectedly to see her.

His surprise visits were a continuous nightmare for Imgard and the others, as was the fear of detection from other causes. Since Imgard lived alone, her Jewish boarders had to be careful not to make the slightest sound when she was at work. They could not walk around, use the faucets, or flush the toilet.

At times the tension was so great that Imgard seemed on the verge of a nervous collapse. At such moments, screaming that she couldn't take it any more, she would threaten to jump off the balcony. But whenever Cecilia suggested that it might be best for her and the others to leave, Imgard would pull herself together and refuse to let them go.

A year passed, and in May 1944, with the Red Army drawing closer to Lwow, it became evident that Imgard, along with the administration's other civilian personnel, would soon be evacuated. Since a new refuge would be needed from the time of her departure until the arrival of the Russians, Podoszyn got in touch with his priest friends, and they hid him, his wife, Cecilia, and Lily in a church until the Russians liberated the city.

After the war, Imgard Wieth emigrated to the United States. On her way there she stopped over in London to visit with Cecilia, who was now living in England.

Cecilia's Yad Vashem deposition says, in part: "Mrs. Wieth is so good and decent a person that today, whenever we attempt to express our gratitude to her, she recoils, claiming that what she did was not heroism, but only discharging her duty to others." (403)

Armin T. Wegner

Armin T. Wegner was an author of some repute in Germany. On Easter Monday of 1933, shortly after the first anti-Jewish boycott by the Nazi regime, he penned the following open letter to the chancellor of the new Germany, Adolf Hitler:

> *Herr Reichskanzler!* On March 29 of this year, you announced that the government was imposing a boycott on all shops owned by Jewish citizens. Offensive inscriptions such as "Cheats!" "Don't buy here!" and "Death to the Jews!" appeared on store windows. Men armed with clubs blocked the entrances to shops, and the capital was transformed into an entertainment arena for the masses. Then, once this odious regulation had made its impression on the public, the boycott was lifted and the streets presented their usual appearance. But is not that which followed

even worse? Jewish judges, prosecutors, and physicians are being forced
out of the posts they so justly earned, their sons and daughters expelled
from school and university professors ejected from their chairs and sent
on vacation (a ruse not fooling anyone); stage managers, actors, and
singers are deprived of their careers; publishers, of their newspapers. .
. . Thus the Jew is being attacked, not necessarily in his profession, but
in the area which is his most noble contribution to society—his spirit.

Herr Reichskanzler, you say that the German people has been
slandered, that its neighbors have accused it of ignoble acts of which it
was innocent; but are not error and calumny the precursors of ability and
glory? Of all peoples, is it not the Jews who taught us to proudly endure
such defamation? It is not by coincidence that so many Jews live on
German soil—but the result of a common fate. Through its wanderings
over the centuries, this unfortunate but great people—driven out of Spain
and denied admission by France—was given shelter for one thousand
years by Germany. The Jew followed an inner call that drew him there,
where life was secure, where the highest erudition attracted his intellect,
so eager to be instructed. Germany, similarly, divided and finding itself
struggling against many enemies, lent an ear to freedom's call and offered
a place of refuge to this hunted people. Is the deed of a thousand years
to be extinguished forever?

We have always given our very best to other people. . . . The German,
an eternal wanderer on the earth, whose emerging homeland claimed but
few colonies, knew that his most important mission would be fulfilled in
the world at large; German bridge builders, merchants, and settlers
added to the wealth and reputation of all the peoples. Have we not been
slandered for these merits in the years before the World War and up to
the present hour? Having only too frequently suffered such wrongs, do
we have the right to inflict the same suffering on someone else who
deserves it just as little as we? Fairness is the crowning virtue, and the
fact that Germany became great in the world is due in part to the
achievements of its Jews. Have they not always shown their gratitude for
the shelter we have given them? Remember, it was Albert Einstein, a
German Jew, a man who shook the concept of space (like Copernicus),
who reached up into the universe and presented the earth with a new
image of the world. Do you remember Emil Rathenau, another German
Jew, who transformed the Allgemeine Gesellschaft into an international
concern? It was Haber, a Jew, who like a magician separated nitrogen
from air in his piston bottle; Ehrlich, a Jew and a wise physician, who with
the help of an anti-syphilis drug, exorcised this lingering disease from our
people. . . . Do you remember? I would have to fill many pages in order
to list the names of all the people whose hard work and wisdom will be
recorded in our history forever. I ask you: Did all these men and women
act in their capacity as Jews or as Germans? Are their writers and poets
part of Jewish or German intellectual history? Have their actors cultivated the German language or a foreign one? . . . We have accepted the
sacrifice of 12,000 Jewish men who fell in the war. In all fairness, have
we any right to rob their parents, their sons, brothers, and grandchildren,
their wives and sisters, of what they earned in the course of many
generations, the right to a homeland and a hearth? . . . Has not the Jew,

whose introverted and brooding character makes him so similar to us, carried the German language and way of life as far as the heart of Russia? Even today, songs in medieval German can be heard on the Jewish streets of Polish villages. The ancestors of the expelled Jews took with them not the gold of these countries but songs that even today still move us when we hear them sung by the Jew, songs that we ourselves neglected and forgot. If a German in a foreign country needs help and looks for someone who speaks his language, where does he find that help? In the shop of a Jewish pharmacist in the Caucasus, in a Jewish tailor's workshop near an Arabian oasis. Jewish families were robbed in Poland and thrown into prison because they remained loyal to Germany, and now, after fleeing to Germany, they are subjected to the very same fate. What unrequited love! Surely you do not believe that belonging to a foreign people makes the Jews incapable of loving our country. Are not many tribes intermixed with the German people—Franks, Frisians, Wends? Was not Napoleon born in Corsica? Are not you yourself from a neighboring country? . . . If you had only seen, together with me, the tears shed by Jewish mothers, the troubled, pale faces of Jewish fathers, the eyes of the children, you would understand the fervent love that can be felt only by generations of people who have been wandering without rest for many centuries. For them, the soil is a stronger link than for those who have never lost it. "I love Germany," that is what I heard the other day from a daughter and a son whose parents, worried about the continuous threats, intended to leave the country for good. "Go alone," they told their parents. "We prefer to die here, for we cannot be happy in a foreign land." Is not such powerful feeling to be admired?

Herr Reichskanzler, this question does not concern our Jewish brothers alone; it concerns the German people. In the name of the people, whom I have not only the right to represent but the obligation to raise my voice in their behalf, like everyone who has been formed through its blood—as a German whose heart is contracted with indignation—I turn to you. Order a stoppage to all this! Judaism has survived the bondage of Egypt, the Spanish Inquisition, the suffering of the Crusades, and sixteen hundred pogroms in Russia. The Jews will survive this threat too, thanks to the toughness that has matured them as a people. But the shame and misfortune that have befallen Germany will be remembered for a long time to come. Who will one day be hurt by the blow now aimed at the Jews? Only we ourselves. Just as the Jews have adopted German ways and increased our wealth, their destruction must necessarily bring about the destruction of German property. History teaches us that the countries that expelled the Jews were made to suffer poverty; they became miserable and despised. . . . A hundred years after Goethe and Lessing we are returning to the most cruel suffering of all times, to blind superstition. . . .

And what will be the inevitable outcome of all this? In place of the moral principle of justice we find [the highest value] in membership in a tribe. . . . Today the most incompetent and amoral person may say: "I am qualified to hold this office simply because I am not a Jew; being a German is enough. I can even get away with doing evil, because I am German." . . . As the distinctions between good and evil are eliminated, we must ask ourselves, what will become of the unity of our people? You will reply: "Our German blood will not let us do anything dishonorable." Certainly, decency and our heritage oblige, but I feel that we are much more obligated to fight for the Jew than against him. It may be true that there are not many heros of the sword among the Jews compared with our own warriors. But they have produced many wise men, martyrs, and holy men. Even the saviors of this awakened [German] people must admit that they cannot do without righteous persons, just as they equally need this [Jewish] people whose voice has never been silenced as they perpetuated an age-old prophecy and the highest moral law. I ask: why are these curious strangers in the world so persecuted and hated? It is because this people has placed law and justice above everything else, because it has always loved and honored the law like a bride, and because those who pursue evil detest nothing more than this people which demands justice.

Herr Reichskanzler! Neither nations nor peoples know each other well, and that is their most serious shortcoming. Have the Germans ever made an effort to observe something which they have shunned since their childhood and regarded as unclean, a prejudice affecting even some Jews who have become ashamed of their admirable heritage. . . . You turn to the Almighty in your speeches. Is it not that same Almighty who has mixed the dispersed members of this people among the Germans like salt in the dough? Do we not need them in the social and moral spheres, for their way of judging helps us to distinguish the weaknesses as well as the good qualities in our own character? You refer to the fact that Germany is in an emergency situation, but instead of dealing with the problems affecting all the oppressed, the misfortunes of one part of the populace are mollified by inflicting misfortune on another part. It is even admitted that Jewish guilt is necessary for the salvation of the homeland. However, a homeland without justice cannot exist. . . . A mighty nation degrades itself by abandoning helpless people to the hatred of the frustrated masses. You say that the Jew arouses animosity because of his insolence. Is this quite so without our doing? Indignant because they are treated unfairly, the Jews take up revolutionary ideas. Have we not offended them since their childhood, and does not every common fate result in common justice as well as common guilt? I protest against the foolish belief that Jews are responsible for all of the world's misfortunes. I protest on the ground of the proof of centuries, and if I turn to you with these words, I do so because I do not know any other way to make my voice heard. I am turning to you not as a friend of the Jews but as a friend of the German people, as a descendant of a Prussian family which can trace its roots back to the days of the crusaders; it is because I love my own people that I turn to you. Even if everyone remains silent in this hour, I do not want to keep silent in the face of the dangers threatening Germany because of that silence.

The opinion of the masses waxes and wanes only too easily. It condemns one day what it strenuously upheld the previous day. Even if a long time passes, the hour of deliverance from torture will arrive, and so will the hour of punishment for the culprits. The day will come when the memory of April 1st of this year will elicit pangs of shameful remorse in the minds of all Germans after they have judged their actions in their hearts. . . .

Herr Reichskanzler, from the depth of a tormented heart I turn to you with words that are not only my words but express the voice of fate, which exhorts you, through me, to protect Germany by protecting the Jews. Do not permit those who fight alongside you to mislead you. They give you bad advice. Consult your own conscience, as you did when you started your lonely struggle upon your return from the war in a world that was in turmoil. It has always been the privilege of great men to admit having erred. The masses are in need of a visible act. Lead back to their offices the men who have been cast out, the physicians to their hospitals, the judges to their courts. Do not keep the schools closed to their children, heal the troubled hearts of the mothers and all the people will thank you. For even if Germany may be able to do without the Jews, it cannot do without its honor and virtue!

Immanuel Kant wisely admonishes you from his hundred-year-old grave: "There is only one true faith, even if there are many denominations." Follow this teaching; it will help you to understand those against whom you fight today. What would Germany be today without truth, beauty, and justice. True, once the cities have been destroyed, the generations bled to death, after the teaching of tolerance has been silenced forever, the mountains of our homeland will still point to the sky in defiance and the eternal forest will still rustle in the wind—but they will no longer stand for freedom and justice as our fathers practiced them. With shame and revulsion, they will relate the story of the generation that not merely thoughtlessly gambled away our country's fortune but also disgraced its name forever. We ask for dignity when we demand justice. I beseech thee: maintain the noble-mindedness, the pride, the conscience that we need in order to exist. Preserve the dignity of the German people.

Since no newspaper would have been willing to print this letter, Wegner mailed it to the Brown House in Munich, the headquarters of the Nazi Party, with a request that it be forwarded to Hitler. In due course he received a letter of acknowledgment from Martin Bormann. Soon thereafter he was arrested and taken to the Columbia House prison, where he was gagged, thrown on a table, and beaten until he lost consciousness, while the Nazi officer in charge gloated, "Now you won't write anything against us!" Wegner ended up in a concentration camp but managed to escape while on a furlough and made his way across the border. He has never returned to Germany.

Armin Wegner did not save anyone during the Holocaust, but he spoke out against the Nazi regime's antisemitism long before the rest of the world had come to understand its implications. In recognition of his courage, Yad Vashem, in 1967, added his name to the roll of the Righteous Among the Nations. (306)

Armin Wegner, who wrote an open letter to Hitler protesting the persecution of Jews (1986). Courtesy of Yad Vashem.

Poland

The Historical Setting

When Germany invaded Poland on September 1, 1939, launching World War II, the Polish people hardly knew what the Nazi leadership had in store for them. According to General Plan East, the Nazi grand design for the solution of Germany's so-called lack of space (*lebensraum* in German historiography), the whole of Polish territory was gradually to be cleared of its native population for colonization by German ethnic populations and eventually incorporated into the Greater German Reich. Considered as an inferior race (as other Slav nations), the fiercely nationalistic Poles in their considerable majority (some 80-85 percent of the population), after a careful sorting of those elements within it considered capable of being "re-Germanized" on strictly racist lines, would have to abandon their ancestral home and be removed to distant Siberia. The several million remaining Poles, reduced to the status of helots, would be expected to obediently serve their new masters.

The transformation of Poland into a German province was to be carried out over a short period of twenty-five or thirty years. Hence, no mercy was to be shown to this population, no temporary alliances formed with collaborationist elements (as in other, even Slavic, occupied territories), no rudimentary forms of autonomy to be tolerated. "It is clear as daylight that the Vistula [Poland's main river] country will be as German as the Rhineland," Hans Frank, the Nazi military governor, triumphantly gloated in his diary.[1]

1. For sources of quotations in this introduction, please refer to "Suggestions for Further Reading, Poland," pp. 382.

To guarantee the success of this vast despoliation, the intelligentsia was to be liquidated. "It sounds cruel," Hitler reportedly told Hans Frank, "but such is the law of life." "The whole of the Government General [the name given to occupied Poland, with the exception of the western provinces, which were immediately annexed to Germany] was simply to be treated as a concentraiton camp," Hans Frank noted in his diary. "The only people who would be allowed any freedom of movement would be the guards."

Through restrictions on marriages, lowering of sanitary conditions, a severe reduction of rations (half of what German nationals were entitled to), and the removal of hundreds of thousands of able-bodied men for labor in Germany, a biological campaign was carried out to bring about a sharp reduction of the population. Polish children in institutions and orphanages in the annexed territories who were considered racially akin to Germans were forcibly abducted and removed to Germany for "re-Germanization" (250,000 children, according to some figures), for the "lost blood" of previous generations had to be salvaged and restored to its original heirs. Polish families, claiming Germanic ancestry were reclassified as ethnic Germans ("Volksdeutsche") and accorded preferential treatment. In the annexed provinces, the Polish language was banned from use in all public offices, and Polish towns were given Germanic names (such as Lodz, renamed Litzmannstadt). Universities and secondary schools were closed, and cultural activities were severely hampered. In the eastern Zamosc region, some 110,000 Poles were evacuated from villages and replaced with 25,000 German colonists.

This premeditated and constant harassment of the Polish population led to an unremitting reign of terror, which stands out as exceptionally ruthless and severe by contrast to other occupied countries, and which lasted for the full duration of the occupation. Individual arrests were conducted on a massive scale, and street roundups for labor in Germany became a common, frightening reality. The Germans reserved the right to impose the death penalty for even minor infractions (such as removing German posters), and any German could shoot any Pole with impunity, and for almost no reason. With the exception of the Jewish population, the Poles suffered more losses of life than the people of any other Nazi-occupied country. It is estimated that close to two million Poles lost their lives during the war years and over a million were consigned to forced labor in Germany.

Given all this pervasive cruelty, a wide gulf, nevertheless, separated the sufferings of the Poles from Jews. As told to Polish underground commander Jan Karski by Jewish leaders at the height of the Holocaust: "After the war Poland will be resurrected. Your cities will be rebuilt and your wounds will slowly heal. From this ocean of tears, pain, rage, and humiliation your country will emerge again, but the Polish Jews will no longer exist. . . . The Jewish people will be murdered."

* * *

The country slated for destruction by the fiercely antisemitic Nazi German state, by a tragic twist of history, also contained the largest concentration of Jews on the European continent—some 3,250,000 Jews, a tenth of the population. Although present on Polish soil since the early Middle Ages, they were, at the dawn of the twentieth century, still by far a nonassimilable community. Apart from the language barrier (most Jews still claimed Yiddish as their native tongue), Jews stood out from the general population in dress, habits, names and surnames, and nonverbal language, such as gestures, facial expressions, and mannerisms—but mostly in the very different religious practice of Judaism in a country considering itself profoundly Catholic. All these factors, coupled with the concentration of Jews in the larger cities (where they constituted between one-third and one-fourth of the total population) and a no less significant presence in smaller ones, contributed to make most Jews easily recognizable, and frankly resented by the majority of Poles.

Again, by an additional historical paradox, the Polish Jews, accused by antisemites of secretly hoarding wealth for dishonorable purposes, were actually the poorest of all Jewish continental communities, and many were literally subsisting below the poverty level. This process was accelerated in the 1930s by government economic measures (aimed at transferring most enterprises into Polish hands) which amounted to economic strangulation of broad sections of the Jewish population, and was also exacerbated by other discriminatory measures, such as the restriction of Jewish students in universities (the infamous "numerus clausus"), random violence on streets and schools, and open adulation of Nazi anti-Jewish measures across the border. The powerful Catholic Church failed to take a stand against the official antisemitic policies of the ruling class (some even condoned it, accusing the Jews, as in Cardinal Hlond's 1936 pastoral letter, of corroding the morals of the youth).

Most Jews saw no future for themselves in Poland and wished to emigrate. The Polish government, seeing in the Jews a surplus population, strongly supported these aspirations, going so as as to petition the League of Nations to place colonies under a Polish mandate so as to enable Poland to settle its Jews there. Thus, the general wish of the majority of Poles to see the country cleared of most Jews tragically coincided with what the Nazis had in store for Polish Jews, as well as those of other conquered European nations.

In the Nazi world, there was to be no place for Jews, not even for dehumanized and enslaved Jews. For reasons not yet fully explainable, Poland was chosen as the main killing site (most serious authorities point out the linkage of geographical feasibility, Jewish population figures, and local anti-Jewish sentiments as the configuration which helped mold the Nazi decision), as the slaughterhouse of millions of Jews (and other nationals); of those inhabiting the country and others who would be transported there by train. Thus the Polish countryside was dotted by an array of death camps whose names (such as Auschwitz, Treblinka, Belzec, Majdanek, Chelmno) will forever remain indelible stains on the human record. There the practice of death was developed into a science and sank to unfathomable depths of depravity, as millions were done to death in various gruesome forms, with gassing eventually becoming the main killing device.

The killing operation went through several stages. At first, the Nazis experimented with various repressive measures—random mass shootings and hard physical labor—causing death to thousands. But this was only a temporary expedient. More rational and "scientific" methods were in store for the hapless trapped Jews. They were expelled from smaller locations and herded into ghettos, where they were restricted to an area which before the war supported only a fraction of the population now inhabiting it. This was coupled with a severe lack of sanitary conditions and starvation-level rations (half of what the underfed Polish population was allotted) causing large-scale deaths inside the ghettos (tens of thousands in the Warsaw ghetto alone). Then, starting mid-1941, coinciding with the invasion of Russia, special liquidation units, known as *Einsatzgruppen*, practiced wholesale murder in the newly conquered territories, killing hundreds of thousands.

When this proved ineffective (not enough were being killed), the Nazi hierarchy decided that the principal method of death would henceforth be gassing, in especially constructed sites, and almost all of them on Polish soil. A special government-sponsored conference was convened in January 1942 in Berlin (known as the Wannsee Conference) to coordinate this vast official killing operation, comprising all European conquered Jewish communities. All Jews were to be transported in cattle cars to death camps in Poland, where, save for able-bodied persons, they would immediately be gassed. Those capable of performing heavy labor would be done to death gradually, as a result of brutal treatment and exhaustion. In all such camps, crematoria and other forms of incineration were to take care of the quick disposal of bodies, thereby also preventing the outbreak of infectious diseases (always the bane of Nazi fears).

Following this master plan, close to four million Jews saw the last light of day on Polish soil, comprising whole communities from as far as Holland, Belgium, and France in the west; Norway in the north; and Italy, Yugoslavia, and Greece (even the island of Rhodes, off the Turkish mainland) in the south. The vast majority of Polish Jewry, close to three million men, women, and children, were trapped in this vast inferno and perished in the conflagration.

All this took place within view of the local population, who could not help but watch the constant movement of trains and hear the desperate cries of their harried occupants as the cars inched their way slowly toward the death camps; nor could they avoid witnessing the incessant smoke billlowing out of crematoria furnaces and the concomitant stench of human flesh, nor the occasional massacres on the streets and near open ditches in the countryside. Horrid tales of mass killings would also be confirmed to them by their own kinfolk, imprisoned in many of these notorious camps, for various offenses, who as camp inmates were treated harshly, but less so than the Jewish ones, and were able to communicate with the outside world.

* * *

How would the Polish population react to the massive slaughter of the Jews in their midst—in their own backyard? This question is especially crucial in light of the unenviably difficult situation Jews found themselves at the height of the killings. They were physically trapped, with all escape valves tightly shut. Surrounding Poland were territories under the control of German and S.S. troops or collaborationist paramilitary units (Lithuanian, Latvian, and Ukrainian). Facing them inside Poland was an immense array of German military and security forces (including S.S., Gestapo, Kripo, S.D., Schutzpolizei), of a magnitude not known in other occupied countries. On the local scene, the Polish police, willy-nilly, became accomplices in this giant murder conspiracy.

Shorn of outside aid, fearing resistance would only aggravate an already impossible situation and definitely doom them, the Jews had no other recourse than to turn for guidance to their own German-appointed leaders. These, cowed into submission by the Nazis, and having nothing practical to suggest, counseled patience and strict obedience, in the hope that the murderous appetite of the Nazis would eventually slacken and thus a remnant would be saved (this, for instance, was the gist of Haim Rumkowski's position, head of the Lodz ghetto).

When the 50,000 remnants of the once close to 500,000 Jews of the Warsaw ghetto rose in rebellion in April 1943, it was not meant to be a rescue operation but simply a last desperate effort to go down fighting and thus save the honor of the condemned Jews. If any Jews were to survive this unprecedented crime in the annals of history in order to tell the world of what their eyes had beheld, this would be the result of either sheer luck (survival in the camps) or of enduring the occupation through help by the non-Jewish population, itself suffering from the lashes of the Nazi whip, but not threatened with immediate destruction. Thus, survival for many Jews was a function of the attitude of the local population. How would the people of Poland react to the plight of the Jews, and how would they respond to the tearful pleadings for aid by an ethnic group which was being swiftly decimated, and would soon disappear for good from the Polish landscape?

The weight of evidence from eyewitness accounts and documentary material, it must be said in full candor, points to a widespread antisemitism that militated against a serious attempt to render succor to the afflicted Jews—difficult as such undertakings would have been in light of the Nazi terror machine which operated with a special brutality against the Polish population. In many quarters, there was even sort of an eerie satisfaction that the Jewish Question in Poland (an irritating 10 percent of the population) was at long last being solved for the good of the country, coupled with a revulsion among some at the methods used to achieve this end.

The opinion that the Poles only stood to profit from the disappearance of the Jews was, however, commonplace. All the blame for this sordid deed would, for good measure, fall squarely on the shoulders of the German nation. This feeling—relief at the disappearance of the Jews coupled with revulsion at the methods employed—may be said to have been quite widespread, other than for those elements who openly gloated over the tragic demise of the Jews (and even participated in the killings) and the few others, at the other end of the spectrum, who risked their lives to save Jews from certain death and to whom this study is dedicated. To overlook or minimize the antisemitism in Poland, one would have to close one's eyes to the welter of data from many sources (even non-Jewish), evidence which no serious historian would dare ignore with impunity.

Antisemitism in Poland had already reached high proportions in the immediate years before the war (although Jews enjoyed unprecedented liberties during the Middle Ages, at a time when their brethren suffered persecution in the rest of Europe). This antisemitism played into the hands of the Nazis, who needed, if not the outright cooperation, then at least the silent acquiescence of the conquered populations if their genocidal plans were to succeed.

It is interesting that Emmanuel Ringelblum, the noted Polish-Jewish historian (whose authority is also lauded by non-Jewish Polish historians), castigated Polish society for its antisemitism; he labeled the Poland of the prewar years "the leading anti-Semitic country in Europe, second to Germany alone." He condemned the Polish police for playing "a most lamentable role in the extermination of the Jews of Poland," and for being "enthusiastic executors of all the German directives regarding the Jews." Ringelblum wrote these words in a major study he was preparing on Polish-Jewish relations, from his hiding place in Warsaw. Ringelblum lamented the antisemitism of the non-Jewish population and their satisfaction "that Warsaw had in the end become *judenrein*."

Ringelblum's gloomy analysis of the anti-Jewish sentiment in Poland is borne out by numerous testimonies of survivors, even of those whose lives were saved through the courageous help of non-Jews. As stated by the historian Hersztein, "the historical account must conform to the documents, not the other way around." Testimonies by survivors, even of those who survived thanks to the aid of benevolent persons, are replete with accounts of unfriendliness shown toward Jews, which in many cases took violent form.

This prevalence of a deeply ingrained dislike of Jews, coupled with the severe economic conditions of the German occupation, created a new profession in the large cities, unknown elsewhere on the conquered continent. These were the professional blackmailers, better known as "schmaltzovniks" (literally "fat fleecers"), who tried to entrap Jews. In league with German and Polish police agents, these included smugglers, speculators, criminal underworld types, but also ideological and otherwise enthusiastic antisemites who did this work for its own sake and not for reward. Roaming the streets in broad daylight, frequenting public squares, cafes, restaurants, railroad stations, and invading private dwellings with impunity, they were at liberty to stop anyone suspected of being Jewish (by his demeanor, appearance, furtive look and hesitating walk, to mention only a few of discerning charateristics in this despicable profession).

Insofar as males were concerned, a quick check of their private parts would indicate whether the man was circumcised or not. If he was, there could be no doubt that the man was Jewish. For women more subtle tactics were used (such as kangaroo court interrogations on the finer points of the religious practices of the Catholic religion with which most Jews were unfamiliar). Then both men and women were offered the choice of either buying their lives in return for stupendous sums or being taken to the nearest police station.

Ringelblum terms these gangs "an endless nightmare" to the Jews on the Aryan side (the term generally used for the area of habitation outside the ghetto, forbidden to Jews on the pain of death). The evidence shows that there was hardly a Jew in hiding who did not have an encounter with them at least once, and who did not have to buy himself free for a sum of money. They brought disaster to thousands of Jews who had succeeded in eluding the Nazis. Numerous eyewitness accounts from other survivors (even of rescuers whose lives was made doubly dangerous and miserable from fear of blackmailers from among their own kinsmen) only tend to confirm this shameful phenomenon for which there was no parallel (to such an extent) in any other Nazi-occupied country.

The plague of the blackmailers was so widespread that the Polish underground felt it necessary to begrudgingly take measures, if not to fully eradicate it, at least to contain it. In practice, only a few informers were actually punished. The few steps taken in this direction bore absolutely no proportion to the magnitude of the crimes committed by the Nazis and, hence, had little effect in reducing the blackmailing plague, which continued festering undiminished till the last days of the occupation.

* * *

This lack of enthusiasm for helping Jews can also be applied to the powerful Polish underground movement. It was indeed the largest of its kind in Nazi-occupied Europe, with the participation of the broad masses of the people. Of all the occupied countries, Poland did not produce anything remotely resembling a pro-German collaborationist movement, as German intentions regarding the country's future left no room for any form of cooperation. The underground rose to count some 380,000 men in its ranks, and was involved in various clandestine military operations throughout the country, culminating in the heroic 1944 Warsaw uprising, surpressed by the Germans after a heavy two-month fighting period which left the city literally in ruins.

The Armja Krajowa ("Home Army"), the predominant umbrella organization in the underground, looked askance at Jews wishing to join its ranks unless, of course, if the Jewishnesss of the combatant could remain hidden from the rank and file. Quite shocking are the stories of partisan sorties against Jews hiding in the forests, openly ordered to do so by underground heads. Many Jews, including men and women of all ages, were mercilessly hunted down and systematically slain—by Polish partisans, with local peasants sometimes joining the fray—again, a phenomenon without any parallel in other occupied countries, save for Ukraine and Lithuania.

As the war drew nearer to a close, fiercely antisemitic units within the underground (such as the NSZ), openly launched killing raids against the remaining Jews. This killing frenzy lasted till the last days of the war and extended even beyond it. In the immediate postwar months, all over Poland, there were secret murders of Jews who had been saved as well as Jews who had come back from the camps and from partisan units, including women and children. Thus the Holocaust of Polish Jewry did little to stem a centuries-inbred antisemitism by many segments of the population.

A measure of this ongoing antisemitism may be garnered by the behavior of the population in the postwar period. Blaming the Jews for the communist takeover of Poland, restless at the thought of surviving Jews returning to reclaim their homes, presently occupied by others, and generally unhappy at seeing even a fraction of the Jews still alive and ready to start new lives, many Poles took matters into their own hands. In no other country were Jews killed after the eviction of the Germans by roaming armed bands, some of them affiliated with the underground; and pogroms were staged in several cities, the most infamous taking place in Kielce in 1946.

Fearing for their lives, most Jews who had survived the Holocaust by the skin of their teeth now fled the country for friendlier skies elsewhere. The Polish government tried to stem the antisemitic avalanche, but it proved unequal to the task. The new communist regime finally brought things under control. Then, in 1968, the same regime launched a renewed antisemitic drive (again, unique in Europe), causing a stampede of the remaining Polish Jews, some 80,000, to across the border. Today, there are only vestiges, dying embers, of a Jewish community in Poland—only recently the vanguard of Jewish cultural and religious life.

* * *

Under the impossible conditions in which Jews found themselves in Nazi-occupied Poland, help by non-Jews was an inescapable precondition for any Jew hoping to survive the Holocaust. The most common form was providing shelter in the rescuer's home. For the Jewish person on the run, help meant escape from certain death; for the rescuer, the risk of apprehension through betrayal and Nazi-style punishment for an infraction that was parallel to a capital offense. How so?

The occupation authorities threatened with death any person who obstructed Nazi designs to destroy the Jews. This dire punishment was not only written in the law and known to studious attorneys but made public by posters on bulletin boards in all major cities. Any Pole caught hiding a Jew could be shot on the spot. If lucky, he would be dispatched to a concentration camp. The murder of Polish inhabitants by the Nazis was common even for lesser infractions, let alone for rendering assistance to Jews. As early as October 15, 1941, Governor General Hans Frank published an ordinance which under paragraph 4b1 stated: "Jews who, without permission leave the district to which they have been confined are subject to punishment by death. Persons who deliberately offer a hiding place to such Jews are also subject to this punishment." On November 10, 1941 the death penalty was enlarged to apply to those who help Jews "in any way: by taking them in for a night, giving them a lift in a vehicle of any sort."

These stern admonitions were repeated throughout all major cities in occupied Poland and worded in three languages (German, Polish, and Russian). That the minutest form of aid was also to be withheld was made clear by Dr. Boettcher, the German police chief of the Radom district, who exacted the death penalty to anyone "who feed[s] the runaway Jews or sell[s] them foodstuffs, even if they do not offer them shelter." Similar threats were issued by other district governors.

Those caught violating these admonitions were either shot on the spot (usually in outlying farms or smaller towns and villages) or haled before military tribunals for quick sentencing. "Sentences will be imposed by special court in Warsaw," Dr. Fischer warned the residents of Warsaw in late 1941. "I forcefully drawn the attention of the entire population of the Warsaw district to this decree, as henceforth it will be applied with utmost severity."

Death could also come less ceremoniously, by hanging on the nearest pole or by setting fire to the farm and burning the residents. At times, the Nazis buried the bodies of those shot for aiding Jews in unconsecrated ground: in the open field, woods, or in Jewish cemeteries, which to Catholic Poles was viewed as a sign of disrespect to the martyred victim. Those fortunate enough to escape the firing squad were dispatched to concentration camps for "special treatment." In no other occupied country was aid to Jews punished with such severity as in Poland.

The threat facing would-be rescuers, however, also came from the direction of the local population. There were not a few Poles who exerted pressure on rescuers to expel their Jewish wards. These coercions came not only from strangers, but also from next-door neighbors and members of the rescuer's family, who were infuriated at the rescuer for risking the lives of his family, of neighbors, and the local community (who could suffer retribution at the hands of the Germans), all for the sake of the "despised" Jews. Many are the stories of rescuers who, under intense pressure, felt constrained to suddenly let their Jews go (in some cases only momentarily, until the pressure had somehow abated), or hurriedly made alternative arrangements for their wards to be hidden elsewhere. Not a few rescuers suffered violence after the war at the hands of their own kinsmen, when through indiscretion the story of their courageous deeds became known; others hurriedly moved to new locations to escape the wrath of their infuriated neighbors.

Thus, Polish rescuers had to overcome greater pressures and fears than their counterparts in other occupied countries, especially in Western Europe. In Ringelblum's own case, a bunker was prepared where he and many other Jews lived in daily fear for a nine-month period, and were cared by Mieczyslaw Wolski and his family, including the family's matron, Malgorzata. The hiding place was, unfortunately, betrayed to the Gestapo on March 7, 1944, and all thirty-four residents were put to death, in addition to the rescuers Mieczyslaw Wolski and his nephew Janusz Wysocki.

The threats faced by would-be rescuers, both from the Germans and blackmailers alike, make us place Polish rescuers of Jews in a special category, for they exemplified a courage, fortiude, and lofty humanitarianism unequaled in other occupied countries. When to these dangers are added the severe economic hardships experienced by the population, the uniqueness and outstanding humanity of those that decided to help, in spite of such unbearable risks, are the more praiseworthy and their deeds close to legendary.

* * *

At the height of the deportation of Jews from the Warsaw ghetto, a clandestine organization was created by several underground political organizations to help Jews escape the Nazi clutches. Inspired by Zofia Kossak-Szczucka, a prewar Catholic author of historical novels (also known for her antisemitic sentiments, but the Nazi methods caused her to experience a change of heart), the Council for Aid to Jews, better known by its code-word *Zegota*, was set up in Warsaw in the latter part of 1942. It dedicated itself with much zeal to helping Jews in hiding or passing as non-Jews in Warsaw and other cities, in several of which it established branches.

Supported by the London-based government-in-exile (with funds funneled by Jewish organizations in the United States), Zegota created departments to deal with children in hiding (in private homes or institutions), medical assistance, acquirement of false certificates, and pay-off money for blackmailers. In this endeavour, it also cooperated with other Jewish clandestine organizations, such as the Warsaw-based Jewish National Committee, headed by Dr. A. Berman.

Throughout its two-year period of activities, Zegota rendered assistance to some 2,000 Jews (some estimates place it slightly higher), mostly in the Greater Warsaw region, where an estimated 20,000 Jews were in hiding. The zeal and dedication of its members is lauded by all eyewitnesses. Stirred by humanitarian and religious convictions, as well as by patriotic zeal (to save the honor of the Polish nation), it endeavored to try rescuing as many Jews as possible, given the limited resources at its command. At a time when the Nazi Moloch was consuming hundreds of thousands monthly, the activities of Zegota were disproportionate and fell far short of the needs of the day. Yet it remains a beacon of light in an otherwise dark setting.

The number of Jews saved in hiding is hard to determine, but reliable estimates place the figure at between 20,000 and 50,000 (over 200,000 Polish Jews survived by fleeing to the interior of Russia). Only a fraction of this figure was saved from altruistic motivations. There are many cases of aid extended to Jews, even at great risks to the rescuers, but for pecuniary considerations. Not infrequently, non-Jews would throw the Jews out when the money ran out. In this study, though, we are concerned with those who helped for mainly altruistic considerations. Those so saved amount to between 15,000 and 25,000 persons. We shall, however, never know for sure.

The few thousand rescue stories emanating from Poland are of great significance to the student of the Holocaust, anxiously searching for traces of humanity in the immense hell of the Holocaust, for they exemplify a spiritual boldness hardly conceivable to the human mind. These Polish rescuers epitomize man as a loving and caring person, in its most elevated form. Their deeds ought to serve as behavioral role models for future generations to come.

Difficult Hiding Conditions

The difficulties and suffering endured by the Jews of Poland in their struggle to survive were extraordinary.

One common form of hiding place was an underground shaft or other hastily prepared hollow spaces. These were invariably congested, stifling, and dark. Those hiding in such places also had to cope with various unforeseen day-to-day hardships, which exacerbated the already highly pitched, tense atmosphere in the shelter.

Seven persons were hidden by Rozalia Paszkiewicz behind a closet in her Strij apartment. The lack of proper nourishment led to illness among them, but their most perilous problem was the birth of a baby to one of the women hiding there. Adults could remain quiet when necessary, but a baby . . . ? For the safety of everyone concerned, the father strangled his newborn child. The danger only came to an end when the body had been stealthily removed and disposed of. (44)

Wiktoria Pokrywka, a fifty-year-old laundress, hid seven Jews in her Lwow flat. Since she did not earn enough to provide for them, starvation set in as soon as the funds of the hidden Jews ran dry. In the words of Clara Eintov, one of the hidden Jews, "My grandfather was the first to succumb .., and Stanislaw [Wiktoria's son] helped to bury him secretly in the cellar. Two months later my grandmother died. She had witnessed the difficulties involved in the burial of her husband and asked before her death that her body be burned in the oven. We all participated in this horrible operation. We kept her ashes in a bowl." Thus they managed to survive till the city's liberation in July 1944. But the harsh conditions in the hiding place affected the health of the survivors even after the war, and several died from exhaustion. Of the original seven, three were able to regain their former strength and commence their lives anew. (1061)

Jan Puchalski

On the eve of a Nazi liquidation raid in the Grodno ghetto, fifteen-year-old Alex Zandman was at his work detail outside the ghetto as a bricklayer. Learning that the ghetto had been surrounded by uniformed men, he decided not to return home. Tearing off the yellow star patch sewn on his coat, he slipped away, and headed for the nearby Lososna forest where his family owned a few cottages for use during vacations. Several cottages had been dismantled during war, but one was still intact, and occupied by the local innkeeper, Jan Puchalski. Alex was acquainted with the Puchalskis, playing with their children during vacations. "I knew that their family had a high respect for our family and liked us."

Alex was warmly received and stayed with them until the end of the war. "I did not have any money, not even a watch to offer them," Alex recalls. "They were extremely poor. Everyone was hungry there, yet they shared what they had."

One day, still in a daze, Alex innocently asked Mrs. Puchalski about her unusual magnanimity, and her willingness to take the risk of hiding him. She responded: "God sent you to us. For years I had been dreaming of someday being able to repay your grandmother, Tema, for her kindness. Whenever I was in trouble, she would help me. One day, when she saw I was about to give birth, she took me to a hospital—the only time I ever had a baby in a hospital—and brought me gifts after my baby was born. I prayed that one day I would be able to repay her, and here you are, God sent you!"

That same night, a relative of Alex's arrived, having escaped an execution squad in Grodno. The following day, four more fleeing Jews joined them. At first, the Puchalskis hid the six Jews in a potato cellar about 50 yards from their house. As that proved too dangerous, a hole was dug under the floor of one of the Puchalskis' bedrooms—measuring 5 feet by 5 feet in length and width and about 3 1/2 feet in height. The dugout was so small and narrow that, according to one survivor, "it was very difficult to change the position of one's body."

Alex and the others stayed there for seventeen months. At first, the Puchalskis received some payment to defray the cost of feeding six additional mouths. When the money ran out, the Puchalskis shared their own meager rations. Jan eked out a small salary as a worker in a tobacco factory. Despite these hardships, the Puchalskis never betrayed their trust. "At no time did they ever hint that we should leave. In moments of despair, Mrs. or Mr. Puchalski and even the children tried to buck up our morale and they prayed for us," Alex emphasizes. During the whole period of hiding, the Puchalskis treated their charges "with the highest respect and love by everyone." (3466)

Jadwiga Suchodolski

Late one evening in April of 1943 a knock was heard at the door of the Suchodolski family in the village of Krzynowloga Wielski (Warsaw region). Adam Suchodolski opened the door and slowly made out the shadow of a man in front of him, his body swollen from hunger. The man fell down on his knees and begged for mercy. "Please help me stay alive." Adam and his teenage daughter Jadwiga painstakingly studied his face and finally perceived that it was none other than Michael Shaft, who, with his family, had lived in the village many years before. Michael had left the village to study law in Warsaw. The vicissitudes of the war had taken him from one place to another, and earlier that same month he had participated in the Warsaw ghetto uprising. Escaping, he had wandered back to his native village. The Suchodolskis—Adam, his wife Stanislawa, and their children

Jadwiga and Stanislaw, hurriedly consulted among themselves, weighing the risks and dangers, and decided to take Michael in.

As danger lurked on all sides, from neighbors and untrustworthy relatives, they decided to keep Michael's presence a secret. A pit was prepared in the granary, the opening of which was covered with animal fodder. There, Michael remained hidden, cut off from the world, for almost two years, till the village's liberation on January 15, 1945. He was regularly fed by a member of the Suchodolski family, who approached the granary through the chicken coop, ostensibly to feed the poultry. "The food was handed to me through a narrow crack. In the winter, rain penetrated the pit. But in spite of the discomforts, I resolved to make it through."

After the liberation, word soon spread that a Jew was being nursed back to life in the village. One day a group of partisans, broke into the Suchodolski house and demanded that Michael be turned over to them. Young Stanislaw held them off long enough to allow Michael to jump out of bed and escape through the back door. Realizing they had been duped, they gave chase but did not catch up with him. In revenge, they ransacked the Suchodolski house. That night Michael came back. Soon thereafter, Michael and Jadwiga were married and left the village, eventually emigrating to Israel in 1957.

"I come from a very devout Catholic family," Jadwiga states in a letter to Mrs. Golda Meir, Prime Minister of Israel, in 1972. "My family and I did what we did because we wished to observe the commandment of 'Thou shalt love thy neighbor as thyself.' I am proud, indeed, to be counted as a Righteous person. At the same time, I am glad that my family and I performed such an important commandment, and I believe that due to this, we have merited a place in the world-to-come." (953)

Jozef Zwonarz

To guarantee the safety of their charges, some rescuers kept the secret even from their immediate families. In July 1942, when rumors became rife that the Germans were planning to liquidate all the children in the Lesko ghetto, Dr. Nathan Wallach contacted Jozef Zwonarz, an acquaintance of his wife's family, who agreed to take their three-and-a-half-year old daughter under his care.

Soon thereafter, Dr. Wallach and his wife were transferred to the nearby Zaslaw labor camp. On December 16, 1942, some 400 young Jewish women were assembled in the main square of the camp and were shot down. Wallach's wife was accidentally felled in the ensuing stampede. She lay motionless for a while, then slipped away unnoticed when the mayhem ended.

The following day, the Wallachs fled to Lesko and again asked Jozef Zwonarz for help. Jozef, an engineer by profession, was forty-five years old at the time, married, and the father of five children. Having already arranged for the Wallach's young daughter to be sheltered by Jan Kakol, a forester, he now resolved to save Nathan and his wife.

Jozef hid them in a specially constructed underground shelter beneath the workshop shack near his home. He kept the matter a secret even from his own family. In the words of Nathan Wallach, "He did not want his wife to know, reasoning that she might say the wrong thing at the wrong place. . . . At times he brought us . . .potatoes or bread from his own house, and sometimes he excused himself for not wanting to eat at the family table, asking instead that his meals be brought to him in the workshop, and these he then turned over to us."

The hiding plave turned out to be quite cramped. "The tomb," as the occupants termed it, measured 5 feet by 3 1/2 feet and was about three feet deep. It was impossible to stand up and even difficult to sit up. "For two years, we could not stand up, but had to sit or lie prone—two persons on one side and two on the other [initially there were four persons in the hideout], with our eight feet intertwined. For two years, we did not see the light of day. We never left the place." Fear of exiting the "tomb" even at night was compounded by the precarious location of the Zwonarz house. To the right—Gestapo headquarters; to the left, the Schutzpolizei (Nazi security police), across the road—the Ukrainian police ("who were worse than the Gestapo," Wallach notes).

Zwonarz's charges could not pay their own expenses. "We had no money with which to buy food on the black market. We did not give him even one cent, for we had escaped from camp empty-handed." To obtain what was needed for the additional expenditures, Jozef hired himself out as a farmhand in return for payment in kind, in the form of barley. "For four days and four nights, we did not see him (he usually visited us at night, bringing food). We had nothing to eat and drink. We could discern noises from outside, but not his voice. We thought the Gestapo had arrested him and we were desperate . . . We felt we should commit suicide." Finally, Jozef suddenly appeared. "There is no way to describe our joy. He said he had barley with him." To provide for the cooking, Jozef ran an electric cable from the hiding place to the city's main circuit, not his own house's line, so that the extra kilowatts would not show up on his meter. He also installed an electric bulb in the pit. From the potatoes he brought them, they fashioned a checkers game which helped to alleviate their boredom and fears.

"He would visit us every evening. Removing the pit cover, he would begin encouraging us." His constant comings and goings aroused his wife's suspicions and she concluded that he was having an affair. She also became aware that food was missing. When a precious ball of cotton was disappeared, she gave free rein to her pent-up anger. Confronting Jozef in the workshop, she accused him of dallying with another woman. Those hidden below could clearly overhear her angry shouting: "You ought to be ashamed, carrying on like this at such a late age, . . . the father of five children." Not knowing how to respond, he remained silent.

As the Russians drew near Lesko in the spring of 1944, the city came under bombardment. A shell struck Jozef's workshop. Jozef deciding to move his charges to the cellar of his house, he finally told his wife the truth. It was imperative that the inmates of the pit get to the Zwornaz home, only 45 yards away but as they emerged they discovered to their consternation that they could not move their limbs. "I was the first one," Dr. Wallach testifies. "I fell and could not get up. I could neither walk nor stand. I had to crawl to the house. We exited at nightfall, but the dim light was like the blazing sun to us, because we had not beheld light for almost two years." Reaching Zwonarz's cellar at last, they hid there for another six weeks until the Red Army moved in.

After the liberation, when they had regained enough strength, they bade farewell to their benefactor, and excused themselves for not being able to reward him. He responded by removing his wristwatch and handing it to them, together with a $10 bill, saying: "Take this, it's all I have. You'll need it to start a new life."

"Our Awakening Angel," the Wallachs term Jozef Zwonarz, referring to the legendary angel who is to rouse the dead from their graves on Judgment Day. Wallach recalls that Zwonarz often told them, "I am a Jew like you, the difference being that I am a Jew freely walking the streets and you are hidden Jews." Reacting to the unfriendly remarks made to him by some of his fellow townsmen, he stated, "I am not ashamed; I did what everyone should have done. They did not do it. They should be ashamed." The Wallachs still find it difficult to compass the boundless goodness of this man. "He took from his family and from his children's mouths." (331)

Manko Szwierszczak

Any obscure hole or inaccesible corner—a murky cellar, an unventilated secluded hole in the ground, even an empty tomb or an unused animal cage—could serve as a place to hide Jews on the run.

As happened to many other Jewish communities, the German invasion of Russia in June 1941 decimated Henry Rosen's hometown of Buczacz in eastern Poland. Soon after the city's occupation, rampaging Volksdeutsche and Ukrainian collaborators attacked the Jewish inhabitants. "I saw many families robbed and killed with knives," Henry reminisces. "I helped bury them in our Jewish cemetery." A few weeks later, a large group of able-bodied Jewish men were marched off to the nearby Fedor Hill, told to dig graves, and unceremoniously shot. The remaining Jews were herded into a ghetto and life returned to normal, or so it seemed, as there was no major killing operation for another year.

However, by the latter part of 1942 it became obvious that the respite was drawing to a close. It was time to explore avenues of escape. Henry

Manko Szwierszczak beside the tomb in Buczacz, Poland, where he hid 4 Jews for close to two years. Courtesy of Yad Vashem.

had, in the meantime, made the acquaintance of a Polish cemetery caretaker by the name of Manko Szwierszczak. Manko lacked a formal education, but, in Henry's words, "was a good Christian and possessed a heart of gold." He was, moreover, prepared to help. With another Nazi roundup in the offing, Henry sought out his newfound friend. Manko agreed to shelter him and about forty other Jews on the top floor of a chapel located in the middle of the cemetery. The fugitives hid in the chapel for several days, during which some 2,000 Jews were deported to their death.

Thanking their benefactor, the forty returned to the ghetto, believing that the worst was now behind them. But the Germans soon sprung another massacre on the already blood-drenched Fedor Hill, and this was followed in February 1943 by still another mass slaughter. Henry, down with fever, had remained hidden under the staircase of his family's house together with his mother and two brothers. "We knew that time was running out," Henry says, "and we decided to leave the ghetto. I was twenty-one years old. My brother was eighteen, and my younger brother was twelve. We got in touch with Manko who had hidden us during the first massacre, and asked if he would help us again." After consulting with his wife, Manko returned with an affirmative response.

In Henry's words, Manko "knew the cemetery like he knew his own pocket," for he was the third generation of his family to work there. Selecting an old tomb that had caved in, he moved the three coffins it contained to another resting place and enlarged the vacated space with the help of the Rosen family. Blankets, pillows and dishes were brought. "At night we all moved into the tomb"—Henry, his two brothers, their mother, and four others, a total of eight fugitives. The arrangement worked out was that the Rosens would pay for food, which Manko would bring each morning, concealed in his tool bag so as to prevent any suspicions about his comings and goings. Before sunset, he would carefully place the food next to the tomb. When night had fallen, the inmates would carefully remove the tombstone and fetch the food. For added security, Manko placed a statue of the Virgin Mary on top of the tomb to make sure that no one would tamper with it. A pipe to the side of the tomb allowed fresh air to flow in from the outside.

One day Manko was observed buying what seemed an excessive amount of food. Hauled off to the police station for questioning, he was mercilessly beaten, but he stood his ground and refuted the charges against him. Released after four days of grueling interrogation, he reappeared with black-and-blue marks on his face from the beatings. "My mother kissed his hands and his wounds. We all hugged him." Four of the hidden men, however, decided they could not go through another such nerve-wracking episode, and taking whatever money they still had with them, they left to seek a better shelter elsewhere. "We never heard from them again," Henry sadly observes. There were now four left in the tomb.

As the autumn winds of 1943 foretold the coming of another harsh winter, the inmates began to fear that Manko's footprints in the snow outside the tomb would reveal their presence. Manko, therefore, moved his charges to an improvised shaft beneath the mortuary at the cemetery's entrance. They remained until March 1944, when an unforeseen accident brought disaster. As the retreating Germans from Russia moved into the area, an artillery unit took up a position around the cemetery's perimeter. During one especially cold night some German soldiers entered the mortuary to escape the night's frost. Gathering on top of the secret shaft, they moved their bodies to and fro in order to warm up. The sudden pressure caused the niche's covering stone to cave in and several German soldiers crashed on top of the four hidden Jews. The soldiers were terror-stricken, believing that the dead were rising to exact vengeance on them for having disturbed their resting place. In the ensuing panic, Henry and his brothers scrambled out and ran to the nearby woods, but their elderly mother, suffering from a swollen foot, and unable to climb out of the shaft in time, was shot by the Germans. Henry and his brothers found a new refuge with Michal Dukiewicz, a prewar acquaintance in a nearby village, who hid them in the hay loft of his barn. There they remained until the village was liberated by the Russians. (2644-45)

Dr. Jan Zabinsky

Dr. Jan Zabinsky was an agricultural engineer by training and a zoologist by profession. During his school days, he had many Jewish friends. "I often quarreled with them; at times we even exchanged punches, but without any hard feelings. To me they were like everyone else." When the war began, Zabinsky was director of the spacious Warsaw Zoo, a post to which he had been appointed in 1929. The Germans also named him superintendent of the city's public parks. Zabinsky lived with his wife Antonina and son Ryszard in a comfortable house on the zoo's grounds.

The German bombardment of Warsaw in September 1939 caused severe damage to the zoo. Most of the animals had been moved at the beginning of the war, and Zabinsky decided to use the zoo's facilities for the purpose of hiding Jews. To begin, a family of five (one of whom was mentally deranged and had to be constantly guarded) moved into Zabinsky's house early in the German occupation and stayed there for four years. Soon thereafter, the empty animal cages began to fill up with Jews fleeing from the Warsaw ghetto, where lack of food and proper hygiene was felling tens of thousands of victims even before the start of the mass killings. Synchronizing these efforts with Jewish underground leaders (such as Dr. Adolf Berman, Rachel Auerbach, and Jozef Zemian), fleeing Jews were temporarily sheltered in the zoo until more permanent arrangements could be worked out for them with host families on the Aryan side of the city. "The largest group that ever stayed simultaneously included 50 persons," Zabinsky notes. This is aside from the Jews who were hidden on a long-term basis in Zabinsky's house.

Whenever Zabinsky had visitors and it was time to feed the hidden Jews, he would suddenly nod toward his son and say, in a code of their own devising, "Ryszard, it's time to feed the peacocks," or "Go feed the lizards." Among them was Regina with her three children. Zabinsky was especially fond of Regina, for her father had, before the war, supplied the zoo with fresh fruits and vegetables. Regina describes Zabinsky's zoo as "a Noah's ark, where men and animals resided." After a two-month stay, Regina left to take up residence in a hiding place elsewhere in the sprawling city.

After the war, Zabinsky discounted his personal role in this unique rescue operation: "Sure, I helped a bit. I hid Jews and provided them with food. Nothing more." He later pointed to his wife as his principal support. "My wife is the real hero . . . She was afraid of the possible consequences, she feared the likely revenge of the Nazis toward us and our young son. She feared dying, but she kept silent and helped me. She never asked me to stop. She never said: 'Enough!' I knew how she felt, and I can therefore affirm that I was not the real hero, she was the true hero in our family."

In August 1944, after the supression of the Polish uprising, Zabinsky was taken prisoner to Germany. Antonina and Ryszard continued looking after the Jews left behind in the ruins of the city.

When the war ended, Dr. Zabinsky resumed his previous profession and continued his studies of the animal kingdom. Some of his several dozen monographs give an idea of the scope of his scientific interests: *Developmental Stages of the Beetles*, *First Birth of a Lycaor Pictus in Captivity*, *Anthology of the Deer*, *Psychology of Animals*, *How Insects were Created*, and *Evolution* (2 volumes).

Questioned about his motivations in rescuing Jews, Zabinsky responded modestly, "I risked my life and extended my hospitality not because they were Jews, but because they were persecuted persons . . . They had been condemned to destruction for no offense on their part. This was shocking. I fulfilled a simple human obligation." (170)

Ten Persons and More in One Hiding Place

As we have seen, hiding conditions in Poland were difficult enough when only a few individuals were involved; but they were extraordinary when large numbers of people hid in one place.

Such as the Duda and Ogonowski families, in the Kielce region, who together hid ten persons in a hole, covered with potatoes, with just a small opening through which the Duda children were able to pass food for the inmates. Another hiding place was located in a pit underneath the barn, covered with twigs. During their twenty-month-stay in the bunker, a pregnant woman went into labor. To hide her screams since an outpost of the army of the Russian general Vlasov (allied to the Nazis) was located nearby, the Ogonowskis began banging pots and pans and moving furniture to and fro.

A more dangerous threat later developed when anti-Semitic Polish partisans raided the Ogonowski house, killing 30-year-old Wladyslaw and severely wounding his 32-year-old brother Stefan. When they left, Franciszka Ogonowski, the mother of the two victims, rushed to the secret hideout to reassure the frightened inmates. "She said it was God's will," Yitzhaq Mintz recalls. (141)

Stanislaw Sobczak

Samuel Maler slipped away during a Nazi *Aktion* in Frampol, in the Lublin region, and after several narrow escapes, made it to the home of Stanislaw Sobczak, a family acquaintance. Sobczak's wife led the frightened Samuel to a ladder and told him to climb up to the attic. There he found seven Jews in hiding. Eventually others joined them. In Samuel's words: "Stach [Stanislaw] used to say that one pays with one's life for hiding one Jew. So it makes no difference if seven or ten Jews are hidden. The punishment is the same. The problem is how to feed them all." In time, however, fear of betrayal by neighbors and a brush with the authorities set Stanislaw's nerves on edges. As he later wrote, "During their stay with me (some seventeen months), I never fully closed my eyes at night. I was constantly terror-stricken, afraid that they would somehow be discovered. . . . But I could not bring myself to tell them to leave for a while and find a hiding place elsewhere. My conscience would not allow me to take such a step, which would have ended in disaster." Later, after a group of German soldiers were billeted in the barn where the hideout was located, he did ask Samuel and the others to leave, at least for a little while. Samuel explains: "He was asking for a respite, for the opportunity to sleep soundly for at least one night." Memories of this incident still terrify Stanislav, "Even today, when I write these lines," he says, "I shake with fright. . . . I feel cold and hot tremors ravaging my body." Another problem beset Stanislaw when one of his wards died and had to be buried in the barn. "She is still buried there," Samuel notes sadly in his 1967 deposition.

Thanks to Stanislaw's courage, eleven Jews saw the light of freedom, although five were later shot by roving partisans, He himself, however, was mercilessly beaten by a group of partisans who were hostile to Jews. The beating left him bedridden for two weeks. "I could not move at all; I could not even lift my head! The daughter of the local dentist took part in this brutal assault." Samuel and the five other survivors left Poland to build new lives elsewhere, forever grateful to "Stach," the Good Samaritan in faraway Poland. (589)

Alexander and Leokadia Mikolajkow

Alexander Mikolajkow was a physician in the city of Debica. Soon after the German conquest of Poland, he hired one of his patients, the youthful Efraim Reich, as an errand boy. This was to be of monumental importance for Efraim's whole family in the ensuing months. On the eve of an *Aktion* in Debica in July 1942, Efraim was at work at the hospital when Leokadia Mikolajkow, the doctor's wife, suddenly appeared and reported that the city's Jews were all to be liquidated within a few days. "She gave me the keys to her attic and said I should try to hide as many as possible there," Efraim recalls.

In the next few hours, Efraim smuggled out of the ghetto, one by one, his parents, sisters, brothers, and other relatives, a total of eleven persons. They stealthily made their way to Mikolajkow's home, located just opposite the ghetto's main gate. There they were quickly hidden in the doctor's attic. "It was just a floor under the roof for storage space," Efraim recalls. "You could not stand up there."

Mikolajkow's house was three stories high. His office was on the first floor; he and his family, and a maid used all of the other rooms as living quarters, except for one on the top floor which was occupied by a bachelor tenant. Late at night when the maid and tenant were asleep, Mikolajkow would bring food to the attic and empty the bucket used as a toilet. "The doctor carried it down every night. He never complained."

In the meantime, the Nazi angel of death reaped his harvest on the Jews of the Debica ghetto. Between 5,000 and 8,000 Jews were killed during the particular roundup. Some 3,000 remained in the reduced ghetto as slave laborers. With the *Aktion* over, the Reich family decided not to endanger Mikolajkow any further. "We slipped out, one by one, after dark and returned to our house, hoping only that the war would end soon."

Soon thereafter, the doctor slipped a note to the Reichs with the message: "The end is near. Come as soon as possible." It was November and the final *Aktion* was in the offing. "Within a few days, thirteen of us were in the attic," Efraim states. "Another cousin and a child of three had joined us. We were to remain under the doctor's protection for two years, until the Russians came in August of 1944."

For the first nine months, though, they hid in a previously unused basement, located behind the garage, in the back of the house. "We lived in darkness. We couldn't have even a candle, because it would have consumed too much oxygen. When it rained, the water would rise as high as our necks and we would spend two or three days submerged. But the wetness kept out insects. They could not live there. Only we were able to live there." Then, after nine months, the Gestapo asked the doctor for the key to his garage which they wanted for their own cars. That night, the thirteen Jews tiptoed out of the garage and filed through the garden that screened the doctor's office from the Gestapo station, which was located across the street. From there, they made their way back to the attic, where they stayed until the city's liberation.

When one of the hidden women took ill from a stomach ailment and died, she was buried at night in the yard. On another occasion, when the Germans staged a house-to-house search for underground members, a Gestapo agent was about to ascend the ladder to the attic but was fortuitously distracted by a noise from another part of the house.

Sadly Dr. Mikolajkow was killed by a stray shell on the last day of the battle that led to Debica's liberation. As the Red Army entered the city, the thirteen Jews left their hiding place. "We looked like animals," Efraim recalls. "Almost everything human had disappeared. We were swollen from hunger. We were almost blind from never seeing light. The Russians examined us. They said nine of us would surely die. But we did not. All of us rallied save one. He died of TB a few months later . . . We couldn't believe we'd lead normal lives again. But life is so strong. For a time, we could do nothing. Some just sat. Some cried . . . But the doctor did not see it. What a horrible irony! . . . He suffered so to keep us alive. And he didn't live to see that we were free."

Reflecting on the sad outcome, Efraim, now a rabbi, adds pensively, "Every year I remember the day he died. I believe in a life after death. I believe he is one of the great people there." As for Leokadia's motivation, "She told me she remembered the Bible. She remembered that Abraham had asked God if He would spare Sodom if there were fifty good people there. And finally God agreed to spare the city if He found only ten good people. She said it looked so dark for all Europe. She felt it was her duty to save the dignity of human beings—so that there would be a little opening left for life."

During a visit to the United States for a reunion with the survivors, Leokadia Mikolajkow added, "My helping to save Jews during the war was based mainly on a religious attitude. In my early life I was influenced by enlightened priests who believed in brotherhood, in the real Christian spirit. True Catholicism shouldn't have any antagonism based on race or religion . . . The Ten Commandments were meant for all mankind. They are not something to be applied just to one's own kind. And that is how I brought up my children." (90)

Jerzy Kozminski and Family

Jerzy Kozminski was a seventeen-year-old lad who supplemented his father's income by smuggling hard-to-get food into the Warsaw ghetto. The Glazer family had done some business with him. On April 18, 1943 Jerzy was in the ghetto on one of his errands. It was late in the day and past curfew time, so he was invited to sleep over at the Glazers'. Early the following morning, the Warsaw ghetto uprising broke out. Since fighting was still in its early stages and had not yet spread throughout the ghetto area, it was still possible to escape. Samuel Glazer turned to Jerzy and said, "We are Jews and doomed to die, but you don't have to sacrifice your life," urging him to jump over the wall and flee. Before doing so, Jerzy gave Samuel his family's address in Wawer, a Warsaw suburb on the right bank of the Vistula River, and told him that if a miracle occurred and they got out alive, they should immediately get in touch with his family.

On April 30, 1943, with the Germans using flame throwers to flush the remaining defenders out of their shelters, the Glazer family managed to escape from the burning ghetto. Their group initially comprised only five persons: Samuel, his wife, his father, a sister-in-law, and a twelve-year-old niece. Subsequently members of three additional families joined them, making an overall total of twelve persons. Desparately hoping that Jerzy's promise to help would not be compromised by the group's large size, they sent a note to him through a messenger. Before long Teresa Kozminski, her husband, and Jerzy, her stepson, came for them. Teresa's husband was at first fearful that the presence of such a large group would jeopardize their safety, but, Samuel relates, "Teresa, infused with exemplary courage, insisted that we all remain,"

The Kozminskis took the group home and built an shelter under the floor of the building they lived in to accommodate all fourteen of them. There they remained for sixteen months, until the Soviet liberation of Wawer on September 10, 1944. At first, the group paid for their upkeep with whatever money they had managed to take along. When this source dried up, the Kozminskis, especially Teresa ("the household's living spirit"), continued to care for them. At times, the group expanded to twenty-two persons, including distant relatives, who were forced to abandon their previous hideouts as a result of betrayals. Jerzy was eventually arrested by the Germans for his underground work, taken to the notorious Pawiak jail, and brutally tortured. He lost all his teeth, yet remained silent. Dispatched to Auschwitz and later to Mauthausen, he survived the war and is now a professional engineer in Poland. "The interesting thing about this family," Samuel notes, "is that we did not know them before," and in spite of this "the whole family, including Teresa's elderly father, was enlisted to help us."

In late August 1944, fighting between the advancing Russians and the retreating Germans reached the area where the Kozminskis lived. When the Germans ordered the civilian population evacuated, all of them left except for Teresa, who stayed with the fourteen people in their shelter, bringing along her three-year-old son. "She came down to us in the bunker. This lasted four weeks. Mrs. Kozminski would leave the hiding place, under a hail of bullets, in order to fetch some food." The hiders and their protector all breathed freely when the Russians entered Wawer on September 10, 1944. (115)

Wladyslav Kowalski

Ten-year-old Bruno Berl had roamed the streets of Warsaw for three days without food and shelter in September 1940. Unable to control his hunger any longer, he decided to stop the first person who came his way and ask for food. That was how he met Wladyslaw Kowalski. A retired Polish army colonel, Kowalski was the Warsaw representative of the Dutch-based Philips concern. Nazi Germany's interest in Philips and its foreign subsidiaries afforded him freedom of movement in all parts of Warsaw, including the generally closed-off Jewish ghetto. But his first opportunity to help took place outside the ghetto, on the so-called Aryan side, when he encountered Bruno. Taking the boy home, Kowalski fed him and provided him with a new identity and a home with friends. This initial altruistic deed generated a desire to do more, spurring him to additional acts of rescue.

He soon undertook to find shelter for more Jews. Exploiting his freedom of movement, he smuggled seven Jews out of the Warsaw ghetto during February 1943 by bribing the Polish guards at the gate, and found them safe havens on the Aryan side. Then, on November 17, 1943, he helped a family of four move from the Izbica ghetto to a safer place in Warsaw. He likewise offered refuge to twelve Jews in his Warsaw home. Roman Fisher, a construction worker whom Kowalski aided as well, helped prepare an underground shelter, using building materials that

Wladyslaw Kowalski, who rescued 50 Jews in Warsaw, at a ceremony in his honor (Yad Vashem, 1967). Courtesy of Yad Vashem.

Kowalski fetched in heavy suitcases. The group staying in his home was kept busy manufacturing toys which Kowalski sold, thus helping defray the expenses for their upkeep.

With the suppression of the Polish uprising in the fall of 1944, and the forced evacuation of the city's inhabitants by the Germans, Kowalski decided to convert the basement of a razed building into a large bunker. He hid there together with forty-nine Jews in a city now populated only by enemy troops. Their daily rations consisted of three glasses of water per person, a lump of sugar, and some vitamin pills. The Jews begged him to leave. He replied: "Either we'll all survive or none of us will." Thus they remained hidden for 105 days during which time one person died from an infection and three left to reconnoiter and never returned. By the time they were liberated by the Russians in mid-January 1945, they had been reduced to eating fuel.

In 1961, Wladyslaw Kowalski said, "I don't consider myself a hero, for I was only fulfilling my human obligations toward the persecuted and the suffering. . . They counted on me, so I could not abandon them to the danger of certain death. . . . I wish to reiterate that I did no more than help forty-nine Jews to survive! . . . I could not sit idly by and remain indifferent in the face of the barbaric acts of the Nazis and their attempt at mass murder." (4)

Leopold Socha

Zipporah Wind waited helplessly for her execution in a dark cell in the notorious Weisenhof prison, located in the Lwow ghetto. Zipporah had fled to Lwow from Turka, a town in the foothills of the Carpathian Mountains in southern Poland, where her whole family had perished in a Nazi *Aktion* (save for one brother who had luckily left for the United States before the war). Before she departed, her mother had placed a Virgin Mary medallion around her neck. Her father had warned her, "Remember, your name is Halina Naszkiewicz. You must forget us, your home, your real name."

On November 10, 1942, Zipporah boarded a train for Lwow. She never saw her parents again. For a time she lodged with a family. On Christmas Eve of 1942, at services in her landlord's flat, she inadvertently gave herself away by reaching for the communion wafer instead of receiving the wafer on her tongue. The others gasped. The secret was out: Halina was Jewish. Betrayed to the authorities, she was arrested, brutally beaten, and made to sign her own death warrant. It was now February 1943 and her time had come.

At the last moment, a stroke of good luck saved her. Ordered to fetch the prisoners' excrement bucket and take it across the courtyard, she noticed that the prison gate had been left unguarded. Quickly darting out of the prison compound into the ghetto proper, she found streets and houses almost deserted. Some friendly Jews quickly snatched her off the streets and into their basement hideout. There she was given a new identity and registered as a seamstress in a German-operated establishment where army uniforms were mended and the clothing of murdered Jews was deloused and reprocessed for shipment to Germany.

For the time being Halina felt secure. Then, on June 1, 1943, a final German *Aktion* took place for the liquidation of the remaining residents of the ghetto. Halina's group were in a hideout not far from the Peltew River, which flows through the city. "We escaped while there was still time, through underground tunnels," Halina recounts, "until we found ourselves walking and crawling through the sewers. Finally we came to a strip of ground where we could sit, leaning against a wall covered with sewage pipes. There we were met by Leopold Socha."

Socha was employed as a sewer worker, but he had also dabbled in theft and he used the sewers as a place to hide his loot. While serving a term in prison before the war, he had met and fallen in love with Magdalena, a prison cleaning woman. The war with its turmoil had brought a change in the man.

Moved by the suffering of the Jews, he decided to help Halina and her associates. Leading them to a niche in the sewer close to the river, Socha told them to stay there through the evening, promising to return with food and some dry clothes. "In the meantime, don't budge from here. Just trust me," he assured them. They really had no choice. Their clothes sopping wet, and without food, they remained through the damp night, crawling on their hands and knees. Around them untold number of Jews were groveling in the dark sewers, lighting their way with lamps. Occasionally a splash in the water would be heard. It was someone who had accidentally, or purposely, jumped into the sewer to be flushed into the Peltew River, hoping to somehow swim his way to safety or, perhaps, to simply drown and be done with all his suffering.

The next day, Socha and a friend returned with the promised provisions. "The ghetto is burning," he told them. "There are bodies everywhere. . . . There are a lot of bodies on the outskirts of the city, where the Peltew comes out [flushing out those who had slipped into the sewers]. Now only you are left." Every day, Socha reappeared to them through a different opening with a load of foodstuff (some of it stolen, some bought with money given him by his charges). Once a week, Magdalena washed and ironed the people's underwear. Socha also brought them a prayer book, reading material, and, most important, words of encouragement.

To stay clear of the filthy foul-smelling waters that flowed through the underground cavern that had become their refuge, the men gathered boards and stones and built a barrier of sorts. Each day was marked by a struggle with the sewer rats. To keep the little food they had secure from these rodents, they stored it in a portable kerosene stove suspended from the roof with a cord.

A deeply religious man, Socha respected the religious sentiments of the Jews. He brought them Sabbath candles to be lit on Friday evenings. For Passover, mindful that Jewish practice prohibited eating bread at that time, he shoveled a wagonload of potatoes through the sewage grating. The rats got to many of the potatoes, but the sewer dwellers were able to retrieve enough to feed themselves during the Passover holiday period.

When their money ran out, some of Halina's friends felt they ought to leave. But Socha's response was blunt: "Either you all survive, or nobody. As long as you are my responsibility, you are all equal to me. How do you know which one of you is destined to live?" Some could not stand up to the existence in the sewer and left of their own accord. Their dead bodies were later seen stretched out on the streets overhead.

During heavy storms, the water level in the sewers rose dangerously high, threatening to drown the inmates. The children had to be lifted and held aloft until the waters had subsided to their previous level. One of the women had been pregnant when she joined the group. Her baby boy was safely delivered, but later died of starvation.

That winter the snow on the street above the sewer tunnel where they were hidden began to melt in the outline of the letter L, identical to the configuration of the tunnel. Socha explained to suspicious observers that this was due to heat emanating from a kitchen in a nearby monastery or from the damp catacombs. The Germans, however, suspected that the pattern of melting indicated the presence of people below. Sewer workers were dispatched to reconnoiter but did not find the hidden persons.

On July 17, 1944 Socha jubilantly announced to his charges that the Russians had occupied Lwow and that they were now free. Crawling their way out of the sewers, they were blinded by the sun's natural light. After a full year of crouching in the sewers, they could hardly stand up. Magdalena was waiting for them with a freshly baked cake and a bottle of vodka. As some of the local population did not take kindly to the sight of surviving Jews, they hid in Socha's home for another week, then parted ways. Of the more than two hundred persons who had descended into the sewers on the night of the ghetto's liquidation, only a handful crawled out upon the city's liberation. Socha's Jews were among the few. (1379)

Stanislaw Jackow

In February 1943, Stanislawow, a city in southeastern Poland, was declared *judenrein* ("clean of Jews"). Two years earlier the city had counted some 50,000 Jews. All had been murdered save for a handful who continued a subterranean life with the help of their protectors. When the city was liberated by the Russians in July 1944, sixty-five Jews came out of hiding—half of them from the hideout run by Stanislaw Jackow.

It all started when Jackow, a carriage-maker by profession, decided to rescue Max Saginur, a Jewish friend from his high school years. On the night of January 31, 1943, Stanislaw ("Staszek") picked up Max, his bride, Gitya, and two other relatives just outside the ghetto wall and hid them in a wooden partition behind his kitchen.

When that proved unsatisfactory, since there was no air and the slightest sound could be detected, Staszek decided to convert his cellar into a hiding place. For beds, he brought upholstered leather cushions from the carriages in his factory and set them on wooden benches. Encouraged by his success, Staszek decided to enlarge the shelter to be able to accommodate more than just a handful of persons. Eventually he took in thirty-one persons. Most came penniless, in rags, after spending months in the forests hunted by Germans and local anti-Semites. Certain facilities were essential for such a large group, so Staszek provided a drill, some pipes, and a hand-operated water pump. With these implements, the men drilled a well twenty-five feet deep and built an indoor toilet. Upstairs, Jackow's family had no plumbing, but in the cellar, there was water for everything—even for washing.

The cellar came alive when Staszek rapped on the trapdoor. His coming was heralded by a red light that flashed in Max Saginur's bunker. Staszek would stay with them for hours, playing chess and cards, and often joking about how he ran "the biggest underground hotel in Stanislawow," deceiving not only the Gestapo but his own mother and sisters, who were aware of his commitment to help Jews, but had no inkling of the magnitude and scope of his rescue operation. He profited from the help of friendly Poles. One, a baker, supplied him freely with fresh bread and at times also cookies; another, a nurse at a local dispensary, provided medicines, still others undertook vital errands to procure other necessities and make contact with Jews on the run.

Outside the shelter, terror and death stalked every Jew still alive. In Staszek's bunkers, with ample food, warmth, and even laughter, a semblance of normal life was restored. Gitya and her sister-in-law, Wanda, both became pregnant. The apparent security was, however, soon put to a harrowing test.

One day a Ukrainian friend informed Staszek that antisemitic Ukrainian partisans had learned about the elaborate hideout and were planning to attack it. Staszek called the people together and told them they had to be prepared to evacuate in case of an emergency. In anticipation of this, they were to dig a tunnel to the town sewer, some 125 feet from the house; from there, they might be able to escape. For seven sleepless days and nights, they worked in shifts, burrowing a tunnel 8 feet under the street.

As they were digging, a piece of the sidewalk suddenly caved in. Mountains of dirt fell on Max Feuer. In the ensuing panic, Gitya, Saginur's wife, went into labor. The baby was born dead but the placenta would not move. She bled for five hours. Finally, one of the group members who was a dentist washed his hands with alcohol and removed it. Gitya lived. Max Feuer, meanwhile, had been able to extricate himself from the dirt without anyone on the outside noticing and the Ukrainians never showed up. Taking no chances, Staszek had previously armed his wards with two hand grenades and four revolvers obtained from the underground in the event of an encounter with Germans or Ukrainian militiamen.

Then, danger appeared from a new direction. Staszek was suddenly conscripted for forced labor and marched off with hundreds of others to an assembly point for transport to Germany. This meant that the thirty-one Jews would henceforth have to cope by themselves. But Staszek managed to elude his captors. Detouring through open fields and back streets, he reached his home and immediately joined his charges in the hideout. The Germans rampaged through the house but found neither Staszek nor the trapdoor leading to the underground hideout.

On July 29, 1944, the Red Army entered Stanislawow. For twenty-four hours thereafter, Staszek checked out the town. Then, convinced that the Germans had definitely been routed, he knocked on the trapdoor and shouted, "We're free, really free."

"I never thought there would be thirty-one," Staszek once kidded his friend Max Saginur one evening in the underground "hotel." "I did it for you . . . If they caught me saving only you, they would kill me. I might as well be killed for thirty-one as for one. But they won't catch us," he assured Max. "This house is blessed." (277)

Wanderings and On the Run

For many fugitive Jews, survival in Poland meant wandering from place to place, especially in off-the-beaten track places, passing the night outdoors in inclement weather, and begging for food and an occasional roof over their heads. Lest we forget, it was open season on Jews, so approaching local inhabitants for help was fraught with great risks. Such as for Josef Czarny, who escaped from Treblinka (one of the most notorious of the Nazi death camps, where some 750,000 Jews perished) during the short-lived rebellion in August 1943 and wandered in the nearby woods for about a month. At the end of his strength, he knocked on the door of a farmer, near the town of Prysow, and was warmly received by Szymon Celka. At first Josef suspected that Szymon intended to betray him to the police a reward, but as he turned to leave the hamlet, Szymon stopped him with the following words: "My son, don't go. I am helping a group of Jews in the vicinity and you shall join them. It is enough for you and them to have escaped from that camp. You must remain alive so as to tell the world what the Nazis did to your people." At this, Josef burst into tears. Szymon Celka continued to care for Josef Czarny in the coming weeks. "I could write a whole book about this man's qualities. . . . An angel, indeed," Josef says. Of the fewer than 500 Jews who escaped from Treblinka, only about fifty survived. Josef Czarny was one of them, thanks to Szymon Celka. (467)

Jan Sagan

In December 1942, fifteen-year-old Morris Krantz, hunted, hungry and forlorn, found himself alone in a cold forest near Janow Lubelski in southern Poland after witnessing the brutal massacre of his whole family. He later described his condition at the time: "I was in a daze, stumbling along in the freezing cold, weakened by hunger and scarcely knowing where to turn . . . My mind was reeling, trying to grapple all at once with grief for my loss, fear about the present situation, and dread of my uncertain future. These tumultuous waves of emotion converged to create a feeling of panic that drove me on, until I stopped for a brief rest and realized that I had no definite destination. . . . I was blue from the cold, swollen from hunger, and literally in tatters. My sparse diet had taken its toll. I was weak and barely able to walk . . . I could not keep going much longer. I needed the help of another human being."

Before the war, Morris's father, a cattle merchant and storekeeper, had business with the peasant families in the surrounding area. Morris decided to approach them for help but was rebuffed. Fearing that these self-exposures would eventually land him in the hands of the Germans, he weighed his next steps carefully. He decided to make one further try before he would passively succumb to whatever fate had in store for him. Mentally assessing the business reliability of the local peasants, based on his recollection of his father's accounts, and grading them accordingly. Morris decided to try out Jan Sagan, whose name topped the list.

One night, Morris slipped into Sagan's pigsty, which was connected to the main building and also contained a mill that his late father had often visited. Hiding in an alcove above the animals, he survived on raw potatoes and beets for the next few days while secretly watching Jan at his daily chores and eavesdropping on his conversations with neighbors who had come by to grind their grain. Once Morris overhead Jan berating a person who had expressed joy at the wholesale massacre of the Jews. "Never rejoice in another man's tragedy," Jan admonished. "We don't know what God has in store for us." At that, Morris decided Jan could be trusted.

The following morning, Morris approached Jan as the latter came into the pigsty—and begged for help. At first Jan hesitated, fearing German retribution on his family (a wife, several children and his parents). Overcoming his fear, he agreed to feed and clothe Morris and shelter him in the barn, and to do so, at least initially, without telling his wife. Morris thus remained hidden for fourteen months, until April 1944, when he left to join up with advancing partisans.

In conversations with Morris, Jan revealed something about his thinking and motivations. On one occasion he said: "It makes me feel good to help another human being at a time of so much killing and cruelty." Jan also told Morris about the excruciating pain he had felt on the day when Morris appeared to him out of nowhere. "That morning will not leave me as long as I live. I was startled by the sight of you—overgrown hair, face swollen from the cold, all in rags—a ghost, a wild man, a barely human creature. When I asked you to leave I was reacting to my first impulse, to shock. But I was in a turmoil over it for two days. I considered it the greatest crisis of my life, either jeopardize my family by allowing you to stay, or turn you out to certain death. . . . You made me aware what a precious gift life is, and the God-given power in it. When I considered your presence on the farm and its effect on me, I suddenly realized that whatever I had done for you had resulted in as much good for me—more. I had never felt so good, so alive. I was convinced that it was the work of a higher power."

When Morris told this story to a friend who had known Jan before the war, the friend replied: "Of all the people your father knew and dealt with, no one would have believed that Sagan would do such a thing. I can only use the word "miracle" to explain your coming to his place. It was God's will." Morris, who is devoutly religious, refers to Jan Sagan as "the man who gave me a new life, my second father." (2743)

Jozef Job

In late 1942, Helen Szturm and her father were caught up in a German *Aktion* in Debica, in southern Poland. As they, along with other Jews, were marched off to be "relocated" (the Nazi code-word for murder), the head of the Jewish police force, who was walking beside them, managed a whisper: "Whoever is able—save himself, save himself!" Helen and her father slipped away and sought out Polish friends and prewar business acquaintances, but they were politely rebuffed. No one wanted to risk German retribution for extending assistance to Jews on the run. Distressed, Helen and her father decided to head for Tarnow.

Avoiding the main highway, they followed byroads through the woods. A man confronted them and said he knew they were Jewish but would not turn them in if they gave him all their possessions. Helen and her father grudgingly consented. They continued walking. It was very cold and the ground was covered with a thick snow. At nightfall they made out the distant light of an isolated forest house. The house owners were decent people and agreed to shelter the two overnight.

The following morning, Helen and her father continued walking in the direction of Tarnow. A Polish woman in a log cabin allowed them to come in and warm up. She also gave them some bread. Continuing in the deep snow, Helen felt her strength failing her.

"It was Sunday morning," she says in her deposition. "My father walked fifty feet ahead of me so as not to arouse suspicion (what were a man and a girl doing walking together in the deep snow on a country road, on Sunday morning?). My legs were swollen and I could hardly drag myself along behind my father. Suddenly a Polish girl passed by me. When she saw the condition I was in, she whispered: 'Don't be afraid. I know you are Jewish, but I won't harm you. . . . Let's walk together.' It seemed as though a miracle had occurred and she had come from heaven."

As the girl disappeared from view, Helen felt she could no longer go on. Her father had to carry her in snow up to his knees. Then his strength gave way too. At that moment she saw a man coming toward them. "He picked me up and carried me to his home. He was the girl's father. Her name was Stefka (short for Stefania)."

Stefka's parents, Jozef and Wiktoria Job, her two brothers, and a younger sister were shocked by the physical condition of Helen and her father and provided them with food, hot drinks, and proper clothing, and invited them to remain for an indefinite period.

The Jobs sheltered Helen and her father in the attic of a half-finished new house next door, taking turns to bring food to them. On exceptionally cold nights, Helen and her father would slip across to the Jobs' house in order to warm up. There they passed the winter of 1942-1943. The following spring, Stefka received a call-up notice for labor in Germany. When Jozef decided to go in her stead, the operation of the family's farm fell squarely on the shoulders of Wiktoria and the children. Eventually one of the sons was also taken to Germany for work.

A year later as the front moved ever closer to Lipiny, the village in which the Job family lived, the Germans ordered the inhabitants to evacuate. The Jobs hid Helena and her father in the forest, where Stefania and her brother took turns bringing food to them. Later, Helen and her father returned to Stefania Job's house where they hid in the barn until the area was liberated. (1828)

Wladyslaw Jeziorski

In mid-1944, Abraham Sheiner was working in the Hermann Goering arms factory in Starachowie, to the northeast of Kielce. When the Germans decided to close down the factory because of the Soviet advance into Poland, rumors ran wild that the 2,000 Jewish workers were about to be liquidated. On July 19, 1944, several hundred Jews tried to cut their way through the camp's barbed wire, but were mowed down by machine-gun fire from the German and Ukrainian guards.

The following morning, Abraham was assigned to a burial detail digging a common grave for those felled in the escape attempt. Deciding to try his luck and attempt flight during the change of guards, he muttered the *Adon Olam* prayer, then ran through a break in the barbed-wire fence. Several other workers joined him, and all headed for the nearby woods. The Germans quickly gave chase and bullets whizzed over the heads of the fugitives. All were eventually apprehended and shot, save two, Abraham and his friend Arieh. They ran that entire day, and then lay down to rest inside the thick forest, wondering what was in store for them.

Over the next few days, Abraham and Arieh penetrated more deeply into the forest as the German pursuit continued without letup. They were fed by friendly peasants, and on three occasions escaped death at the hands of partisans belonging to the intensely antisemitic NSZ faction.

Eventually, totally exhausted, they lay down on the damp ground, oblivious to the rain and cold. "My whole body ached," Abraham recalls. "But I was troubled most by the swellings and wounds on my knees and feet. I was no longer able to walk and my mind was completely disordered. I was running a high fever and felt as if I were near death."

Helpless and destitute, Abraham and his companion awaited fate's judgment. And then, as if in a dream, a young man was looking down at them. "Be careful," he said. "The Germans are only half a mile away."

The young man offered the two some vokda to warm up their cold bodies and, indicating the proper direction, told them to come to his house once it was dark. Abraham was so weak that he could not even drink the vodka. That evening he and Arieh dragged themselves to the farmhouse. The young man, Marian, took them into the house to meet his parents, Wladyslaw and Anna Jeziorski. Anna nursed Abraham's wounds, spreading horseradish leaves over his swollen body, which burned his skin and caused him extreme pain but eventually they made the swellings and his fever disappear completely.

The two men hid in the Jeziorskis' barn as the Germans, with the front only miles away, combed the area for fleeing workers and deserters. As the fighting moved close Wladyslaw Jeziorski sent them off with instructions on how to reach friendly partisans. Instead they ran into advancing Russian soldiers and were finally free. (366)

Tadeusz Soroka

Tadeusz Soroka was a twenty-year-old young man in 1943 when the three persons whose testimony earned him Yad Vashem's recognition met him near the Grodno ghetto in northern Poland. Aron Derman, Lisa Nussbaum, and Robert Ness had come to Grodno from Slonim, where Lisa's mother, sister, and aunt had been caught in one of the Nazi roundups and disappeared. In Grodno, Aron was assigned various repair jobs outside the ghetto. Soroka, who worked for the railroad, stopped occasionally at the work sites to trade food for clothes, and that is how the two met.

One day, Tadeusz Soroka told Aron that the ghetto had been surrounded by German police units and its liquidation was imminent. He volunteered to hide Aron. Aron responded that he had no money, whereupon Soroka said, "I don't need your money; I want to help you." Aron hedged, suspecting a trap that would enable Tadeusz to claim a German bounty for informing on an escaped Jew.

Aron, who had lost all his family to the Germans, decided to bide his time. But after narrowly escaping another German *Aktion* by hiding in the synagogue coal room, he reasoned that the risks of staying in the ghetto outweighed those of fleeing to Vilna with the help of Soroka. Vilna, some 110 miles away, was relatively safer. Its ghetto was larger; it had an underground, and in case one had to flee, the nearby forests offered many hiding places and the opportunity to join up with partisan units known to be operating in the region. Aron decided to take along Lisa, to whom he was romantically linked, and her brother Robert.

Fleeing the ghetto through a hole in the wall, on March 9, 1943, they met Soroka, as arranged, at a public washroom about a mile and a quarter away. From there they walked to the railroad station, Soroka leading the way and intermittently blinking his flashlight to signal the others. When they reached the station, Soroka had them lie down near one of the platform embankments until a German military train had finished loading ammmunition, then they were to jump aboard as the train headed out of the station.

As the train moved past, the three men leaped on and climbed to the roof of a boxcar as planned but sixteen-year-old Lisa missed a step and was left dangling with her feet off the ground. Soroka, ran along the train until he spotted her; then, as the others hung on to his legs, he leaned over and pulled her up. As if that were, he had brought along sandwiches and tea for the journey. He also added words of encouragement.

As the train pulled into Vilna, he had the three blacken their faces with coal dust to make it look as if they were railroad workers returning from the night shift; he then had them jump off the train at a bend with instructions to hide in a certain farmer's shed. Later on, he placed them at the tail end of a work detail of Jews returning home, and thus they were able to enter the ghetto unnoticed.

The rescue by Soroka was just in the nick of time, for two days thereafter a large contingent of Grodno Jews was deported to concentration camps. Soroka made a total of four such journeys, saving a total of nine lives. In one instance he outwitted a German guard who wanted to check the boxcar where a Jewish escapee was hiding.

During an emotional reunion in 1982 in the United States with those he had saved, Soroka said, "We were all taught the second great commandment: 'You shall love your neighbor as yourself.' So I knew what I had to do. . . . It was no big thing." He did not consider himself a hero: "I lived by my religion and I still do." Regarding the significance of his deeds, he said, "I believe that every good deed is permanently enshrined in history." (2695)

Irena Gut

Fanka Wilner and her husband were assigned labor in a German firm doing the laundry for German officers outside the Tarnopol ghetto. The agent in charge at work was a Polish woman by the name of Irena Gut. From the start Irena showed a special sensitivity to the needs of the Jewish workers, providing them with additional necessities whenever possible. Ultimate responsibility for the firm's operations lay with a German major, a man suffering from digestive ailments. Irena prepared special meals for him; he in turn showed his gratitude by overlooking her peccadillos and transgression of regulations. With his connivance, she acquired special passes making it possible for her Jewish workers and their families to leave the ghetto and spend several days in the laundry while raids on the inhabitants of the Tarnopol ghetto were taking place.

In July 1943, the camp where the laundry firm was located was slated for liquidation. Irena urged the 300 Jewish residents to attempt fleeing immediately before the *Aktion* was launched. On top of this, Irena hid numbers of Jews intermittently in the major's private apartment, in the cellar or attic, without his knowledge.

One day, the major returned home sooner than usual and found several Jews in his home. Calling Irena before him, he berated her for placing him in such great jeopardy by sheltering nine Jews in his private quarters. Not able to control himself, he left. Irena ran after him, imploring him to show mercy and charity to these innocent persons. It is not clear how she managed it, but not only did she sway him from whatever he had on his mind but he also agreed to have his home cellar furnished with some conveniences to make the stay of the hidden Jews less difficult.

As suspicions mounted, someone informed the authorities of strange noises and movements emanating from the major's house. The Gestapo came to investigate. Irena refused to allow the premises to be searched, stating it was the private residence of a major in the German army. Instead she suggested they call him on the phone at his office. The ruse worked and the Gestapo men left without initiating a search. The nine hidden people had a close brush with death. So did the major and his trusted aide, Irena Gut.

As the situation worsened for the Germans at the front, Irena Gut, together with other personnel in the German civil administration, were ordered to evacuate the town and move toward Germany proper. Instead, Irena went into hiding with her Jews in the cellar. Together they then fled to the woods, where they remained out of sight. Before she parted from her friends, she arranged for a Polish woman to look after the Jews in the forest, giving her a silver-adorned powder compact as compensation.

On March 23, 1944, the Jews in the forest outside Tarnopol were liberated by the advancing Russians. Irena Gut had been moved with the retreating Germans to Kielce, in central Poland. She managed to elude her captors, flee, and join up with a partisan unit. Both rescuer and rescued survived to tell the unbelievable story of a group of doomed Jews, rescued by a Polish woman, with the assent of a German officer. (2317)

After the war, Irena moved to the United States, married, and generally kept to herself. But in 1975, when she heard claims that the Holocaust was a hoax, she decided to start talking. Her favorite groups are the children. She tells them, "You can do what I did! Right now! Stand up when you hear name-calling, when you see skinheads. You are the future of the nation." She adds, "we all have to reach out to know we're not alone in the world. You have to give not just money, but you must give of yourself."[1]

Waclaw Nowinski

It was the late afternoon of April 9, 1943, on a busy Warsaw street on the Aryan side, and Alexander Bronowski had been spotted by two plainclothesmen. Something in his demeanor and walk aroused the suspicion of the two police agents that the man might be Jewish, in spite of his non-Semitic looks. It was only days before the start of the Warsaw Ghetto uprising, and the Germans, sensing the Jews were going to give them a stiff fight, had brought in reinforcements, whose presence on the streets could not be avoided. Sensing he was being tailed, Bronowski slipped into a church where Mass was being celebrated and mingled with the crowd. When he exited, two hands grabbed him by the shoulder. He was asked to present his credentials. All seemed in order, as well as his impeccable Polish. Yet the two secret police agents suspected otherwise.

1. G. Block, *Rescuers*, p. 196.

As it was already late in the day, they decided to drop him off at a local Polish police station, promising to return the next morning to fetch their prey and take him to Gestapo headquarters for a more grueling interrogation. The police officer at the desk noted down in the register that Bronowski was suspected of being Jewish and was to be jailed till the following morning.

Alexander Bronowski, a noted Lublin lawyer, had had various brushes with death since the start of hostilities in September 1939 and had wandered from place to place to elude the Nazis. With the help of non-Jewish Poles, he had finally found a nest in the cosmopolitan city of Warsaw. His wife and daughter were sheltered separately in the city. Now it seemed he had reached the end of the road.

Sitting in his damp and cold cell, Bronowski tested the vigilance and kind-heartedness of the Polish sergeant-major in charge and found it was wanting. Bronowski ventured to offer the man payment in return for a phone call to a friend. The policeman took the money and showed Bronowski back to his cell. From the guard on duty outside the cell, Bronowski learned that the desk sergeant had been replaced by another person. It was eleven in the evening, and Bronowski, wishing to test the new desk sergeant's humanitarian feelings, asked the cell guard to take him to the lavatory. To get to the lavatory he had to pass near the hallway where the desk sergeant sat. Bronowski asked whether he could sit in the hallway for a few minutes to warm up his cold body next to the stove. The desk sergeant agreed. "I sat in the hall and began to talk to the sergeant-major. He introduced himself as Waclaw Nowinski. We talked for three hours, from eleven o'clock at night until two in the morning." During that long conversation, Bronowski admitted to his being Jewish and pleaded with the policeman to do something to help him avoid being turned over to the Gestapo the following morning.

At two o'clock in the morning, Sgt. Nowinski suddenly called a halt to their conversation with the words: "I must save you." As Bronowski stared in astonishment, Nowinski got up, left his desk, and walked out of the building. Leaving a police post unattended constituted a serious breach of regulations and a major dereliction of duty for the sergeant-major. Four hours later, at six in the morning, he suddenly reappeared and said to the stunned Bronowski, still sitting in the hallway, "I've arranged everything. In another hour, two secret police agents will come for you. They asked me for 5,000 zloty. I'll pay them. Don't worry; you won't have to pay me back." Bronowski could not believe his ears. Perhaps it was a setup? But, having no other alternative, he decided to cooperate and play the game.

An hour later, two German security police agents arrived, made a note in the police register to the fact that Bronowski had been erroneously arrested; that his credentials were in order as well as his non-Jewish identity. They then took Bronowski outside. He gave them the 5,000 zloty as instructed and walked off.

The next day, Bronowski returned to the police station in order to repay Nowinski the money owed to him and add an additional 2,000 zloty as a reward. "Mr. Nowinski was terribly incensed at this, and only with great difficulty did I convince him to utilize the money to try saving another Jew. As for the additional reward money, he was greatly offended, and I felt it necessary to apologize. Our friendship dates from that moment."

Nine days later, the Germans stormed the Warsaw Ghetto, and the last Jewish defenders fell in combat after putting up a stiff fight. In May 1943, Warsaw was officially *judenrein*, except for those leading an underground existence, aided by well-meaning Poles. Alexander Bronowski availed himself of Nowinski's help to survive the Nazi terror. "He used to warn me if I was in danger, and occasionally I hid in his house." There, Bronowski discovered several other Jews in hiding, helped by Waclaw's wife Janina and their seventeen-year old son.

After the war, Bronowski moved to Israel and he heads a Yad Vashem-sponsored subcommittee dealing with honoring non-Jews who risked their lives to save Jews in distress, bestowing on them the title of Righteous Among the Nations. The list of those so honored includes the unforgettable Polish police sergeant Waclaw Nowinski. (611)

Sister Dolorosa

In January 1942, Sister Dolorosa (Genowefa Czubak) of the Order of St. Ignatius of Loyola, at Pruzana, northeastern Poland, took ill. There were no non-Jewish physicians in Pruzana at the time, and all Jews had been incarcerated in the ghetto by the Germans. The sisters took counsel and agreed to seek medical aid from the Jewish Dr. Olga Goldfein. Sister Marianne was dispatched to the ghetto, ostensibly to seek dental treatment. The Germans allowed such visits inside the ghetto by non-Jews. Sister Marianne contacted Dr. Goldfein. who consented to follow her outside the ghetto, again by means of a dental surgeon's permit. They both hurried to the cloistered walls of the convent. "She made a good impression on all the sisters and myself as well," Sister Dolorosa relates. Quickly recovering from her illness, Sister Dolorosa did not forget this brief encounter with the Jewish doctor.

In August 1942, Nazi anti-Jewish measures increased in ferocity. Many were taken out the ghetto and shot over graves the victims had themselves been forced to dig. Olga Goldfein managed to drop in on Sister Dolorosa for a quick visit, ostensibly to see how her patient was recovering. "Mrs. Goldfein remarked that it might be the last time we would be seeing her," Sister Dolorosa stated. "I tried to comfort her. She then asked me whether I would be prepared to shelter her if necessary. I did not answer in the negative in order not to sadden her but, not anticipating such a request, I was not thinking seriously about what I was saying." Sister Dolorosa heard herself saying she would help in one way or another.

On November 2, 1942, the Germans launched a massive raid on the Pruzana ghetto's Jews. Two days later, Sister Dolorosa received a secret message from Olga Goldfein asking her to meet her at a certain spot near the ghetto's barbed wires. "She looked terrible. Mrs. Goldfein admitted to me that she had tried committing suicide but the injection had proved not potent enough. Seeing the hand of destiny in this, she begged me to hide her. Overcome with pity, I told her to come see me that same evening." Returning to the convent, she consulted with the other Sisters, urging them not to mention this to anyone. "I was quite worried. Maybe I was wrong to consent to hide her," Sister Dolorosa agonized silently.

That evening, Mrs. Goldfein came, looking very depressed. She remained hidden in the convent for five weeks, until matters had quieted down in the ghetto and she felt safe to return. It was now December 1942. When this incident was reported to her superior in Bialystok, Sister Dolorosa was reprimanded. She was also informed that she was demoted as punishment for affording shelter in the convent to a secular person, against the order's regulations, and would no longer be teaching in the town's elementary school. Sister Dolorosa took all this in stride.

On January 28, 1943, the Nazis launched another *Aktion* on the ghetto's diminishing Jewish population. Posters appeared in public places warning the population that the death penalty would be meted out to anyone caught helping a Jew trying to escape the Nazi dragnet. "That evening, I could not eat anything," Sister Dolorosa relates. After prayers, Sister Dolorosa was informed by the convent's superior that she had better not repeat her previous "mistake." "Very depressed, I took sleeping pills, hoping to immediately fall asleep."

At 2:00 a.m., Sister Dolorosa woke up suddenly. "My heart seemed to have turned to stone, so heavily did it weigh on me." Several minutes later, the night-guard Sister ran up to Sister Dolorosa's room with the news that Dr. Goldfein was at the convent's gate. She had escaped from a column of Jews about to board a train transporting them to their death. That January 30, 1943, Dr. Goldfein was given a nun's habit. Armed with two legally issued work-permit cards, one in her name, the other in the name of a Sister from another city who had left her card while on a visit at the convent, both women walked out of the convent. Dr. Goldfein was henceforth to be known as Sister Helena.

That evening, the two women slept in the home of a forester. They were committed to the life of wandering nuns, supporting themselves with alms from kindhearted souls. They passed through various towns and villages, on foot or by horse-drawn carriage or by train. Arriving in Bialystok, the two wandering nuns spent the night at the home of a poor family. That evening, Sister Dolorosa kept her ears open to the shots emanating from the Jewish ghetto, where a large-scale deportation raid was in process. "I remained awake with anxiety. I heard shots. I saw myself standing before the unfortunate inhabitants of the ghetto, who were surely trying to save themselves by escaping and were being shot down by Nazi bullets."

The two women continued their peregrinations. Passing through Wielka Dabrowa, they saw trains packed with Jews on their way to Treblinka camp. Sister Dolorosa recalls that "the condemned persons broke holes in the sides of some of the cars, throwing out their small children through the openings. At times, adults too jumped, so as to die on the spot and bring their sufferings to an end. Poles could not help them, for Nazi guards guarded the tracks. There were some who pillaged the dead, exploiting the tragedy of others. The preceding Sunday, the priest at Sokolow had cursed, in his sermon, this shameful behavior of some Catholics." They reached Sister Dolorosa's hometown of Olszyny, where they remained in the security of Sister Dolorosa's family for a full fifteen months. Sister Dolorosa traveled to the cathedral in Lowicz, where she made her confession while Sister Helena mixed with the crowd. One Sunday, Olga asked to be allowed to join Sister Dolorosa for Mass. "If people see us together, it will be safer," Olga reasoned. "I refused," Sister Dolorosa relates. "For me, holy communion is God, for you it's bread. The fact that you belong to a different religion does not disturb God, but my behavior must conform to the regulations and teachings of the church."

To others, Sister Helena was introduced as a former student nurse who had undergone a religious experience and taken nun's vows. Sister Helena freely treated the sick and ill. Her reputation as a healer began to spread. All her prescriptions produced wonders. In one case, she countered the diagnosis of two local physicians, who did not hesitate to denounce the mysterious Sister to the authorities. Summoned by Dr. Dietrich, the German district doctor of Rozyce, she was told she could give injections, but only on doctor's orders. "Or else, both of you will be deported to Germany."

Sister Helena continued to give free medical advice. In one case, she treated an ill child, then turned to its mother (a refugee from another region), saying, "And you, Madam, you don't look well yourself. Perhaps you're ill." "Yes, Sister!" the woman replied. "I was healed by a good doctor, a certain Mrs. Goldfein. She is probably no longer alive, since she was Jewish. I pray for her soul everyday." At this, Sister Helena, lowered her head and left the room.

After the liberation of Poland, Sister Dolorosa was informed that she had been expelled from the Order of St. Ignatius of Loyola. Accepting the verdict, she removed her nun's habit and resumed her maiden name of Genowefa Czubak. She remained faithful to her religion. Mrs. Goldfein left Poland and eventually reached Israel, where she was appointed a physician in a hospital. She died in 1974, not before giving a most treasured memento of her wartime years to the Beit Lohamei Hagetaot Museum, outside Haifa, for permanent safekeeping: a photograph of herself and her benefactress, both in nun's habits. (1851)

Anna Borkowska

Before the war, Vilna, claimed a Jewish population of 80,000. Immediately upon the entry of the Germans in June 1941, 35,000 Jews were massacred in the woods of Ponary, some 10 miles away. The rest were herded inside a ghetto and liquidated in stages.

In 1941, Anna Borkowska was mother superior of a small cloister of Dominican Sisters in Kolonia Wilenska, near Vilna. After the Ponary massacres of 1941, Anna was asked by a friend to allow members of a Zionist pioneering group to hide in the convent for brief spells of time. Anna Borkowska agreed. She describes the fugitives: "Some of them had lost their nearest and dearest—but they were calm and taciturn; only their eyes revealed their pain." Soon the convent of less than a dozen nuns was bristling with activity, for the young Jewish men and women were busily plotting an uprising in the ghetto. "If we are to die," Sister Borkowska remembers them saying, "let us die the death of free people, with arms in our hands." Resignation was replaced by a tragic obstinacy.

"They called me Ima [mother]," Anna fondly recalls. "I felt as if I were indeed their mother. I was pleased with the arrival of each new member, and was sorry that I could not shelter more of them." She evokes with sadness the names of "my girls" who passed through the convent, most of whom did not survive: Tauba, "who loved life so much, gentle, pleasant"; Margalit, "crying for her baby while working in the kitchen"; Chuma, "brave and energetic"; Wirka, liaison officer from the ghetto, "who placed mines on the nearby tracks and came rushing over to us for a cup of tea." She recalls the men as well: Michas, who had arrived at the convent "his face as pale as a holy wafer" after being hidden by his mother in an attic hole for weeks without light and air, "he helped us during the harvest, got tanned"; Israel, "good-natured and quiet . . . He [later] suffered terrible misery in the Warsaw ghetto. He wrote me a most cordial note which I shall never forget. He perished in Treblinka." There was Arieh Wilner, "I gave him the name 'Jurek,'" which was the code-name under which he was to be known for his exploits in Warsaw. where he eventually perished. "In spirit Jurek was the closest to me."

And there was, of course, Abba Kovner, the moving spirit of the Vilna underground; "my right hand," in Sister Borkowska's words. Kovner presided over secret conclaves in the convent where plans were hatched for an uprising in the Vilna ghetto. Until these plans could mature, Kovner and his sixteen colleagues worked side by side with the convent's nine nuns doing laborious work in the fields. To conceal the Jewish group's presence, they were all given nun's habits and thus they cultivated the nearby fields.

A former Jewish resident of the convent calls it "the only spark of light that shined in the general darkness; the only place where one found brotherhood and humane compassion."

In the convent cells, Abba Kovner issued his famous call for rebellion, the first of its kind in Nazi-occupied Europe, which began with the clarion words, "Let us not be led like sheep to the slaughter!" This manifesto, secretly printed in the convent, was distributed in the ghetto on January 1, 1942, and served as inspiration to many ghetto and partisan fighters.

When the time came for Abba Kovner and his comrades to return to the ghetto to lead the struggle against the Nazis, Anna Borkowska rushed to join them. "I want to go with you to the ghetto," she implored Abba Kovner, "to fight and fall alongside you. Your war is a holy war. Even though of Marxist inclination and free of religion, you are a noble people, for there is religion in your heart. A great God—now you are closer to Him than I." Kovner told her she could help the cause by smuggling in weapons. And so it was. Abraham Sutzkever, the noted Yiddish poet, relates: "The first four grenades . . . were the gift of the mother superior, who instructed Abba Kovner in their proper use. . . . She later supplied other weapons." Concealing the weapons inside her habit, she brought them to the ghetto gates and stealthily transferred them to Kovner's waiting and trembling hands. "I have come to join you," she repeated on this occasion, "for God is with you." With great difficulty, Kovner succeeded in dissuading her from that course. She returned to her convent and continued to aid those inside the ghetto from the outside. As suspicions mounted, the Germans eventually had Anna Borkowska arrested in September 1943, the convent shut, and the sisters dispersed. One sister was dispatched to a labor camp.

After the war, Abba Kovner, now in Israel, dedicated a poem to her entitled "My Little Sister." He sought in vain to reestablish contact with her but was erroneously informed that she had passed away. In 1984, learning that she was indeed still alive, he rushed to her side in a tiny Warsaw apartment and presented her with the Yad Vashem award of Righteous Among the Nations. She wondered, "Why do I deserve this honor?" Responding to her modest query, Abba Kovner evoked her selfless devotion to the cause of the harried Jews during the Holocaust. "You are Anna of the Angels," he told her. (2862)

Karolina Kmita

Sara Gewirtzman survived German liquidation raids in Lwow and Kowel during 1941 and 1942, losing most of her family in the process. On July 27, 1942 she fled from the Kowel ghetto and headed for the home of Elza Kmita, hoping to receive a valid identity card belonging to Elza's distant relative, with which she would register as a Pole for labor in Germany—at the time, a surer place to survive than in conquered Poland. While talking things over with Elza, she met Elza's mother-in-law, Karolina Kmita, commonly referred to as "Grandma Karolina," who had dropped in for a visit. Karolina suggested that Sara accompany her to her hometown village of Boza Darowka, to ride out the current wave of Nazi liquidation raids. Bandaging one of Sara's eyes to make it appear as though she were suffering from some ailment, Grandma Karolina took the twenty-year-old woman to her farmstead, where she was passed off as a distant relative by the name of Wanda. There, Sara helped them with harvesting the crops. Soon afterwards, four Jews fled from Holoby to the Kmitas' farm. They dug a pit between the field and the garden and hid therein. Sara was allowed to join them; Karolina looked after the lot.

After about a week, the four men decided things had sufficiently calmed to allow them to leave the pit. Karolina saw them off with food, money, and clothes. Sara decided to remain behind, freely circulating in the house during daylight hours and passing the night in the dark pit. The Germans then announced that Jews in hiding could return to Holoby and no harm would befall them. Karolina's motherly instincts told her differently. She warned Sara not to fall for this trick; instead, she was invited to prolong her stay with the Kmitas. Karolina's suspicions proved correct. On September 15, the Nazis unleashed a second *Aktion* on the city's remaining Jews, netting those who had willingly returned to their former dwellings. The town was declared *judenrein*, and a reward was offered for anyone turning in a Jew in hiding. The Ukrainian police, ever anxious to please and outdo their masters in this regard, immediately went on the hunt.

The Kmita family was overcome with great fear. Mikolaj Kmita, Karolina's husband, pleaded with Sara to leave them. "My dear girl," he told the speechless Sara, "if it meant only placing my property and life on the line, I would be prepared to take the risk and shelter you. But when I look at my little grandchildren, frightful fear overcomes me." Others in the family backed Mikolaj in the decision to send Sara off. But Karolina, overhearing her husband's words, had different plans for the hapless young woman. That afternoon she took Sara to a nearby forest with a supply of warm clothes and food. When they settled down, safe from any intruding eyes, Grandma Karolina told Sara: "You are my child. I shall not forsake you and I shall continue to hide you with us." She returned later that evening and took Sara to the house garden, placed her on the ground between two heaps of potatoes, and covered her with leaves. Late that same night, with everyone else sound asleep, Karolina returned to move Sara to a small pit which she had dug in a field a little distance from the house. There Sara lay motionless, covered with straw for almost two months. During those lonely cold nights, Sara reports, "Karolina used to crawl from her house [in order not to be seen] when she came to see me and to bring me food." When the others in the Kmita household were convinced that Sara was gone for good, Karolina returned and took Sara back to the pit near the house. There, Sara remained through the winter of 1942-1943 and until June 1943. At night, Karolina brought hot food and removed and washed the pan used as a chamber pot. "In the winter, she came wrapped up in a white sheet so as not to stand out against the snow, and she blurred her footprints with a twig. From time to time, she brought me clean underwear." Sara's feet were wrapped in a sack full of cotton wool and she covered herself with a warm blanket.

In June 1943, the Ukrainian police left the city, and Karolina felt safe to bring Sara into her house. It was just in time, for a shepherd had discovered the woman in the pit when one of his sheep strayed. In Karolina's home, Sara was kept hidden in the attic. With her formerly apprehensive husband now supporting her, Karolina added three more Jewish women to her household. All four survived the Holocaust and witnessed the liberation on March 6, 1944. Recalling her rescue by Grandma Karolina, in a deposition twenty years later, Sara terms her "a saint in Sodom." (301)

Surviving as a Threatened Child

At Yad Vashem a monument stands for the 1.5 million Jewish children murdered during the Holocaust. The Nazis, in their zeal to be rid of all Jews, did not differentiate between adults, teenagers and infants. The plight of helpless children, separated or orphaned from their parents, is especially poignant, and the written word cannot capture the immensity of the suffering or the awesomeness of the crime. Human language was not created to cope with such monstrosity.

The psychological wounds inflicted on children of a tender age in hiding, especially toddlers, is especially harrowing. Forced to change identities quickly and transfer their sympathies and trust to new parents, many found their forced separation from their wartime guardians after the war very painful.

Sister Alfonsa

Hedy Rosen (a four-year-old child in the summer of 1942) and her mother had wandered through the woods for two years, seeking shelter from the fury of the Nazi Final Solution. One day they arrived outside the walls of a convent in Przemysl in southern Poland. Panting for breath and on the verge of collapse, Hedy's mother looked into her daughter's eyes and told her quietly: "You have no choice. From now on your name is Jadwiga Kozowska and you are a Christian Pole." After repeating with her several verses of a Catholic prayer, she placed Hedy near the convent's entrance and disappeared behind a tree. Hedy stood there alone and wept. Her cries alerted the nuns. who opened the gates and fetched the child inside. There she stayed for two full years. She was the first Jewish child to be admitted. Twelve others followed in her wake.

St. Joseph's Heart was a children's orphanage with main offices in Cracow. In 1942, Sister Alfonsa (Eugenia Wasowska) was sent from Cracow to the Przemysl convent to help the other five nuns and one priest

A nun from the convent of St. Joseph's Heart, Przemysl, Poland, visits the children after their return to Jewish hands in 1945. Courtesy of Yad Vashem.

to care for the forty-seven orphaned Catholic children. With the approval of her Cracow superiors, the Przemysl mother superior decided to give shelter to Jewish children; she then suddenly took ill and expired. When her successor in turn fell ill, Sister Alfonsa was made responsible for the "Jewish Section" of the Catholic orphanage. Under her stewardship, a total of thirteen Jewish children (ten girls and three boys) were sheltered in the orphanage until the city's liberation in July 1944.

Przemysl had a Jewish population of 20,000 at the start of the war. When the city was liberated in 1944, only some 250 Jews had survived the Nazi terror.

Hedy's mother had in the meantime found work in a nearby village, under a new identity, and on occasion brought food to the orphanage for her daughter's sake. "I was forbidden to show the slightest sign that I knew her," relates Hedy, "for fear of the other children. I had to disregard her completely." The fear of detection was a constant threat to the children and the orphanage as well. Various tactics were used. One was to tell the Jewish boys "that if a stranger comes to the convent and asks a boy what he wants to be when he grows up, he should say a priest," Sister Alfonsa relates, adding, "We took the children to church along with Polish children, not because we were trying to make them Catholics but just so nobody would suspect they were Jews."

Miriam Klein, during a 1978 visit with the three nuns who rescued her during the war. Courtesy of Yad Vashem.

Sister Alfonsa was committed, soul and heart, to her charges. She saw to it that the children did not lack food or clothing during those years of dearth and want for the local population. Not able to repress the severe traumatic experience which had preceded their placement in the orphanage, the Jewish children were prone to sudden bursts of hysterical weeping. "Sometimes at mealtime a child would cry and throw his food on the floor," Sister Alfonsa recalls. Miriam Klein remembers some of the children screaming at night and wetting their beds. "Sister Alfonsa always knew how to calm us. Sleeping with us in the small room she was alert to every noise and often got up at night to place an additional blanket on the frightened children."

Immediately upon the city's liberation, Sister Alfonsa took the thirteen Jewish children to the newly constituted Jewish Committee in Przemysl and promptly turned them over. "They were Jewish children and belonged with Jews," Sister Alfonsa emphasized. In one case, a father who was a shoemaker, made a pair of new shoes for Sister Alfonsa as a sign of his appreciation.

After the war, Sister Alfonsa was cautioned not to discuss her wartime saving of Jewish children because of the prevalent antisemitism in many circles. She left for Australia. In 1980, she went to Israel searching for "my children." Six of them were located and reunited with their rescuer. "The image of these children were with me these past forty years. Now that I am together with them, this is the happiest moment of my life." Recalling her stay at the orphanage, Miriam Klein remarks, "I was privileged to experience calm and mental relaxation, and there I discovered the best and most beautiful of women." (1929)

Zofia Boczkowska

"I was born in Lwow in 1937," Hanna Podoszyn starts her searing testimony. "My parents were killed in one of the deportation actions of 1942." Hanna faintly remembers being placed in an Ukrainian orphanage for several days and then being fetched by her aunt, a dentist, who hid her with others behind her dental office in Busk, a town near Lwow. She then remembers being taken to a stranger—woman who treated her badly, made her sleep on the floor, and fed her starvation diets. After a few days, a friend of the woman came over to visit. Hanna was told to fetch her overcoat. They were going for a walk. When they reached a bridge spanning a river, the woman and her companion suddenly grabbed Hanna by her hands and feet and threw her into the river. "I felt a swell of cold water but I held on to a tree branch and was cast off on the riverbank." Hanna remained alone beside the river through that night, shivering in her wet clothes. When day dawned, she began to walk aimlessly. Approaching a hut, she was fed some potatoes, then taken to the nearest police post. Questioned about her background, Hanna's instincts told her to deny her Jewish origins. The German post commander suspected otherwise. Outside the post, a group of Jews, about to be shot, were digging their own graves. The commander, not sure whether to add the five-year old girl to the others, told her to stand aside while he deliberated on her fate.

At this point a woman drove up in a horse-drawn coach. Zofia Boczkowska, on her way to town for some errand. beheld from a distance a mass execution of Jews in progress, similar to those that had taken place earlier in that region. There was nothing she could do, so she drove on. Suddenly her attention was drawn to a small girl, standing alone, talking to herself, gesticulating, hopping, and dancing. "A child [among the group of adults]? But that's impossible," Zofia said to herself. She ordered the coachman to pull up. Dismounting, she approached the German commander, while not for a moment removing her eyes from the girl. She could now discern the girl's big black eyes and curly hair. She was definitely Jewish, Zofia thought to herself. The child looked terribly thin, was dressed in a long water-soaked dress, and was performing what seemed a mysterious ritual. She danced, then bent down courteously, enacted several bows, made the sign of the cross and murmured a prayer—repeating the performance several times. "I was stunned and frightened;

not knowing what to do, although I had to do something to save this little creature. I realized I must save her, otherwise I would never know peace and tranquillity again."

Approaching the German commander, she was told to leave the area forthwith. She responded that she had come to fetch the girl, whom she knew to be non-Jewish, orphaned as a result of the recent war, and with no one to turn to. Zofia reinforced her argument by assuring the commander she was prepared to return with the necessary credentials proving the girl's non-Jewish origin and added (in a quick afterthought) that she wanted to reward the commander and his aides with freshly prepared goose, other delicacies, and, of course, choice vodka. The commander agreed to spare the girl, if only for a while, letting her stay in the guardhouse for a day or two until Zofia returned with the proper papers. In the meantime, Zofia was told she could return to feed the starving child. She then sped off home.

Zofia told her husband, Stanislaw, about her encounter with the little girl at the execution site. "What are you doing, woman?" Stanislaw demurred, "You are endangering us all, and the girl will surely not be saved." Zofia's two sisters had been sent to Auschwitz by the Germans for some offense. Zofia had hoped to use whatever little money they had saved to ransom her sisters. Much of the money had already been spent in that effort but without success. Would Zofia use the remainder of her savings to acquire false credentials to rescue this little girl (Hanna), or would she follow her husband's advice and drop the whole thing? "We discussed the matter a lot during the evening. I could not ask my husband for support, though he was equally saddened by Hanna's fate. A way out had to be found. Everywhere, bulletin board notices threatened the population with the death punishment for helping Jews. We lived in a village where everyone knew us. . . . In addition, Hanna looked so Semitic. What to do? What to do?" The following morning, Zofia saw clear through her doubts and fears. A decision was reached. "The nightmarish night over, we both decided to save the little one in spite of everything!"

With this, Zofia rose briskly and hurried to prepare the food and liquor she promised the German commander, as well as some fresh nourishing soup for the hungry girl, and she returned to the German police post. The commander was happy to receive the promised delicacies and allowed Zofia to feed the girl. The little girl, unsure of Zofia's intentions and fearing another ordeal, began her ritual of dance, gesticulation, bows, and prayers. Making her sit, Zofia stroked her hair and fed her, slowly—since the girl's body was no longer used to food. The girl then fell asleep and was placed on two chairs which were joined together; she was then covered with a rough blanket. Leaving the girl, Zofia sped off to Lwow to see some friends, who helped her acquire the necessary credentials, including a false baptismal certificate, with which she sped back to the police post and obtained Hanna's release.

From that moment, Hanna became a full-fledged member of the Boczkowski family and sister to Jolanta, the daughter of her benefactors. Raised in a spirit of warmth, love, and care, Hanna for once knew peace and security. When she was a little older, she was told that the other girl in her hosts' care was also Jewish. Janka Stiglitz was the sole survivor of a family of Jews, previously employed on the landowner's estate where Stanislaw was employed; her whole family had been killed in a sudden German raid in 1943. The young Janka had been found hiding in the bushes. She had first been taken by Zofia to her brother, then at a later point she was brought to the Boczkowskis' own home.

After the war, Hanna studied medicine and married a Jewish fellow student; both left for Israel in 1954. When Hanna wrote from Israel, offering financial help to her adoptive mother, Zofia replied, "Not for this; we did not give in order to take something in return from you. Your love is for us the most beautiful payment. We shall somehow survive." (239)

Marja Maciarz

Before they were transported to the notorious Plaszow camp, during the liquidation of the Cracow ghetto in March 1943, Natalia and David Twersky arranged for their three-year-old son Jack to be sheltered by Natalia's school friend. During a previous German *Aktion* in the ghetto, the boy had already been hidden in her home in the suburb of Podgorze. The woman promised the worried parents to look after their only child for as long as it might require.

However, the harsh punitive measures by the Nazis against Poles who sheltered Jews, and the constant search for hidden Jews by Gestapo agents, finally broke the willpower of this woman. No longer willing to jeopardize her own two daughters, she decided to deliver Natalia's son to the Gestapo. In the hallway on her way out with the little boy, she ran into her mother-in-law, Marja Maciarz, who lived in the same building. Not suspecting her daughter-in-law's intentions, Marja cautioned her not to take the child out on the street because of the danger of detection. To which Helena answered that the boy would no longer be a cause of danger to others, for he was about to be turned over to the Gestapo. Marja Maciarz was appalled. She reminded Helena that she had promised to care for the boy until the end of war, and had even been rewarded for this well in advance, but to no avail. Finally, Marja grabbed the boy's hand and said she would take care of the boy herself and that she would accompany him to the Gestapo if her daughter-in-law reported the boy. "Neither I nor my husband knew Marja Maciarz personally before and she didn't know us," Natalia Twersky writes. Her husband David was able to learn of Marja's magnanimous deed from inside the camp and to establish contact with her. "Our financial help to Marja was minimal—old clothing which she sold in the market."

In August 1944, David was transported to Mauthausen camp, while Natalia was moved in October of that year to Auschwitz, then to Ravensbrück. "Our contact with Marja Maciarz and our son came to an end." Luckily for both, they survived. Walking on foot all the way back to Poland from Germany at the end of war (there was as yet no organized transportation), they met the rescuer of their child. "I found our son Jack in Marja Maciarz's apartment in good health and surrounded by love," Natalia notes. Jack called her *babci*, "grandma." It was later learned that Marja had cared for and sheltered two additional distraught Jewish persons.

Before parting from Marja and Poland to start a new life elsewhere, Natalia turned her parents' home over to Marja. Marja signed the deed with the sign of the cross. "Illiterate, but with the heart and feelings of a saint," Natalia notes. (2960)

Alexander Roslan

In early 1943, the Warsaw ghetto was going through its death throes. From an original population of some 500,000 Jews, it had been reduced by Nazi deportations to less than 50,000. Hanna, the aunt of the three Gutgold brothers, was at her wits' end, trying to figure out a scheme to save the young boys. The boys' father had earlier fled to Russia, hoping to be able to fetch his sons out of Warsaw in due time. The German attack on Russia in June 1941 scuttled these plans. The boys' mother had died before the war.

Aunt Hanna decided to approach the family's prewar chauffeur, living on the Aryan side, and seek his advice on how best to smuggle the children out of the doomed ghetto. She made it to the chauffeur's home without being recognized or stopped, only to learn to her dismay that he had been arrested on a smuggling charge and shot. The owner of the chauffeur's one-room flat noticed Hanna's dejected look and volunteered his assistance. When told of Hanna's efforts to find a safe refuge for the three boys, this stranger suggested that they move into his flat. Not believing her ears, Hanna instinctively promised the man a rich reward after the war was over. To this he responded, "If we succeed in getting out of the Nazi hell alive, reward me then. If not, what use is money?" The die was cast. The man had not even consulted his wife. His name was Alexander Roslan.

"We stole out of the ghetto in the dark of the night," David (then five years old) relates. David's two brothers, Shalom (seven years old) and Jacob (ten years old) were taken to Roslan's home, whereas David was temporarily moved to the home of Roslan's brother-in-law. This man, it turned out, was an unstable person, given to drinking too much and to physically abusing his wife, so Alexander Roslan removed David and brought him to his own home.

In addition to the Roslans' own two children they were now sheltering the three Gutgold boys in their home. Yet this did not deter Alexander from suggesting to Hanna that she and her other relatives flee the ghetto immediately and join the boys in his home. They gratefully acknowledged this offer but asked that the move be postponed until after Passover, for they wished to celebrate the traditional Seder in the company of their coreligionists inside the ghetto. This proved to be a fateful decision, for the final Nazi *Aktion* was launched on the first day of Passover. Hanna was taken to Auschwitz. For a time Alexander managed to have gold coins smuggled to her through a third party. Soon all traces of Hanna were lost and it was presumed that she had perished in that notorious camp. But the three boys were safe and sound in Roslan's home.

After a while, Jacob and Shalom came down with scarlet fever. Alexander made arrangements to have them admitted to a hospital under false pretenses. They were smuggled out of his home hidden in a sofa in which holes were bored to allow for fresh air. Shalom died on the operating table, but Jacob survived. His recovery, though, proved to be longer than originally anticipated and this involved additional expenses. Roslan moved with his family from their three-room apartment to a one-room apartment in order to be able to cover the costs of the additional treatment.

Jacob and David remained hidden underneath the bed or in the kitchen closet whenever strangers visited. In order to compensate for the lack of sunlight in the boys' hiding place, Alexander bought an ultraviolet lamp for their use. He also bought them rare and expensive fruit. "He neglected his own children for our sakes," David relates. One day, Jacob remembers, the Polish police came to check on a neighbor's report of having seen a strange boy. "But the Roslans got them drunk and entertained them all night," David says, "and by the time they left they had forgotten they were looking for Jews."

With the destruction of Warsaw, following the aborted Polish uprising of August-October 1944 (during which the Roslans lost their son in a German bombardment), and the forcible expulsion of its inhabitants, the Roslans wandered with their charges from place to place for six months, hiding in barns and eating scraps of food.

After the war, Alexander Roslan took his family to Germany as the first step in a hoped-for emigration to the United States. David and Jacob joined him. They parted ways at one of the DP camps. The two boys continued to Palestine to be reunited with their father, who had arrived there in 1941 by way of Russia. Until that moment, the Roslans had cared for the two boys, even paying for their education. The Roslans, including their surviving child, Mary, reached the United States in 1947 and settled in New York, where Alexander found a job as a foreman for a construction company.

In 1962, Jacob, an Israel nuclear chemist, finally managed to locate his former benefactors after a frustrating fifteen years search. Arriving in the United States for research work in his field, Jacob took his wife and little daughter for a reunion with the Roslan family. "It was just like a homecoming," Jacob exulted. "He was just like our own son," Alexander replied, adding "I have no words to describe the attitude, devotion, and self-sacrifice of this man for all the time we spent in his house [four years]. It seems to me that only a talented and conscientious author would be capable of encompassing and exhausting the deeds of this very dear person." (427)

Nannies and Household Maids to the Rescue

As was customary throughout Europe, nannies, maids, and governesses were inseparable household members of many families, including Jewish families. These devoted women stood many Jews in good stead during the Holocaust.

Gertruda Babilinska

In late 1939, Michael Stolowicki's mother fled the Germans to Vilna, which was then occupied by the Russians. There she learned that her husband had died in France under mysterious circumstances. Gravely ill, she had the family nursemaid, Gertruda Babilinska, make a vow that four-year-old Michael would be taken to safety in Palestine after the war. After the death of her mistress, Gertruda passed the child off as her own son, and induced a priest to admit the boy into a church choir. Michael's task included sprinkling holy water during services, even on German officers and soldiers who attended mass. To support herself, Gertruda helped local inhabitants draft petitions to the occupation authorities in German, a language with which she, as a native of Danzig (now Gdansk), was familiar. In exchange, she received payment in the form of eggs, dairy products, and other foodstuff.

After the war, she learned that her fiancee had been killed as a partisan. Keeping faith with the vow she had taken taken in 1939, she bade farewell to her family and set out with the child for Palestine. In Italy she and Michael boarded the illegal refugee ship *Exodus*. On its way to Palestine, the ship was intercepted on the high seas by the British navy in 1947, and its occupants were sent back to a displaced refugee camp in Hamburg, Germany. Gertruda and Michael eventually reached the newly founded State of Israel in 1948, and they both settled there. Gertruda remained faithful to the Catholic religion, but she raised Michael in the Jewish tradition, in accordance with the wishes of his late parents. (11)

Janina Pawlicka

At times, housemaids transferred their allegiance to other threatened Jews when conditions under Nazi rule caused them to be separated from the host family that had originally employed them.

Janina Pawlicka's story is a classic example of such faithfulness. "I was born in 1910," she states in a 1962 deposition to Yad Vashem. "As a young girl on my own, I was forced to find a job to support myself. I was hired as a housemaid by the Aaronson family: a good and well-to-do family, owners of a large textile firm. I looked after the two children in the family. I felt very good there because of the wonderful treatment I received."

When the war broke out, the Aaronsons fled. They eventually reached Warsaw, where they were required, as were other Jews, to move into the restricted Jewish ghetto. Janina joined them in the ghetto despite the fact that as a non-Jew she could have lived freely on the Aryan side. The Aaronsons were able to acquire foreign visas in 1942, and they left the ghetto, with German approval, to take up residence at the Hotel Polski on the Aryan side. It later turned out to be trap. All who fell prey to this ruse were transported to Vittel camp in France; thence to concentration camps.

Janina, left behind, decided to help other Jews in distress. She accepted the proposition of several ghetto families that she use money they provided to rent an apartment on the Aryan side in which they could hide after escaping the ghetto. Janina found a third-story, three-room apartment. After some interior structural rearrangements, eleven people moved in (including the famous Bund leader Bernard Goldstein) and remained hidden in one of the rooms, whose entrance was camouflaged from the rest of the apartment by a stove. Janina was known to be poor and living by herself, and in order to camouflage the buying of food for such a large group of people she made shopping trips to various parts of the city. Every morning, Janina left for work (doing knitting), locking the apartment behind her, and she returned in the evening to care for her charges.

This arrangement worked well for a year, when in September 1943 the apartment was suddenly raided by two Gestapo agents. The raid was so sudden that none of those inside had time to flee to their separate room, which was concealed from the rest of the apartment. They were now at the mercy of the two agents. Luckily for Janina and her charges, the agents contented themselves with looting the apartment. Five days later, they returned to resume their looting spree, collecting everything of value— jewelry, trinkets, ornaments, and other household items—which they stuffed in three valises. Before leaving, one of the agents turned around and said: "We won't be back, but you should know that others may turn up." The implication was clear; they had better flee immediately. That same day, all vacated the apartment. They spent one evening in a toy store which had closed down, then took up residence in an unused darkroom in a photographer's studio. Space was limited so they all slept on the floor, including Janina, allowing one elderly woman to occupy the lone bed. After the war, as in her youthful days, Janina was hired as a housemaid by a new Jewish family, who took her along with them when they moved to Israel in 1957. (76)

Humanitarianism as a Crime

Julian Ney and Anna Bogdanowicz

Soon after Poland's defeat and the end of hostilities in September 1939, scores of refugees flooded the town of Jaslo, in southern Poland, among them Anna Bogdanowicz and her family. Originally from Jaslo, before the war she had moved to Kielce, where her husband, Marcel, was district attorney. Anna decided to prolong her stay in Jaslo together with her two sons, so as to be near her mother during this troublesome period, while her husband returned to Kielce to resume his prewar post in the municipality.

As the Germans forbade the reopening of schools, Anna arranged private tutoring for her two sons. She hired her friend Sara Diller, who had been a teacher before the war, as the children's tutor. Thus began a relationship that would eventually bring tragedy to one and deliverance to the other.

A promising young physician named Julian Ney lived on the same street as Sara. They knew of each other but had not met before the war. Sara's mother suffered from a heart ailment. Since the town's experienced doctors had fled eastward, Sara enlisted Ney's services. Her mother was unimpressed when she first saw him; too young, in her opinion, to be taken seriously as a doctor. The fact that he did not sport a beard, as other doctors did, was added proof for the ailing mother that he lacked experience. But this was no time to be too fussy about choosing a doctor, so Julian Ney's services were retained. His frequent visits to Sara's mother's bedside led to a growing romantic relationship between the young non-Jewish doctor and the Jewish teacher. Ney came often, ostensibly to receive lessons in German from Sara, but in truth to be as close as possible to the object of his affections. When the first *Aktionen* began in the summer of 1942, Ney urged Sara to flee. Acquiring new credentials for her, Ney had her move to the non-Jewish section of the city. Her name was now Maria Janina Dubiel.

Soon thereafter, a train was seen waiting several miles outside the city; rumors circulated that it was intended for the town's last Jews. Julian and Anna decided to act quickly. On August 14, 1942, as Sara returned from work (manufacturing bags for the German army), her mother informed her that a ticket had been purchased for her for a train leaving that evening. "I said goodbye to my mother and grandmother, with the premonition that I was probably seeing them for the last time." At the station, Anna and her elder son, Antoni ("Tosiek"), were waiting. Before the train departed, Ney appeared, in time to bid Sara farewell, assuring her that all would turn out fine and urging her to write him often. During the journey, the conversation in the compartment turned on the *Aktion* against the Jews which was just unfolding at that moment. Most of the other passengers expressed satisfaction that the Jews were finally being removed. Anna gritted her teeth and kept quiet.

Arriving in Kielce, Anna could not admit Sara into her spacious home because of her husband's pronounced antisemitism. He was now the appointed mayor of the city. Sara was initially placed with a teaching couple, friends of Anna's, who were not aware of Sara's true identity. She was presented to them as Maria Dubiel. From that moment, Anna Bogdanowicz devoted herself to Sara's welfare. "She watched over my every step with maternal care, and occupied herself with the minutest detail, in spite of the fact that I was an adult."

Through a municipality official (and unbeknownst to her husband, the mayor), Anna obtained for Sara a legitimate ID card under her adopted name. She then took Sara to be registered as a Kielce resident. At the municipality, Anna and Sara accidentally ran into Anna's husband. Marcel had known Sara from the time when she gave lessons to his two sons and he had come to Jaslo to visit his family. "He stared at me in terror, then greeted me politely and sped off," Sara relates. The following day, Anna told Sara of the furor raised by her husband the previous evening after he arrived home from work. He accused her of unnecessarily endangering the whole family for a Jewess. He told her bluntly, "You know that I hate Jews. I shall do nothing to help them. On the contrary, I'll do everything to help be rid of them. Of course, I have no objection to Miss Sara being saved. However, if you should get in trouble because of her, I shall not be able to help you."

Sara moved to several locations, supporting herself by tutoring and doing household chores. Anna shared with her some of the food received from Anna's mother in Jaslo (where food was less scarce than in Kielce) and visited her constantly. Anna usually came on Sundays, skipping the obligatory mass. She was a devout Catholic, but felt that under the present circumstances, her absence from mass was not a violation of her religious obligations. She felt that encouraging and uplifting the spirits of the person in her care was a comparable if not greater duty.

In November 1942, coinciding with the final liquidation of the Jaslo ghetto, Anna Bogdanowicz received a letter from her mother, worded in cryptic language. It spoke of danger. Dr. Ney had been arrested by the Gestapo, and Anna's mother urged that Sara flee immediately.

Anna deliberated what to do next and decided that she would maintain Sara under her care, come what may. It was a fateful decision. At the time, Sara was staying with a forester's family at the edge of a forest outside Kielce. There, she tutored the children and did various household chores. One day, soon after the receipt of the ominous letter, Sara rode into town, ostensibly to buy Christmas presents for her hosts but in truth to learn if anything new had transpired. Stopping off at the home of the teaching couple with whom she had stayed when she first reached Kielce, she was received coldly. The wife blurted out, "What? A Jewess in my home! Get away from here, get away. How dare you?" Not giving Sara time to catch her breath, the woman informed her of the arrest of the whole Bogdanowicz family.

Sara was stiff with fear, but, regaining her composure, responded, "Don't shout at me. . . I'm going directly to the Gestapo to confess and get Anna released. My life is no longer of any consideration." Finally admitting Sara into her home, the woman told of a message from the imprisoned Anna for Sara, smuggled out of jail, urging her to flee the city but not to use the train, for Sara's picture, drawn from her ID card (a duplicate was on file at the municipality), had been distributed to police agents at the station. If she was apprehended, she was to deny any role by Anna in her rescue, and only admit knowing her from school days and meeting her accidentally on the streets of Kielce for a brief forty-five-minute conversation. She was to do this for the sake of Anna's family.

Sara fled to Cracow and then to Warsaw, where, with the help of friends, she survived on the Aryan side until September 1943, when she was dispatched as a Pole to Austria (then part of Germany) for forced labor. In April 1945, on the eve of Nazi Germany's fall, she crossed into Switzerland through the principality of Lichtenstein. There she learned from a Jewish refugee from Kielce that Anna Bogdanowicz had been deported to Auschwitz "for something having to do with helping a Jewess."

She left for Israel, where in 1948 she learned of the fate of her two benefactors. Under interrogation, Anna had taken full responsibility for Sara's disappearance, making possible the freeing of her husband and her eldest son, Antoni. Sent to Auschwitz, she contracted typhus and died. Her body was consumed in the crematorium flames. Julian Ney was tortured to force him to reveal Sara's whereabouts. Refusing to speak, he died under mysterious circumstances—by his own hand, according to one version, so as to spare himself further torture. As a further punishment, the Germans ordered his body buried in a Jewish cemetery.

In 1963, Sara renewed contact with both her benefactors' families. Visiting Israel in 1984 to plant a tree in his mother's memory at Yad Vashem, Antoni stated that he viewed the tree as symbolizing his mother's final resting place. He would return to the tree as often as possible. There was no other place he could commune with his mother's memory. "Now I know where my mother lies buried—here in Jerusalem." (2685,2686)

Jakub and Zofia Gargasz

Jakub Gargasz and his wife Zofia lived in the town of Brzozow in the Krosno district, where they owned a farm. During the war, they gave shelter in their home to Henia Katz, an elderly Jewish woman whom they knew from before the war, after she was found hiding in the attic of their house. Mrs. Katz had escaped deportation in nearby Sanok in November

1942. She was sick, lonely and terrified. Jakub and Zofia, both members of fthe Seventh-Day Adventist Church, decided after some hesitation to nurse the sixty-five-year old Henia back to health and care for her. Mrs. Katz had some valuables and jewelry in her possession from which she paid for her maintenance. Betrayed by a neighbor, all three were arrested. Henia Katz was shot, whereas her protectors were charged with the offense of *Judenbegünstigung*—extending help to Jews. The court was presided over by three learned judges, two of whom had earned doctoral degrees. On April 26, 1944, the court pronounced its sentence: death for both defendants. The grounds for such harsh punishment, as meticulously spelled out by the learned judges, and neatly typed in the official court minutes, read in part as follows:

> The defendant claims that as an Adventist, her religion forbids expelling a sick person from one's home. This compelled her to keep the Jewess until she had recovered. . . . According to paragraph 1 of police regulations for the establishment of a Jewish quarter in the district of Radom, Cracow, and Galicia, dated November 10, 1942 (VOB1, p. 683), Jewish residential quarters were ordered established in the various cities in the Cracow district. Brzezow is not part of these cities. It was hence forbidden for the Jewess Katz to be found in Brzezow after December 1, 1942 (paragraph 2/2 of above regulation). Therefore, the moment the defendant decided, in spite of the above, to keep the Jewess in her home, she was guilty as charged (in accordance with paragraph 3/2 of above). . . . The defendant's claim that her religion obligates her to help a sick person and forbids her to remove him are of no consequence. Police regulations were enacted for state security reasons, and the religious motivations of individual persons cannot controvert such regulations. It is therefore necessary to impose on the defendant the only penalty which the law prescribes—the death penalty. As for the defendant's husband, he too must bear this penalty, for the moment he discovered the Jewess in his home and did not expel her immediately but, on the contrary, together with his wife nursed the Jewess back to health, he too was an accomplice to the act of sheltering her. . . . As the law allows only the death penalty for extending aid to Jews, this too must be imposed on the husband. In accordance with paragraph 465 (St.Po.), the defendants must bear the court costs.

This death sentence for the "sin" of trying to save the life of a sixty-five-year old Jewess was signed by Justices Pooth, Stumpel, and Dr. Aldenhoff, and witnessed by Dr. Voltereck and Dr. Naumann, all respected jurists—"on behalf of the German people."

In this instance, Jakub and Zofia Gargasz were more fortunate than others of their countrymen who were sentenced to death for similar offenses. On June 6, 1944 (with the Red Army speedily approaching the prewar Polish-Soviet border), Hans Frank, the Nazi governor-general of occupied Poland, decided to commute the Gargaszes' death sentences to incarceration in concentration camps. They survived the war and were liberated by Allied troops. (1622)

Irena Sendler

Irena Sendler was one of the most active members in the Council for Aid to Jews (code name "Zegota"), a Polish underground organization, which operated primarily in the Warsaw area. In the early days of the German occupation, she worked to alleviate the sufferings of many of her prewar Jewish friends and acquaintances. Employed by the Social Welfare Department of the Warsaw municipality, she carried a special permit allowing her to visit the ghetto area at all times, ostensibly for the purpose of combating contagious diseases. This afforded her ample opportunities to furnish many Jews with clothing, medicine, and money. When she walked through the ghetto streets, Irena wore the "star" armband as a sign of solidarity with the Jewish people; wearing the armband also helped prevent attracting attention that might have interfered with her valuable work.

In the summer of 1942, Irena was invited to join the newly founded Council for Aid to Jews. She became a valuable asset to Zegota, for she already claimed a large group of people dedicated to her charitable work, including her companion Irena Schulz, and she had a widespread network of contacts inside and outside the ghetto. Under the code name "Jolanta," she arranged for Jewish children to be smuggled out of the ghetto and for secure places to be found for them with non-Jewish families in the Warsaw region. Each of her coworkers was made responsible for several building blocks where Jewish children were sheltered. "I myself had eight or ten flats where Jews were hiding under my care," Irena proudly states. The sheltering families received financial supported from Zegota.

In October 1943, Irena was arrested by the Gestapo, taken to the infamous Pawiak prison, and brutally tortured. Failing to get information they wanted, her inquisitors told her she was doomed. In the meantime, however, her Jewish underground companions had bribed one of the Gestapo agents, and on the day she was to be executed, she was freed, although she was officially listed among those executed. Forced to stay out of sight for the remainder of the German occupation, Irena conducted her humanitarian activities from her hiding place.

Irena Sendler explained that her actions were driven by lessons learned in the unique atmosphere at her parents' home. Her father was a physician, and "most of his patients were poor Jews; I grew up among these people. All my life, I had Jewish friends." She then added, "My family taught me that what matters is whether people are honest or dishonest, not what religion they belong to." (153)

* * *

The concluding story in this chapter encapsulates many of the issues facing would-be rescuers. These individuals were forced to struggle many times over not only with the Germans but also with their own conflicted feelings: self-preservation against self-respect; hesitation against determination; fear against courage; suffering against comfort; resignation against tenacity. Ultimately, however, their love for their fellow human beings prevailed.

Miron Tarasiewicz

On May 1, 1943, Eliezer Livyatan and his friend were again out in the woods in the Vilna region (which before the war belonged to Poland), heading for a new and as yet unknown destination. After escaping from a German labor camp, they had found temporary shelter in a Polish peasant home. After two weeks, apologizing for not being able to keep them any longer, he referred them to another peasant, Miron Tarasiewicz, who, in his opinion, might agree to shelter them for a week or two. Approaching Tarasiewicz, they were led to a barn and invited to spend the night there. Eliezer and his friend, exhausted from the day's events, immediately fell asleep—just as their host dropped in for a chat. As Eliezer relates, "The man was shocked at our appearance. He felt great pain listening to our sufferings and wept as we narrated our experiences. We too wept." In the ensuing conversation, Miron asked the two men, "But why did you decide to approach me?" "Because your friend Sztom told us you had a reputation as a good man," Eliezer replied. At this, Miron embraced both men and said, "If my friend endangered himself by hosting you for two weeks, for sure I shall do likewise!"

Alerting his family (a wife and three children), Miron made sure the two men received the best food available. Eliezer asked for water, but was instead offered fresh milk. "It is completely fresh," Mrs. Tarasiewicz assured the startled Eliezer. "I have just milked the cows." Two weeks passed, and the two guests prepared themselves to thank their host and continue their wanderings. On their final evening, Miron's daughter, Irka, brought them dinner in the barn with the following message: "Daddy asked me to inform you that due to the inclement weather he wishes you to stay for a while longer. As you can see, it is raining outside." As Eliezer learned later, Miron had been led to believe by too-optimistic rumors that a giant Russian offensive was developing which would, in two weeks time, rid the area of the Germans. Eliezer knew better; the Germans had still not been dislodged from their fortified positions at the gates of Leningrad, several hundred miles away.

The two additional weeks passed and Eliezer and his friend again bade farewell to their benefactor. "We thanked our host in moving words for his good deeds toward us; we embraced and kissed one another. Tears streamed from the eyes of the peasant." Then Miron said: "Poor souls! Where will you go? Who will take you in? Please, stay with me for another two weeks! Let's wait and see what the coming days have in store for us!

Perhaps the period of sufferings will pass. It is very likely that the Germans will be fully defeated and this terrible war will end!"

The two men thanked their benefactor profusely and accepted his invitation to stay on. They were very fortunate indeed, for they had no place to go. The dangers for Miron and his family were immense. German soldiers stopped at his home almost every day, for fresh sausage, eggs, butter, honey, and a never-to-be-missed gulp of vodka. Miron Tarasiewicz forced himself to act the role of a charming host to these uninvited intruders, while at the back of his mind he worried about the safety of his two charges, tucked away in the hayloft of his barn.

Six weeks had now passed and Eliezer and his friend felt they no longer wished to abuse their benefactor's hospitality. They decided to peremptorily thank him and leave, not giving him time to change his mind. The evening preceding their departure they were surprised not to receive their customary dinner, usually brought to them by a member of the family. Early the following morning, Miron came to the barn and told the two men: "Do you know what we were thinking and deliberating during the whole evening? We are perfectly aware that if we are fated to die, we shall die together! So, from now on you remain at ease. You may stay with us for as long as you wish." Writing years later, Eliezer tried to recapture his feelings at Miron's exceptional generosity:

> His words seemed to have been uttered in a dream. Perhaps this is all just a dream? Is it reality? No, no—it must be a dream! But it is really otherwise! Here, before us, stands Tarasiewicz, excited and shivering. Tears unashamedly stream down from his eyes and he is speaking: "Together we shall await deliverance. Through a common effort, we shall overcome all obstacles." We embraced and wept. Our joy was limitless. We responded to this noble-minded farmer: "But we have no money, and how shall we pay you? How shall we reward you for your deeds? With what shall we pay for the food you provided us after arriving here as though from the grave, exhausted, battered, naked, hungry, and thirsty? How shall we repay you?" "Never mind," Tarasiewicz calmed us. "We shall stay together. In due time we'll talk about the costs. My only wish is to see you through alive and happy . . . I am confident that we shall both yet see good times."

The Russian army liberated the area on July 7, 1944. Tarasiewicz's fears, however, did not pass with the end of the German occupation. Some of his neighbors, upon learning of the man's help to Jews, vandalized his home, causing extensive damage, and took off with his few cattle. They tried harming him but he managed to elude them. Then came an eight-year stay in distant Siberia for as yet unknown reasons. at a time when Stalin ruled over the Soviet Union, including the region where the Tarasiewicz home was located. "For two years, we wandered to and fro until we met Tarasiewicz," Eliezer Livyatan states in his deposition. "What a man! He symbolized, in our eyes, the best in man. He was, indeed, an angel!" (283)

Polish woman photographed by the Germans with the two Jews she tried to rescue; pinned to her dress a sign stating that she was being punished for her "offense." On display in the Auschwitz (Oswiecim) museum. Origin unknown. Courtesy of Yad Vashem.

Lithuania and Latvia

On June 22, 1941, when Nazi Germany launched its armies against Soviet Russia, some 250,000 Jews resided in Lithuania, which had been annexed to the U.S.S.R. in 1940. Before the year was out, most of them had been murdered in an orgy of bloodshed unprecedented in its fury, cruelty, and thoroughness even by contrast with what happened in Ukraine!

The most shocking aspect of this mass slaughter was that it was perpetrated mostly by Lithuanians, who started the killings as soon as the Russian forces withdrew. Once the Germans arrived on the scene, they were more than happy to let Lithuanian auxiliary units continue the bloody business and did little more than supervise the carnage. When a halt was finally called, about 80 percent of the country's prewar Jewish population had been wiped out.

The survivors were herded into ghettos in Vilnius (Vilna), Kaunas (Kovno), and Siauliai (Shavli), where they were decimated in the next few years. The Kaunas ghetto was liquidated in July 1944, most of its residents murdered by Lithuanian auxiliaries at the notorious Forts 7 and 9; the same fate soon befell the Jews of the other two cities. Those from Vilnius were killed in the nearby Ponary forest. By the time the Red Army liberated the country, there were hardly any Jews left, save for those who had joined or formed partisan bands and less than 1,000 who were in hiding with non-Jews.

This tragic finale to Lithuanian Jewry comes as a surprise in a country which does not claim a history of antisemitic outbreaks, none to compare with the Russian pogroms of the nineteenth century or the Ukrainian massacres in the seventeenth century. Antisemitic feelings hardly made a dent before World War I, when Lithuania, as well as Latvia and Estonia, was part of the Russian Empire.

237

In the wake of the short-lived Nazi-Soviet nonaggression pact of 1939, the Russians occupied the country and outrightly annexed it in July 1940. The new authorities, wishing to remove nationalist persons from influential positions in the local government, eased the employment of Jews favoring the new communist regime. This led to a growing resentment against the Jews by most classes in Lithuanian society, overlooking the fact that the Soviet authorities persecuted non-communist Jewish movements (such as the various Zionist factions) with as much vigor as they applied against Lithuanian nationalist elements, and even more so.

Thus on June 14, 1941, on the eve of the German invasion, the Russians staged a roundup of leading Lithuanian nationalists. Some 40,000 were exiled to the interior of Russia. When the German army opened hostilities on June 22, 1941, the overwhelming majority of Lithuanians welcomed them as liberators. Cables sent to Berlin, and signed by leading representatives of Lithuanian society, including the heads of the churches, congratulated Hitler on "liberating" Lithuania from the Soviet yoke and committed themselves to further German aims in the region, in which there was no room for Jews.

To translate intentions into deeds, Lithuanian irregular and regular units (the so-called battalions) staged massive killings of Jews, including the destruction of whole communities in the provinces, almost to the last person, utilizing especially horrid methods which even at times shocked the Germans. German military dispatches to Berlin report not only the friendly reception of the German military by Lithuanians, but also their avidity in taking the lead in the slaying of Jews, much to the satisfaction of the German *Einsatzgruppen*, the Nazi mobile killing units, mainly responsible for the "solution of the Jewish question" in the area. One of these units, under direct German supervision, was indeed made up solely by Lithuanian volunteers—not counting the other Lithuanian formations, which enthusiastically collaborated with their masters in ridding the country of the unwanted Jews.

But if many Lithuanians believed that their work as executioners for the Germans, and their willingness to volunteer for "extra work" by lending a hand in liquidation operations across the border, in Byelorussia and Poland, would be liberally rewarded, they were soon in for a heartbreaking disappointment. Hitler and the top Nazis (with the exception perhaps of Alfred Rosenberg, who did not pull much weight in the Nazi hierarchy) had other designs for Lithuania, considered an inferior country, though not on the same low scale as Poland.

Administratively, the country was lumped together with Latvia, Estonia, and Byelorussia as the Reich Commissariat Ostland, and ruled by a German-appointed commissioner. Although not as rudely treated as the Polish people, and even granted a measure of cultural autonomy for a brief spell, the Lithuanians did not fare too well under the Nazi heel.

It did not take them too long to wake up to the realization that they had replaced one tyranny for another, no less baneful to Lithuanian aspirations. At first, Lithuanian nationalists appealed to the Germans for a greater understanding of local aspirations. When such pleadings struck no responsive chord in Berlin, and with the onset of German military reverses, starting with the great defeat at Stalingrad in February 1943, Lithuanians began to gradually distance themselves from a too close affiliation with their German overlords. Feelers were sent out to the Western Allies, in the hope of staving off a renewed Soviet occupation of the country.

This period coincided with the increase of rescue attempts of Jews by individual Lithuanians, although the killings by Lithuanian auxiliary forces went on until the bitter end. Underground cells were formed with the aim of combating both Germans and Russians. However, no major effort whatsoever was undertaken by any clandestine organization to help save the remnants of this once-proud Jewish community. All rescue undertakings were the work of individuals. Among the helpers, one finds persons from all walks of life and occupations, including the clergy (although the church hierarchy, previously sympathetic to Germany, stayed aloof from any pro-rescue undertakings).

The record for Jews in nearby Latvia is no more inspiring. The majority of the local population gave the Germans a rapturous welcome, regarding them as liberators from the Soviet regime. Many enlisted in special German-led units to help with work of the liquidation of unwanted elements, with the Jews topping the list. With this, and with no help by the country's civic leaders, the fate of the country's 95,000 Jews was sealed. Most were massacred in the months immediately following the German occupation, led to nearby forests and shot near prepared ditches (such as the Rumbuli forest outside Riga, where 10,600 Jews were shot in one day alone). In the Riga ghetto, some 5,000 able-bodied Jews remained to meet German labor needs. These too were slowly decimated. By the time the country was liberated, in late 1944, hardly 1,000 Jews had survived the Nazi nightmare.

* * *

Vilnius, Lithuania's largest city, was part of Poland before World War II but was included in the territories taken by Russia in 1939. Known as the Jerusalem of the North, it had long been a major center of Jewish cultural and religious life. Around 57,000 Jews lived there at the time of the German invasion in June 1941. Barely 600 were still alive when the city was liberated in July 1944.

The chapter on Poland tells about Anna Borkowska and other Polish residents of the Vilnius area who extended aid to Jews. The three stories that follow are about Lithuanians who did the same.

Ona Simaite

Ona Simaite, a librarian at the University of Vilnius, was distressed by what the Germans and their Lithuanian collaborators were doing to the city's Jews. "I was unable to work," she wrote. "I was unable to remain in my study. I was unable to eat. I was ashamed not to be Jewish myself. I knew how dangerous it would be, but it didn't matter. A force stronger than myself was at work."

Hoping to serve as a go-between the Jews and the outside world, Ona obtained permission to enter the ghetto on the pretext of recovering library books borrowed by Jewish students before the German invasion. This made it possible for her to save many valuable literary and historical works from YIVO and other Jewish institutions and from the collections of private individuals like the Yiddish poet Abraham Sutzkever. She cached them in a variety of places, hiding some under the floor of her flat.

On her daily visits to the ghetto, Ona smuggled in food and other necessities. In addition, she helped some of her friends there to raise money for food by bringing them possessions they had left with non-Jews, often having to undergo abuse, and even threats of physical violence, from the people she had to call on to recover the property. Ona also made arrangements for temporary accommodations for Jews who managed to escape from the ghetto. In her modest flat, she washed the lice-ridden clothes of the escapees, returning them clean and neatly pressed.

In due course Ona befriended Tanya Sterntal, a lone Jewish girl, and decided to rescue her. Sneaking her past the guards at the entrance to the ghetto, Ona took Tanya home with her. "She brought me to her room and cared for me like the mother of an unfortunate child," Tanya relates. For a while Tanya lived in the attic of the university library, but when two thieves happened on her hiding place, Ona moved her to another location.

Under surveillance by the Nazis for some time, Ona Simaite was finally arrested in the summer of 1944 when she adopted a ten-year old Jewish girl, registering her as a war orphan from a bombed-out town which, upon investigation, turned out to be nonexistent. She was brutally tortured but refused to divulge any information about her Jewish contacts. "I prayed that I wouldn't say anything when they tortured me," Ona later said. "I would purposely mix up names and addresses in order to forget them. I am not a believer, but at that moment I prayed with all my heart." The torture ruptured Ona's spine, leaving her in pain for the rest of her life.

The Nazis intended to execute Ona, but her friends at the university bribed them to reduce her sentence to imprisonment in a concentration camp. She was sent to Dachau and later was transferred to southern France, where she gained her freedom after the Allied invasion in August 1944. Except for a brief spell in Israel, Ona Simaite lived in France until her death in 1970.

Ona Simaite consistently refused to accept any honors stemming from her wartime activities. The Jews, she said, were the war's true heroes.

According to Abba Kovner, the poet-fighter of the Vilnius ghetto: "If there are ten Righteous Among the Nations, Ona Simaite is certainly to be counted among them." Tanya Sterntal describes her as one of those unique people "who reach out to give but are incapable of taking." (191)

Father Juzas Stakauskas

Grzegorz Jaszunski was born in 1910 in St. Petersburg (Leningrad). His father, Jozef Jaszunski, was the secretary of the editorial board of the *Russian Encyclopedia*. Both of his parents were fully Russianized, but in 1917, after the Bolshevik revolution, they moved back to their hometown, Grodno, Poland, and then to Vilnius, where Jozef Jaszunski was appointed principal of a Jewish school. In 1928 Jozef became the head of the ORT vocational school network in Poland and the family moved again, this time to Warsaw.

When the Germans invaded Poland in September 1939, Grzegorz, his wife Irena, and their son fled to Vilnius, which had been occupied by Russia in accordance with the Hitler-Stalin pact. Grzegorz's parents and his brother Michal, a physician, remained in Warsaw, and he never saw them again. All three perished in Treblinka in January 1943.

Following the German conquest of Lithuania in June 1941, Grzegorz and his family, like the other Jews of Vilnius, had to move into the ghetto. There Grzegorz served as head of the cultural department and joined the FPO, a Jewish underground organization headed by Abba Kovner.

Over the next couple of years Grzegorz carried out several FPO missions on the other side of the ghetto walls. In October 1943 he and Irena left the ghetto for the last time, with orders to establish a link between the FPO and the outside world. They had been given the address of a sympathetic Polish woman and told to contact her, but there was no one home when they got to her house. With danger lurking at every turn, and having no other alternative, they decided to ask for help at the former Benedictine convent, now an archives depot, where Grzegorz had worked under the Germans for several months cataloguing books and documents they had stolen during their advance into Russia.

The building's doorkeeper was Sister Maria Mikulsa, the only nun who had been allowed to remain when the convent was closed by Soviet officials in 1940. "I opened the door. It was about five or six in the afternoon," Grzegorz recalls. "Sister Maria was sitting just inside the entrance. As soon as she saw the anxious expressions on our faces, she said, 'Quick, come in and wait; Father Stakauskas will be here in two or three hours.'" As Grzegorz later commented, "She knew that we needed a place to hide without my having to tell her. We went in and waited."

Father Juzas Stakauskas, who was of mixed Lithuanian and Polish ancestry, was the Lithuanian government's chief archivist and as such was in charge of the storage depot at the convent. During the months that

Grzegorz had worked there, Stakaukas had been impressed by his knowledge of languages. As Grzegorz later wrote, "He was a strange man; not very practical-minded, but very dedicated. An idealist, I would say. He considered it his duty to save people, particularly Jews."

When Stakauskas arrived that evening, he told the Jaszunskis: "You can stay here in this building under my protection, and I'll take care of both of you." He stunned them by adding that he was already hiding eleven other Jews. "By confiding this information," Grzegorz reminisces, "he showed how much he trusted me."

Father Stakauskas and Sister Maria then led the Jaszunskis downstairs to the basement. "At the end of a long corridor, he stopped and knocked on the wall. The people behind the wall knew the signal and opened. . . . There I saw a number of Jews. The only one I had ever met before was Dr. Aleksander Libo."

The entrance to the room where the Jews were concealed was blocked by a false wall with shelves on which six or seven folio volumes were stacked. Father Stakauskas had come up with the idea for this, but it had actually been designed and built by Vladas Zemaitis, a mathematics teacher who was also a skilled carpenter. "Years later I asked Stakauskas what prompted him to make the decision [to save Jews]," Jaszunski recalls. "His response: 'It was my Christian duty.' There we stayed until the liberation in July 1944."

Dr. Alexander Libo had met Father Stakauskas while working at the state archives building, where he was assigned to unpack and sort books. From time to time, as he did his work, Stakauskas had quietly whispered a few words of encouragment, adding, "If things get worse in the ghetto, come to the archives and I will hide you."

On September 25, 1943, having learned that the Germans were planning a major *Aktion*, Libo fled the ghetto with his wife and daughter. When they got to the archives building and told Stakauskas what had happened, he replied, "You did well by coming here." He hid them temporarily in the attic, where Libo was able to watch through an aperture, over the next few days, as groups of Jews were marched off to the notorious Lokishki prison.

A month later Father Stakauskas took the Libos to the nearby Benedictine convent, which was now the city's main archives center. As soon as they entered the building and encountered Sister Maria, Libo says, Stakauskas asked her pointblank whether she was willing to help hide Jews. She responded: "If the archives director is willing to be hanged on a tree, so am I." (Recently a Pole had been strung up on a tree in the center of town after being caught sheltering a Jew.)

With this detail settled, Stakauskas had Zemaitis prepare a secret room at the end of a long corridor in the convent's basement. In due course Stakauskas brought in several other Jews, and by the time the Jaszunskis joined them, several weeks later, there were eleven people living in the room.

According to Esther Kanterowitz, who was also one of the workers assigned to Father Stakauskas, it was the Germans, in need of storage space for the vast quantity of books and manuscripts looted during the invasion of Russia, who first had the idea of transferring the archives to the unused convent.

The centuries-old building was a huge maze of cellars, garrets, and corridors that seemed to lead nowhere. When Stakauskas was ordered to draw up a plan showing how it could be used as an archives depot, he purposely left out the far end of one of the basement corridors, which he then, with the help of Jewish workers, blocked off from the rest of the corridor with huge bookshelves, as was mentioned earlier. The workers knew nothing about the purpose of the mysterious enclosure until the day he invited them to move in.

The group living in the convent's basement included both adults and children. They had to maintain complete silence during working hours because the upstairs rooms were filled with Germans and Lithuanians. When the last employees left, usually around four in the afternoon, Sister Maria gave the signal by stamping on the floor three times. The hideout and the adjoining rooms then became a beehive of activity: washing, cleaning, cooking, and conversation. "We had primitive bunks, made of straw, to sleep on," Grzegorz remembers. "Most of the time was passed by reading books from the volumes stored in the archives."

The group ate once a day. Father Stakauskas bought the food, sometimes paying for it with money and valuables provided by members of the group. He purchased it in small quantities in different stores, often located quite far away from the convent, so as not to arouse suspicion, and Zemaitis brought it down to the hideout. Stakauskas visited his charges every three or four days to try to cheer them up and to help settle the quarrels that inevitably arose from such a large group being cooped up together for so long a time.

Father Stakauskas used to say, "Either all of us will survive, or all of us will perish." Sometimes he would hold his head and moan, "My poor head! What shall I do with all of you? The war is going to last another two years, and none of us will be able to hold out that long!"

One survivor says that Stakauskas was obsessed by the idea of saving Jews. He was so dedicated, and so determined not to profit from what he was doing, that he even refused to accept little gifts from his wards. During the winter of 1943-44, for instance, one of them gave him a gold watch and a fur collar as a token of gratitude. Stakauskas would not take the watch and bartered the collar for some coal.

On the day Vilnius was liberated, July 14, 1944, the survivors left the convent and went their separate ways, cherishing the memory of the courageous trio who had saved their lives, Father Juzas Stakauskas, Sister Maria Mikulska, and Vladas Zemaitis. In the words of Esther Kanterowitz: "The three of them risked their lives for people they did not know, and without receiving any reward, putting themselves in danger strictly out of love for others, and with the sole aim of helping people whose fate had been sealed for death and annihilation. They acted in full conscience and well knew what dangers awaited them in the event of disclosure. They saved our lives. They restored our faith in man." (917)

Stase & Jonas Ruzgys

After the Germans occupied Vilnius on June 22, 1941, thousands of Jews were taken to the nearby Ponary forest and shot. The rest were herded into a ghetto, and the populace was warned that anyone who had any contact with a Jew would be punished severely. Stase Ruzgys and her husband, Jonas, disregarded the Nazi directive and went to the ghetto to visit their friend Lisa Aizenberg, whose husband had been killed at the beginning of the occupation.

"You, Stasia, were the only person to extend a helping hand to me, the only one to open her heart, to offer me a warm, encouraging word," Lisa Aizenberg wrote to Stase from the United States, many years after the war. "Each of your visits uplifted me and strengthened my will to go on."

Stase began urging Lisa to let her save her two-year-old daughter, Rita. Reluctant at first to part with the child, Lisa finally agreed. In accordanace with the plan worked out by Stase and Jonas, Rita was taken to the hospital, ostensibly with an eye infection, and admitted as a Karaite.[1] After her release she lived temporarily with a Polish family.

Meanwhile, Stase and Jonas arranged Lisa's escape from the ghetto. Once she was safely outside the walls she joined them at a prearranged location where they were waiting with a change of clothes. Disguised as a peasant woman, she accompanied them to their house. "Once again you were like guardian angels," Lisa wrote, taking me from the ghetto into your home. During our meeting at the pharmacy, where you waited for me to change my clothes so I wouldn't be recognized, and during the long trek from the city to the outlying district where you lived, both of you played your roles like calm, experienced actors. However, what went on in your minds only I could know. Nobody else could have understood you as I did."

At the Ruzgys house Lisa and Rita were reunited. The two of them were hidden in a recess behind the wall of a back room, a "dark hole in which we hid and which we reached by walking through a clothing closet. We had to lie there for hours on end with a blanket covering our heads to muffle the sound of breathing or any sign of human existence."

---

1. The Karaites separated from mainstream Judaism in the ninth century and eventually became a separate sect. By the 1930s there were only about 12,000 of them, mostly in the Crimea and southern Russia, but Vilnius was also one of their main centers. Nazi racial specialists ruled that the Karaites were descended from converts and therefore not members of the Jewish "race," and as a result they were generally not persecuted during the Holocaust.

Some while later Stase was denounced by an informer and summoned to the Gestapo for questioning. Hoping to keep her friend from getting in trouble, Lisa decided to take Rita and hide in the forest—"to go anyplace, wherever my eyes might lead me, with only one thought, that the two of you would not pay with your lives for having given me shelter."

Stase, however, would hear nothing of it. In Lisa's words: "Then you turned to me, and calmly, without the slightest reproach or hostility, in a voice expressing compassion as well as authority, said, 'Lisa, you're not going anywhere. If we are going to die, we will all die together!' The feeling of love and esteem this evoked prevented me from leaving. Your voice still rings in my ears. I shall remember it for the rest of my life."

At virtually the same moment as this incident, on one of the main streets of Vilnius, three bodies were hanging from a utility pole. Affixed to the chest of each one was a placard bearing the words: "Any citizen harboring a Jew will look like this."

Both rescuer and rescued survived the horrors of the German occupation. After the war Lisa and Rita went to the United States. Writing to her friends in 1961, Lisa expressed her eternal gratitude in profoundly moving words. "I consider Rita to be the daughter of all three of us. You, my dear friends, couldn't have done more for her if she had been your own daughter. I want to share my joy with you; I want you to know all about her. I'm sure it will make you very happy."

Eight years later, terminally ill with cancer, Lisa Aizenberg stated on her deathbed that her last wish was to have Stase and Jonas Ruzgys recognized by Yad Vashem as Righteous Among the Nations. (1192)

Sofia Binkiene

The following two accounts involve a writer's wife and an itinerant monk. Both took place in Kaunas, the capital of Lithuania between the two world wars and the seat of the country's second largest Jewish population, some 35,000 souls at the start of the Nazi avalanche.

Sofia Binkiene, the wife of Kazys Binkiene, a well-known Lithuanian poet and dramatist, had virtually no contacts with Jews before the war. But when the anti-Jewish excesses began in 1941, she resolved to do whatever she could to help in her limited capacity as a housewife married to an ailing man and burdened with four children.

In the months that followed, many Jews escaping from the Kaunas ghetto found their first refuge in the Binkiene home. At times, especially during the final liquidation of the ghetto in 1944, Sofia roamed the streets in the hope of picking up stragglers and giving them a place to hide.

Gita Yudelevitz was twelve years old when Sofia took her in. Born in 1929, she was the only daughter of Yitzhak and Raysa Yudelevitz. During the anti-Jewish riot on the eve of the German army's arrival in Kaunas, Gita's parents had her stay with Jadwiga Muzaliene, a friendly Lithuanian woman. Back with her parents, but now living in the ghetto rather than in their former home, she witnessed incessant liquidation *Aktionen*, including the forced march of German Jews to the notorious Fort 9 outside the city, where they were shot.

Determined to protect their only child, the Yudelevitzes once again entrusted her to Jadwiga Muzaliene. Jadwiga in turn took her to the home of Sofia Binkiene, where she received a warm welcome. "Sofia seated me on a couch, smiled, and spoke softly to me in Lithuanian. Lilianne, one of her daughters, came in, kissed me, and then began weeping so uncontrollably that she had to be taken out of the room before she could calm down."

Gradually, Gita was introduced to the rest of the family and given a new name, Vale Vilkauskete, with a corresponding identity card. Occasionally she was sent out on errands. During the summer, she accompanied the Binkienes to their summer house in Pasvelis, on the Dangiene River.

During the years she lived with the Binkienes, Gita recalls, Jewish escapees were constantly coming and going, moving in for brief spells or staying just long enough to get advice and encouragment from Sofia. Whatever food was available in those trying days, and usually there was not very much, was shared by everyone. "We were constantly on the verge of starvation. We shared the food to the last crumb." After Kazys died of a heart condition in 1942, Sofia's children went out to work to support the family.

Gita's parents, meanwhile, had fled to the forest, where her father was captured and sent to Dachau. He survived and in 1947 went to Palestine. Gita did not see her mother until the end of the war, but she was once taken to a farm in Utena so that her mother, hidden nearby, could observe her from a safe distance. Mother and daughter went to Israel in 1971, and there Gita was reunited with her father.

After the war, Sofia worked for the national radio network on a program for children. She also edited a book about Lithuanians who had saved Jews. Because of her activities during the war she was ostracized in some circles as the "Queen of the Jews." Nonetheless she is fondly remembered by many and has become a legendary figure for Lithuanian Jews. (383)

Bronius Gotautas

Sarah Finkelbrand's husband was killed at Fort 9 soon after the beginning of the German occupation. Every day she watched as scores of others were marched from the ghetto to the murder site. Assigned to a job at the municipal airport, and able to take her four-year-old son with her to work, Sarah began seeking an opportunity to escape.

One day she and the child were able to sneak away. They asked for assistance at a nearby church but the priest rebuffed them. It was against the law to help Jews, he said, and was apparently unmoved by Sarah's reply, "What about the commandment 'Thou shalt love thy neighbor as thyself'? Which law comes first?"

From the church Sarah went to a pharmacy whose owner she knew and asked him for a dose of cyanide "to help me and my child in a difficult hour, so we needn't suffer too long." The pharmacist told Sarah not to lose hope, explaining that he knew someone who might be able to help her.

Following the pharmacist's instructions, Sarah went back to work and returned to the pharmacy a week later. A woman was waiting there to meet her. She introduced herself to Sarah by announcing that she prayed every day for Lithuania to be saved from the Antichrist, by which she meant Hitler, adding that she was helping the "Little Brother" to save Jews.

Suddenly a door opened and in walked a barefoot man in a tattered brown cassock, his face almost hidden by a bushy brown beard. He pulled two identity cards from his knapsack, one for Sarah and the other for her sister-in-law back in the ghetto.

His keen black eyes gleaming, the man helped Sarah to memorize the name and biographical information on the card. When she had it down pat, he handed her a slip of paper and told her that she and her sister were to wait one week, then leave the ghetto and go directly to the address written on it.

The following week Sarah, her son, and her sister-in-law slipped through the barbed-wire fence around the ghetto and went to the designated place. The next day the man called for them and took them to Panemune, where separate living arrangements had been made for them under their new names. Thus all three were enabled to survive. But who was their mysterious benefactor?

His name was Bronius Gotautas, and he was born in 1901 on a farm near the city of Taurage. Gotautas never went to school and never learned to read and write, but he was reared in a devoutly Catholic atmosphere and dreamed of becoming a monk. When he was old enough he applied to a monastery. Rejected as a novice because of his lack of education, he was allowed to live at the monastery as a kind of factotum and among other things was charged with peddling religious books and pamphlets in the surrounding countryside.

Every summer, a knapsack full of religious literature on his back, Gotautas set out on his book-selling circuit, visiting towns and villages, isolated farms, and market fairs. He ate sparingly and never knew in the morning where he would sleep that night. Nicknamed "Broliukas" (Little Brother), and sometimes also called "Knygnesys" (Book-peddler), he soon became a well-known local figure. His austere way of life, his personal warmth, and his intuitive grasp of human nature won the admiration of the peasantry, as did his accomplishments as a healer, and many began to think of him as a holy man.

Appalled by the Nazis' treatment of the Jews, Gotautas was unable to stand idly by while others were suffering. Motivated and given courage by his faith in God, and ready to give his life, if necessary, to let the world know that there were still some decent people in Lithuania, he set about the task of snatching victims from the Nazi whirlwind.

Gotautas was a shrewd judge of character. Carefully sizing up the inner strengths and weaknesses of those he turned to for help, he never asked more of anyone than they were able give. In order to protect those who aided him, he always tried to arrange things so that the blame would fall on him if anything went wrong.

Gotautas's wide range of contacts helped him to carry out his self-imposed mission. In order to obtain the documents needed to establish new identities, for example, he turned to some of the priests he knew from his book-selling circuit because in Lithuania the clergy was empowered to issue birth and death certificates. Over the years Gotautas saved a very large number of people, most of them Jews but also including several Russian prisoners of war.

The Gestapo soon found out about Gotatutas but was unable to track him down because he had no permanent abode. They finally caught him with the aid of an informer and sent him to the notorious Stutthof concentration camp. He survived the camp's rigors but emerged at the end of the war ill and impoverished. Known to be a staunch anti-Communist, he could not return home now that Lithuania was once again part of the Soviet empire. Instead he remained in West Germany. There, his friends, many of them people he had saved, arranged for him to be admitted to a nursing home where they could keep in close touch with him.

Gotautas's asceticism and saintly generosity were proverbial. Sarah Finkelbrand, for instance, tells how she gave him her dead husband's sweater during the harsh winter of 1941-42. The next time she saw him it was gone. When she asked where it was, he replied that he had given the sweater to someone who needed it more.

A woman he saved, now the wife of a rabbi in the United States, describes Bronius Gotautas as "the image of an angel." Sarah Finkelbrand, who lives in Israel, concluded her testimony with the following statement: "Peace to his soul. May many follow his example. Would that our children learn from him to love their fellow man and to be loyal to the ideals to which he held fast. As a pure soul, he saw the command 'Thou shalt love thy neighbor as thyself' as the essence of Christianity, a course which he pursued throughout his life. Gotautas serves as an example of what a simple and illiterate man can do when possessed with the will to do it. . . May his memory be a blessing." (780)

Jonas Paulavicus

The following two stories also took place in the Kaunas area.

Jonas Paulavicus, a carpenter by trade, lived with his wife Antosia and their two children in Panemune, just a stone's throw from the Niemen River. Employed by the railroad to refurbish sleeping cars, he used materials obtained on the job to build underground hideouts in which some two dozen people ultimately found a refuge.

It all began when Jonas's son, Kestutis, asked Jonas to hide Johanan Fein, a fourteen-year-old fellow student whom he lauded as a future Paganini because of the violin recitals he had given at school. Jonas went to see Johanan's sister at her workplace outside the ghetto. "I want to do a good deed," Jonas told her. At first she refused to give her consent, puzzled by his offer to shelter a boy he had never met and fearful of a trap, but she eventually gave in.

Jonas and Antosia treated Johanan as if he were a member of the family and gave him the freedom of their home. Later on, when the danger of detection increased because of the heavy volume of German military traffic on the nearby bridge spanning the Niemen River, they made a hiding place for him in the attic.

Soon afterward Jonas also took in the Shames family—husband, wife, and four-year-old son. He asked Shames to seek out other Jewish professionals so that, as he put it, the Jewish people would have an intellectual elite after the war to restore their communal life. Curiously, these words were uttered by a man whose own intellectual pursuits and formal education were quite limited.

Shames brought in Chaim and Tania Ipp, both of whom were physicians. At first, like Johanan Fein's sister, Chaim was suspicious when told of Jonas's offer. "My husband couldn't believe that a Lithuanian would do it only for the sake of saving a Jew," Tania recalls, and without asking to be paid.

Before long Moshe Gershenman, an engineer, and his wife, Musia, had also joined the group. They were followed by Miriam Krakinowsky, David Rubin, and several others.

David's story illustrates how Jonas made a point of frequenting places where he was likely to encounter Jews on the run. David escaped in July 1944 while in a group being transported to a concentration camp in Germany. Hoping to get across the Niemen and link up with advanced units of the Red Army, he was wandering along the riverbank when a man in a boat approached him. The man—it was Jonas—warned that there were German troops in the vicinity and offered to hide him.

The refuge Jonas offered turned out to be an underground room that was set up much like a railroad sleeping car. Actually there were two such underground hideouts near Jonas's house, both provided with radios and electricity. The occupants had to remain inside at all times, and neither group knew about the other, but Jonas visited both shelters every day.

Miriam Krakinowsky tells a story similar to David's. She too escaped in July 1944, slipping away from a column of Jews being marched across the Niemen bridge. Uncertain what to do next she was walking along the riverside when she noticed that a man in a boat seemed to be following her. She asked what he wanted, and he replied that he wanted to help her.

At first Miriam thought that the man was after the bounty the Germans would pay if he turned her in, but he insisted, warning her that the retreating Germans were shooting anyone who had no papers. "I told him that I didn't have any money or jewelry to give him and asked why he wanted to save me. The man told me to trust him. I didn't really trust him, but I had nowhere to go."

Accompanying him to his home, Miriam was led down into a cellar. There Jonas removed some planks and knocked several times on the floor. A small door was pushed up. "I was told to go down the steps. I found myself in a very small hot room filled with half-naked Jews." Amazed at finding so many fellow Jews sheltered by a man she had feared was about to betray her, she could not contain her emotions. "I began to cry as they asked questions about the fate of the ghetto. I remained there (together with seven adults and one four-year-old boy) for three weeks until liberation."

All told, the Paulavicius family saved twenty-four people—twelve Jews, and twelve escaped Russian and Lithuanian prisoners.

It is hard to say what motivated Jonas, a simple, uneducated man, to perform this heroic humanitarian feat, especially in light of the intense antisemitism so prevalent among his countrymen. Those he saved recall him as being a very serious man, socialist by inclination and given to long spells of brooding silence. On the other hand, there were times when he would sit up with his charges until late in the night, lifting their spirits and cheerfully encouraging them to look forward to the liberation. Perhaps, one survivor has surmised, Jonas saw saving Jews as a form of resistance against the Nazis.

Miriam recalls that Jonas Paulavicius had a very high regard for Jews. He once remarked to her, "You come from the family that epitomizes the highest level of human achievement." After the war, Jonas took pride in having saved so many Jews. Antisemitic compatriots, however, dubbed him "Father of the Jews," and eventually he was murdered by members of a pro-Nazi organization that would not forgive him his "sin."

Before the tragic finale to his life, however, Jonas Paulavicius was able to do one more act of kindness for his Jewish friends. In 1946, he helped them to get out of Lithuania on the first stage of their journey to Palestine, giving them provisions for the journey and money with which to bribe the border guards.

At the moment of parting Jonas warned them to be careful. A mother's love for her newborn babe, he said, is largely due to the pain she experiences in giving birth to it. He felt like their mother, he continued, for through him, and at the price of great suffering for himself, they had been reborn and given a new lease on life.

At the Yad Vashem ceremony where a tree was dedicated in his memory, David Rubin apostrophized Jonas as "the dearest of all men," and lamented his tragic end. "Lo! I was not there with you when your life was snuffed out, and my ears did not hear your agonized cries! My heart is torn from much sorrow. How thou hast fallen! How thou hast been struck down on a day of sorrow!" Then, on behalf of the survivors, David vowed "to cherish your memory in our hearts forever, and to educate our children to cherish your memory with respect, reverence, and love." (2472)

Mykolas Simelis

Mykolas Simelis was a forester, and before the war he supplied pine roots to Meir Korn, who owned a turpentine factory. Meir, who knew Mykolas for many years, describes him as an honest, kindhearted man of noble character who had always been well disposed toward Jews.

In October 1941, after escaping a German raid on the factory, Meir and his family fled to the Kaunas ghetto. One day, while Meir was doing forced labor, someone tapped his shoulder. It was Mykolas Simelis. He said: "There is room for you at my place." Mykolas disappeared as suddenly as he had appeared.

Since Meir was working for the Germans as an auto mechanic, he had access to a truck. And so it happened that one cold night in November 1943, all eight members of the Korn family slipped out of the ghetto to a waiting truck and then drove the 45 kilometers across the Lithuanian countryside to the town of Veyvis.

Parking at a safe distance from the Simelis house in order not to leave any incriminating tire tracks in the snow, they finished their journey on foot and knocked on the door. Their old friend flung it open and greeted them with his usual broad smile and hearty handshake. His five children greeted them too; they had been told that the newcomers were war refugees but not that they were Jewish.

At first the Korns stayed in a small room at the back of the house, but this was too dangerous. One day, for instance, the housekeeper ran into Meir while she was cleaning one of the other rooms. She told Mykolas that she knew who he was and intended to quit so as not to be involved, but eventually his wife, Jadvyga, persuaded her to stay on and and say nothing.

This hardly solved the problem, however, because people were con-tinually coming to the house for one reason or another. Eventually Mykolas decided that there was only one alternative: an underground bunker. Both families threw themselves into the arduous task of excavat-ing. All the earth they dug up had to be carried to the attic, because disposing of it outdoors might have attracted attention.

The completed bunker had two entrances, one through a trapdoor under a cupboard in the living room and the other behind the oven in an adjacent room. It had electricity and a stove, and was amply provided with straw and blankets for sleeping. A few trusted friends helped Mykolas to get food for his eight charges, buying it in small amounts at different shops to avoid arousing suspicion.

In January 1944, four more fugitive Jews were added to the group in the bunker, then two more, for a total of fourteen persons. Late each night, when there was no longer any likelihood of unexpected visitors, Mykolas would open the trapdoor and the occupants would emerge to breathe some fresh air and listen to radio bulletins on the war's progress. When his charges once told him how sorry they were to cause him so much trouble, he replied: "The world is not without good people. . . . I would have helped anyone who came knocking at my door."

In April 1944, at the age of thirty-eight, Jadvyga Simelis died of blood poisoning in a Kaunas hospital. Mykolas took his three oldest children with him to the funeral, leaving the other two with a neighbor.

On the very day that Mykolas was expected home, German soldiers and Ukrainian auxiliaries staged a raid in the area, looking for hidden Jews. Stopping at the Simelis house, they made a thorough search, meticulously checking every nook and cranny. Mykolas walked in just as a soldier began to move the living-room cupboard. Hardly stopping to think, he ran into the kitchen, grabbed a bottle of vodka, and invited the soldiers to join him in a toast to the Third Reich.

Later on Mykolas told the others that he had learned about the raid at the railroad station upon returning from the funeral. Certain that the bunker had been discovered or was about to be discovered, he had momentarily been tempted to take his children and make for the forest. But then he decided to play it out, saying to himself, "You can only die once. Maybe, despite everything, I can still help them." And he set out for home— arriving just in time to stop the soldier from moving the cupboard that concealed the trapdoor.

In July 1944, the area was liberated by the Red Army. The following year, some former Nazi collaborators lured Mykolas into the forest, ostensibly to discuss a business deal, and murdered him. Then they ransacked his house, telling the maid, "This is what happens to anyone who helps Jews!" (2550)

Sempo Sugihara

We end the section on Kaunas with the story of a humanitarian par excellence, a Japanese diplomat whose scorecard of lives saved numbers in the thousands.

In the fall of 1939, Sempo Sugihara, a member of the Japanese diplomatic service, opened a consulate in Kaunas, which was then the capital of Lithuania. Almost one year later, in August 1940, the Soviet government, which had occupied and annexed Lithuania that summer, ordered all foreign legations in Kaunas closed by August 31.

One morning in the early part of August, as he was busy packing and winding up operations, Sugihara was surprised to see a huge crowd on the street outside the consulate. He sent his Polish-speaking secretary to see

Sempo Sugihara, the Japanese consul-general in Kaunas, Lithuania (1940). Courtesy of Yad Vashem.

what the trouble was and received the following message in reply: "We are Jews from Poland. We will be killed if the Nazis catch us, but we can't get away without visas. We want you to issue Japanese visas."

Until that moment Sugihara had been quite indifferent to the Jewish question and had paid no attention to the frenzied antisemitism engulfing his country's German ally. His interest in the war had been strictly political, focusing on the advantages Japan could glean from the global conflict, but now something inside him would not allow him to ignore the people milling about outside.

Sugihara agreed to meet with a delegation and found himself moved by their pleas. With tears in their eyes, they begged him to issue Japanese transit visas so that they could obtain permission to travel across Russia on their way to other destinations. Most hoped to reach one or another Latin American country, others the United States or Palestine.

According to Dr. Zorach Warhaftig, who was a member of the delegation and years later became Israel's Minister for Religious Affairs, the meeting with Sugihara turned out to be a fateful encounter for thousands of Polish yeshiva students and faculty who had escaped en masse to Lithuania after the German invasion in September 1939.

They had been stranded in Kaunas ever since, unable to leave because they could not get the necessary documents. Quite by chance, two students had learned that visas were not needed to enter the Dutch West

Jewish refugees near the Japanese legation in Kaunas (August 1940).
Courtesy of Yad Vashem.

Indian island of Curaçao. This seemed to provide a way out, since they
could claim that Curaçao was their ultimate destination. Nonetheless,
they could not get transit visas allowing them to travel across the Soviet
Union unless they also had visas permitting them to continue their
journey by way of a contiguous country.

As Warhaftig tells the story, he spread out a map and said to Sugihara:
"You see, we have visas for Curaçao. We can get there by way of Japan,
sailing on a Japanese ship. Please give us transit visas that will permit us
to travel through Japan." Sugihara was taken aback by this request but
promised to give them a reply in a few days.

He began looking into it almost at once. A check with the Soviet
authorities confirmed what Warhaftig had said about the Soviet transit
visas being conditional on having visas for a contiguous country. Sugihara
then cabled Tokyo with an account of the situation and asked if it would
be all right to issue the visas. The reply was negative; he sent another cable,
but this time there was no response. A third cable also went unanswered.

Recalling these dramatic August days many years later, Sugihara told
how he had struggled to make a decision. "I really had a difficult time, and
for two whole nights was unable to sleep. I eventually decided to issue
transit visas . . . on my own authority as consul. I could not allow these
people to die, people who had come to me for help with death staring them
in the eyes. Whatever punishment might be imposed upon me [for
disobeying orders], I knew I had to follow my conscience."

On August 10, taking full responsibility for his acts, Sugihara began
issuing Japanese transit visas to the refugees regardless of whether or not
they had the necessary supporting documents. When the Japanese

Foreign Ministry learned what he was doing, it ordered him to cease and desist. "But I totally disregarded their cables," Sugihara proudly recalls; "I knew the Foreign Ministry would fire me, but I continued to issue travel visas until the day I left Kovno."

By his own estimate, Sugihara issued around 3,500 visas (Warhaftig places the figure closer to 1,600). In order to complete all the necessary paperwork, he worked without letup for twelve consecutive days and enlisted several rabbinical students to stamp documents for him. According to one source, Sugihara continued to issue visas even after boarding the train for Berlin on August 31.

The thousands of refugees lucky enough to obtain visas from Sugihara were all spared the ravages of the Holocaust, which came upon Lithuania like a thunderclap with the German invasion in June 1941. Ironically, none of them ever got to Curaçao. From Japan the great majority went on to Shanghai. Many remained there for the duration; others were able to continue on to the United States, Canada, or Palestine.[2]

When Sugihara got to Berlin he was temporarily assigned to the Japanese legation in Königsberg and then was sent to Romania, where he remained until the end of the war. Two years later, when he returned to Tokyo, Japan's new Minister of Foreign Affairs presented him with a dismissal notice without offering any explanation. Other officials, however, hinted that it was because of his insubordination seven years earlier when he had issued the visas despite clear orders from Tokyo.

In the years that followed Sugihara moved from one job to another. For a while he was a purchasing agent for the U.S. Army, then worked as a translator for the Japan Broadcasting Corporation and for private companies. In 1961, he went to Moscow as a sales representative for a Japanese exporting firm.

As time went on the story of Sugihara's humanitarianism gained a wider hearing, and in 1985, when he was officially designated one of the Righteous Among the Nations, the Japanese press give it extensive coverage. Sugihara was bedridden and unable to attend, but at a ceremony hosted by the Israeli ambassador to Japan, his wife received the medal and certificate on his behalf. Several months later a tree in his name was planted in the Garden of the Righteous at Yad Vashem. (2861)

Mykolas Juskevicius

The last three stories from Lithuania pertain to incidents in other parts of the country.

---

2. In 1965 Warhaftig asked the former Dutch governor of Curaçao whether the refugees would have been allowed to land if they had reached the island. The governor candidly replied, "By no means! I would have made the ship put to sea again just as the United States and Cuba did with the *St. Louis*."

Before the war Azriel Abramowitz was a lawyer in Siauliai (Shavli), and Mykolas Juskevicius, a local farmer, was one of his clients. When the Germans occupied Siauliai, Azriel and many other Jewish men were arrested and shot. The rest of the city's Jews, among them Azriel's wife, Manya, and their daughter, Salomea, were herded into the ghetto.

When Mykolas learned of this, he sent a message to Manya stating that he would hide them if they could manage to escape. Manya was unable to act on his offer because she was in the last stages of pregnancy. Soon thereafter she gave birth to a son.

Despite the terrible conditions in the ghetto Manya and her two children, together with Lyuba, Manya's sister, managed to survive. Early in 1944 Mykolas Juskevicius again got in touch, warning that if she did not escape now it would soon be too late, because the Germans were strengthening the ghetto walls in preparation for a final *Aktion* against the residents.

Manya left the two-year-old in the care of a friendly Lithuanian family. Then she, Salomea, and Lyuba made good their escape and outside the ghetto, as planned, were met by Mykolas, who was waiting with a horsedrawn cart. He took them to a bunker he had prepared in the forest, and there Manya and Lyuba were reunited with their mother, who had escaped sometime before.

Although they themselves had barely enough, and five children of their own to feed, Mykolas Jusekevicius and his wife, Nastia, brought food to the bunker every day. When Manya's mother fell ill, Mykolas decided to move the whole group to the loft of his barn.

They lived there for five months, but one day the farm was raided by Lithuanian partisans looking for Jews. The four Abramowitz women were discovered and taken outside to be shot. For good measure the partisans set the Juskevicius house on fire. This attracted the attention of a German patrol. As soon as the partisans saw the Germans approaching, they fled, leaving the women behind.

The German soldiers, assuming that the women were connected with the partisans, took them in for questioning, but that night Manya, Lyuba, and Salomea escaped through an open window. They sought refuge in a nearby convent, and as it was almost time for Mass, the nuns hid them behind the church organ. Just as the service ended some German soldiers came in and began searching the premises.

Desperately afraid to be captured, Manya began trying to slash her wrists with a piece of tin she had found on the floor and signaled the others to do likewise. Fortunately the tin was not sharp enough, because a few moments later the Germans left. As soon as they were gone the three women left also.

They headed for the forest. There Manya and Salomea joined a partisan band and thus were able to survive the final phase of the war. Not so for Manya's sister, however. Unable to bear the strain any longer, Lyuba let herself be captured by a German patrol. Her fate remains unknown.

Fearing the worst when their house was burned down and the Abramowitz women were arrested, Mykolas and Nastia also fled to the forest, leaving their five children behind to be cared for by neighbors. The family was reunited several months later when the area was liberated. (1848)

Petras and Ursule Maladauskas

When the Germans entered Vilkaviskis in southwestern Lithuania in July 1941, they sacked the homes of its Jewish inhabitants and massacred many of the men. The survivors were held in an abandoned army barracks declared "off limits" to Lithuanians, any attempt to contact them being punishable by death. Every morning, wearing the yellow star on their coats or dresses, Jews from the barracks, now locally known as the ghetto, were assembled in the marketplace and assigned to work details.

"One day I was stopped in the street by three German soldiers on motorcycles," Judith Sperling states in her deposition. "They knew that I was Jewish because I was walking in the middle of the street, with the yellow patch conspicuously displayed, and my head down so that I wouldn't have to salute them." Judith was frightened at first, but the men told her that they were members of the anti-Nazi resistance, "and they urged me to flee and hide as they had learned that the Jews in the surrounding towns were being slaughtered."

When she returned to the ghetto that night Judith relayed this news to her family. But what were they to do? "There was no place for us to run or go, because of the hostility of the Lithuanians. The law was against us. Any German soldier or Lithuanian civilian could rob us, and they did." The situation seemed hopeless. "We were caught in a trap with nowhere to flee."

The next day a friend told Judith that he and his family had been offered a refuge by a Lithuanian they knew and invited her to come along. She did so, but when the group got to the village where Petras and Ursule Maladauskas lived and went to their house, which had belonged to a Jew just a few weeks earlier, a disappointment was in store. Judith's friend and his parents looked too Jewish, so they had to be sent on to the home of Petras's parents, who lived quite far away in a more isolated area. Since Judith was blonde and blue-eyed, she stayed with the Maladauskas family. "I put a chain with a cross round my neck and worked in the field and the house."

Judith and the others had escaped just in time, for several weeks later, in September 1941, armed Lithuanian auxiliaries surrounded the Vilkaviskis ghetto, made its residents dig a mass grave, and then killed all of them. Judith learned about this from Antanas Maladauskas, Petras's brother. As a police officer he had participated in the massacre, and he exultantly gave her all the details, never imagining that she was Jewish.

A while later, after a tip-off that Jews were hiding there, the police searched the Maladauskas farm. Judith hid in the barn, buried under some hay, and was not discovered, but her hosts, alarmed by the close call, decided to move her to the home of friends whom they knew to be sympathetic to the Jews.

As a result, Judith now found herself living with Petras and Adele Jureviciene, who "received me warmly on the day of my arrival." Although Petras and Ursule Maladauskas knew nothing about it, she soon learned that her new benefactors had already taken in a Jewish girl from Germany.

Petras Jureviciene, who was a carpenter, built a hiding place under a heavy wooden table, and whenever danger threatened the two girls took refuge there. The Jureviciennes shared their meager food with them and never said a word about being repaid after the war. "I want only one thing," Adele told the girls, "When you are free again, I want you to remain good people and to help those in need."

Judith stayed with the Jureviciennes for a year, then returned to Petras and Ursule Maladauskas, who in the meantime had built themselves a new house with a more adequate hiding place for her. While living there she helped with the chores and also learned weaving from Petras. From time to time Adele Jureviciene came over to cheer her up and encourage her to hope for better days to come.

Adele's father and mother, Juozas and Antonina Sneideris, were also sympathetic to the Jews. For two years they hid three Jewish sisters who wandered onto their farm after another sister and their mother had been killed by a Lithuanian mob. On May 5, 1945, ten months after the area's liberation, Juozas Sneideris was murdered by a fanatical antisemite.

Judith went to the United States after the war, but she still keeps in touch with her former benefactors. Petras Jureviciene died of tuberculosis shortly after the liberation, but Adele refuses all offers of financial aid. "She was happy that I had survived and was free," Judith states. "That was her greatest compensation." (1327, 1328, 1328a)

Elena Ivanauskiene

Leah was one of the many refugees who hid either alone or in small groups in Lithuania's dense forests. Early in 1944 she happened to pass through the village of Skovagaliai. Hoping to get some food, she knocked at the door of a peasant's house. It was opened by Elena Ivanauskiene, who took one look at the rag-clad, underfed girl shivering in the cold and motioned her to come in.

Elena was a deaf mute, but she and Leah were able to communicate in writing. Leah told Elena that she was the widow of a Russian officer murdered by the Germans. Elena believed her, and when she learned that Leah could sew and do other household tasks, she invited her to stay.

Later on Elena discovered that Leah was a Jew, but this only made her more protective and kind, and she readily agreed when Leah asked if her friend Samuel Ingel, whom she married after the war, could come join them. Elena consented, but because she was uncertain of her husband's attitude, did not tell him they were Jewish.

One day the Germans staged a raid in the area, tipped off by an informer that there were Jews in hiding. Elena took Leah into one of the fields and told her to lie flat on the ground until she came back. She returned home and watched the soldiers search her house, then, while they moved on through the rest of the village, composed the following poem for Leah:

> Like a lonesome bird
> In the darkest night,
> In the fields
> Trembling, she clings closely
> To the gray earth.
> The heart weakens from pain,
> Pain over your fate.
> Death seeks you out,
> It is forbidden for you to live.
> With every step you take
> Suffering accompanies you.
> Will the darkness surrounding you
> Ever shine with light?
> Will anyone share your suffering?

When the Germans were gone Elena went out to the field and brought Leah home. Soon afterward Leah rejoined Samuel in the woods. There, together with other Jewish refugees, they awaited the arrival of the Red Army.

"Elena was like a star shining through the darkness that we lived in," Samuel and Leah said in Jerusalem, after planting a tree in honor of their benefactress. (2854)

Jan Lipke

The following two tales took place in Latvia, Lithuania's northern neighbor.

The Germans occupied Riga, the capital of Latvia, on July 1, 1941. By December Nazi *Einsatzgruppen* and Latvian auxiliary units had killed three-quarters of the city's 40,000 Jews. Over the next few years they killed almost all of the remainder plus an additional 20,000 Jews deported o Riga from Germany and Austria. When the Russians entered the city on October 14, 1944, fewer than 100 Jews were still alive. Forty-two of them had been saved by one man, a dock worker named Jan Lipke.

The story begins on November 30, 1941, during a massive liquidation operation in which 10,000 residents of the Riga ghetto were slaughtered. Lipke watched in horror as the broken bodies of children were thrown into the street. Turning to Zygmund, his son, he said, in an emotion-choked voice, "Look well, my boy, and never forget."

This terrifying vision out of Dante's *Inferno* determined Lipke's future. Bent on doing everything he could to save Jews, he quit his job on the docks and got a new one with a civilian contracting firm that did work for the Luftwaffe (German Air Force).

Lipke took the job because he knew that the firm used Jewish workers from the ghetto. With the aid of a trusted friend, he was able to help several of them to escape. As foreman, Lipke would make sure that the coast was

Jan Lipke, who rescued several dozen Jews in and around Riga, Latvia. Courtesy of Yad Vashem.

clear, then the Jewish worker would slip away. When it was time for the detail to return to the ghetto, Lipke's friend, wearing a yellow star, would take his place. Since the final count would come out right, the guards never noticed anything, and the next morning the friend would leave the ghetto with a work detail assigned to some other contractor.

Lipke also helped Jews to escape from the labor camps the Nazis set up in Riga. Sometimes he would contact those he hoped to save by means of written messages left at their worksites or in some public place like a phone booth; other times they might meet and talk through the barbed-wire fence surrounding the camp. However it was done, Lipke would help plan the escape and in some instances provide money or jewelry (often given him by the escapee's friends or relatives) with which to bribe the camp guards.

Once the inmate was out of the camp, Lipke would be waiting nearby at an agreed-upon spot and would get him away either by streetcar or hidden in the back of a truck driven by a friend of his named Karlis. At the outset, Lipke brought most of the escapees to his own home and hid them in a specially constructed shelter. Naturally he had the full cooperation of Johanna, his wife, and of Zygmund.

Lipke had originally planned for the escapees to go to neutral Sweden, and he began building a boat for the voyage across the Baltic Sea. Unfortunately the police took an interest in the project. He and a Jewish fellow conspirator were arrested. The Jew was killed, but Lipke was able to talk himself out of trouble and was soon released. The boat project, of course, had to be abandoned.

As an alternative Lipke purchased a farm near the hamlet of Dobele as a place to hide Jews whom he helped to escape. He also arranged for several of them to be taken in by friendly Lithuanians on farms in Miltini and other villages just outside Riga. Regardless of where the escapees were placed, Lipke kept in close touch and arranged for them to be moved if the situation warranted.

Jan Lipke began rescuing Jews in December 1941 and continued until the Russian liberation of Latvia in October 1944. He never asked anything from anyone, and once, when a Jew he offered to help replied that he couldn't pay him, Lipke said, "You seem to think I'm doing this for money, but there's not enough money in the world to make me risk my life this way."

Some idea of Lipke's methods can be derived from the account given by David Fishkin. Late in 1941 Fishkin was assigned to work in a Luftwaffe warehouse, and it was there that he and Jan Lipke first met. Lipke offered to help him escape, but David did not accept, confident that his ability to do useful work would guarantee his safety.

About two years later David was standing near the fence around the labor camp when he heard someone whistle from a nearby field. "I turned my head in the direction of the sound and saw Lipke hiding in the tall grass." Making sure that no one was watching, David moved closer to the fence. "He asked me if I needed any food or clothing and when I would be ready to come with him." As David hesitatingly tried to formulate an answer, Lipke handed him some jewelry to use as a bribe should he decide to escape.

On July 24, 1944, with the Russians only 25 miles away, the Germans staged another *Aktion*. David noticed that the guards were on edge. It was obvious that the German army was about to withdraw from Latvia, and he began to fear that they would kill the remaining prisoners or take them along. When the guards had the prisoners begin constructing wooden crates for their possessions he knew that it was now or never.

Helped by two Ukrainians whom he paid off with the jewelry Lipke had given him, David got over the fence. As arranged, Lipke was waiting on the other side, and the two men immediately boarded a crowded streetcar.

To their dismay they discovered that several of the passengers were German soldiers. Fearful that someone would notice David's semitic features, Lipke quickly told him to look out the window and began an impromptu speech on the evils of Bolshevism and how all true Latvians should help the Germans defeat the Red Army.

The other passengers were so distracted that no one noticed David, and in due course they reached their destination, the home of a woman associate of Lipke's. David remained in her cellar, along with several other Jews who were already hidden there, until August 14, when the Russians arrived.

In 1977 a tree in honor of Jan Lipke was planted in the Garden of the Righteous at Yad Vashem. Several speakers praised his heroism at great length, and then Lipke was invited to respond. He stood up, looked straight ahead, and tried to find some words appropriate to the occasion. Finally, after several moments of silence, he said "thank you" and sat down. Forty-two people owed their lives to this taciturn dock-worker from Riga. (207)

Vladimir Micko

Carolina Taitz and her parents were among the lucky ones: they had survived the first massacre of the Riga ghetto Jews in 1941, which took place in the Rumbuli forest. But the threat to their lives was not over, for soon thereafter the Nazis ordered all Jews to prepare to transfer to a nearby concentration camp. The Taitz family was one of the last, out of the 30,000 ghetto inhabitants, to leave on this journey.

"It was four o'clock in the morning and the Jews were driven from the ghetto with sticks and whips," Carolina recalls. It was November 1941, and the earth was covered with snow. On the way, many people realized that they were being led in the direction of the Rumbuli forest, the site of the original massacre, but there was no turning back.

Suddenly the order came to stop. In Carolina's words: "We could see that a mass grave had already been dug for us. We were told to undress. People screamed. I will never forget the snow mixed with blood, the children who were shot. . . . Naked, the people were shot by machine-gun fire and fell into the grave."

Slowly the line progressed to where Carolina and her family were standing. It seemed that the end had come. Suddenly the Nazis asked if any of the women on line were seamstresses, for they needed some for a labor camp, and Carolina grabbed at the opportunity, although there was no guarantee that the Nazis would honor their word. Several Jews, including Carolina and several members of her family, stepped aside and were led to a nearby prison, thence to the empty Riga ghetto.

Carolina had been saved, but she had lost her father and brother in the massacre, and she decided that her only chance of survival was to run away—but how and where?

Carolina's plan was to find her old nursemaid, a Baptist woman, and hide with her. She was warned of the danger in walking alone in the open: the roads were infested with Nazi troops and the local collaborationist militia; and antisemites along the way might turn her in to the authorities. But Carolina's mind was made up. She was determined to make a supreme effort to have at least a remnant of her family survive this terrible conflagration.

She dressed in men's clothing and a coat marked with the obligatory yellow star sign. A hat with earflaps covered her hair. She was going to slip out of the barbed-wire camp together with a group of men on their way for a day's hard labor. "Everyone thought me crazy, but dressed as a man, I slipped into the formation of marching workers and managed to get past the guards of the ghetto."

Once outside the ghetto perimeter, Carolina became terrified as her dirty clothes made her obvious to passersby. Looking around her, she saw a house with some logs piled up for firewood. She hurried there and hid between the logs. Night had fallen, and Carolina was hungry. She decided to bet her chance and knock on the door of the house.

Two German shepherd dogs began to bark violently. Then a woman's voice shot out: "Who's there?" The dogs' barking stopped and the door swung open. She saw a man and a woman standing before her. "I told them my story, that I had run away from the ghetto, that I was trying to get to my maid, a Baptist, who perhaps would hide me."

Tense, filled with fright and anxiety, Carolina waited for the response. "Come in, my child," the man responded. "My child," he continued, "last night I had a vision. God came to me and said, 'You will save someone who will come to you in need.'" He was convinced that the forlorn girl standing before him was the person God had sent to be saved. The man's name was Vladimir Micko, and the woman next to him was his sister, Olga Kateneva.

"The whole family (including Vladimir's parents) accepted me immediately and surrounded me with love," Carolina recalls. Since it was very dangerous to keep Carolina openly in the home, Vladimir decided to build for her an underground shelter. For this, he removed the floor boards and dug out a hole about 3 feet deep, 6 feet long, and 6 feet wide.

Vladimir had to be very careful when preparing the hiding nest. Disposing of the earth he dug out was the biggest problem, because the Germans had built a garage on his property, and the guards carefully watched everything that happened in the vicinity. Since getting rid of the earth in buckets or a cart would have aroused suspicion, he carried it out in small increments hidden in specially made inner pockets in his clothing. Literally hundreds of trips between the house and a place where he could dump the earth were required before the job was finished.

Carolina normally spent most of her time in her benefactor's living quarters, but when danger threatened, or when a neighbor suddenly dropped in for a visit, she would in seconds make her way to the pit and secure the cover with a lock from the inside. The entrance to the hiding place was masked with a carpet, above which stood the dinner table.

Vladimir also volunteered to bring provisions to Carolina's mother and sister, who had survived the November 1941 massacre, carefully passing food, clothing, and medicine to them through the ghetto's barbed-wire fence.. "Without his unselfish help, which was extremely dangerous to his life, both my mother and my sister would have starved from hunger in the ghetto," Carolina remarks.

At other times, Vladimir, a Christian Evangelist by belief, sewed on his coat the Jewish yellow star, so as to pretend to be a Jew and thus gain entrance to the ghetto. "I was petrified by his behavior and begged him not to do such things any more. But he went often to the ghetto, past the Nazi guard post, and brought to my mother and sister bread, sugar, butter, cheese, etc. His pockets were filled with food, and in many cases he indiscriminately distributed food to every Jew who came his way. . . . It was a truly divine miracle that the Nazis did not recognize him."

Vladimir bore the extra expenses from his own pocket, in spite of the fact that he earned a meager income as a stoker in a nearby kindergarten.

The Nazis raided Vladmir's house several Nazi time in search of hidden Jews and army deserters. He recalls instances of persons found sheltering Jews who were hanged in Riga's marketplace, "and the corpses were left hanging for weeks in order to frighten the local population not to provide help and shelter to the persecuted and doomed Jews."

Thus, Carolina remained hidden in the home of the Micko family for three full years, until the area's liberation in October 1944. "They cared for me as a member of the family, and never demanded any payment or monetary reward for their kindness," Carolina states in her deposition to Yad Vashem. "Without their selfless love, their courage, and their humane actions, I would never have survived." (4838)

Ukraine and Byelorussia

In 1939 there were about 1.5 million Jews in Ukraine. The number increased considerably following the outbreak of the war because of the Russian annexation of eastern Poland, which became part of the Ukrainian Soviet Socialist Republic, and also because many Jews from German-occupied Poland fled eastward to escape the Nazi terror.

Nazi ideology held all Slav peoples to be an inferior race and consigned them to a degrading position in the Nazi New Order. However, tactical short-time considerations called for allowing, and even encouraging, national aspirations to concretize—but only to a limited degree—in Slavic countries which were not, as Poland, on Germany's immediate annexation list. However, even on this point there were conflicting opinions within the top Nazi hierarchy, with Alfred Rosenberg, formally in charge of the conquered eastern territories, favoring a more lenient policy vis-à-vis the national aspirations of the Ukrainians, and Hitler desiring the total enslavement of all the peoples in the conquered territories of the Soviet Union and the intensive colonization of its lands by German and kindred peoples, as fast as possible.

This bifurcation of views at the highest level of the Nazi hierarchy throughout the war years caused the occupation of Ukraine and Byelorussia to be quite severe indeed, by contrast to conquered countries in the west, but slightly less oppressive than in Poland. This was especially so insofar as Ukraine was concerned.

The Ukrainians counted in 1939 some 40 million persons, with 29 million residing in the Soviet Ukraine and the rest in adjacent territories inside Poland, Czechoslovkia, and Romania. Over 5 million Ukrainians lived within the prewar frontiers of Poland, mainly in the eastern provinces. Through the centuries the Ukrainians had developed a national conscious which clamored for independence, especially from Tsarist

265

Russia, but always suffered setbacks and defeats. A short-lived independent Ukrainian state, headed by Petliura, was suppressed by the Red Army in 1921. Stalin's forced collectivization of Ukrainain farmlands decimated the peasantry, and hundreds of thousands perished from malnutrition and repressions. In newly reconstituted Poland, where the Ukrainians constituted a sizable minority, the new regime restricted Ukrainian national and cultural aspirations.

These continuous frustrations bred within the Ukrainians intense feelings of revenge against those considered to thwart their national goals, with the Jews (viewed as either pro-Polish or pro-communist) bearing the brunt of this resentment. With Hitler's rise to power, Ukrainian goals centered on an alliance with Nazi Germany, which it was hoped would favor an independent Ukraine at the expense of the Soviet Union. With German backing, a fully independent Ukrainian state would rise on the debris of the dismembered Polish and Russian states, as a full-fledged ally of Hitler's Germany.

None but the most astute (and these were few) could detect the wide gaps separating these wishful thoughts from Hitler's true intentions. For him, the fertile lands of Ukraine were none but virgin soil for a German massive colonization program with the majority of the indigenous population to be resettled in the lands farther east. This long-range goal was not made public; on the contrary, Ukrainian youths were mobilized into German-commanded battalions which spearheaded the Nazi invasion of Russia in June 1941, with others joining the fray, in auxiliary and paramilitary units, in the hope of cementing an imaginary German-Ukrainian alliance.

The dust of the invading armies had hardly settled when disenchantment set in. When the Ukrainian nationalist movement under the leadership of Stepan Bandera proclaimed an independent state in western Ukraine, the German reaction was swift and drastic. The leadership was arrested and carted of to concentration camps. The same fate befell the competing group, headed by Andrew Melnyk, with some of its members executed. The Ukrainian militia was disbanded and reorganized into more German-controlled auxiliary units.

Further disillusionments with German occupation policies opened the eyes many Ukrainians as to the real intentions of their "liberators," but they still placed hope on an alliance with Germany, preferring the latter to Stalin's Russia. This led to the continuation of an unenthusiastic, though continuing, collaboration with Nazi Germany throughout the war years (by October 1944, some 220,000 Ukrainians were fighting on the German side), and to an almost-frenzied participation in the liquidation of Jews. In this area, Ukrainian nationalist sometimes outdid the Nazis, launching mass pogroms even before the arrival of the S.S. troops and outdoing the Nazis in zealously pursuing the Jews throughout Ukraine and adjacent territories with large Ukrainian populations.

The tenacity of this anti-Jewish drive led the Nazis to use Ukrainian auxiliaries in various liquidation operations in places as faraway as Lithuania. They were to be found in most major liquidation actions in Poland and served as well as guards in the most infamous concentration camps. Historically, Jews had suffered tremendously during Ukrainian nationalist uprisings, with the pogroms of Bogdan Chemielnicki, in the seventeenth century and Semyon Petliura (in the 1920s)—considered national heroes by the Ukrainians—topping the list. But these were far surpassed by the mass exterminations of the 1940s, perpetrated with especially brutal methods and in front of the local population, who were invited to join the fray. Under Nazi rule, many Ukrainians who had not before manifested open hostility toward Jews were now eager to demonstrate their antisemitism, since this was a quick means of acquiring wealth, prestige, and power in the new political constellation as well as of demonstrating loyalty to Hitler's Germany.

Those who risked their lives to save Jews were few and far between, but they were to be found in many quarters. Among the 1,500 Ukrainians sentenced to death for various offenses in October 1943, some 100 were executed for helping or concealing Jews (*Judenbegünstigung* in Nazi parlance). This is not an inconsiderable figure when we take into consideration that only a fraction of the Ukrainians who helped Jews were apprehended (and of those arrested, actually executed); that in many instances those guilty were executed on the spot and do not figure in the official statistics; that the report covers only a part of the Galicia district, and only the period of October 1943 to June 1944 solely.

Members of the small Baptist and Seventh-Day Adventist churches were prominent in the rescue of Jews, for mostly ideological reasons. In some cases, church dignitaries personally intervened to rescue individual Jewish persons, as in the case of Metropolitan Andreas Szeptycki, the head of the Catholic Uniate Church. However, he equally favored a pro-German alliance and called upon his people to help Nazi Germany win the war, while at the same time not specifically condemning the killing of Jews by his followers.

Estimates of Jews saved during the Nazi occupation of Ukrainian-inhabited regions are hard to arrive at. Most Jews who survived owe their lives to the good foresight of fleeing into the interior of Russia on the eve of the German invasion rather than to the magnanimity of the local population. But rescuers there were, as the following stories will illustrate.

Rescue stories at the hands of Ukrainians will be presented regardless of whether they took place in strictly Ukrainian-populated regions or in cities and towns with mixed populations (as in many parts of prewar Poland).

Anton Suchinski

Anton ("Antos") Suchinski, a bachelor who barely managed to eke out a living as a tinker, lived alone in a modest house in Zborów. He had existed on the edge of poverty for the greater part of his life, and as far as the neighbors were concerned, he was a naive person of no consequense.

In July 1941 Zborów fell to the Germans. A series of murderous actions against the town's Jews followed. During one of these Eva Halperin lost her father, mother, and two brothers, and was sent to a labor camp.

In April 1943, just a few days before everyone in the camp was liquidated, she escaped together with four members of the Zeiger family. They went to Suchinski's house and begged him for help. Antos let them in and hid them in an underground cellar together with a sixteen-year-old girl who was already hiding there.

As time went by, some of the neighbors noticed telltale signs that there was more than one person in Suchinski's house and concluded that he was hiding Jews. Before long a delegation of villagers dropped in to tell him that they would inform the police unless they were paid off. The Zeigers had some money, and at first complied, but after a while, realizing that the demands were not going to stop, they refused to pay any more.

One night in October 1943 the gang returned with rifles and opened fire on the house. An elderly Jewish woman was killed and Eva was wounded. The six Jews fled in panic and for the next three days sought a refuge in the surrounding countryside, where friendly peasants fed them but insisted that they move on.

Having no other place to go, they returned to Suchinski's house in the dark of the night. "Our feet stumbled over stones and sank into the half-frozen puddles of muddy water," Eva relates. "Our clothes were so wet that they stuck to our bodies." Antos was relieved to see that they were still alive. "Opening his arms, and weeping from joy, he kissed us emotionally," Eva writes. Whispering to make sure that none of the neighbors overheard, he said, "My precious ones, I am so happy you have come back to me. I'll make sure that they never torment you again. From now on I'll fix it so that no one will be able to see you."

For the time being he hid them in the attic, but over the next three nights, with the help of the two Zeiger brothers, he dug an underground hideout beneath the house. It was about 8 feet wide, 4 feet long, and less than 3 feet high, and had two entrances; one, camouflaged with bundles of straw, was just outside the house, the other led to his bedroom by means of a trapdoor.

The six escapees lived cramped together in this dismal hole for the next nine months. There was a single kerosene lamp for light and virtually no room to move, although they were able to sit up. Without Antos they would have starved or suffocated. "Every night he used to let down food for us through the trapdoor (mostly beets and potatoes) and remove the bucket which we used as a chamberpot."

Providing food for six hungry mouths was a major problem. Suchinski's brother and sister, who lived next door, helped, but sometimes, when he was unable to obtain anything extra, he gave the six his own meal and then went to bed hungry. "We were happy that Antos was taking care of us," Eva continues, "but unimaginable new troubles arose for him, and he was only able to endure because of his saintly patience and his tremendous love of life coupled with his determination to save us."

Ever since October the neighbors had been wondering what had happened to the six Jews, and in due course they began to suspect that Antos was still hiding them. They reported their suspicions, and one day a party of German soldiers and Ukrainian militiamen descended on the Suchinski house. The six people in the cellar, able to hear every word, listened fearfully as the soldiers searched the room above them and questioned Antos at gunpoint. Despite threats and abuse he revealed nothing, and eventually the soldiers left.

"Another time Antos learned that the Germans were going to search the farm with dogs trained to find people," Shelley Zeiger recalls. "He stayed up all night, spreading waste from the outhouses and pepper over the surface of the fields to throw off the scent. They did come with the dogs, but they never found us."

On July 24, 1944, the occupants of the hideout watched in terror as the trapdoor opened without the usual signal from Antos. "Our blood froze from fear, thinking the Germans had discovered us," Eva recalls. Instead, it was good news. In a gentle voice, Antos joyfully exclaimed: "My friends, you may leave. You are saved. The Russians have arrived." As it turned out, the liberation took place at the eleventh hour, for the roof of their hiding place collapsed just two days after they vacated it.

When the war ended, Suchinski's six wards left the Ukraine, some of them going to Israel and others to the United States. In America, starting from scratch, Shelley Zeiger became a successful businessman who headed several companies. The dehumanizing experience of his early years had a profound effect on him. "It made me a stronger person. I fear nothing except God. When things get really rough, I think of how much worse it was. We never let our own children forget. And their children will know it too. It will be a good stabilizer."

In the early postwar years, Zeiger regularly sent parcels of food and clothing to Antos Suchinski, but in the late 1950s the acknowledgments stopped. In 1988 Shelley Zeiger was able to find Suchinski again. Overcome with excitement, he phoned his mother: "Antos is alive!" He then journeyed to Zborów (now part of Ukraine) for an emotional reunion with his benefactor.

As Shelley and his wife approached Suchinski's home, "Antos walked toward us carrying a loaf of bread covered with a traditionally decorated Ukrainian cloth. I knew the custom. I kissed the bread," Zeiger relates. He recalls that Suchinski once said to him, "Don't be taken in by people who are always saying prayers; the important thing is to give food and shelter when it is needed." Concludes Zeiger: "What matters most is to send the message that when you do good, good will come back to you. When you do good, you will not be forgotten." (910)

Ivan Kaczerowski

Kalman Katz's father owned a general store in a village near Przemyslany. Toward the end of 1941, when it became apparent that the Germans intended to round up all the local Jews, the Katz family fled to the nearby woods. Kalman's father was acquainted with a Ukrainian peasant, Ivan Kaczerowski, who was willing to hide one person. Kalman, twenty years old at the time, was the one selected.

Kaczerowski prepared two hiding places for Kalman in his barn. One, entered through a feeding trough in a corner of the pigpen, was where he spent his days. The other, up in the hay loft, was where he slept. Except for a few minutes late at night when he was able to get some fresh air, Kalman never left the barn and was always in one or the other of the two places. By July 1943, when all the Jews in the area, except those in hiding, had been killed, neighbors began to suspect that Kaczerowski was sheltering someone. Kaczerowski persistently denied the allegations, but one night the *soltys*, or headman, of the village stopped by with a friendly warning that if he didn't get rid of his Jew he'd have to face a police raid.

After the *soltys* left Ivan went to the barn to tell Kalman about the visit. "He was very nervous, smoking one cigarette after another, and said to me: 'Look, I won't tell you what to do, because if anything happens to you it will be on my conscience for the rest of my life. You'll have to make up your own mind in this situation.'" To which Kalman adds: "He knew perfectly well that if I was caught there, he and his family would be ruined and all his possesions would be burned."

Kalman kept putting off the moment of decision, and a few days later the raid came sooner than expected. When the police arrived he was in the hayloft. "I heard loud voices outside on the road speaking in German and Ukrainian." A moment later three Ukrainian militiamen burst into the barn while the Germans went into the house.

The Ukrainians searched everywhere. When they began removing the hay from the loft, Kalman thought the jig was up. "At one point, one of the Ukrainian murderers came so close to me that I could see his outstretched hand right before my eyes. I buried my head in the hay and held my breath. For some reason, he did not go any farther, and I heard him say to his companion in Ukrainian: '*Tut Zidiw nema*' [There are no Jews here]. It was the most frightening moment in my life—I saw the angel of death in front of me."

The militiamen left after searching the farm. They moved on to other houses in the village, and later that day it was learned that a total of eleven

Jews had been found. All had promptly been shot.

Meanwhile, ever since their separation from Kalman, the rest of the Katz family had been hiding in the forest. Ukrainian militamen eventually tracked them down and killed his brother and two sisters, but his parents escaped to the Kaczerowski farm. "Mr. Kaczerowski was happy to keep us all together till the war's end," Kalman Katz writes. Moreover, his testimony continues, "He did it entirely out of good will; not for money or a reward. . . . He wanted nothing. Those people were really *zadikim* [righteous]." (2474)

* * *

The following two stories recount rescues effected by Ukrainian Baptists. We begin with another story from Tarnopol and continue with one from the Wolyn area.

Wasyl Dzywulski

Wasyl Dzywulski, his wife Marina, and their five daughters were all members of the Baptist church in the village of Kotasiwka. At one time Wasyl had worked as a night-watchman for the Ehrlich family, who were cattle-dealers in Potok Zloty.

When the Germans occupied Potok Zloty in June 1941, Michael Ehrlich fled into the woods. The seventeen-year-old lad wandered aimlessly for a while but eventually came to the outskirts of Kotasiwka. One day, while hiding behind some bushes, Michael saw a man approaching. "I started to run away. He called to me, 'Don't be afraid, I want to help you.' I overcame my fear for the moment and went toward him. As I drew closer he recognized me because he had so often been a guest in my parents' home."

Learning that the frightened youth had not eaten in two days, Dzywulski invited him home for a meal. Michael hardly remembered Dzywulski and therefore didn't trust him. When they got to the house, Michael remained outside in a grove of trees and insisted that Dzywulski bring the food to him. Dzywulski did as he asked, "then told me that I should come to him every night and knock on the window."

The next night, and the next, and the next, Michael warily approached the house and Dzywulski brought food out to him. When he finally won the boy's confidence, Michael began coming inside. All this, of course, took place late at night "so that his neighbors would not observe our activities." Nonetheless, whenever Michael was in the house the whole family kept watch, both outside and at the windows, to make sure that no unexpected visitor came along and caught a glimpse of the youngster.

"This man risked his life, and the lives of all of the members of his family to help me at the time," Michael emphasizes, adding: "If he had been discovered helping me and had been reported to the authorities, he, his family, and I would unquestionably have been killed."

After a while Michael asked permission to build himself a hideout in the stable, and Dzywulski consented. It took him more than two months to dig a suitable pit because all of the earth had to be loaded into a bag and dumped in a nearby stream. The entrance to the hideout was in the floor of the cow stall. Whenever Dzywulski fed the cows, he would put some food for Michael in the bucket with the fodder and then slip it through the hidden opening.

It was now September 1942, and the Germans had proclaimed Potok Zloty *Judenfrei* after moving the few remaining Jews to the ghetto in nearby Buczacz. Michael thought his family might be among the ones taken there but knew they wouldn't survive long. One day he asked Dzywulski if he would be willing to hide them as well. Dzywulski answered with a simple yes.

Michael set out for Buczacz to find his family. "Of course, I didn't know exactly where my family was at this time, or even whether I had any family left." When he got there he learned that his parents were dead, as were all the others except for his brother Israel and Israel's wife.

Michael brought their nine-month-old daughter Zipporah back to the farm with him, and the Dzywulskis took her in, renaming her Marusia and pretending that she was their own child. A short while later Israel died of typhus, but his wife and a dozen of her relatives made their way from Buczacz to the Dzywulski farm. There were now a total of thirteen people in the bunker beneath the stable, and together with Zipporah, as Michael points out in his statement, this made a total of "fourteen people whose lives were saved by Wasyl Dzywulski."

Naturally the bunker had to be enlarged to accommodate the newcomers, but it remained sorely inadequate by any reasonable standard. Measuring 6 by 8 by 6 feet, "the hideout was," in the words of Yaffa Kirschenbaum, "cramped, dark, and airless. As a result of which we were afflicted with many illnesses from which we still suffer [written in 1974], such as poor eyesight and rheumatism."

Taking in so many people was very dangerous. Several Jews had already been discovered in the village: they and their benefactors had all been shot, and the benefactors' houses had been burned down. Nonetheless, fortified by their religious faith, the Dzywulskis were willing to take a chance.

Feeding the escapees was one of the biggest problems. Marina Dzywulski regularly traveled long distances in order to get food. "If she had bought too much in her own village, this would at once have aroused suspicion that she was hiding Jews."

At the outset the Jews in the bunker were able to provide Marina with food money, but before long their funds ran out; the Dzywulskis then tapped their own savings, but this source too was soon exhausted. From then on they improvised. Some nights, for example, Marina and her daughters would sneak into the fields of other peasants and harvest enough to feed the bunker for a few days.

In March 1944 the area filled up with German troops retreating before the inexorable advance of the Red Army. With Germans everywhere it was impossible to obtain extra food or risk going to the bunker. Dzywulski gave the hidden Jews a small supply of potatoes and bread and told them that he would not be back until the Germans were gone. Over the next several days, while tensely waiting for the German withdrawal to resume, the Dzywulski family lived in constant fear, drawing the strength to get through this difficult period from their belief in God.

After the liberation, unfortunately, hard times began in earnest for the Dzywulskis, for they were uprooted from their home and deported to the interior of Russia, where they were forced to live in exile for several years. "It was impossible to repay this most wonderful human being and his family for saving our lives," Michael Ehrlich wrote in his 1973 deposition from the United States. "We had nothing tangible that we could give them. Their philosophy was that they and we, all together, would live or die. We live because of him, and our lives are richer and fuller for having known these beautiful human beings." (265)

Ivan Jaciuk
Sawko & Okseniya Mironiuk

The city of Lutsk was taken by the Germans on June 21, 1941. By November 1942 almost all of its prewar Jewish population of 20,000 had been massacred, most of them in the nearby Polanka forest.

David Prital, a teenager, had been sent to a labor camp just outside the city when the roundups of Jews began. In December 1941, seeing the handwriting on the wall, he knew he had to get away if he was going to survive. While on a work detail he sought out a Pole who was said to help Jews for a fee. On the way back to the camp after talking to the Pole, he noticed a large number of German and Ukrainian troops in the streets. Concluding that an *Aktion* against the city's Jews was in the offing, David decided right then and there to flee.

Since he had no money he could hardly return to the Pole. Instead he decided to throw himself on the mercy of the Bron family, Polish acquaintances of the Pritals from prewar days, who lived in a nearby village. When he got there, Zygmund Bron agreed to give him a bed for the night but said he would have to leave the next day.

In the morning, hoping Bron would let him stay if he made himself useful, David began doing the household chores. By and by Bron came over and said: "It wasn't really that bad. The night is over and no Germans turned up." All things considered, he continued, it would probably be all right for David to stay just a little bit longer. David could see that Bron was going through some sort of internal struggle. "Please," he said, "just let me stay for the winter. In March I'll try my luck in the forest." Bron agreed.

A former Red Army officer, Zygmund Bron was not a devout Christian but had an abiding faith in man. Once, in a thoughtful and rather solemn mood, he said to David: "I am an old man. In my time I've seen a lot, and I have come to the conclusion that nothing in this world lasts forever. Rest assured, even the German occupation will come to an end, like a bad dream."

Zygmund Bron's wife, Wanda, displayed a motherly affection toward David. Of their two daughters. Irena, the youngest, was very sympathetic to him. Once, during a family argument about David's presence, Irena tearfully said to the frightened lad: "I am serene and calm, for the simple reason that we didn't decide to hide you because of money. God will surely help us!" The older sister, in contrast, was bitterly antisemitic and made no effort to hide her feelings.

With the arrival of spring, and spurred on by the growing tension in the Bron household, David decided it was time to leave. He hoped to join up with a partisan band, but this was easier said than done. First he would have to find out where the partisans were, and then he would have to get to them without been captured on the way by one of the Ukrainian nationalist gangs that were roaming the countryside. It was quit certain that he would never reach the partisans on his own, but whom could he possibly ask, and where would he find anyone willing to help him?

This dilemma gave David many sleepless nights. Then, in a flash, the answer came to him. Back home, before the war, the family's maid had been a Baptist, and David still fondly recalled her piety and her love for the Jewish people so much in contrast to the usual Ukrainian antisemitism.

And he also remembered a saintly old Baptist peasant he had met when his grandfather once took him along on a business trip to the countryside. He too had been friendly toward Jews, and David had been fascinated by the hymns the old man and his friends sang, and by their baptismal ceremony on the banks of the river Styr.

David decided to seek out some Baptists and ask them for help. With their assistance he would go to Ludmir, where the ghetto had not yet been liquidated, and someone there would tell him how to find the partisans.

Passing through Lutsk on his way to an area where he knew there was a Baptist community, David stopped off at Witold Fomienko's barbershop to find out if there were any other Jews in hiding. Fomienko, a Ukrainian, was a legendary figure. He used to go into the ghetto with sacks of bread and distribute it free to the wives of Jewish barbers who had been killed or sent to camps. Then, in good tonsorial style, he would regale anyone would would listen with jokes and funny stories in which the Germans were invariably the butt. Fomienko was glad to see David, but he was already hiding eight Jews in his home and could not make room for another.

The region David passed through after leaving Lutsk had been part of Poland before the war and had a mixed population. Now it was ablaze with civil strife as the Ukrainian majority burned Polish farms and terrorized their hapless owners.

One morning David came to the home of a Polish peasant outside a small village. The Pole, who had just received an anonymous letter threatening him with death if he did not leave the area, had several Jews in his barn. He let David rest there for a few days. When David told him his plans, the Pole confirmed that the Baptists were good friends of the Jews and gave him directions to a nearby farm owned by a Baptist family.

That evening David bade farewell to his Polish friend, who was later killed by Ukrainian partisans, and made his way to the Baptist farm. As he approached it a man emerged from the farmhouse and walked straight toward him. When the man got close enough he looked David over for a few moments, then, hesitating briefly, took him by the hand and led him inside.

"God has brought us an important guest," he joyfully called out to his wife. "Come, let us thank the Lord." The man's name was Ivan Jaciuk. He and his wife fell on their knees, praising God for having granted them the privilege of meeting a son of Israel and imploring Him to save the remnant of Jews who were hiding in the fields and forests. David could hardly believe his ears. So it was true! The Baptists really were friends of the Jews, just like the ones he had known as a child.

Their prayer completed, the Jaciuks stood up and invited David to dine with them. Ivan's wife served milk with potatoes. Before eating, Ivan read from the Bible. Over dinner, he said to David, "Try to understand; I too am Jewish." When David's puzzlement became apparent, Ivan continued: "Spiritually I am a Jew, and this encounter with you gives me a lot to think about, because it verifies the prophet's word that a saving remnant will be spared."

Ivan began pressing David to discuss his religious beliefs, but David demurred, explaining that with thousands of his brethren being slaughtered while the world looked on, and with his own family among the victims, he was hardly in the right frame of mind for a conversation about religion. Ivan, his eyes wet with tears, apologized. "You're right; you are right."

Ivan's house could only serve as a temporary haven because the next-door neighbor was a rabid Jew-hater who would certainly report anything unusual to the police. Late that night, however, Ivan took David to the home of another Baptist family. In the weeks and months that followed he was rotated from one Baptist household to another, never staying with one family long enough to arouse suspicion.

One evening Ivan called him aside. "We usually trust our fellow believers, " he said. "But in the final reckoning man is tested in adversity and difficult situations. Tonight we shall take you to someone who doesn't know you. His attitude and response will test the sincerity of his faith. There is no danger in this for you. At worst he will refuse you his hospitality, and in that case we'll take you somewhere else. But to us his response will be a serious indication of the strength and depth of his faith."

David knocked at the indicated door and said he was a homeless person seeking shelter for a few nights. Behind the closed door the man and his wife began arguing. She strenuously objected to letting a stranger in, and finally the man told David that he was not going to open the door. David replied: "What a world this is, that refuses shelter to a Jew!" The Baptist peasant, overwhelmed by this revelation, said to his wife: "But it's a Jew; how can we refuse?" The door swung open and David was given a hearty welcome.

Another time, the Baptist peasant with whom he was staying sat down beside David and said: "I see you are sad and depressed. Allow me to sing you a song that will strengthen your spirit." Then, in the original Hebrew, he began to chant Psalm 126, which begins with the words, "When the Lord brought back those that returned to Zion"!

When he was taken to the house of Sawko and Okseniya Mironiuk, David discovered that another Jewish boy was already living there. Unbelievably, it was a distant relative of his named Ignac. And to make it all still more unbelievable, Ignac claimed that he had been led there by the spirit of his dead mother, which had risen up out of the flames of the ghetto and appeared to him in a dream. David learned that Ignac had begun writing hymns and was a celebrity of sorts among the local Baptists. He later was killed while serving as an officer in the Russian army.

Jaslenski, another Baptist with whom David stayed for a few nights, saved his life when nationalist guerillas, tipped off by an informer, raided the farm. They had pulled David out of the barn and were about to shoot him when Jaslenski began shouting: "You don't know what you are doing! This Jew is a wanderer—estranged and homeless. What has he done to you? If you kill this Jew, his blood will cry out for all eternity and will haunt you for the rest of your lives. Let him go!" Overcome with superstitious awe, the guerillas released him and skulked off.

Eventually, David left the Baptist community and joined a partisan band in the forest. Now a member of an Israeli kibbutz, he still corresponds with some of his rescuers. In a recent response to a letter from David, Ivan Jaciuk wrote as follows:

> Many friends were in tears when they read the parts of your letter about the reclamation of the wilderness—barren for a thousand years. I see it as the fulfillment of God's promise to Israel, for we read in the Holy Scriptures that the desert will bloom in the end of days and will be transformed into the Lord's own garden (Isaiah 51:3, Ezekiel 36:33)... When we sing "When the Lord brought back those that returned to Zion, we were like unto them that dream," for us the dream has come true. "The

Lord hath done great things with us." I am grateful that even though so many years have passed since you left us, you have not forgotten me. I am told that a tree will be planted in my honor in that majestic city of Jerusalem, city of all nations. But I am not worthy of it or of any other honor, for with death they all pass away. There is a blot on my conscience. Perhaps I could have done more for your people during those terrible days when I saw your starved brethren carrying heavy stones and begging for a crumb of bread from passersby—so-called Christians. Oh, how much I long to see you before leaving this woeful world! . . . The years of my youth have gone, and now I am afflicted with old age and sickness. I showed your letter to Sawko and Okseniya. They wept like small children as they recalled you. We constantly pray for you. May the Lord bless and keep you. . . . I shall continue praying for you. (2655—56)

* * *

The following two stories also took place in Wolyn.

Fiodor Kalenczuk

Fiodor Kalenczuk was a Ukrainian peasant from a village near Rovno. Over the years he had often done business with Pesach Kranzberg, a Jewish grain merchant, and the two families had been friendly.

Early in the war all of the Jews from the Rovno area were confined in a ghetto in the town of Hoszcza. In September 1942, word got out that the Germans were planning to liquidate the ghetto. The night before this took place the Kranzberg family escaped and fled to the Kalenczuk farm.

The Kranzbergs hid in the house for two days while Kalenczuk prepared an underground hideout for them beneath the barn. They moved in on the third day. It was a pit measuring about 12 feet wide, 16 feet long, and 7 feet high, and they remained there from September 1942 to February 1944—a full seventeen months.

Throughout this period, Rasya, Pesach Kranzberg's daughter, relates, "our rescuer brought us meals three times a day." Her father, she says, was very punctilious about the dietary laws and refused to touch any food that had not been cooked under kosher supervision. For this reason Kalenczuk "also tried to bring special food for father, such as bread, eggs, milk, potatoes, steamed fish, fruit, and vegetables."

Fiodor Kalenczuk's wife had never wanted to take in the Kranzbergs. When she and her husband began having money problems, she insisted that he get rid of them. This led to noisy arguments punctuated by accusations that "he was taking food from his own children for the damned Jews." During one of their fights she threatened to either set the barn on fire or tell the nationalist militia. Fiodor had the last word, though, pacifying her with promises that the Kranzbergs would reward them after the war.

The area was liberated by the Red Army in February 1944, but Kalenczuk did not let the Kranzbergs out for another two weeks. It would have been too dangerous, for in the aftermath of the Soviet advance, Ukrainian nationalist bands were running wild, killing every Jew in sight. (346)

Ivan and Domka Semeniuk

In May 1942 all the "nonproductive" Jews in the ghetto of Dubno were shot. Fifteen-year-old Frieda Binshtok and her aunt Anna were among the few who survived. They fled to nearby Studinka, where they were drafted into a labor gang working in the fields under the watchful eyes of hostile Ukrainian militiamen. Every day news trickled in of massacres of Jews in the surrounding area, town after town, village after village. "Our turn will surely come," Frieda thought to herself.

When the local people learned that Anna was a nurse, they began coming to her for medical assistance. One of them, a forester, offered to hide Anna and Frieda in a cave not far from his home in the forest. They accepted, and just two days after they escaped they learned that the entire labor gang had been shot.

Anna and Frieda remained in the cave, as planned, and every night the forester's wife brought them food and water. After about three weeks, however, she told them they would have to find a new hiding place because her husband, while drunk, had told people he was taking care of two women in the forest.

"To this day," says Frieda, "I don't know if it was the truth or simply a way to get rid of us." In any case, the two women moved to another hideout deeper in the forest. The forester's wife kept bringing them food for a while but then stopped coming.

By now it was late December and snow was beginning to fall. Suffering badly from the cold, and with nothing left to eat except a few lumps of sugar, the two women decided to see if they could find a family that would be willing to help them. On their way out of the forest they saw a man with an axe heading in the direction of their hideout.

Assuming that he had been sent to kill them they began walking as fast as they could, and before long they were back in Studinka. The village was a hotbed of antisemitism, and many of its inhabitants were members of the pro-Nazi Ukrainian militia, but Anna and Frieda were so worn out that they couldn't go on. Having no other alternative, they decided to take a chance on Ivan Semeniuk, another man whose family Anna had helped.

Late that night they approached his house. They were afraid to knock, but the dog began barking, and Domka Semeniuk, Ivan's wife, came outside to see what was wrong. "When she saw us hiding behind the house, she almost fainted," Frieda writes. "We said nothing but waited to see what she would do. At first she hesitated; then she told us to hide in the barn because there was a guest in the house."

When the guest left, the Semeniuks brought Frieda and Anna inside. Their house was a typical peasant hut with thatched roof and beaten-earth floor, but poor as it was, it was a safe haven for two women on the run. Ivan and Domka apologetically offered what they described as a poor man's dinner, but the fugitives saw it differently. "For the first time in a month we had a decent meal." After the two women had eaten, the Semeniuks took them to the loft of their barn, where they immediately fell asleep.

The next morning Domka warned the children not to say anything about Anna and Frieda and assigned them to help in caring for the guests. As quickly as possible the Semeniuks made an underground hideout for them in the barn. "Domka's husband, who was suffering from tuberculosis, dug the hiding place together with her, while the children removed the earth."

Most of the time the two women stayed in the barn, but when the weather was very cold they spent the nights in the house with the family. In case an emergency arose while they were there, a second hiding place was prepared behind the large stove.

Wherever one went in Studinka there were militiamen boasting about how many Jews they had killed. As a result, the Semeniuks lived in constant fear of being discovered. In the spring of 1943, on his deathbed, Ivan begged his children to continue to protect and feed the two women.

His eldest daughter, Alina, aged sixteen, died of pneumonia contracted while bringing food to the barn. "She had done this barefoot so that the neighbors would not hear her footsteps," Anna writes, adding, "I feel that I had a large part in the death of this young woman, in addition to all the fears and troubles I caused her. She bore the heaviest burden after the death of her father."

After the war, fearful about what the neighbors might do when it got out that they had saved two Jewish women, the surviving Semeniuks left Studinka and moved to Rovno.(14)

Pelagia Lozinska

As in Poland, so too in the Ukraine, Jews utilized every imaginable means of escaping the Nazis. In at least one case, hiding in a grave seemed a sure way to avoid detection.

Before the war, Pelagia Lozinska, an ethnic Ukrainian, was employed as a housekeeper by the Sperber family in Lwów. Early in the war she married Julius Sperber, an attorney and musician. When the Nazis instituted a full-blown anti-Jewish campaign in the conquered city, she made up her mind that she was going to save her husband, her mother-in-law, and several Jewish friends. Although Pelagia had little formal education, she kept a diary from June 1941 until the city's liberation in July 1944. It is an invaluable historical document.

Pelagia hid her husband in several different places as the situation warranted, among them her apartment, a cemetery, and a botanical garden, whose caretaker let Julius stay there as a way of reciprocating the free violin lessons he had given his son before the war.

The following two excerpts from Pelagia's diary are of special interest:

> *August 17, 1942.* I went back to the cemetery to help my husband find a hiding place. An idea suddenly struck me, and I asked the gravedigger if he would be willing to hide my husband in an empty grave. He said he would for 500 zloty. Suddenly a lawyer named Fuks, who knew my husband, turned up and asked the gravedigger to bury him too. In the end, the gravedigger agreed to hide Fuks and seven of his relatives as well as my husband for 1,000 zloty, and I paid him what he asked. I was somewhat relieved, because now my husband would not be all alone in the grave. When it got dark, the gravedigger took the nine of them to an empty grave site. He removed the cover and I saw empty coffins inside. I became terrified—my husband was about to be buried alive! They all tried to calm me down, saying they would gladly stay in a grave until the end of the war, since, as they put it, life in a grave was better than death in a gas chamber. Straw and boards were brought, and they all fixed places for themselves to sit and sleep. *August 23, 1942.* I am beginning to worry about the Jews who are hiding in my attic. I am afraid that the neighbors will find out about them, on top of my worries about having to run back and forth every morning to fetch food for them. In the evening, I usually go to visit my husband, who hides in the grave all day and only comes out at night.(216)

Olena Hryhoryszyn

We end with a moving story about a kind-hearted Ukrainian woman and a Jewish orphan.

Born in Shishori, a town at the foot of the Carpathian Mountains in southeastern Poland, Donia Rosen was orphaned at an early age. After her mother's death, her father remarried and settled near Kolomyja. Donia was raised by her grandparents in Kosov.

Soon after the German invasion in June 1941, Donia and her grandparents were herded into the Kosov ghetto. On September 19 the Nazis began liquidating the ghetto.

A couple of days later Donia and her grandmother were recognized on the street and arrested. The Ukrainian militiamen who took them back to the ghetto made a brief detour to Pistin Hill and forced them to look at the still-unburied bodies of the Jews slain in the *Aktion* just ended.

In April 1942 the residents of the Kosov ghetto were transferred to another ghetto on the banks of a nearby stream. Donia became a slave laborer for the German military, assigned to the work of hauling bricks and cement to a construction site.

On September 19 the Nazis began liquidating the ghetto. Donia, her grandmother, and some other people hid in an attic, but the crying of a baby revealed their presence. There was pandemonium as the Germans forced their way in, and at that moment Donia fainted. She has no memory of what happened next. Apparently someone pushed her into a corner when she passed out and the Germans failed to notice her because of the poor light. In any event, when she regained consciousness she was all alone.

Removing the yellow star from her dress, Donia left the ghetto and ran into the woods. After bypassing several villages, she eventually got to Mikitinitz and went to the house of Parashka Hryhoryszyn, who had known her grandparents. She concealed Donia in her attic for a few days, but said nothing to her husband because he would have objected. When it was time for Donia to leave, Parashka helped her to disguise herself as a peasant girl, giving her the necessary clothing and a cross to wear around her neck, and teaching her how to recite the Lord's Prayer. The twelve-year-old was now on her own.

Donia found work in the neighborhood as a housemaid but returned to Parashka's house when she was recognized by some people who had known her before the war. In the meantime Parashka had told the story to her uncle, Stepan Hryhoryszyn. He in turn sent for his sister, Olena, and told Donia to hide in the forest until her arrival. When Olena got there, Donia begged her for help. As recorded in Donia's testimony, Olena replied: "I will do whatever I can for you, so long as my strength and my spirit last." Olena Hryhoryszyn was then sixty-five years old; she had never married and lived by herself. As she spoke she began weeping. She and Donia embraced.

Donia moved in with Olena and Stepan, but Olena worked at several different jobs and was often not at home. From the outset she warned Donia not to have much confidence in Stepan, for he was not only an antisemite but had been embittered by an unhappy marriage. It was not very long before Stepan began insisting that Donia had to go, and when Olena refused to part with her, he threw them both out of the house.

A period of wandering followed, but they were able to return home once Stepan calmed down. He was usually away for days at a time, which made the situation a bit easier, and whenever anyone knocked at the door Donia hid behind the stove. The militia once searched the house, and when Donia came out of her hiding place afterwards, Olena said to her: "I shall never give up. This terrible struggle gives me strength. So long as I remain alive, you too will live. This is the first time I have ever felt that my life has meaning. This is the first time anyone has needed me. You have saved me from my terrible loneliness. Let me share your fate as a sister and friend. I want to share your difficult and bitter fate. I am not afraid of death, for this is a battle that I have freely chosen for myself. . . . A difficult fate has bound us so closely together that I can no longer conceive of life without you."

One day two Ukrainian soldiers broke into the house, beat up the old woman and the girl, and dragged them outside. Now the secret was out and soon the whole village would know. Olena hurriedly took Donia into the forest, dug a hole on a hillside, and covered it with dry twigs. This became Donia's home during the winter of 1942—43.

Late each night, when everyone in the village was fast asleep, Olena would quietly slip out and walk several kilometers to bring food to Donia and massage her stiff legs. On the way back home, Olena would carefully cover up the footprints she left in the deep snow.

When the spring thaw began and the hole began filling up with muddy water, Olena arranged for a neighbor to keep Donia in his attic for a few days while she built a rude hut for her in the forest. Later, while visiting her in the hut, Olena confided: "I have just one wish—that God will enable me to keep you strong and healthy so that you will live and someday be happy. I ask nothing in return. Only, when I die, I want you to bury me."

Donia and Olena went through more hair-raising confrontations with death than can possibly be recounted here. Time and again they were on the brink of being shot and then miraculously escaped at the last moment. Most of the time Donia stayed in the forest, but every once in a while Olena placed her with trustworthy peasants for a brief respite.

One day in the spring of 1944, with the Red Army drawing steadily closer, Donia was spotted by a Ukrainian militiaman. When he headed toward her, she began running. The chase led through the forest to the edge of the Pruth River. She got across somehow and found that the opposite bank was already in the hands of the Russians. She was safe now, but her joy was mingled with sorrow because she had been unable to bid farewell to the woman who had done so much for her. The two never met again.

From the Pruth Donia went to Kolomyja and then to Czernowicz, where she fell ill and had to be hospitalized. When she recovered she went on to Romania and in 1947 sailed for Palestine aboard an illegal refugee boat. Apprehended on the high seas by a British warship, she and the other passengers were interned in camps on the island of Cyprus, where they remained until Israel became an independent state in 1948.

In 1971 Donia wrote a book about her wartime experiences. The dedication reads:

> Dear, unforgettable Olena. If I were a sculptor, I would make a statue of you and perpetuate your exalted image—that of a mother ready to bear the most brutal suffering for the sake of her children; even ready to sacrifice her life at any moment. You were a mother to me, replacing the mother taken away at the dawn of my life. To my sorrow, I am neither sculptor nor poet. I can only offer you this modest tribute—these

memoirs, written out of a profound spiritual need. Accept them, dear Olena, as the expression of my deep love for you, of my gratitude and esteem. Dear and beloved Olena, I shall never forget you! (144)

* * *

Yad Vashem has only recently been amassing material on the Holocaust in Russia. The following two stories, which took place in Byelorussia (White Russia), were documented many years ago.

Jelena Valendovitch

After the fall of Minsk, in June 1941, the city's 90,000 Jews were herded into a ghetto set up in a nearby suburb. In a single night (November 7, 1941), 12,000 of them were machine-gunned to death alongside the mass graves they had been forced to dig. Two weeks later another 5,000 were killed. More executions followed, and by February 1943, subtracting the 10,000 or so who had managed to escape, only 9,000 Jews were left. They too would all soon die.

Living in the Minsk ghetto in 1941 were Katia Tokarski, her mother, and her two-year-old daughter Vala. Whenever a German raid seemed likely, Katia passed Vala through the barbed-wire fence around the ghetto to a friendly gentile woman outside. Dangerous as this might have been, she reasoned that it was less dangerous than taking Vala into one of the ghetto's underground bunkers. There had been too many cases of babies being smothered so that a bunker's location would not be revealed by the sound of an infant crying.

Katia's mother and daughter, like Katia herself, had blonde hair and fair complexions. Since it was obvious that the raids on the ghetto would continue until there were no Jews left, Katia proposed that the three of them should escape to the Aryan side and try to pass as non-Jews.

"No, my daughter," Katia's mother responded, "I was born Jewish and want to die Jewish. Why go somewhere else only to meet death? I prefer to meet it here." But she urged Katia and Vala to escape without her. "Maybe the two of you will make it. A beautiful blonde girl, speaking good German! Who knows?"

For the time being Katia decided to do what she could for Vala. In the early morning hours of September 1, 1942, she reported to her work detail with Vala tucked in her arms and completely covered up. The day had not yet dawned; and in the semidarkness the guards at the gate did not notice anything. Once outside the ghetto, Katia slipped away as the detail turned a corner and ran into the ruins of a bombed-out building.

What followed was like a modern-day version of the biblical story of Pharaoh's daughter and the infant Moses. Katia set Vala on the pavement in front of the building and hid a short distance away to see what would happen. The child played quietly for a while, then began to cry. Before long a tall man happened past. He picked the child up and studied its face for a moment. Vala, as if instinctively, touched a finger to his neck.

"At first," Katia relates, "I almost ran over to him, but I controlled myself and stayed where I was." With the child in his arms, the man walked away, and Katia followed at a safe distance. Eventually he entered a house. Making a mental note of the address, Katia left and rejoined her work detail.

The man who had taken Vala home was Misha Gromov, an escaped Russian POW. He was living with Jelena Valendovitch, who had found him wounded in the city park, and her young son Eugenyi. When Gromov told Jelena how he had found the infant, she realized at once that the child was Jewish. She decided to protect her, telling the neighbors that the girl was her niece from a distant village.

Back in the ghetto, Katia was uneasy about Vala. She felt she had to see her at least once more to make sure she was being well cared for. One day about six weeks later Katia again managed to slip away from her work detail. Rushing to the house where Gromov had taken the child, she entered, opened the first door she came across, and, pushing aside a curtain, found herself face to face with her daughter.

"When she saw me, Vala stood up in her crib. The woman in the room, thinking that the presence of a 'stranger' had frightened the child, took her in her arms." Stepping over to the crib, Katia silently caressed Vala's leg. "She began to weep, and I wept too. Then the woman understood everything. She sent the man [Misha] away, telling him to lock the door on his way out. And that was the beginning of my friendship with Jelena, my daughter's rescuer."

Jelena offered to hide Katia if the Nazis began to liquidate the ghetto, but Katia would not accept. "Wherever I go death follows," she said. "The safety of your home means more to me than my own life." Deeply moved by Katia's reply, Jelena promised to take care of Vala no matter what. With this, the two women parted.

In the months that followed the makeshift family of Jelena, Gromov, Eugenyi, and Vala managed very nicely. Gromov's illegal earnings as a watchmaker were enough to support them, and whenever a neighbor became too inquisitive they moved to another dwelling. As far as Vala was concerned, Jelena and Misha were her parents.

Meanwhile, with Vala safe Katia was now able to look out for herself. On March 30, 1943, she escaped from the ghetto with some other people and joined a partisan unit operating in the nearby forest. Unknown to her, Jelena had joined a partisan unit operating about 30 kilometers away from her own.

Over the next few months, Katia was told on more than one occasion that her daughter had been seen with the other band. One day she decided to find out whether there was any truth to the stories. The journey through the forest was dangerous, but at its end she was tearfully reunited with Jelena and Vala. Katia arranged for them to be housed in a village about 4 kilometers from her unit's camp and from then until the liberation in July 1944 visited them every two or three days.

As for Misha Gromov, he too joined a partisan unit, but he did not live to see the end of the war. Several days before the liberation of Minsk, he fell in battle. (1620)

Ignacy Kurjanowicz

Brest-Litovsk fell to the Germans at the very beginning of their invasion of Russia. On June 28, 1941, just a few days later, the Nazis rounded up and massacred 5,000 of the city's 30,000 Jews. More mass killings following, and disease and starvation took their toll as well. By the end of the war only a handful of Jews were left in the city.

Moshe Smolar was a teacher at a school for orphans run by the CENTOS, a Jewish philanthropic organization. During the roundup on June 28 two German soldiers entered his classroom. "One asked: 'Jewish?' I answered yes. He then said: 'Come with me!' The other said: 'Stay here.' This decided my fate for life and death. It took only a minute. There was no argument. One said 'come,' and the other said 'stay.'" A stroke of good luck had spared Smolar's life, but he would soon be in jeopardy again.

Some while before the German invasion, Smolar's principal had sent him to the local employment office to hire a new school custodian. Several men were sitting on a bench waiting to be interviewed. "Among them, I noticed a middle-aged man, tall and slim. He made a good impression on me."

The man's name was Ignacy Kurjanowicz and he was an ethnic Byelorussian. When Smolar interviewed him, he learned that Kurjanowicz was "not so kosher" in that he was suspected of anti-Communist tendencies. Impressed by his sharp mind and his work experience, Smolar hired him.

Kurjanowicz fit in easily at the school, well liked by teachers and pupils. He struck everyone as being a regular fellow, but as Moshe notes in his testimony, "there was nothing outstanding about him, either positive or negative."

Early in the German occupation of Brest-Litovsk the CENTOS school and all the other Jewish institutions had to discharge their non-Jewish personnel. Soon afterwards the city's Jews were confined to a ghetto occupying about three square blocks and surrounded by a barbed-wire fence.

On December 15, 1941, the last day outsiders were allowed to enter the ghetto, Kurjanowicz visited Smolar to say goodbye, "for he knew he would not see me again." The two men embraced. "He said to me: 'Listen, my friend, if you need me, here's my address. I'll do whatever I can to help you, and even more.' Then he left. The next morning the ghetto was closed off."

There followed a series of killing operations which decimated the ghetto's populace. In October 1942, when word spread that the ghetto would be liquidated on the fourteenth of the month, Moshe Smolar and his father together with Moshe's woman friend and her mother built themselves a camouflaged hiding place on a rooftop.

From this vantage point, over the next few days, they watched as Lithuanian and Ukrainian militiamen rounded up the ghetto's inhabitants and marched them off to be loaded on trains. Anyone who resisted was shot on the spot, and so was anyone found hiding.

After the troops left each day the mob took over. Thousands of peasants flooded the empty houses to loot whatever the Germans and their militia henchmen had overlooked. They even smashed down walls in their search for plunder. For every hidden Jew they found they received a 1,000-zloty reward.

Moshe Smolar's father died while the operation against the ghetto was still in progress, and since there was no way to bury him, Smolar moved the body to another rooftop. Realizing that the militia or the mob would soon ferret them out, he and the two women decided to throw themselves on the mercy of a Polish woman who had promised to help them. Since the two women did not look Jewish, they would go first, depending on their appearance to get them through the mob. Moshe was to follow as closely as possible.

In accordance with the plan, Smolar's woman friend and her mother left the rooftop, but when he tried it was too late. "I had only gotten as far as the stairs when I met some peasants on their way up. I mingled with them, and participated in the looting so that I would seem to be one of them." Once they left, he went back to the rooftop. He waited three days without hearing anything from the women, and later learned that they had been caught and killed.

Smolar was now alone on the roof of a condemned building with no food or water. One night he lowered himself into the cellar by means of a rope, then went to the home of a Polish engineer who had once worked at the CENTOS school. Quite understandably Smolar was in a gloomy mood because of the horrors he had just been through, but the engineer's kindness, and the risk he took in helping him, was like a tonic. "Here at least," he reflected, "is someone in whom the divine image of God is still alive."

Smolar had asked for nothing but water. The engineer had given him some, of course, but had also provided him with money and cigarettes. Taking heart from this, Smolar decided to seek aid from Ignacy Kurjanowicz as well. He made his way back to his rooftop and waited for an opportunity.

Kurjanowicz lived with his wife, his married daughter, and her husband in a suburb on the other side of a railroad right-of-way that could only be crossed by way of a heavily guarded bridge. Taking along a small axe he had found, Smolar pretended to be a laborer going to work. The German sentries on the bridge let him pass, and he arrived safely at Kurjanowicz's home.

"When I knocked at the door, Ignacy and his wife opened it, and both crossed themselves. Trembling, they embraced and kissed each other." So far as Smolar could tell, their reaction was a combination of joy and fear. They hurried him into the house, and once he was inside suggested that he take a bath. "I washed for the first time since the liquidation of the ghetto."

Moshe stayed there for a full day. "That initial meeting with the Kurjanowicz family, and the way I was welcomed, had the greatest influence on my life and on the way I would conduct myself in the future, for thanks to him I was saved spiritually. That day was the beginning of my deliverance—spiritual and physical. I simply couldn't believe that someone would risk his only daughter, his wife, and himself just to save a Jew, and with no compensation in return."

That night Kurjanowicz gave Smolar a knapsack full of food and said, "This will last you for a week. Then come back here." To make sure that no one bothered Smolar on the street, Kurjanowicz accompanied him to the edge of the former ghetto. The following week Smolar returned for more food.

The weekly visits continued for nearly two months, but on January 4, 1943, while up on the roof, Smolar heard loud noises coming from inside the building. Sneaking downstairs to investigate, he came upon two men breaking in the walls in the hope of finding hidden valuables. They were as dumbfounded as Smolar, for they had not expected to encounter anyone alive in the building, much less a desperate-looking man armed with an axe. They fled, but Smolar knew they would soon be back with reinforcements.

Abandoning his rooftop shelter, Smolar set out for the Kurjanowicz house. By the time he got there he was a bundle of nerves. Kurjanowicz was able to calm him and gave him something to eat, but later in the day Smolar began weeping. Kurjanowicz and his wife tried to cheer him up. "Listen here, my friend, don't worry; we've found a solution. It is now January, and you won't be able to survive outside in this cold. We'll keep you here for the winter; then we'll see."

Kurjanowicz began digging out a hiding place in the wall behind the oven. There was only enough room for a cubicle about 2.5 feet by 4 feet, just enough space for Smolar to crouch in with a makeshift chamberpot and a small supply of food and water. After he went inside Kurjanowicz replaced the bricks, telling him to knock with the axe whenever he could no longer stand being cooped up and had to get out for a while.

As members of the Orthodox Church, the Kurjanowicz family cel-ebrated Christmas on January 7 rather than December 25. When the holiday occurred, ten days after Smolar came to stay with them, they invited him to join in the festivities. Their warmth and kindness, like that of the Polish engineer, strengthened Smolar's resolve to survive. By April, however, the heat in the hiding place had become unbearable, and adding to Kurjanowicz's problems were rumors that his house was slated for demolition.

Determined to save Smolar, Kuranowicz came up with a daring scheme. He somehow managed to purchase papers identifying him as a Ukrainian worker named Mikhail Aleksandrovitch Timoshenko who was home on leave and would soon be returning to his job in Germany. While going from Brest-Litovsk to Germany might seem like jumping from the frying pan into the fire, Kurjanowicz felt that the credentials would pass review and therefore that the scheme would be sure to work.

Smolar, however, was terrified, convinced that he would never be able to play the role adequately, and when it came time for him to join the other workers for the return trip to Germany, he desperately tried to cut his wrists. Kurjanowicz grabbed his hand and forced him to drop the knife. "He was an intelligent man," Moshe relates, "and he understood that I had come to the end of the line. He did everything he could to persuade me that life was still worth living."

Smolar eventually reached Germany and he remained there under the assumed Ukrainian name until the end of the war. He and Kurjanowicz met again in August 1945. Writing of their reunion, Smolar said, "It would be impossible to describe our meeting without a profound analysis of man's passions and all the components of the human soul." Moshe stayed in Kurjanowicz's house for several weeks, then set out to start a new life for himself. (819)

Czechoslovakia

Czechoslovakia, which came into existence at the end of World War I, was a composite of ethnic groups, the most dominant of which were the Czechs and Slovaks. In March 1939, the country's fabric came apart, as the Germans extended their sovereignty by proclaiming a Protectorate over Bohemia and Moravia, while subtly giving birth to a satellite, though literally independent, state in Slovakia. Over 100,000 Jews were reported living in the Protectorate region, and 70,000 of these were deported to the Theresienstadt camp, located on Czech soil, on the first leg of the journey to their further deportation to the infamous Auschwitz camp. Of the 60,000 Theresienstadt Jews arriving at Auschwitz, it is estimated that only 3,200 survived. The remainding 10,000 Jews eluded the Nazi net, including several thousands who were specifically not deported because they could claim Aryan spouses.

Next-door Slovakia presented a different picture. With a population of 3 million, the newborn independent state claimed some 90,000 Jews. The country was overwhelmingly Catholic and very loyal to the church and its institutions. When Slovakia came to birth with Hitler's blessings, on March 14, 1939, its head of state was a priest—Monsignor Josef Tiso. All the factions in the new government favored strong anti-Jewish measures, without the Germans having to exert pressure in that regard. Indeed, on April 18, 1939 (before the start of the war!), the month-old government enacted its first anti-Jewish decree with a definition of who is a Jew closely modeled on the Nazi pattern.

More restrictive laws followed in September 1941, severely restricting Jewish economic and civic privileges. That same year, forced-labor camps were set up for able-bodied Jews, and many Jews were ordered evicted from the country's capital, Bratislava. This was but a prelude to the final grand step to clear the country of Jews, by turning them over to the Germans. To guarantee the irrevocable nature of the expulsion of the country's Jews, the Slovak authorities (who perhaps were not at the time aware of the final fate awaiting the deportees) were willing to pay no less than 500 German marks per head, in return for the promise that none of the deported Jews would ever be brought back to Slovakia. The Slovak government prided itself that this arrangement was wholly its own initiative, without any pressure exerted on it from the direction of Berlin.

This cleared the way for the start of the large-scale deportation of Jews from the country, which commenced in March 1942 and proceeded with alacrity until November of that year, netting some 52,000 Jews who were dispatched to the death faclities in Auschwitz. The Hlinka Guard, the Slovak equivalent of the German S.S. units, lent themselves to this task with much dedication.

Toward the end of 1942 the deportations slowed down and ground to a halt as a result of increasing pressure from the Vatican, as well as of the changing fortunes of the German arms, which suffered a stinging defeat at Stalingrad in early 1943. An untold number of Jews, viewed as economically indispensable to the country, as well as others who had converted to Christianity or were married to Christian spouses, received special dispensations and were exempt from deportation.

For a country priding itself for its Catholic loyalty, it is interesting to study the role of the church in trying to stem the destructive process. Initially, the Vatican showed an interest only in Jews converted to the Catholic faith, for whom it sought exemption from the anti-Jewish laws of 1939 and 1941. Vatican entreaties in this regard met with some success with the government of Father Tiso.

As for the Jewish population per se, the bishops' pastoral letter to the faithful on April 26, 1942 gave its blessing to the recent anti-Jewish measures, basing itself on the traditional theolological antisemitic arguments of the deicide guilt of the Jews. "The greatest tragedy of the Jewish nation," read the pastoral letter, "lies in the fact of not having recognized the Redeemer and of having prepared a terrible and ignominious death for Him on the cross." The bishops continued with a condemnation of the "pernicious" influence of the Jews on the morals of the Slovakian people, concluding with the statement: "The Church cannot be opposed, therefore, if the state with legal regulations hinders the dangerous influence of the Jews." This was tempered with a reaffirmation of the need to act as humanely as possible toward the disenfranchised Jews.

A year later, amid mounting reports of the liquidation of Jews deported to Poland (and appeals to the Vatican to intervene and exert its influence), the tone of Vatican protests sharpened and became more stringent. The pressure now shifted to saving Jews not yet affected by the recent mass deportations. By then, the Slovak government, for reasons for its own had decided to suspend further deportations of Jews. This policy remained unchanged until the fall of the Tiso government in August 1944.

That month, a local uprising was suppressed by the Germans, who proceeded to occupy the country. The destruction process could now be tackled by the more efficient and experienced S.S. elite troops. Some 13,000 of the remaining 16,000 Jews were caught in a swift roundup operation and dispatched to the killing center of Auschwitz. Those who survived inside the country did so through either fleeing into the forest or seeking shelter by hiding with non-Jewish families.

Michael and Anna Majercik

Janka-Hetty Fisch was born in 1932 in Bratislava, where her father was a well-known dentist. Hetty's mother had died in childbirth, so her father's sister Beate moved in to keep house and take care of her, but after a few years she married and with her husband, Julius Weiner, settled in the city of Zilina.

In 1939, when Hetty was seven, Slovakia became an independent state. She still remembers the persecution that ensued. "At first we were thrown out of our apartment and all our valuables were stolen," Hetty writes. Next Jews were forced to wear the yellow star and Jewish schools were closed, although for a while classes were conducted in the public kitchen run by the Jewish community. In addition a curfew was imposed on the Jews and certain streets were closed to them, as were all athletic facilities. "Insults were hurled at us; we were beaten, undressed, and spat upon. Tormenting children and old people became a kind of sport or recreation."

By the summer of 1943 conditions in Bratislava had become unbearable, so Hetty's father, who subsequently died in Auschwitz, sent her to live with the Weiners. Zilina was the site of a transit camp for Jews on the way to Auschwitz, but Hetty's aunt and uncle, because they were employed in the construction of a stadium, were permitted to live outside the camp and exempted from deportation.

After the Slovak uprising in August 1944 the Germans decided to liquidate the country's remaining Jews. Toward the end of the month a Gestapo unit appeared at the stadium site and rounded up all the Jewish workers. The Weiners were given permission to go home and pack a few things before joining the others in the camp.

Four guards escorted them to the house and two waited at the entrance while they went upstairs to their apartment. When they left the apartment, Hetty was in the lead, followed by the Weiners, and with the two other guards bringing up the rear. Hetty was downstairs, walking along the first-floor corridor, she says, when suddenly "a door opened, and a man I had never seen before stretched out his arm, drew me inside, and shut the door. He said to me, 'Don't be afraid, child. I only want to help you. Don't say a word and don't make any noise,' then led me into the bedroom where a baby was asleep in a crib."

The man was Dr. Michael Majercik. He and his wife, Anna, quickly took the baby and the bedding out of the crib, put Hetty in, put the mattress and the sheet on top of her and the baby on top of that, and then covered him with a down quilt. About half an hour later the Germans guards came looking "for the child who had not come downstairs."

The Germans turned everything upside down, emptying the closets, moving all the furniture, even looking inside the stove. One of them warned the Majerciks that the punishment for hiding Jews was death for the rescuer's whole family, but the couple insisted they knew nothing about the missing girl. With that the Germans left, but they returned several more times in the days that followed, prodded by the owner of the grocery across the street. A relative of Father Joseph Tiso's, she had seen Hetty go into the building but not come out, and was certain that the girl must still be somewhere inside.

Hetty spent the first few days hidden in the crib, which was in the Majerciks' bedroom, but at night slept with them in their bed. When things settled down a bit, the couple moved their two-year-old daughter into their room and gave hers to Hetty. She was now rather comfortably fixed, for she had her own closet, table, chair, and bookcase, and "Mrs. Majercik made sure that I always had flowers on my table."

Hetty's presence forced the Majerciks to change their lifestyle. They no longer went visiting and stopped inviting friends over. Anna Majercik, who had been scheduled to begin working as a teacher in the local secondary school, decided not to take the job. "They never left me alone because they knew I was frightened. When there were air raids, the Majerciks stayed in the apartment with me instead of going down to the shelter."

As it happened, Dr. Majercik's mother, who lived not far away, was hiding seven Jews in a shed in the courtyard of her house. In February 1945 the Germans searched her place and found them. Since Auschwitz had already been liberated by the Red Army, they were sent to Theresienstadt.

When Dr. Majercik learned what had happened he realized that the Germans might come back the same day for another look at his apartment, so he decided get Hetty off the scene for a while. Putting his infant son in the baby carriage, he told Hetty to take it and go straight to the butcher shop, not stopping or talking to anyone along the way.

It was early in the morning when Hetty set out, and she walked for hours. The day was cold and windy, and before long snow began falling. By late afternoon, when it began to get dark, she knew she was lost. Exhausted and frightened, she sat down on a stone underneath a tree and fell asleep.

After searching for hours the Majerciks found her late that night. When she asked why they had made her and the baby go out in the cold, they answered, "We were afraid they would arrest you if you were alone, but we figured that no one would be suspicious of a child pushing a baby carriage." Looking back forty years later, Hetty said, "Today, as the mother of five children, I can't believe that they were not afraid for their child. If I had been in their shoes I doubt that I would have taken such a chance."

In her deposition to Yad Vashem, Hetty said she was unable to find words that could fully express her gratitude to the Majerciks. "When I came to them, I had nothing but the clothes I was wearing. They took care of all my needs—warm clothing, shoes, even slippers. At night, when I was overcome with longing [for my family], they took me into their bed. They gave me good books to read, provided me with school texts, and tutored me. They were always kind and loving. On Christmas, for example, they would give me a gift just as good as what they gave their son and daughter."

Hetty lived with the Majerciks for a while after the war until her surviving relatives came to fetch her. When they did, they offered to pay the Majerciks, but the couple refused to take anything. Later on they returned all the packages of food and clothing that Hetty and her family sent them from abroad. "The only thing they asked of me," Hetty says, "is that we not lose touch with each other, for in the final analysis, they acted out of love." (2086)

Jan Caraj

Karl Steiner was a grocer in the city of Nitra in southern Slovakia. In 1942, along with most of the other able-bodied Jews in the area, he was conscripted for forced labor on a road-construction project near Deges on the Hungarian border. Several months later, in 1943, he and the other members of his work gang were loaded on cattle cars. They were apparently being sent to Auschwitz, but the train was turned back while it was still in Slovakia because the road had not been finished and the head of the project had angrily demanded the return of "his Jews."

For the time being they were safe, and life in the work camp developed a reassuring routine. Every so often, whenever they were able to hitch a ride on a supply truck, Steiner's two sons, Marcel, twelve, and Moshe, ten, came to visit him in camp for a few days, bringing news of their mother and their seventeen-year-old sister Hedy back in Nitra.

Things took a turn for the worse after the Germans occupied Slovakia in the aftermath of the August 1944 uprising. That September they rounded up the entire Jewish population of Nitra, including Mrs. Steiner and Hedy, both of whom died in Auschwitz, but not the boys, because they were at the work camp at the time.

Word of the disaster at Nitra was accompanied by the news that the Jewish work gangs were also going to be liquidated. Along with three other workers, Steiner and his sons broke out of the camp. At one point they heard some shots and thought the jig was up, but the riflemen turned out to be hunters, not soldiers, and they ignored the Jews because they were after four-footed prey.

For several days the little group lingered in the vicinity of the village of Dolny Taran, hiding in the fields nearby and begging for food at the farmhouses at night. They eventually knocked at the door of Jan Caraj. The owner of a 50-acre spread and a small herd of cattle, Caraj not only fed them but took them to a field about 2 miles from his house and helped them to dig a hiding place inside a gigantic haystack.

Steiner and the others lived in the haystack throughout that autumn; and every night—and sometimes in the daytime too, although that was very dangerous—Caraj brought food to them. One day some passersby heard voices coming from the haystack. Poking around for a while, they discovered the six Jews and robbed them. Afraid they would also tip off the police, Steiner and the others decided to take their chances in Deges, but once there they realized they would be picked up because of the curfew, so they returned to the Caraj farm.

With the onset of winter the haystack became uninhabitable because of the freezing rains and the rats in search of food, so Caraj moved the six into his house, hiding them in a storeroom whose doorway he blocked with a large closet. On several occasions they listened nervously as he explained to inquisitive visitors why the room had been closed off. Other times, late at night, he would pull the closet away and they would come out to join him in listening to news bulletins on the BBC. Finally, around the middle of April 1945, the area was liberated by the Red Army.

Reminiscing twenty years later, Moshe Steiner said: "I want to emphasize that Mr. Caraj acted out of selfless love for others, for he had never had anything to do with Jews until that moment [when we appeared at his house]. Furthermore, money could not possibly have been a consideration, for we were penniless and had no way to pay him."

Marcel Steiner added: "We didn't know anyone from his village or the neighboring villages and certainly did not know Mr. Caraj. Today I ask myself what motivated Mr. Jan Caraj, a farmer quietly pursuing his life, to endanger himself and his five children in order to save six miserable Jews whom he had never seen before. I can only say, as simply as possible, that he did it out of love for others." It may be, Marcel adds, that Caraj's affiliation with a Protestant evangelical church had something to do with his behavior. (204)

Michal Vitus and Viera Vrablova

The Ganz family lived in Mesto-nad-Vahom, a small town in central Slovakia. As the situation steadily worsened, Mrs. Anna Vitus, the Protestant midwife who had delivered several of their children, offered to help them if the need should arise.

On September 4, 1944, when the Germans began rounding up the area's remaining Jews, Mrs. Vitus went to the Ganz house and urged them to come with her. "We left on short notice, leaving everything behind," relates Ladislav Samuel Ganz, now a dentist.

Michal Vitus, Anna's husband, was a builder by trade but did some farming on the side, and behind their house there was a small barn, about 20 by 32 feet in area, where he stored fodder for his animals. Inside the barn Ladislas and his brother Menachem dug a hiding place in the hay large enough for the five members of the Ganz family and two women who had accompanied them.

At first everyone had assumed that the war would soon be over, but when this proved not to be the case, the strain of hiding seven Jews became too much for Mrs. Vitus. Her nervousness was exacerbated by the thrice-daily warnings on the radio that anyone who helped a Jew would be shot and by news reports of the executions of people found harboring Jews.

Toward the end of October, tipped off by an informer, a detachment of the pro-Nazi Hlinka Guard surrounded the Vitus farm and began a methodical search of the house, yard, and outbuildings. Shouting "Where are the Jews?" they made Mrs. Vitus accompany them every step of the way. When they got to the barn, Ladislav Gans recalls, "Twelve of them came inside. They probed the hay with their bayonets but luckily did not find us."

The seven Jews heaved a sigh of relief when the soldiers departed, but not Mrs. Vitus. Already suffering from a heart ailment, and terrified by what she had just gone through, she told them they would have to leave. "I don't want to die because of you. I have young daughters to take care of."

At this juncture, Viera Vrablova, one of Mrs. Vitus's married daughters, intervened. "You can't throw them out," she told her mother; "their lives are in danger. You brought them here, and now you have to keep them here until the end of the war."

"But the Germans will kill us if they find them," Michal Vitus protested. To which Viera replied: "Lots of people die in a war. If the two of you are killed, at least you'll know that you were trying to protect decent people who never did anything wrong."

Finally giving in, Michal Vitus sent Anna to stay with her parents in a town 125 miles away. Since the barn was no longer safe, he moved the seven Jews into the cellar of his house and there, with Ladislav's help, he sealed off an alcove about 8 by 12 feet for them by putting up a double brick wall. Air and a little light were provided by a glazed opening at ground level through which he passed them food and took their waste pail each day. From time to time, when it was safe enough, the inmates were able to crawl out through the opening at night to get some fresh air.

When the alcove was completed, Viera brought two more Jews to join the group and arranged for the two small children of one of the hidden women to stay with host families in the area. Throughout this period Viera was the guardian angel of the Jews in the cellar. As Ladislav Ganz wrote in his deposition, "She looked after us, ran errands for us, sold some gold

for us when we ran out of money, and kept us up to date on the latest news.
. . . Often she invented good news to keep our spirits up, thus giving us
some badly needed moral support."

In December 1944, when they ran out of things to sell in order to help
pay for their upkeep, the little group began worrying about what would
happen. Michal Vitus and Viera realized what was on their minds, and
reassured them in more or less the following words: "We're not doing this
for money and you couldn't pay us for the risks we're taking. We just want
to save you. There's more than enough food to see us through. If you're
discovered, God forbid, we know that it means death for us too, but at least
we'll die knowing that we did the right thing. If, God willing, we all survive
the war, you can give us something if you want to; if not, there'll be no hard
feelings."

On April 7, 1945, the day of liberation, the hidden Jews crawled out
of the cellar, still alive thanks to Michal Vitus and Viera Vrablova. The two
children whom Viera had placed on local farms were also alive, although
they had been mistreated and neglected by the original families and had
been passed from one household to another for several months. Some
years after the war, as a gesture to show his appreciation, one of the
survivors gave Michal some modern farm machinery as a gift. (2935)

Anna Schiller

Olga Ehrlich's nineteen-year-old brother was sent to Majdanek in
1942, but she and her parents were left alone for the time being because
her father, as a dentist, was exempted from deportation. The situation
changed in the autumn of 1944, however.

When the Germans began rounding up the Jews of Bratislava, the
Ehrlichs hid briefly in the homes of various friends. Dr. and Mrs. Ehrlich
were eventually caught and sent to a death camp, but Olga managed to
escape. "For more than a month," she recalls, "I had nowhere to go and
never knew in the morning where I would sleep that night. I had no money
or clothing, I got weaker and weaker; it was winter and I was tempted to
give myself up to the Slovak Gestapo."

Suddenly Olga remembered the Schiller family. Former patients of her
father's, they had often voiced anti-Nazi sentiments, but she not had seen
them in six years and had no idea whether their views were the same.
Having nowhere else to turn, however, she decided to take a chance.
Through a friend she sent them a note: "Mrs. Schiller, you are my last hope.
If you don't help me I will jump in the river."

Upon receiving Olga's message, Anna Schiller hesitated for a moment,
fearing a Nazi trap, but then decided it was genuine. Deeply moved by
Olga's plight, Anna hid her in her own apartment. A week later Olga moved
in with Anna's sister, Gertrude Odriska, who lived with her father and four-

year-old son in a one-room house on the outskirts of Bratislava and was already hiding a bedridden Jewish woman.

Olga had no money, of course, but the Schillers, who were supporting the Odriska household, took care of her maintenance and provided her with clothing and underwear. After the war Olga lived with them until she felt able to strike out on her own. (2352)

Kristof and Ludmila Jahn

Eva Erben was exhausted and barely able to keep up with the column. For days now she and hundreds of other prisoners from the Gross-Rosen concentration camp had been on the move, relentlessly driven forward by S.S. guards. It was April 1945 and everyone knew that Germany had lost the war. But would they manage to keep alive until the surrender?

Four years earlier, in 1941, Eva and her parents had been sent to Theresienstadt and then to Auschwitz. There her father had died. She and her mother had survived and had been transferred to Gross-Rosen, but the past few days had been too much for Mrs. Erben.

"After her death," Eva wrote, "I decided not to continue on the march no matter what. One night when we were allowed to take shelter in a barn, I waited till everyone was asleep, then dug myself into a huge pile of hay." In the morning the column went on without her.

After making sure the coast was clear, Eva left the barn and began looking for a place to stay. "I walked for three days along the railroad tracks until I reached a Czech village. I knocked at the first house, but there was no answer. I opened the door and peeked inside. My eyes went dim. Before me stood a pair of boots, S.S. boots, black and polished! I starting running but at some point collapsed and have no memory of what happened next."

When Eva came to, she found himself wearing a nightgown and lying in a clean bed. A man and a woman, Kristof and Ludmila Jahn, were at the bedside trying to make her eat something.

As they later explained, Kristof had found her lying in their clover field, not far from their home in the village of Postrekov, and had brought her home in his wagon. From then on they had been taking care of her.

For a while Eva was too weak to walk, but the Jahns carried her whenever necessary. As provision for emergencies, they improvised a hiding place for her under the kitchen floor. They plied her with special foods to help her regain her strength, and to allay suspicion in the neighborhood, had her dress in a peasant's outfit with a scarf to cover her shaved head. "Since the village girls all covered their hair, I did not stand out."

In July 1945, several months after the war ended. Eva's aunt came to Postrekov. "She arrived suddenly and wanted to take me with her. I refused to go, but 'Uncle' Jahn persuaded me to go with her, because otherwise I would never be able to get an education and make something of myself."

It was difficult for Eva to part from the Jahns, for they had given her love as well as physical care, but they assured her that she would always be welcome in their house if she could not adjust to life in Israel. In 1966 she and her husband, with their two children, visited the Jahns. It was, Eva said, "like returning home." (2428)

Hungary

Hungary's case during the Holocaust is unique, for the Jews of that country, an ally of Nazi Germany, remained relatively untouched until the middle of 1944. They were decimated in Hitler's final year of power, in a shrinking Nazi-dominated Europe that was definitely going down in defeat. To put it more bluntly, Hungary was the only country in which the perpetrators knew perfectly well that the war was lost when they began to destroy the Jews. Furthermore, the mass deportations in that country could no longer be concealed (as was the case for the other occupied countries during 1942-44); they were carried out openly in full view of the world.

Hungary was one of the German-allied countries termed by a historian as "opportunist;" that is, it joined the Nazi camp in order to gain territory for itself. After Hitler's rise to power in Germany, Admiral Horthy, the ruler of Hungary, cemented an alliance with Germany which he hoped would lead to the aggrandizement of his country. The Nazis, however, placed one condition—the implementation of severe anti-Jewish measures to undo the great influence enjoyed by Jews in Hungary. The antisemitic Hungarian government was only too willing to oblige.

Between 1938 and 1941, several anti-Jewish laws were legislated by the Hungarian parliament, progressively restricting Jewish rights and privileges and economic pursuits. The 1941 law was closest to defining Jews in racial terms, a measure that the churches objected to strenuously, not so much out of concern for the Jewish population as for the welfare of Jewish converts to Christianity. Estimates place the number of such Jewish-Christians as between 62,000 and 95,000 in

299

a country with a Jewish population of some 725,000 (this figure includes the Jewish populations of territories annexed by Hungary from Czechoslovia, Romania, and Yugoslavia during 1938-41).

The heads of the Catholic and Protestant churches were not at all opposed to anti-Jewish measures; they actually welcomed them, but they were infuriated at the lumping of Jewish-Christians together with full-Jews, as a result of the racial character of these laws. The head of the Catholic church, Jusztinian Cardinal Seredi (representing 64 percent of the population), and Bishop Laszlo Ravasz, on behalf of the Protestant churches (24 percent) vehemently protested this "sinful" lumping of Jews and non-Jews by a government priding itself as acting according to Christian principles.

When Hungary joined Germany in the war against Russia, able-bodied Jewish men were conscripted in labor battalions for forced labor at the front. Some 130,000 men passed through these ranks. At its peak, these unarmed auxiliary units contained 80,000 men. Commanded by non-Jewish officers, they were made to understand by their superiors that it was in the best interest of the nation to guarantee a high mortality rate among these laborers. Indeed, some 42,000 perished; mostly, due to mistreatment and inhumanities suffered at the hands of their non-Jewish commanders (with the notable exception of a few, especially of Colonel Imre Reviczky).

However, other than this, and the occasional brutalitiy of the Hungarian military (such as the forcible roundup of 12,000 Jews in the Ruthenia region, annexed to Hungary, and their delivery to Nazi mobile killing units [Einsatzgruppen], who proceeded to slaughter them, or the massacre of 4,000 Jewish laborers in the Hungarian zone in Yugoslavia), the bulk of Hungarian Jews lived in relative security, as they watched one Jewish community after the other go up in flames in Nazi-dominated Europe.

This "abnormal" state of affairs in a country allied to Germany rankled the Nazi leadership. At a meeting in April 1943, Hitler demanded from Horthy stronger physical anti-Jewish measures, not merely economic restrictions. The Jews had to be treated like tubercular bacilli, Hitler fumed, that threatened a healthy body. Nations that hesitated to deal rigorously with the Jews would perish, Hitler warned.

It was now the post-Stalingrad period, where Hungary saw its entire Second Army destroyed in the Russian snows, and Hungary was beginning to look for ways to extricate itself from what appeared a losing war. It was, therefore, good politics not to pursue the anti-Jewish campaign too far, for this might not look too well to the Allies, with whom the Hungarians hoped to reach an understanding. So Horthy returned from his meeting with Hitler determined not to exacerbate anti-Jewish measures in Hungary, and hoping to ride out the storm with the country's new expanded borders intact.

Another year passed, and in March 1944, the Germans (now clearly losing the war) decided to upstage the Hungarians, who were conducting secret negotiations with the Allies, and force the hand of their fledgling ally. On March 19, 1944, German troops occupied Hungary. As the shocked Horthy reported to his government, one additional reason for this German move was that "we are accused of the crime of not having carried out Hitler's wishes, and I am charged with not having permitted the Jews to be massacred."

With the Germans in control, things moved speedily and tragically for the country's 725,000 Jews. A special Nazi unit (*Sondereinsatzkommando*) appeared in the Hungarian capital headed by S.S. chief Eichmann, who was charged with the implementation of the Final Solution throughout Europe. The Nazi overlords forced the new Hungarian government (headed by the more pro-German Sztojay) to issue a series of edicts virtually outlawing the Jews. All Jewish business establishments were ordered shut, bank accounts sequestrated, valuables confiscated, movements severely restricted, and the wearing of the identifying Yellow Star imposed. Within hardly two months of the German occupation, in a country still nominally independent, Jews had been completely disenfranchised and placed outside the pale of the law.

The Star decree hit the Catholic Church with tremendous impact. It was now apparent that tens of thousands of Christians (who had been born Jewish), even including members of the clergy, would soon have to appear in the streets wearing a Jewish symbol. However, Cardinal Seredi's protestations did not avail him this time, since the authorities feared that making an exception for the tens of thousands of converted Jews would cause a stampede of Jews to the churches, in order to save themselves.

In May 1944, the Nazis launched the next and fatal drive. Dividing the entire Hungarian territory into six zones, they proceeded to round up Jews, with the active help of the Hungarian police and gendarmerie, and quickly deport them directly to the Auschwitz killing facility in occupied Poland, which had been alerted to "welcome" them. By the end of June, all Jews had been emptied from the provinces. All told, some 440,000 Jews (including converts to Christianity) were deported to Auschwitz (where most perished) in an operation unparalleled in its efficiency and swiftness, literally before the eyes of the world.

Not waiting to savor the fruits of this success, Eichmann immediately moved to his next prey—the over 200,000 Jews in the capital city of Budapest. At this point, the Hungarian government bowed to mounting outside pressure and called for a halt to the deportations.

Already in May 1944, at the start of the deportation from the provinces, the Vatican nuncio in Budapest, Angelo Rotta, took the initiative in appealing to the authorities "not to continue this war against the Jews beyond the limits prescribed by the laws of nature and the commandments

302 The Path of the Righteous

of God." Rotta and other Catholic prelates exerted strong pressure upon Cardinal Seredi, the Catholic primate of Hungary, to issue a strong denunciatory pastoral letter, but the cardinal hedged. Finally, stung by the constant rejoinders concerning his moral obligations as head of the largest church in the country, Cardinal Seredi finally issued his long-awaited pastoral letter on June 29, 1944. By then all but the capital's Jews had disappeared from the scene.

Seredi's pastoral letter did not mince words on the church's fundamental anti-Judaic feelings. "We do not deny that a number of Jews have executed a wickedly destructive influence on the Hungarian economic, social, and moral life," it read in part. This was followed with words supporting the antisemitic measures adopted by the government before the German invasion of March 1944. Cardinal Seredi then proceeded to condemn the discriminatory measures meted out against Jewish converts to the church and deplored objectionable acts against Jews; this, without as much as mentioning them by name. No sooner had the government became aware of the contents of this harmless letter, than great pressure was exerted on the cardinal not to have it disseminated. With assurances that the deportaion of Christian Jews would henceforth cease, Seredi had the letter rescinded.

Dismayed by the weak stand of the Catholic Church, the Lutheran and Calvinist churches, represented by Bishop Ravasz, issued their separate condemnation of the deportations (not failing to mention the "sin" of lumping Christian Jews with the condemned full Jews). This more strongly worded letter was also withdrawn at the last moment, when Ravasz received assurances that Jewish Christians would be exempt from further deportation, coupled with the threat of consequences to the churches if undue pressure on the government caused the more extremist Arrow Cross (Nyilas) to come to power.

Thus the heads of the of the largest churches of the country refrained from condemning the deportation of the Jews, leaving their flocks with the impression that the mass removal of the Jews was not viewed with disfavor by their spiritual leaders.

In the meantime, a halt to further deportations was brought about as a result of mounting pressure from world leaders, including—for the first time—a personal communication from Pope Pius XII to Horthy, and no doubt also due to the continued military reverses by the Germans (the Allies had by now landed in France). In July 1944, Horthy ordered the stop of all further deportations. A less pro-German prime minister was installed (Lakatos), and Eichmann and his S.S. unit were ordered out of the country. The capital's Jews were spared.

When the German front in Romania collapsed in August 1944, and the Russian army drove up to the Hungarian border, Horthy frantically negotiated with the Allies the conclusion of a separate armistice. Again, the Germans intervened, deposing Horthy in a coup on October 15, 1944, and installing the pro-Nazi Arrow Cross movement, headed by the self-styled "leader" Ferenc Szalasi. He immediately unleashed a wave of terror in the capital city, where thousands of Jews fell prey.

Eichmann immediately returned to the scene and ordered a forced march of all Jews toward the Austrian border. Known as the infamous Death March from Budapest to Hegyeshalom, up to 60,000 men and women of all ages plodded through cold, rain, sleet and mud to the Austrian border with Hungarian gendarmes taking a toll of the sick and disabled. When Szalasi cancelled all further foot marches on November 21, thousands of bodies littered the over 100-mile road. The surviving marchers were turned over to the Germans for the performance of forced labor inside Germany's shrinking frontiers.

In Budapest, a city under siege by the Russian army, all remaining Jews (some 160,000) were herded into two large ghettos, of which 90,000 were confined in the so-called International Ghetto—houses under the protection of neutral countries (Switzerland, Sweden, Portugal, and Spain), the International Red Cross, and the Vatican. These too had to submit to violations and random killings by Arrow Cross guards. Thousands of Jews in the capital lost their lives during the brief period of Arrow Cross terror, from October 15, 1944 until February 13, 1945, when the whole city was liberated by the Russians (the Pest section of the city having fallen earlier, on January 17th).

Those who survived this ferocious onslaught by Nazi and Hungarian collaborators owe their lives to the kindheartedness of individual non-Jewish men and women throughout the country; to the compassion shown by some of the clergy, and the hospitality of various religious and lay institutions; as well as the unflagging help by diplomatic representatives of foreign governments and agencies.

Bishops Vilmos Apor (in Gyor) and Aron Marton (in Kolozsvar-Cluj) were indefatigable in their interventions in behalf of Jews, condemning the atrocities against Jews from their pulpits in no uncertain terms. Sandor Ujvary, on behalf of the papal nunciate, distributed freely hundreds of blank safe conducts to distraught men and women during the infamous Death March of November 1944. Working with forged credentials and faked certificates of baptism, Ujvary received the nuncio's (Angelo Rotta) blessings in the words: "I grant you absolution in advance. Continue your work to the glory of God!" In Budapest, many religious institutions opened their doors to distraught Jews.

In the most difficult period of the siege of Budapest, with Russian shells wreaking havoc everywhere in the city, and rampaging Arrow Cross gangs running wild in the streets, Reverend Gabor Sztehlo, in charge of the children's section of the Jo Pasztor (Good Shepherd) Committee, sheltered 1,500 Jewish children in thirty-two homes with the aid of the Red Cross. Several representatives of foreign governments and agencies, refused to leave the city, as ordered by their superiors, and braved all dangers to their persons to extend help to endangered Jews. Noteworthy of mention are: Raoul Wallenberg, the incomparably heroic Swedish diplomat, representing the Swedish crown (and indirectely the United States government); the Swiss diplomat Carl Lutz; Friedrich Born and Valdemar Langlet, respectively in behalf of the International Red Cross and the Swedish Red Cross in Budapest; and Angel Sanz Briz and Giorgio Perlasca, in behalf of Spain.

Perlasca took over the operation of the Spanish legation in the city when Sanz Briz left for Switzerland upon instructions from Madrid. Posing as the new Spanish charge d'affaires, he threatened, cajoled and negotiated with the vicious Arrow Cross leaders for more lenient treatment of Jews under the protection of the Spanish government (especially of Jews in houses flying the Spanish flag), dangling before them the possibility of direct support of their losing cause by the Franco regime. None suspected that he was in reality an Italian national who was sought by his own government. He is credited with saving up to 1,000 Jewish lives.

All told, Jewish casualties amounted to 500,000 lives lost. Among the lucky survivors are those who withstood the brutalities of the concentration and labor camps, and tens of thousands (mainly in the capital city) who were sheltered by international agencies (estimated at 69,000) as well as by untold individual non-Jewish persons who gave refuge to as many as 25,000 Jews in Budapest alone. The following stories will illustrate this further.

* * *

The stories from Hungary have been divided into several groups. We begin with three where rescuers and rescued knew each other before the war.

Dr. Geza Petenyi

Dr. Geza Petenyi, professor of pediatrics at a Budapest university and head of the pediatrics department at the Feher Kereszt Hospital, was a renowned physician who pioneered new methods of fighting measles, tubercular inflammations of the brain, and other childhood diseases. Petenyi had a Jewish friend named Otto Gordon, and when Germany occupied Hungary in March 1944, he did everything he could for the Gordon family. Most importantly, he regularly provided them with extra food rations, paid for out of his own pocket, and obtained Swiss and Swedish safe-conduct passes that protected them from being rounded up for deportation.

When the antisemitic Arrow Cross came into power on October 15, 1944 and unleashed its militia, Dr. Petenyi threw the pediatrics department open to fleeing Jews. Falsifying X-rays to show that they were suffering from tuberculosis, he admitted everyone he could to the hospital, adults as well as children. Before long the pediatrics ward and every private room under his control were jam-packed with Jews (not to mention a few gentiles posing as Jews), and there were even people sleeping in his office and waiting room.

During the Russian siege of Budapest, Petenyi came into contact with an odd character named Hochner, an Austrian Jew who was hiding several Jewish children in his attic. According to one account, Hochner was posing as an S.S. officer. In any case, he frequently entertained prominent Nazis in his house, and feared that the crying of the children might give him away. The two men made a deal. Petenyi agreed to take the children off Hochner's hands, and in return Hochner opened the attic to a group of adults sent over from the hospital.

The crowding and constant activity in the pediatrics department were quite apparent to the hospital's staff, many of whom were Nazi sympathizers, but no one informed on Petenyi. As Otto Gordon explains, "His enormous prestige and integrity were his sole protection, and his staff dared not denounce him, because they did not wish to destroy him."

Thus, through sheer luck, capitalizing on his popularity and professional standing, Dr. Petenyi was able to rescue scores of Jews without the Arrow Cross ever finding out. All this was done without payment, solely for humanitarian reasons.

After the war Petenyi continued teaching pediatrics, and Dr. Ariel Kedar, who studied under him, recalls the dedication to child health which he instilled in his students. "We learned from him to select the best diagnostic methods available. We learned from him how to become good pediatricians," says Dr. Kedar, adding: "He was a great humanitarian, a representative of the progressive Hungarian intelligentsia. . . . He remained human during inhuman times."

In her January 1983 deposition, Maria Gordon wrote: "Like everyone who knew him, I feel very strongly that this wonderful man, who was so modest and quiet, who hated fuss and praise, should be remembered at Yad Vashem, to remind us all that in those terrible times there were still some heroes who, out of kindness and sheer human decency, risked their lives for others."

In March 1983, just three months before her death from an incurable disease, Maria Gordon's call was answered and Dr. Geza Petenyi was posthumously recognized as one of the Righteous Among the Nations. A year later, survivors and friends planted a tree in his honor in the Garden of the Righteous. (2543)

Augusta and Eva Gervay

In July 1944, Mrs. Augusta Gervay, a devout Catholic, warned her Jewish friend Olga Wolf of an impending roundup and offered her country house outside Budapest as a refuge. Mrs. Wolf, whose husband was serving in a labor battalion, turned down the offer because she did not want to desert her ailing mother and her aunt, but in the weeks that followed Mrs. Gervay returned again and again, bringing gifts of food and urging Olga to reconsider.

Olga came around when Mrs. Gervay offered to provide for all three of them. She had Olga's mother admitted to a hospital, and then took Olga and her aunt to her country place. They soon discovered that several other Jews were already living in Mrs. Gervay's house, which was under the protection of the Swiss embassy and served, as well, as a temporary stopping place for Jews who had escaped from deportation assembly points. Also living there were a number of antifascist non-Jews and some deserters from the Hungarian army.

As unexpected as all this was, it was far from the full extent of Mrs. Gervay's activities. In her city apartment, she and some friends, among them Father Emilian Novak, ran a workshop that turned out baptismal certificates for Jews in need.

Very often, thanks to Father Novak, they were able to provide documentation on authentic forms. In some instances these were reused certificates, for he had mastered the technique of chemically eradicating the original notations without spoiling the paper. Other times, though, they were brand-new certificates from the sacristy of the Basilica of St. Stephen. Accompanied by Mrs. Gervay's daughter Eva, Father Novak would visit the parish priest. While the two men were engaged in conversation, Eva would snatch a handful of baptismal forms from a desk in the room.

Thus a mother and daughter, religious women who under normal circumstances would never have dreamed of doing anything against the law, joined with a kindly priest to help scores of Hungarian Jews survive the Holocaust. (3582)

Erzsebet Fajo

"Erzsi came to us as a thirteen-year-old nursemaid in October 1931. I was three months old; my brother, two and a half years older." So begins the moving testimony of Zsuzsanna Ozsvath (née Abonyi), currently a professor of literature at an American university.

Zsuszanna's parents, Laszlo and Margit Abonyi, were living in Subotica, Yugoslavia, when she and her brother Ivan were born, but in 1931 they returned to their native Hungary. Settling in the small town of Békéscsaba, they opened a pharmacy and hired Erzsebet Fajo, a young girl who had dropped out of school because of economic need and family pressure, to look after their children.

Erzsi Fajo and the Abonyi children hit it off immediately. Ivan and Zsuzsanna soon grew very attached to her and as a result were very upset when their parents, a few years later, put Erzsi to work in the pharmacy and hired a German-speaking governess to take care of them. What Zsuzsanna terms a "four-year war" ensued, but in the end she and Ivan won, and their parents agreed to let Erzsi live with them as before.

By 1941 the shape of things to come in Hungary was evident. In order to forestall the losses he would incur if he waited for his business to be confiscated, Laszlo Abonyi sold the pharmacy for about half its value and bought a bicycle shop in Budapest with the proceeds. Erszi accompanied the family to the capital, continuing to live with them and working in the shop.

When the German occupation began in March 1944, the Abonyis made Erzsi move out of their apartment for her own good. She moved in with a friend, "but visited us every day," Zsuzsanna says, "swearing again and again that she would not let us be killed, that she would save us come what may."

Hoping to protect the Abonyis from unpleasant street incidents after the yellow-star decree was promulgated on April 5, 1944, Erzsi insisted on accompanying them whenever they went anywhere. They rarely had to leave the apartment, however, for she did all their shopping and brought them whatever they needed, from food to books, toys, and anything else that might lift their spirits.

Laszlo Abonyi was much troubled about the problems facing his family and the rest of Hungarian Jewry. When he learned that his only brother had been reported missing while serving in a labor battalion, the news was too much for him. He fell into a severe depression, and his mood so infected the rest of the family that no one objected when Zsuzsanna proposed that they all commit suicide.

At this low point Erzsebet Fajo again came to the rescue. Talking incessantly about how she would save them, she steadily built up their morale. Then, with the help of a janitor she had bribed, she managed to get their clothing, linens, radios, and other portable possessions out of their third-floor apartment and past the eagle eye of the building's pro-Nazi concierge, "a woman . . . who felt not only that Jews were dangerous but also that it was her duty to unmask their activities."

About a month later Erzsi acquired false papers for the Abonyis and came up with a plan to smuggle them out of Budapest. Circumstances forced them to abandon the idea, and in the following weeks several other escape schemes fell through. Deportation now began to seem inevitable, and one day Erzsi announced that when the time came she would go with them. Laszlo Abonyi begged her to get away while it was still possible, but Erzsi replied, "I don't want to live without you! If I can't share your life, I will share your death!"

That same month the Hungarian government called off the deportations, and for the moment the Jews of Budapest were safe, but when the Arrow Cross gained power, the city was turned into a slaughterhouse, and to make a bad situation worse, it came under bombardment by the Red

Army. During this black period Laszlo Abonyi was arrested and taken to a camp just outside Budapest, but Erzsi, wielding a Red Cross letter of protection, secured his release.

A few days later there was a roundup on the street where the Abonyis lived. Fortunately, however, Erzsi got them out of the building and through the streets to a deserted pharmacy where they spent the night. The next day she joined the crowd clamoring for letters of protection at the Vatican embassy and remained there even when German soldiers opened fire, killing and wounding several people, in an effort to disperse the throng. Armed with these new documents, Erzsi was able to get the Abonyis into the so-called Vatican House, a building complex under papal protection where they would be safe for the time being. Once again she visited every day to bring them food and other necessities.

On December 3, 1944, when the government closed the Vatican House, Erzsi had to find new accommodations for the family. While she was away arranging for Lazslo to be admitted to a building under Swedish protection and persuading a cousin to hide Margit, Arrow Cross militiamen marched the remaining residents of the Vatican House, Ivan and Zsuzsanne included, to the central ghetto. Two days later Erzsi turned up there with false papers for both of them. "She got us through all the checkpoints," Zsuzsanna relates. "If she had been caught she would have been executed."

Between then and the end of the month Erzsi had to move Zsuzsanna five different times in order to evade the brutal Arrow Cross gangs that were running amuck in the streets of Budapest. Initially she took Zsuzsanna to a Red Cross children's home, but when it was closed down, she hid her in a vacant apartment in a building near the Danube. Several days later she took her to the Red Cross hospital, where Zsuzsanna was briefly reunited with her parents and Ivan.

Despite the almost continuous Russian bombardment, Zsuzsanna writes, "Erzsi managed to move my parents twice and my brother three times. As we were miles and miles apart from each other . . . and Budapest was under a complete siege, shelled and bombed twenty-four hours a day, without public transportation, she usually came on foot, in snow or freezing rain, running from house to house, hugging the sides of buildings to seek protection from the incessant bombardment." On December 23rd, when the shelling was heavier than usual, it literally took Erzsi from 8:00 a.m. to 8:00 p.m., running, crawling, and groping through the streets, to get Ivan to a new hiding place.

On January 17th, when Russian troops entered Buda, on the right bank of the Danube, the Abonyi family happened to be together. They decided to see how their former home had fared. "Erzsi was waiting for us outside when we got there. . . . We took her in our arms and began weeping. I still weep when I think of that moment."

After the war the Abonyis adopted Erzsebet Fajo. Resuming the education that had been broken off when she went to work at age thirteen, she eventually graduated with a diploma as a lab technician and was employed by a pharmacological firm until her retirement in 1982. When Laszlo died Erzsi shared equally in the estate with Zsuzsanna and Ivan, and as the years passed she helped to raise Ivan's daughter, and then his granddaughter, just as she had raised him and his sister.

"Driven by the desire to save us, Erzsi defied the Germans," Zsuzsanna says in her deposition. "She saved us from death, saved my brother and me from becoming orphans and my parents from the worst anguish that can befall people—losing their children. Her strength and courage gave us life, making it possible for us to grow up and eventually have our own children. Her love has contributed to Jewish life on earth. . . . She truly is our sister, . . . a sister who gave us life when we were sentenced to death, a sister who waged war against the whole world and managed to save us from destruction."

Writing from Budapest, Dr. Ivan Abonyi says that Erzsi's deeds were motivated by humanitarian considerations, not the expectation of reward. "She knew our financial condition and was well aware that we had lost everything." After Budapest was liberated, she sold some of her own possessions to buy food for the starving Abonyi family.

In 1986 Erzsebet Fajo was recognized as one of the Righteous Among the Nations. "I believe that Erzsi was a true heroine of the Holocaust," writes Zsuzsanna Ozsvath at the conclusion of her testimony. (3449)

* * *

In the following three stories rescued and rescuer were initially unacquainted and met by chance at the height of the anti-Jewish excesses.

Elek Horvath

Helena Welwart and her husband lost their two houseware stores when the government began confiscating Jewish businesses. This was bad enough, but when the Germans occupied Hungary in March 1944, they realized that they and their family would now have to worry about staying alive. Their predicament was underscored during the first post-occupation air raid, for the people in their usual shelter shut the doors on them.

When the Welwarts sought access to another shelter, however, the building warden, Elek Horvath, immediately let them in even though he had never seen them before. They continued going to Horvath's shelter, and soon after the Germans began rounding up Jews, he unexpectedly appeared at the Welwart apartment with an offer of help. They accepted, and over the next few days he took the grandmother and two of their seven children to stay with some of his relatives in Pécs, a city south of Budapest, placed two other children with a friend in another city, and hid Helena, her husband, and the rest of the family in a stable, bringing them food every day.

In July 1944, when the Hungarian government ordered the deportations halted, the Welwarts emerged from their hiding places, but everything changed after the Arrow Cross seized power and launched an anti-Jewish reign of terror. Once again Horvath saved them. While he was taking the children to an orphanage run by the Swiss Red Cross, Helena Welwart was caught in a roundup. Escaping from the assembly point before she could be loaded onto an Auschwitz-bound train, she fled to Horvath's house. He let her in, then went back to the assembly point and helped several other Jews to get away.

Soon after this, during the death march of November 1944, Horvath learned that Helena's husband was one of a group of prisoners on the road to Austria. Disguising himself in the uniform of the border police, and armed with a rifle, he caught up with them at the frontier, took Welwart in custody as if on official business, and brought him back to Budapest, where he hid him in the attic of his house. Helena and the other Welwarts had, in the meantime, been moved to one of the houses under Swedish protection, but Horvath helped her to visit her husband from time to time and also made sure that the Welwart children had adequate food during the Russian siege.

After the war the Welwarts emigrated to Israel. In 1951, shortly before his death, Helena Welwart's husband wrote to each of his children urging them never to forget what Horvath had done for them. When Yad Vashem began the Righteous Among the Nations program, the Welwarts nominated the man whom Helena described in her deposition as "a saint, the likes of whom one would not find among thousands."

In 1965 Elek Horvath was elevated to the rank of Righteous Among the Nations. That same year, old and ill, but deeply moved to once again see the people he had saved, he visited Israel and planted a tree in the Garden of the Righteous at Yad Vashem. (136)

The Czismadia Family

In 1942 Maria Czismadia and her three daughters, Olga, Malvina, and Irena, all four of whom were Calvinists, moved from Nové Mesto, a region of Slovakia annexed by Hungary, to the town of Sátoraljaujhely, where twenty-year-old Olga found a job as a sales clerk for a Jewish couple. When her employers were confined to the local ghetto, she began smuggling food to them and came up with an escape plan. The wife was willing to try it, but the husband refused, and in consequence they both ended up in Auschwitz.

In May 1944, the school next door to the Czismadia house was converted into a work camp for the 300 Jewish conscripts of Labor Battalion 107/11, who until then had been building fortifications in the Ukraine. From the outset the four women did everything they could to help, delivering messages and food parcels to the camp, and even allowing their house to be used for secret meetings between inmates and friends or relatives. One former inmate later wrote: "The whole camp knew there was a family you could count on." Another, Karol Fisher, says: "The Czismadia women would bring us a pot filled with cooked food, buy provisions for us in town, and provide us with newspapers and news from the outside world."

On October 10, 1944, the camp commander was ordered to move the battalion to the Austrian border. Everyone knew what this meant: they were going to be turned over to the Germans. The Czismadias swung into action. Olga took Karol Fisher and three friends to a nearby village, and the others found refuges for two dozen other men. "Some were hidden in vineyards," Olga recalls, "some in attics and cellars. . . . My mother brought food to those in one village. I took care of those in another village. My sister Malvina took food to those in town."

One survivor, in his deposition, told what happened when his group left the camp. "We came to a railroad bridge guarded by police with dogs. Malvina approached one of them and asked for a match to light a cigarette. She struck up a conversation with the guard and distracted him long enough for us to cross the tracks. Half an hour later, I collapsed from exhaustion, but Malvina made me keep walking. It required a superhuman effort to do so, what with the all gruesome sights along the road: the bodies of workers from the labor units hanging from the trees, dead cattle in the ditches. . . . There isn't enough paper to list everything this woman did. I can hardly write these few words without crying, for I dare not recall all the horrible things I saw."

On December 7, 1944, the Red Army liberated the area, but for Olga and Karol Fisher one more travail awaited. Karol had come down with pneumonia while in hiding. Since the local hospital was an empty shell without equipment or medicines, Olga had to nurse him back to health on her own. She managed to buy some penicillin from an accommodating doctor, but in order to get it had to go to Miskolc, a three-day journey on foot there and back, through territory where fighting was still going on.

After the war Olga and Karol were married. For the next few years the two of them and Malvina worked for an illicit organization that helped Israel-bound Hungarian Jews get out of the country. In 1949 Olga and Karol also went to Israel, where Malvina later joined them. They have lived there ever since, and both sisters have been recognized as Righteous Among the Nations. (111, 3619)

Maria Olt

On March 22, 1944, three days after the German occupation began, Miriam Kuti, the wife of Dr. Laszlo Kuti, gave birth to a daughter in the Budapest hospital where her husband was employed. The atmosphere in the hospital, and throughout the city, was grim and depressing. "We had to wear the yellow star and many of our friends on the hospital staff committed suicide," Miriam recalls. "My husband and I thought about it too, but several days after Anna was born, Maria Olt appeared on the scene."

Maria, who was then about twenty-one, was one of Dr. Kuti's patients. Stopping in at his office to keep an appointment, she saw his yellow patch and began plying him with questions. When he told her that he and Miriam were worried about what might happen to their newborn infant, Maria, on the spur of the moment, said, "Please let me save the child." The Kutis agreed, and that very day, with Anna in her arms, Maria Olt left Budapest for her native village of Hossuvolgy, in the Zala region.

Several days later Maria returned to Budapest for Miriam. To explain her presence in the village and her connection with Anna, Maria told everyone that she was a gypsy friend who had become pregnant and run away from home to escape punishment. Miriam's curly black hair and dark complexion made the story plausible.

The following week Maria brought Lazslo Kuti to Hossuvolgy and hid him in the cellar of her father's winepress. Since there would have been no way to explain his presence in the village, he had to remain in the 6 foot by 6 foot cellar, but every day Maria slipped in to bring him food and remove his wastes.

After a while, unfortunately, Miriam was recognized by the village midwife, who had studied under her husband and been present at Anna's birth. When she threatened to inform the police, Maria Olt quickly moved Miriam to another village and took Anna, for whom she had been able to obtain identity papers, to the home of Miriam's sister Vera Rozsa, who in turn gave her into the care of a family living near the Czech border.

Having been regaled by the villagers with a gory account of how the local peasants had torn a Jewish shopkeeper limb from limb, Maria knew it was not safe for Miriam to remain where she was. They had to move on, but Miriam had no papers, and to complicate things, neither did Maria, since she had given her identity card to the wife of a friend of Dr. Kuti's.

The days and weeks that followed were a grueling ordeal, for the two women could never stay anywhere long. "We wandered from village to village," Miriam relates. "Once we came across a train packed with Jews heading for Auschwitz. I was so depressed that when the train stopped for a moment, I felt a terrible urge to climb aboard and put an end to my suffering. But Maria said she would go along with me, so I dropped the idea."

In time Maria managed to borrow some money. She rented a room for Miriam, then returned to Hossuvolgy for Laszlo and brought him, concealed beneath a load of hay in her father's wagon, to the place where Miriam was staying. Soon afterward she was able to get a set of papers for him, and arranged for the couple to stay with a family that was already sheltering several other Jews, among them Vera Rozsa.

Around this time Maria's husband left her, unsympathetic to her involvement with Jews and fearing for his own safety. In a way this may have given Maria a free hand, for she soon found others to help now that Miriam and Lazslo Kuti were provided for. Over the next ten months Maria looked after Miriam's parents and the three Stern sisters, who were living in a village near Fot in the same building that housed the area's Gestapo headquarters. She spirited Dr. Kuti's mother and a friend out of the Budapest ghetto and put them up in an abandoned house elsewhere in the city, telling the neighbors that they were relatives and visiting them regularly to allay any suspicions. And she saved the life of a Jewish infant by taking her to St. Istvan Hospital with a set of invented symptoms. The child was admitted for testing and observation, and by the time she was discharged, Maria had found a safe place for her.

After the war Miriam Kuti moved to Israel, where she became an actress and drama instructor. She and Maria kept in touch, and in 1979 she invited Maria to visit for Passover, concurrently nominating her as one of the Righteous Among the Nations.

On her arrival in Israel, Maria Olt learned for the first time of the honor to be conferred on her. After the ceremony in which she planted a tree in the Garden of the Righteous in her own and her father's name, she was asked about her reasons for helping the Kutis and the others.

Maria replied that her first contact with the yellow-star patch had struck her like a bolt of lightning. From that moment, she said, "I felt an urge to help the persecuted. An inner voice spoke to me in those days and guided my every action without consideration for the dangers surrounding me. I would never have forgiven myself if I had done anything else. Those were certainly days of fear and terror. But since I had no time to worry about what would happen to me if I was arrested, I just went on without stopping to think." Looking at the medal she had just received, she added, "I never expected to get anything for what I did."

Someone who was present at the ceremony penned the following poem:

MARIA OLT

On a hillside in Jerusalem
under the pounding sun, she lifts

a little carob tree, the tree of John
the Baptist, and sets it

into its hole. Solid as a house,
she is called Righteous, a Christian

who hid Jews in Hungary. Her hair clings
to her broad face as she bends

with the hoe, carefully heaping the soil
around the roots. She builds a rim of dirt

on the downhill side and pours water from
the heavy bucket. She waits until the earth

sucks the water up, then pours again
with a slow wrist. The workmen

sent to help her, stand aside, helpless.
She straightens up. Her eyes are wet.

Tears come to her easily.
The small Jewish woman she saved

stands beside her, dry-eyed.
Thirty-five years ago, as they watched

the death train pass, faces and hands
begging between the slats, the girl

had cried, I want to go with them!
No, said Maria, you must understand,

if you go, I will go with you. (1636)

* * *

While Hungary's church hierarchies were indifferent to the plight of
the Jews, or at least did nothing about it, many ordinary priests and
members of religious orders were active in rescue efforts. The following two
stories are typical. We also include two stories involving Protestant
ministers.

Sister Margit Slachta

Sister Margit Slachta, who headed the Benedictine Order in Hungary
during the war, was instrumental in saving many Jewish lives. In 1943 she
went to Rome to see the Pope on behalf of the 20,000 Jews in Slovakia who
had not yet been sent to death camps, and she also made a direct appeal
to Archbishop (later Cardinal) Francis Spellman of New York in the same
cause. Moreover, on her instructions, the order's convents and other
institutions throughout Hungary were opened to Jewish refugees.

One of the beneficiaries of Sister Margit's policy was Dr. Magda Gross.
Disguised as a nun, and coached by Sister Margit on how to conduct
herself so as not to arouse suspicion, she was given sanctuary in the

Benedictine convent in Kosice. Some of the nuns opposed taking in Jews but did not realize that Dr. Gross was Jewish. On the other hand, one of them, Sister Shalkhaz, was not only in favor of helping Jews but was killed while trying to protect several who were arrested and later shot.

Attached to the convent was a convalescent home for children. One day, Dr. Gross relates, the police lined everyone up and began questioning the youngsters about their family backgrounds. All of a sudden Sister Margit burst in, went up to the officer in charge, and angrily said, "Do you think we are raising bulls here that you need to know their pedigree? Our work is saving souls." The policeman snapped, "You've all been paid off by the Jews," but he took his men and left.

After the war Sister Margit emigrated to the United States. She led her life in accordance with the same principles she taught her nuns: "Do not let yourself become preoccupied with evil in the negative sense, but strive to achieve good. Zeal for the good rather than fear of evil. Good deeds rather than fear and trembling brought on by sin." (495)

Brother Albert Pfleger

During the turbulent days of November 1944, when Budapest was being ravaged by Eichmann's S.S. squads and the pro-Nazi Arrow Cross, Brother Albert Pfleger, a French-born monk of the Marist Order, decided that it was God's will and his Christian duty to save as many Jews as possible. With the authorization of his superior, Brother Louis Pruczer, he opened the gates of the Champagnat monastery to fleeing Jews and also began bringing people from the ghetto to the safety of the Marist cloister.

Turning to Valdémar and Nina Langlet of the Swedish Red Cross for assistance, Brother Albert obtained letters of protection and supplies of food for the children in the monastery. Nina Langlet, in her account of their meeting, describes Brother Albert as "one of the most courageous collaborators" of the Red Cross in its efforts to save Jewish children. When she warned him to be careful, pointing out that Arrow Cross toughs were running wild in the very neighborhood where the Marist cloister was situated, he answered: "If the Nazis attack us, we shall go to jail with our proteges. If not, our task will only be half done."

Margit Schneller tells how she and her family were saved by Brother Albert. On November 8, 1944, he offered them a refuge in the monastery; they accepted and remained there until the liberation of Budapest in February 1945. Brother Albert gave the seven of them his own tiny room and slept on the hall stairway outside. When he learned that Judith Szilagyi, Margit's niece, had been left stranded after her former hiding place, the convent of the Society of the Sacred Heart, was closed, he went to the ghetto, literally "snatched" her out, and brought her to Champagnat.

For obvious reasons, conditions in the monastery were very crowded, and sometimes as many as fifteen people had to share a room. Altogether, there were sixty or seventy Jewish families living in the monastery compound. Inspired by Brother Albert's leadership and example, the other members of the order did everything they could, obtaining false papers and extra food, and, when the crowding got too bad, locating new hiding places in other religious houses or in private homes. Olga Vértes, another of the Jews saved by the Marists, tells how she once saw Brother Alexander Hegedüs, known as Frère Joseph, carrying an old Jew into the cloister on his back after finding him collapsed in the street.

On December 9, 1944, the monks and some of the Jews were arrested by the Gestapo. Though tortured, starved, and deprived of medical care, the monks refused to reveal the whereabouts of the other Jews or the names of those who had helped in the rescue operation. Several weeks later, thanks to the intercession of the Swedish Red Cross and the papal nuncio, they were released.

Writing of Brother Albert and the other Marist monks, one of the survivors said: "They considered it the most natural thing to help us. Having thrown themselves into this rescue operation with great courage, and without regard for the danger that threatened them, they suffered much. If not for their humane deeds, I would not be here today able to testify on their behalf. We survivors render homage to them from the depths of our hearts and express our deepest gratitude." (2008)

Pastor Laszlo Michnai

Laszlo Michnai, an Adventist minister in Budapest, had befriended many Jews before the war. When the Germans occupied Hungary, he and his family gave their identity cards to Jews in need, making it possible for them to live unmolested outside the ghetto. After the Arrow Cross coup d'état on October 15, 1944, and the intensification of the anti-Jewish terror, Pastor Michnai hid thirty Jews in the attic of his home and found refuges for others with friends in the neighborhood. Ultimately, however, he moved all of them out of Budapest in two groups and placed them with Adventist farmers in the countryside around Vác, a city about 16 miles north of Budapest, where they remained until the liberation.

Pastor Michnai refused to accept any compensation from those he saved, some of whom were quite well off, and in addition, in order to fulfill the "mitzvah" of helping Jews in need, he insisted on paying for the food and other requirements of his charges with funds from his church treasury. While Pastor Michnai knew some of the people he helped, many of them were total strangers and some were deserters from the Jewish labor battalions. Judith Carmeli, one of the people he saved, says of Laszlo Michnai, "he thanked God for giving him the privilege of saving some Jews." Roman Vilmosz, another of them, says he was "as good as God himself." (18)

Pastor Gabor Sztehlo

In November 1944, with the Arrow Cross terror campaign in full swing, hundreds of Jewish children whose parents had been killed were wandering the streets of Budapest. Many of them were saved by Pastor Gabor Sztehlo, the head of the Protestant Jó Pásztor (Good Shepherd) Committee, an organization originally founded to assist Jewish converts to Christianity, who conducted his rescue operation in conjunction with the International Red Cross.

In addition to orphaned children from the streets, Pastor Sztehlo also took in young deserters from the Jewish labor battalions. One of them, Samuel Ben Dov, was seventeen when he left his unit. He went to ask Sztehlo for help, but had no idea that the minister was running a large-scale rescue operation. Studying the youth's credentials for a moment, Sztehlo said: "This document is forged and you are Jewish, but don't worry. I shall place you in one of our institutions in the city." On his arrival there Ben Dov soon soon noticed many familiar Jewish faces among the hundreds of children, and also among the nurses and attendants.

One day Arrow Cross guards broke into the building and carried the children away to the ghetto. Samuel Ben Dov managed to escape. He went to the office of an organization affiliated with Pastor Sztehlo's committee but was thrown out. Retracing his steps, and being careful to avoid encounters with Arrow Cross patrols, he made his way to Sztehlo's office. There he was given a certificate identifying him as a Red Cross messenger.

During the Russian bombardment of Budapest the children's home run by Sztehlo's committee was hit several times. With the building no longer fit for habitation, Sztehlo transferred thirty-three children to the cellar of his house, where they, he, and his family huddled for twenty frightening days while German troops on the upper floor of the building exchanged fire with Russians several blocks away.

When the city was liberated, Pastor Sztehlo found new quarters for the children and cared for them until their families or representatives of Jewish organizations came to claim them. Sensitive to their religious needs, he set up a synagogue and made them attend services while in his care. Survivors credit Pastor Sztehlo with having saved at least 500 Jewish children. (722)

* * *

As mentioned earlier, several foreign officials in Budapest actively participated in rescuing Jews. Among them were Monsignor Angelo Rotta, the papal nuncio; Angel Sanz Briz and Giorgio Perlasca of the Spanish embassy; and Friedrich Born of of the International Red Cross. Unfortunately, we have space here only for the stories of Carl Lutz of Switzerland and Raoul Wallenberg of Sweden.

Carl Lutz

Born in 1895, Carl Lutz was educated in the United States and in 1935 became the Swiss consul in Tel Aviv. When the war broke out in September 1939, he intervened on behalf of the 2,500 German nationals in Palestine who were being deported as enemy aliens by the British. Late in 1941 Lutz was reassigned to Budapest, and he arrived there on January 2, 1942, charged with representing the interests of the United States, Britain, and other countries that had severed relations with Hungary because of its alliance with Germany.

Starting in March 1944, when the German army occupied Hungary and the deportation of the country's Jews began, Lutz took steps that resulted in thousands of lives being saved. He began by providing several hundred Jews with certificates identifying them as nationals of El Salvador (and therefore exempt from deportation) and went on to issue numerous letters of protection (*schutzbriefe*), also referred to as safe-conduct passes, stipulating that the bearer was protected by the Swiss embassy for one reason or another, such as while waiting to emigrate to Palestine.

Lutz ultimately brought almost 45,000 people under the Swiss umbrella. Sometimes, thanks to his inventive manipulations of diplomatic protocol and his broad reading of the rules set down for him, he even managed to obtain the inadvertent acquiescence of the Germans, as when he interpreted the 7,500 *schutzbriefe* they had authorized as applying to entire families rather than to individuals. When Raoul Wallenberg arrived in Budapest in July 1944, Lutz gave him a crash course in how safe conducts could be used to save Jews. His activities also served as a model for rescue operations conducted by the Spanish, Portuguese, and Vatican embassies.

After the pro-Nazi Arrow Cross movement seized power on October 15, 1944, Lutz persuaded the new regime to validate the letters of protection he had issued, holding up as a quid pro quo the possibility of Swiss diplomatic recognition. He also obtained permission to lodge the holders of the safe conducts in twenty-five apartment houses officially designated as under Swiss protection.

In November of 1944, desperately in need of workers, the Germans rounded up 60,000 Budapest Jews, herding them across Hungary and into Austria under the most appalling conditions. Much to the consternation of the Nazis, however, a good many prisoners disappeared during the course of what came to be known as the death march. Carl Lutz deserved much of the credit for this. Even while the columns of prisoners were forming up he continued to issue certificates of Salvadoran nationality, and the guards, for whatever reason, tended to release the certificate holders.

Reminiscing years later, Lutz wrote: "My wife and I once stood for hours, in the snow and ice, at the former Obuda Brick Works (which served as the assembly point for Jews being sent on the death march), busy with the sad task of issuing protective passes. Heart-rending scenes took place before us. Five thousand unfortunate people stood stiffly in line, freezing, shaking, hungry, clutching precious packages. . . . I shall never forget their anxious faces. They pleaded for my help so fiercely that they almost ripped my clothes off, and the police had to step in. It was a final expression of the will to live before the passivity that so often ended in death. . . . How often I drove along the lines of people being taken to the brickyard just to show them that all was not lost, but the heavily armed guards finally closed the road to me."

In December 1944, as the Soviet siege intensified, all foreign representatives were ordered to leave Budapest. The Swiss ambassador had departed the preceding month, but Lutz decided to stay on, unwilling to abandon the 30,000 Jews in the so-called International Ghetto, an area of residential buildings under the protection of the neutral governments. Lutz later described his remaining in the beleaguered city as "a matter of conscience." A German diplomat, he explained, had told him that the Nazis, in gratitude for his help to the German aliens in Palestine in 1939—40, had ordered the Arrow Cross to leave the International Ghetto alone as long as Lutz was on the scene.

Over the next three months Lutz and his wife, together with some Jewish refugees, led a precarious existence in the basement of the abandoned British embassy, which was located in Pest, on the left bank of the Danube. They had almost no food or water, he wrote later on, and their nerves were at the breaking point from tension and lack of sleep. During the final bombardment the embassy building was hit by nineteen shells and burned for two days and nights. Pest was stormed by Russian troops on January 15, 1945. With gunfire coming from all directions, Lutz and his wife escaped through a window and managed to reach Buda, across the Danube River, which did not fall to the Russians until a month later.

In 1965 Yad Vashem designated Carl Lutz as one of the Righteous Among the Nations. He retired from the diplomatic service the following year and died in 1975, at the age of eighty. (46)

Raoul Wallenberg

The story of Raoul Wallenberg is an account of selfless devotion to the cause of a community threatened with destruction. In the lines that follow we shall try to do justice to the noble spirit that animated this great soul.

Wallenberg was born into an aristocratic Swedish banking family in 1912, three months after his father's death. Educated under the guidance of his grandfather, he traveled widely and studied architecture. In 1936 he worked for six months in the Holland Bank in Haifa, Palestine, where he first came into contact with Jews fleeing from Nazi persecution. Soon thereafter, on his grandfather's death, he returned to Sweden and became an executive of an import-export company, headed by a Hungarian Jew, that did a considerable amount of business in Central Europe.

A letter of protection issued by Raoul Wallenberg in Budapest (September 1944), and signed by the Swedish Ambassador Carl Danielsson. Courtesy of Yad Vashem.

During the early years of the war, Wallenberg led a lively social life and seemed indifferent to world events, but there was an inner restlessness that seemed to be looking for a cause, and in due course he developed an intense, even single-minded concern about the fate of the Jews. Meanwhile, in the spring of 1944, the Swedish government, responding to pressure by the United States, agreed to do what it could to help what was left of Hungarian Jewry. It delegated the task to Wallenberg, appointing him First Secretary of the Swedish embassy in Budapest.

On July 9, 1944, when Wallenberg arrived there, the Hungarian government had just halted the deportations begun in March and seemed eager to dissociate itself from the the Nazis and the Final Solution. Armed with supreme confidence, virtually unlimited funds, and a businessman's pragmatic willingness to do anything that worked, Wallenberg threw himself into his work. His unconventional methods sometimes shocked traditionalist colleagues, but none could deny that he got results.

Early on, for instance, having learned from Carl Lutz and others about the many uses that *schutzbriefe* could be put to, he applied to the Hungarian Foreign Ministry for authority to issue them. When permission was granted for only 1,500, he used some judiciously placed bribes to up the figure to 15,000. Similarly, he sliced through shortages, red tape, and other complications to set up an extensive network of hospitals, day-care centers, and soup kitchens for the Jews under his protection.

By October 1944, satisfied that the situation was well in hand, Wallenberg wrote a final report summing up what he had done and prepared to return to Stockholm. Then, with the Arrow Cross coup on October 15th, everything changed. Gangs of toughs began beating and killing Jews in the streets, and the deportations were resumed with a vengeance.

As one of its first acts, the new government canceled the safe-conduct passes Wallenberg had issued in the preceding months. Though its officials had nothing but contempt for his efforts to save Jews, he got them to revalidate the documents by adroitly dangling the possibility of Swedish diplomatic recognition as bait.

Wallenberg also played a key role in the establishment of the International Ghetto, an area of several square blocks in which more than 30,000 Jews were concentrated under the protection of the neutral embassies and the Red Cross. Using the great sum of money at his disposal, he organized a paid staff of 335 for the ghetto, including guards and house wardens, and enough medical personnel for two hospitals with a capacity of 150 beds.

In November, when the death march began, Wallenberg followed the columns of Jewish prisoners in his car, distributing hundreds of safe-conduct documents, some genuine, many others not, whenever they were allowed to stop for a rest. One of the people he saved in this manner was Miriam Herzog, who gave some details in her deposition:

The conditions were frightful. We had to walk 20 or 30 miles a day in freezing rain, relentlessly driven on by the Hungarian police. Our group was made up entirely of women and girls, and I was seventeen at the time. The police were brutal, beating those who could not keep up, leaving others to die in the ditches along the road. . . . Suddenly [while we were resting in an abandoned building] I heard a great commotion among the women. "It's Wallenberg," they said. I didn't think he'd be able to help me, and in any case I was too weak now to move, so I lay there on the floor while dozens of women clustered around him, crying "Save us, save us." I remember being struck by how handsome he was—and how clean—in his leather coat and fur hat, like a being from another world, and I thought, "Why does he bother with wretched creatures like us?" As the women clustered around him, he said to them, "Please forgive me, but I can't help all of you. I only have a hundred certificates." Then he said something which really surprised me. He said: "I feel I have a mission to save the Jewish nation, and so I must rescue the young ones first." The idea of a Jewish nation was brand-new to me. Jewish people, of course, but not a Jewish nation. He looked around the room and began putting names down on a list, and when he saw me lying on the floor he came over. He asked my name and added it to the list. After a day or two, the hundred of us whose names had been taken were moved out and put into a cattle car on a train bound for Budapest. There were plenty of dangers and hardships still in store for us, but we were alive—and it was thanks entirely to Wallenberg.

In another incident of this kind, Zvi Eres, also a survivor of the death march, watched disbelievingly as Wallenberg leaped from his car, brandishing a list of names, and became embroiled in a shouting match with some Hungarian officers and German S.S. men. "I was too far away to hear exactly what they were saying," Eres writes, "but clearly there was a tremendous argument going on. In the end, to our amazement, Wallenberg won his point and between 280 and 300 of us were allowed to go back to Budapest." There they were assigned accommodations in one of the Swedish houses in the International Ghetto.

He also sometimes turned up at the assembly points in Budapest. Sandor Ardai, an eyewitness, tells what happened one day at the railroad station:

Wallenberg walked past the S.S. officer supervising the deportation train, climbed up on the roof of the train, and began handing safe-conduct passes through the doors, which had not yet been locked. He paid no attention when the Germans ordered him to get down, or when the Arrow Cross men began firing their guns and shouting at him to go away. Ignoring them, he calmly continued giving passes to the outstretched hands. . . . After Wallenberg had distributed the last of the passes, he told everyone who had one to get off the train and walk over to a caravan of cars parked nearby, all marked with the Swedish colors. I don't remember exactly how many, but he saved dozens from the train, and the Germans and the Arrow Cross were so dumbfounded that they let him get away with it.

Wallenberg repeatedly confronted death without faltering, facing down angry guards in situations like the ones described above and carrying on with his work despite rumors that the S.S. and the Arrow Cross were engineering an "accident" that would eliminate him without violating his diplomatic immunity. Even at the very end, when he heard that the retreating Germans intended to blow up the central ghetto and its 70,000 Jewish inmates before leaving the city, he rushed to the office of the garrison commander and, indifferent to his own safety, threatened to have him prosecuted for war crimes if he dared carry out the plan.

On January 17, 1945, several days after the liberation of Pest, where the ghettos were located, Wallenberg set out to see the Russian commander, Marshal Malinovsky, at Debrecen, about 125 miles to the east, to propose a plan for the rehabilitation of the Jewish community. He said that he would be back in a week, but as he left, under Soviet military escort, he remarked to a colleague: "I don't know if they're protecting me or

Swedish diplomat Per Anger, who worked with Raoul Wallenberg, in Budapest, at Yad Vashem (1983), with Gideon Hausner, chairman of Yad Vashem International Advisory Council, left, and Torsten Orn, the Swedish ambassador to Israel, right. Courtesy of Yad Vashem.

watching me. I'm not sure if I'm their guest or their prisoner." He was never seen again.

No one has ever satisfactorily explained why the Russians arrested Raoul Wallenberg and why he was never heard from again. The Red Army held the other diplomatic personnel in Budapest for a short time but eventually released all of them, including everyone attached to the Swedish legation. Perhaps they suspected Wallenberg of being a spy for the West. As Lars Berg, a former official at the Swedish embassy, states: "For the Russians, with their understanding, or more accurately their lack of understanding, of human problems, it was completely inconceivable that Wallenberg, a Swede, would have come down to Budapest to rescue Hungarian Jews."

Over the years the Swedish government made inquiries about Wallenberg, and, in 1957, the Soviets officially announced that he had died from a heart attack in 1947 while in Moscow's Lubianka Prison and had been cremated. No evidence was provided, however, and as a result Wallenberg's family and many of his admirers did not believe the story. Reports that he had been seen alive in Soviet prisons and mental institutions persisted into the 1980s.

In 1963, the year it came into existence, the Commission for the Designation of the Righteous at Yad Vashem recognized Raoul Wallenberg as one of the Righteous Among the Nations. His mother, who continued to believe he was alive, declined an invitation to plant a tree in the Garden of the Righteous, saying she would do so when he was released and standing at her side. In 1979, after her death, a tree was planted in his honor near the Hall of Remembrance, where an eternal flame recalls the martyrs of the Holocaust.

The last time Wallenberg spoke with Per Anger, a fellow official at the Swedish embassy, he said: "I'd never be able to go back to Stockholm without knowing deep down that I'd done all anyone could do to save as many Jews as possible." In the few short months he spent in Budapest Raoul Wallenberg rescued tens of thousands of Jews—some say up to 50,000. He was barely thirty-three years old when he disappeared. (31)

Yugoslavia

The Jewish community of what is now Yugoslavia dates back to Roman times. On April 6, 1941, Germany, joined by Italy, Hungary, and Bulgaria, occupied Yugoslavia in a military operation that lasted hardly a fortnight. The victors then divided the spoils. Germany annexed Slovenia in the north and set up an occupation administration in Serbia, the country's largest and most important region; Italy occupied Dalmatia in the west; Hungary and Bulgaria, respectively, took Vojvodina in the northeast and Macedonia in the southeast; and Yugoslavia's second-largest region, Croatia, became a nominally independent German client state, its government headed by Dr. Ante Pavelic, leader of the pro-Nazi Ustase movement.

With the exception of the Italian zone of occupation, the 75,000 Jews of Yugoslavia were to fare badly in all parts of the country. Almost everywhere the German invasion was followed by the enactment of harsh new laws which, in just a few weeks, completely disenfranchised them, relegating them to the status of aliens, and even worse. In Serbia and Croatia, this was quickly followed by the physical decimation of the local Jewish populace. By June 1942, a German security official named Dr. Emanuel Schaefer was able to report that "there is no longer any Jewish problem in Serbia," as most of its 12,000 Jews had either been shot or gassed to death.

In the puppet-state of Croatia, the Ustase auxiliaries were only too glad to oblige the Nazis by solving the "Jewish problem" without outside help. By mid-October 1941, most of Croatia's 30,000 Jews had been sent to labor camps, including the infamous Jasenovac camp, where thousands of Jews and tens of thousands of Serbs were killed in such gruesome ways that even the Germans, who preferred more "sanitized" methods, were appalled. Jews not immediately killed were handed over for transportation

325

to Germany, with the Croatian government paying the German government 30 Reichsmarks for each deported Jew—a contribution to the "final solution of the Jewish problem in Croatia," in the words of Finance Minister Koshak.

In Vojvodina, and especially in its principal city, Novi Sad, the Jews suffered depredations and murderous raids at the hands of the Hungarian occupation forces even before the Germans took direct control of the region in March 1944. Similarly, the Jews in Skoplje, Macedonia, under Bulgarian control, were rounded up in a massive operation in February 1943 and dispatched to the death camps in Poland.

It was only in the Italian zone, which included part of Croatia, that Jews experienced a spell of relief and were not physically harmed. As news of the Italians' humane policy spread like wildfire in nearby Croatia, thousands of Jews fled the brutal Ustase. They were generally permitted to cross into the Italian zone and, to their utter disbelief, were sometimes even welcomed by the Italian soldiers guarding the border.

As is discussed at greater length in the chapter on Italy, the Italians found it hard to digest the racist ideology of their Nazi ally and regarded the persecution of the Jews as incomprehensible and revolting. Not surprisingly, the 3,000 to 5,000 Jews who found a sanctuary in the Italian zone became a bone of contention between the two Axis states at the highest governmental level.

Claiming that their continued presence in the Italian zone was a grave military threat, the German Foreign Minister, Ribbentrop, exerted all the pressure he could to persuade the hesitant and inconsistent Mussolini to hand over the Jews to the Ustase. Matters came to a head in March 1943. With Italy completely dependent on German military aid to offset its many serious losses, Mussolini (who earlier had issued contradictory orders) consented to Ribbentrop's demand that 3,000 Jews be turned over to Germany.

When one of his aides objected, declaring that many high Foreign Ministry officials as well as the Italian commanders in Yugoslavia felt that helping the Nazi death machine would sully Italy's national honor, Mussolini replied: "All right, all right, I had to consent to the extradiction, but you can invent all the excuses you want to make sure that not even one Jew is deported. Say that we don't have any boats available to transport them by sea and that there is no possibility of moving them by land."

As a sop to the Germans, most of the Jews in the Italian zone were interned in camps on Rab, an island off the Dalmatian coast, where they continued to enjoy the protection of the Italian army. Some Jews fled to Albania, which was also under Italian rule, or to Italy itself, although this was forbidden by Italian law.

The circumvention of Italy's anti-Jewish laws by officials at all levels, and the protection of foreign Jews, lasted until September 1943, when

Germany occupied Italy following its capitulation to the Allies. Many of the 3,000 Jews in the former Italian zone were apprehended and deported, but a great number managed to elude the Nazis and flee to the hills, where they eventually joined up with Tito's partisans, taking up arms against their obdurate oppressors.

Of the 75,000 Jews in Yugoslavia at the start of the Nazi invasion, it is estimated that only 12,000 were still alive in April 1945. Most of them had survived by hiding in the mountains; others had served in partisan units or had been hidden here and there by friendly non-Jews.

Borivoje Bondice and Slobodan Knezevic

Of the few rescue stories from Yugoslavia in the Yad Vashem files, we have selected several which reflect the special circumstances in that country during the Holocaust.

Ladislav and Julija Dajc, a Jewish couple, were physicians employed by the sick fund of an agricultural cooperative in the township of Aleksandrovac Krusevacki. After the German occupation they were fired. Like other Jews, they had to wear the yellow patch on their coats.

At first the Dajcs kept out of sight, taking refuge with a friend who lived on the outskirts of the township, but in December 1941, when the search for Jews intensified, they felt it was better to leave. "We decided to disappear and go underground," Julija relates.

At times, they stayed together; more frequently they lived apart. In the summer of 1942, they found themselves in a forest hideout with a group of escapees from a labor battalion in a nearby mine. Unexpectedly the group was forced to scatter, and Julija suddenly found herself separated from her husband, alone—and pregnant.

Having no other alternative, Julija approached Predrag Zdravokvic, a man with whom she was slightly acquainted from the days of her medical practice. He and his wife, Stana, took her in and hid her for six weeks, even though sheltering Jews was punishable by death.

Recognized by a prewar female acquaintance and fearing betrayal to the authorities, Julija left the Zdravokvics and moved in with Borivoje and Grodzana Bondice, who willingly hid the distraught pregnant woman even though their house was on a road heavily traveled by German military vehicles. "I slept with Grodzana in the bedroom; we kept the light off to make sure that the children wouldn't see me if they woke up," Julija says.

The following week the Bondices took Julija to the house of a peasant in the village of Lakovac who had promised to let her stay with him during her confinement. Meanwhile, however, a rumor spread through the countryside to the effect that the Germans had arrested Zdravkovic for hiding a Jewish woman after an informer tipped them off.

The peasant, terrified, threw Julija out on the street. "I was alone, on the point of giving birth, and had no food or money," Julija recalls. At this moment of dire need, a compassionate couple by the name of Slobodan and Milenija Knezevic took her in. The next day she gave birth to a son. It was March 3, 1943, a date that remains etched in Julija's memory.

Subsequently, she wandered from house to house and from village to village. From the day of her son's birth until the end of June 1943, she took refuge with twenty-four different families in the vicinity of Aleksandrovac, thanks to arrangements made for her by Borijove Bondice. "Slobodan Knezevic used to come for me from time to time at night on his donkey and, in spite of the curfew, would take me by roundabout ways from one hideout to another, carrying my baby in his arms." Thanks to Bondice and Knezevic, Julija and her son survived the war. (1810)

Mustafa and Zayneba Hardaga

The region of Bosnia just to the west of Serbia has a substantial Moslem community dating from the period it was part of the Ottoman Empire. Sitting out the war in Berlin, Haj Amin el Husseini, the Grand Mufti of Jerusalem, sought to win his Bosnian coreligionists over to the Nazi cause, calling upon them to join with Germany in a common struggle against the Jews, and thus prevent the rise of a Jewish state in Palestine. Many of them succumbed to his harangues, enlisting in German-led Moslem paramilitary units. But not Mustafa Hardaga, who decided that his Moslem creed required him to take a different course.

Mustafa Hardaga, who lived in Saravejo with his wife, Zayneba, owned a building in which Josef Cavilio, a Jew, had a workshop that manufactured steel pipes. Over the years the two men had become friends. As a result, in April 1941, when Cavilio was planning to move his family into the factory because his house had been destroyed in a German air raid, Hardaga would not hear of it, insisting that they come stay with him.

Arriving at the Hardaga house, the Cavilios were greeted with the words: "Josef, you are our brother, Rivka our sister, and your children our children. Feel just as at home here as you would in your own house. Everything we have is yours."

The Hardagas were devout Moslems, and the women of the household customarily veiled their faces in the presence of strangers. Hardaga's hospitality was all-encompassing, however. "Our wives will not hide their faces from you," he assured Cavilio, "for you are like our own family. You are in danger, and we shall not abandon you." As Zayneba remarks in her statement, this was the first time that a man who was not a relative had ever slept in their house.

When the Germans entered Sarajevo, the situation of the city's Jews rapidly worsened. The old synagogue was looted and the Torah scrolls put to the torch. Mustafa consoled Josef, assuring him that he and his family would be all right. But Josef, fearing denunciation, moved Rivka and the children to Mustar, which was under Italian administration and thus safer for Jews, while he stayed behind to look after his remaining assets and his factory, which, by government order, had been turned over to his bookkeeper, an ethnic German. When the latter proceeded to accuse Josef of sabotage, he had to flee.

With the help of a friend, Josef was accepted into a military hospital, but soon afterwards he was arrested and transferred to prison. One morning, during the winter of 1941–42, while he and some other inmates were at work clearing snow from the streets, he noticed a veiled woman standing nearby and weeping. It was Zayneba. For the next month she brought food for him and his fellow inmates.

Soon thereafter Josef managed to escape. He returned to the Hardagas, who hid him for ten days and told him that they had looked after his family during his absence. At night, Josef could hear the screams of prisoners being tortured in the Gestapo building nearby. Posters on the streets warned people against giving shelter to Communists and Jews. Deciding that it was too dangerous to remain in Sarajevo, Josef escaped to Mustar, where he was reunited with his family. Somewhat later he joined the partisans and fought for Yugoslavia's liberation.

After the war, the Cavilios returned to Sarajevo, again staying with the Hardagas until they could find a suitable dwelling. Mustafa Hardaga returned the valuables which Josef Cavilio had left with him for safekeeping four years earlier. In 1950 the Cavilio family moved to Israel.

Mrs. Zayneba Hardaga-Susic, fourth from right, *planting a tree in the Garden of the Righteous 1985.* Second from right, *Mr. Josef Cavilio, the man she and her late husband Mustafa rescued. Courtesy of Yad Vashem.*

In Jerusalem to plant a tree in her family's name in the Garden of the Righteous, Zayneba recalled the wartime martyrdom of her father, Ahmed Rahmateli. While at the railroad station in Konice, Ahmed noticed a Jewish acquaintance about to board a train for Sarajevo. He ran over and warned him not to go there because all the Jews in the city were being rounded up. The Jew and his family stood spellbound, uncertain what to do next, but Ahmed took them to his home, obtained false papers for them, and arranged their transfer to the Italian zone.

"They were all saved except my father," Zayneba sadly recounts. "He was denounced and taken to the Jasenovic camp and was killed on the charge of aiding Jews." She then said, "As his burial place is unknown, may this tree that I plant here be a memorial for him. May this tree became a symbol of the man Ahmed Rahmateli."

Congratulating her on behalf of the Moslem Religious Council, a sheik assured Zayneba that her deeds, and those of her late husband, were in the spirit of the prophet Mohammed and in full accord with Islam's teachings on the importance of aiding strangers in distress. (2811)

Stephan and Anna Popstephanova

The next two stories took place in Macedonia, which was annexed by Bulgaria in April 1941.

Soon after the annexation, Stephan Popstephanova, the head of a Bulgarian police training school, was appointed regional police commander in Skoplje, the Macedonian capital. When he and his wife, Anna, a former actress, arrived there, they stayed at a local hotel and then found a comfortable house with the help of Rachel Kariv, who with her husband, Moni, was a long-standing Jewish resident of Skoplje.

In other parts of Yugoslavia, and especially in Serbia and Croatia, the killing of Jews began immediately after the German invasion, but the situation remained relatively calm in the Bulgarian zone. In March 1943, under intense German pressure, the Bulgarian government agreed to hand over the Jewish populace of the newly annexed territories. Alexander Balev, Bulgaria's Commissioner for Jewish Affairs, was sent to Skoplje to supervise the operation.

Popstephanova, outraged at his country's collusion with the Nazis, sent Anna to warn the Karivs of the impending roundup and tell them to keep off the streets for the next ten days. In addition, he enlisted a trusted police officer named Ogenien to move the Kariv family, all told numbering five persons, out of the area to be covered in the operation.

Ogenien was to have done this under the cover of darkness while the Bulgarian officialdom of Skoplje was attending a party in honor of Balev, but at the last minute the plan fell through because the Macedonian who had agreed to hide them changed his mind. Around 11:00 p.m. Ogenien showed up at the party and with a nod of his head signaled to Popstephanova that he had not been able to get the Karivs to safety. Anna, sitting next to her husband, excused herself and left the room. Outside, Ogenien explained what had happened.

Anna went to see the Karivs, and they dejectedly told her that they were going to turn themselves in the next morning. On hearing this, and without consulting her husband, Anna decided to hide them in her own house. Still accompanied by Ogenien, she and the Karivs made their way through the darkened streets, passing the hall where the party for Balev was in full swing.

Leaving the Karivs at home, with Ogenien to watch over them, Anna hurried back to the party and, asking her husband to dance with her, gave him a whispered account of what she had done. The following morning, March 11, 1943, all the Jews in Skoplje were rounded up and assembled in a tobacco warehouse. There they were relieved of their possessions and loaded on waiting trains.

Four days later, Popstephanova bribed an Albanian consular official to arrange for the Karivs to cross over into Albania, which at the time was occupied by Italy. He then moved them to the apartment of a friend who was a theatrical impresario—ironically, located on the ground floor of a building occupied mainly by German officers—and set about getting them to their destination.

On the appointed day, Ogenien came by with a wagon and picked up the Karivs. Armed with a machine gun in case of trouble, Stephan joined them in the wagon, as did Anna. During the journey to the frontier he took out a map and showed the Karivs the route they were to follow. When they were as close as possible to the area separating the two zones, Stephan and Anna bid their charges farewell, providing them with sandwiches as a final gesture.

The Karivs safely reached Albania. There they experienced many hardships and had several narrow escapes, but nonetheless conditions were much better than in Skoplje, and they survived the war.

Returning to Skoplje, they learned that Ogenien had been arrested and shot for hiding a Jewish child. They also learned how the Popstephanovas had tried to save Moni's sister-in-law, Stella Baruch. During the mass roundup, Stella and her children had been put on a deportation train. As soon as they heard about this, Stephan and Anna had rushed to the station. After a frantic search, Anna saw Stella hanging out of the window of a railroad car and begging a German guard on the platform to allow her child, who had been assigned to another car, to join her.

Anna desperately but unsuccessfully tried to obtain Stella's release, then approached a German soldier and said brusquely: "This is Bulgaria! My husband is a police commander . . . . Separating a woman from her child is an outrage!" Stephan, standing at her side, ordered the Germans to return the child to its mother. The guards did so, apparently deciding that the least they could do for the doomed mother was to let her spend her last few days in the company of her child.

About a year after this incident, misfortune struck the Popstephanovas. Arrested by the new Communist regime because he had been an official of the former government, Stephan Popstephanova was executed on September 9, 1944, just a few days after the Red Army entered Bulgaria. Anna was not harmed. The Karivs left to build new lives in Israel. (2551)

Aleksander and Blaga Todorov

Betty was born in 1939, in Skoplje, to Aaron and Rivkah Bechar. Her father owned an electrical appliance business in partnership with a non-Jew named Aleksander Todorov, an old friend. The partnership cemented the close relationship between the two families, and after Todorov married, little Betty spent much of her time with him and his wife. "They loved me and spoiled me. On many occasions, I slept over at their place," Betty recalls.

In 1943, when Betty was four years old, conditions for Jews began to worsen. They were made to wear the yellow star, and many were conscripted into labor battalions. Todorov obtained new identity cards for the Bechars so that they could escape to Albania, where things were better. Using these, they made their way to the frontier but lost heart when they saw how well it was guarded and returned to Skoplje.

They had walked into a trap, for on March 10, 1943, the Germans and the Bulgarians launched a major roundup of the city's Jews. At the time, Betty was staying with the Todorovs. When Aaron and Rivkah received the order requiring them to report for deportation to an unstated destination, they naturally wanted to take their daughter along, reasoning that the family ought to remain together, but when they called for her, she began weeping uncontrollably at the thought of being separated from the Todorovs.

Aaron and Rivkah decided to leave Betty with the Todorovs for the time being, hoping that the separation would not be very lengthy and also left all their valuables with them. On March 11, the Bechars reported as ordered and were taken to a nearby internment camp. Aleksander Todorov regularly sent them food packages and even visited them at the camp. In time, however, the internees were shipped to Poland. It was later learned that they were all killed.

Meanwhile, Betty continued to live with her devoted adoptive parents. From time to time Gestapo agents raided households suspected of harboring Jews, including the Todorov house, but they never imagined that Betty, who now sported the name Christina, was anything but the Todorovs' natural daughter. However, the neighbors knew that she was not, and rumors about her began to circulate. Blaga Todorov countered by claiming that Betty was the offspring of a premarital relationship with another man.

Betty lived with the Todorovs throughout the war. She had no reason to think that she was not their daughter, and that Sergej, their infant son, was not her brother, but sometimes her supposed father did things that aroused her curiosity. "I remember as a little girl," she says, "my father would send me with some money wrapped up in a newspaper to the office of the local Jewish communal organization, with instructions that it was a donation for Jewish war orphans. I was forbidden to give the donor's name or even my own."

In 1948 the Communists arrested Todorov, charging him with capitalist tendencies. The valuables the Bechars had left in his care were used as evidence to support the charges. Todorov's property was confiscated and he was sentenced to a long term in prison. In his absence, the burden of supporting Betty and Sergej fell squarely on Blaga's shoulders. She took on odd jobs like knitting and embroidery.

In the meantime, Betty continued to be the subject of rumors about her origins and parentage. One day, in 1952, she found a cryptic note between the pages of one of Todorov's books: "Binbenita Bechar shall remain with Aleksander Todorov until our return." It was signed: Aaron Bechar.

"The name Aaron Bechar meant nothing to me," Betty admits, but now she began to pay more attention to the incessant rumors and whispers. Todorov's continued imprisonment contributed to Betty's transformation. Her thoughts became more somber. "I began to think and fear that I might not be their daughter."

One day, passing the Jewish communal offices, she entered and asked an official whether the name Aaron Bechar meant anything. At last she learned the truth. "I was told that I was Jewish and that the Todorov family had rescued me; that my parents had perished in the Holocaust. . . . I was in shock."

Betty kept the secret to herself for half a year. She made several more visits to the Jewish communal organization. A friend of the family saw her going in, and one day, when she came home, Blaga asked her what she had been doing there. In reply Betty told Blaga what she had discovered. "She wept, and the lights were on all that night. Mother told me who I was, what had happened to my parents, about the package which my natural father had left for me, and about my parents' property."

Betty was now determined to rejoin her people by moving to Israel, but Blaga tried to discourage her. "She loved me very much, and my decision affected her health. But she said I should do as I felt best." Betty's adoptive father was still in prison. "I had to struggle with my feelings; I could not bring myself to leave my parents, and especially my beloved Sergej; it was difficult for me to part with him. But in the end I decided to leave for Israel."

Blaga Todorov outfitted Betty with new clothes for the voyage, and her father was given a furlough from prison to see her off. Their parting was very emotional, because they were the only parents she had ever really known, and they genuinely regarded her as their own child.

In 1952, when she arrived in Israel, Betty joined a kibbutz. Later on she studied nursing while in the army, and she has been a nurse ever since. Her ties with the Todorovs remained strong, and when she married, she and her husband went to Yugoslavia on their honeymoon to visit them.

"Today," Betty wrote in 1979, "I have two children, a son and a daughter. During each pregnancy, close to the date of delivery, my mother came to Israel to look after me, and she stayed until after the child's birth. My brother Sergej, a professional architect, is married and has a child. He too visited me a few years ago, and we remain in close contact until this very day." (1766)

Olga Bartulovic

When the Germans invaded Yugoslavia in April 1941, Erna and Samuel Nachmias and their three children lived in Bania Lokia, Croatia. Their hometown ceased to be safe after the Germans set up a nominally independent Croatian republic, for as soon as the puppet regime came into being, its ruler, Pavelic, and the Ustase fascist movement turned on the local Jews and Serbs, killing them by the thousands. During this reign of terror Samuel Nachmias fled to Belgrade, in German-occupied Serbia. Sometime later he escaped to Split, in Italian-occupied Dalmatia, and Erna and the children joined him there.

The situation changed overnight when Italy surrendered to the Allies in September 1943 and German forces overran the former Italian zone. The day after the Germans entered Split, posters went up informing the populace of the draconian new laws concerning Jews, warning that stiff penalties would be meted out to anyone found harboring Jews in their homes. All Jews were ordered to register with the police.

At the time the Nachmias family was peacefully residing in the home of Olga Bartulovic. Learning of the new anti-Jewish measures, Olga urged her boarders not to register but to keep out of sight in the days to come. Samuel Nachmias, fearing he would be arrested, decided to take his chances and register, but Olga refused to let him go. In Erna's words, "she actually used force and coercion to make us stay with her." Moreover, she persuaded Erna to ask for sanctuary at the Marjan convent in Split.

Following Olga's instructions to the letter, Erna claimed to be a Greek Orthodox woman married to a Jew threatened by the new measures. She and Samuel were admitted to the convent and given separate quarters. "We were always afraid," Erna recalls, "for the Germans staged searches in the city and were persecuting the Jews. The danger was great."

Olga visited them frequently at the convent to keep their spirits up, and eventually recommended that they flee to the mountainous area held by Tito's partisans. Once again they did as she advised. Guided by Olga, Samuel Nachmias made the difficult 25-mile trek past German patrols and into the mountains to the town of Trogir, which was controlled by the partisans.

Olga then returned to Split for Erna, whom she had hidden in the home of a trusted friend. Two months passed before the coast was clear, but Olga then had a friend guide Erna to Trogir while she and her sister-in-law, Dragica, traveling separately along parallel routes, brought the Nachmias children there, armed with false papers claiming they were their own children.

It was December 1943. Olga rented a room for her charges and arranged for Samuel, who had joined the partisans, to be reunited with his family. Olga and Dragica left them money and food for three days, as well as bedding and cigarettes, and then returned home. "And that's how Olga Bartulovic saved my husband and son, while her sister-in-law saved my daughter and my second son," Erna states in her deposition. When the war ended, Olga sought out the Nachmias family. Finding them alive and well, she was happy to know that her efforts to save them had been worthwhile. (185)

Ivan Vranetic

Many Jewish refugees found a temporary heaven on the Italian-occupied island of Rab in the northern part of the Adriatic. When Italy capitulated in September 1943, Yugoslav partisans landed on Rab. Forced to withdraw by the Germans, they took most of the Jews with them when they returned to the mainland. The able-bodied men joined the partisans, while the elderly, the women, and the children set out for Toposko, an inland town located in an area infested with pro-German Ustase troops. On several occasions Ustase militiamen raided and sacked Toposko, wreaking vengeance on those suspected of pro-Tito sympathies, and showing no mercy to any Jews who fell into their hands.

Ivan Vranetic, a seventeen-year-old Croatian lad, dedicated himself to helping Jews trying to escape the Nazis and their Ustase collaborators. Whenever a Ustase attack was expected, Vranetic warned the Jews to take refuge in the woods, arranging transportation for those who were unable to walk. When necessary he carried children, old, and sick people on his back, urging others to act likewise.

Among the people whom Vranetic helped were Erna Montilio, a widow whose husband had perished in the Jasenovac camp, her young daughter, and her elderly mother. When Erna fell ill, he hid her in his parents' house, where she found other Jews in hiding. As Erna relates, "I cannot imagine how the three of us would have survived without his help." Another survivor adds: "This young man made a special point of helping the old and the sick and those burdened with children. There was a great shortage of suitable dwellings, even for an overnight stay; this lad ran from place to place in search of vacant places; he would clean up rundown shacks in order to make them suitable for habitation. He put up some people in his parents' house. He also scoured the countryside to find extra food for his charges."

After the war, Ivan Vranetic wanted to marry Erna Montilio, but her mother objected. Instead she married a Jewish man and bore him two children, but the marriage did not last. In 1963 Vranetic visited Israel and met Erna Montilo after a twenty-year separation. He returned the next year—for good.

"She was my first love," he says shyly, "and I cannot leave her." He supports Erna and all three of her children. As Ivan says, "Everyone does what is best for him. Everyone plans his own life. I did not come here to make money. I came here for love." To these candid words, Abraham Alteretz, one of the survivors, adds: "As he once admitted to me, he also came here out of a deep urge to be with us." (561)

* * *

We close with a story from nearby Albania, to which many Jews from Yugoslavia fled.

Refik Veseli

In June 1990, Gavra Mandil wrote an impassioned letter from Israel to President Ramiz Alia, head of the Communist regime of Albania, asking that Refik Veseli be allowed temporarily to leave that self-isolated country, in order to be reunited with those that he and his family had helped during the Nazi period. Israel and Albania had no diplomatic relations at the time, so there was no guarantee that the request would be granted. However, in this instance, the Albanian government showed itself true to its humanitarian tradition during World War II, and that same year Refik Veseli arrived in Israel and was feted at Yad Vashem as a Rigtheous Among the Nations, the first of his country to be awarded this title.

The story unfolds during the German occupation of neighboring Yugoslavia during World War II. When Gavra's father flouted German orders to report to the authorities so he as well as other Jews could be deported to the camps, he knew he had to flee immediately. With the help of local Serbs, the Mandil family (Gavra was then four and a half years old) fled from the capital city of Belgrade to the area under Italian occupation. At first, Mandil's family together with other Jewish refugees were interned in a camp in Prishtina, but with the help of the Italians many of them were able to proceed to Albania—also under Italian occupation—and to the cities of Kavaja and Tirana.

When Italy capitulated to the Allies in September 1943, the Germans reacted immediately by occupying Italy and all other areas administered by the Italian army; and thus the Holocaust reached mountainous and isolated Albania and its over 1,000 Jews, most of whom had fled to the safety of this hospitable country from nearby Yugoslavia. Many Jews immediately took to the hills, forests, and outlying villages, and in the words of Gavra Mandil:

> In those dark days, when danger and death were all around, the small and brave Albanian people proved their greatness. Without any fuss and without asking anything in return, the Albanian people performed the elementary human duty, and saved the lives of their Jewish refugees. Each Jewish family found shelter with an Albanian family—and at the risk of their own lives, they saved and protected their guests. It was more than just hospitality; it was the highest sacrifice and devotion to duty!

Gavra's father, a photographer by profession, had earlier hired a fifteen-year-old Albanian apprentice by the name of Refik Veseli to whom he taught the art of photography. "Refik became like a son to him, and an older brother to me," Gavra recalls. When Mandil's family found it necessary to flee the Germans again, Refik immediately offered his parents' home in the village of Kruja as a place of refuge. The village's location, between almost unpassable mountains, seemed an ideal place to hide.

Together with another Jewish family, a total of seven persons made the arduous journey on the back of donkeys, riding by night and remaining hidden in caves by day, and were welcomed into the Veseli household. Gavra's parents were lodged in an alcove above the barn, whereas Gavra and the other refugee children shared the household children's quarters.

With the increase of anti-Nazi partisan activities, the Germans intensified their searches of isolated villages, including Kruja. Refik's parents, who had not known these refugee Jews before, calmed his wards and assured them that "only over his family's dead bodies would the German Nazis get to us."

Gavra also notes in this context that most Albanians are simple people, "but kind, warm-hearted, and very humanitarian," and adds the following observation: "Perhaps they were not educated in the culture of Goethe or Schiller, but they accorded, in a most natural and instinctive manner, the highest importance to man's existence. During those dark days, when the life of Jews in Europe mattered for nothing, the Albanians protected the Jews in their midst with love, devotion, and self-sacrifice."

At the end of the war, when the Mandil family returned to Yugoslavia, Refik joined it in order to complement his training in photography under the tutoring of Gavra's father. At the end of a two-year training period, Refik returned to his native country, a fully proficient photographer, whereas in 1948 the Mandil family left for Israel.

In 1990, Gavra and Refik (both professional photographers) met in Israel, after a separation of forty-two years. This near-miraculous reunion

(Albania at that time still did not allow its citizens to travel abroad) galvanized other rescued Jews residing in Israel to seek out their erstwhile rescuers in Albania and bring to light the epic story of the contribution of many Albanians to the rescue of Jews.

Refik Veseli and Gavra Mandil, in a picture from the war years in Albania. Courtesy of Yad Vashem.

Refik and Mrs. Veseli kneel before the Eternal Flame at Yad Vashem (1990). Behind: Gavra Mandil and relatives. Courtesy of Yad Vashem.

Greece

The Germans invaded Greece in April 1941 after Italy's attempt to conquer the country met with defeat. Most of Greece, including Athens, the capital, was turned over to the Italians, but the northeastern province of Thrace went to Bulgaria, while Germany occupied the militarily valuable Aegean islands as well as the city of Salonika (also known as Thessaloniki) and its environs. Of the country's 77,000 Jews, 55,000 lived in and around Salonika, and thus came under German jurisdiction; another 13,000 were in the Italian zone, the remainder in Thrace and the Dodecanese Islands.

For some time, the Germans took no action against the Jews under their control, except for the customary incidental harrassment and, in July 1942, the conscription of 6,000 men into labor units for work in malaria-infested swamps. During the period before the Nazis set their machinery of destruction into operation, some 3,000 Jews managed to flee from Salonika southward to the Italian zone.

In February 1943, however, the Germans established a ghetto in Salonika, and with this act began the destruction of the city's Jewish community, one of the oldest in Europe and a major center of Sephardic culture since the expulsion from Spain. Around February 25, the Germans announced that the residents of the ghetto would be relocated to Cracow, in Poland, where they would do useful work under the auspices of the local Jewish community. Polish currency was distributed to substantiate this tale, which was, of course, totally false, since the last remaining Jews in Cracow were being liquidated at that very time.

Starting in mid-March and continuing until May, trains carrying 2,000 to 2,500 Jews a day left Salonika for the death camps. In all, about 46,000 Jews were deported, most of them to Auschwitz. Of these, only 5 percent survived.

The Italians, as was their wont in matters related to the Final Solution, gave the Germans a hard time whenever possible. Zamboni, the Italian consul general in Salonika, distributed Italian naturalization papers to hundreds of Jews without carefully scrutinizing the documents they presented to support the issuing of such papers. The Germans protested vehemently but dared not move against their ally. Some 320 Jews were allowed to leave Salonika aboard an Italian military train heading for Athens. The Spanish government also interceded for some 600 Jews claiming Spanish nationality, and these, though deported to Bergen-Belsen, received "preferential" treatment after they arrived there.

In Thrace, the Bulgarians, complying with German requests, rounded up over 4,000 Jews. The operation was accompanied by savage brutalities in sharp contrast to the way the Bulgarians treated the Jews of their own country. Most of the Jews of Bulgaria proper were never deported, whereas the great majority of the Thracian Jews were not only rounded up but sent to the death camps.

The 16,000 Jews under Italian jurisdiction enjoyed relative freedom and were not physically harmed until the capitulation of Italy in September 1943, when the Germans took over the Italian zone, including the Dodecanese Islands. The Germans immediately set about rounding them up but ran into opposition from priests and civilian officials, especially in Athens, where Metropolitan Damaskinos, the Greek Orthodox prelate, ordered that Jews be given refuge in all monasteries and convents, and Angelos Evert, the police chief, secretly provided Jews with false papers that enabled them to pass as non-Jews. German raids netted about 5,400 victims, all of whom were deported, but many others were hidden by non-Jewish families or by resistance units. Some managed to escape across the Aegean Sea to the Turkish coast.

Most of the Jews who resided on the Greek islands were also eliminated. Of the 2,000 Jews of Corfu, for instance, close to 1,800 were transported to the mainland and then by train to the death camps. Likewise the 260 Jews of Crete. In contrast, the 275 Jews of Zakinthos (Zante) were helped to escape to the mountains by the island's bishop and the mayor. The 1,500 Jews of Rhodes, off the Turkish coast, survived until July 1944, when a special unit landed on the island, rounded them up, and started them on the journey to Auschwitz, where most perished.

All told, more than 60,000 Greek Jews (about 85 percent of the country's total Jewish population) were sent to the death camps. Some 12,000 eluded the Nazis, most by escaping across the sea or hiding in the mountains; some were taken in or aided by compassionate non-Jews.

We begin with several rescue stories originating in Salonika, the hub of Jewish life in Greece until the coming of the Nazis.

Dimitris Spiliakos

Dimitris Spiliakos, a noted Salonikan attorney, had many Jewish clients in the years before the war. During the early part of the occupation, when the Germans assured the city's Jews that they would not be harmed, he continually urged his friends to flee while it was still possible, warning that German promises could not be relied on. In most cases, however, his warnings were not heeded.

In 1942, when a new German regulation required all Jews to register with the authorities, Spiliakos advised the Simantov family not to comply. "Unfortunately I did not do as he suggested," Albert Simantov relates, "and as a result, I was taken as a forced laborer for over six months, until the Jewish forced laborers were released upon payment of a large ransom."

The following January (1943) the Jews of Salonika were confined to a ghetto, and two months later the deportations began. Spiliakos urgently warned all his Jewish friends to get away while it was still possible. In particular, he went to the home of Isaac Covo, an old-time business associate and offered to help him and his family to escape. Covo, who was an official of the Jewish community, refused, explaining that he had recently persuaded the Germans to spare an orphanage that was part of his communal responsibility, and if he now disappeared, they might harm the children in revenge.

Spiliakos refused to take no for an answer.In the words of Ida Covo, Isaac's wife, Spiliakos "confronted us with a fait accompli. He had obtained a student identity card for my son Albert [then seventeen years old] as well as a ticket for an Italian train leaving for Athens." The Covos hedged. Then, in the words of Albert Covo, "Mr. Spiliakos took me out of the ghetto by force" and, the same evening, put him on the Athens-bound train. "And that is how I was saved."

Several months passed, and in August 1943, the Germans decided to round up the city's remaining Jews. Having learned of the German plan, Spiliakos sent his sister to tell the Covos that he would be coming for them later that evening. While she was inside the ghetto, the Germans suddenly launched their *Aktion* and began loading children on trucks. Spiliakos's sister immediately tore the yellow star from Ida Covo's coat, and they both slipped out of the ghetto. That same evening Dimitris Spiliakos managed to spirit Isaac Covo out of the ghetto.

Both Covos were hidden in the home of friends of Spiliakos (his own home was unsafe because the authorities knew that he had Jewish friends and therefore might have searched it). A few days later, Spiliakos learned that a trainload of Jews who claimed Italian nationality would soon be departing from Salonika. If he could somehow manage to get the names of the two Covos added to the passenger list, it might be possible to get them out of Salonika even though the Germans were looking for them.

After several visits to the Italian consulate, Spiliakos obtained permission for the Covos to board the train. "That day, attorney Spiliakos came to fetch us at dawn," Mrs. Covo recalls. "He accompanied us to the station, where we had to pass a checkpoint. We had some trouble when the Germans couldn't find our names on their list. But Spiliakos, sporting a safe-conduct pass and with great determination, succeeded in getting us on the train."

Spiliakos helped other Jewish families in much the same way. "On April 5, 1943," Albert Simantov recalls, "Mr. Spiliakos helped me to leave Salonika for Athens aboard an Italian military train, dressed in an Italian uniform." Two days later, he arranged for Albert's mother to be transferred to Athens as well. Mrs. Daisy Navarro recalls that Spiliakos pretended to be a drunk on a spree when he got her parents out of the ghetto so that the guards would not bother him.

A similar story is told by Laura Nissim (whose ancestors had settled in Salonika in the fifteenth century after they were expelled from Spain). Spiliakos spirited out all nine members of the Nissim family, one at a time. Once again, he camouflaged what he was doing by pretending to be drunk. At 5 a.m., accompanied by two seemingly inebriated friends, Spiliakos stumbled his way into the ghetto. "Acting as if they were coming home from a party, they crossed the empty ghetto, singing like drunken sailors," Laura Nissim relates. "It should be noted," she adds, "that whenever a sector of the ghetto was emptied, it would be well controlled by armed Germans at all corners. Here, again, Spiliakos demonstrated enormous courage and dedication."

After getting them out of the ghetto, Spiliakos hid Nissim's parents for several days and then arranged for them to go to Athens. The situation there had deteriorated, however, after Italy's capitulation in September 1943 and the city's subsequent occupation by the Germans. Here again, Spiliakos came to the rescue. "For a second time, attorney Spiliakos was at our side," Ida Covo testifies. "He hid us with a married sister who lived in Athens."

Spiliakos also found places for all ten Simantovs to hide out, according to Albert, and obtained false papers for them as well. "Mr. Spiliakos claimed that my mother and I were relatives from his native village. Hardly anyone believed it, though, because of my mother's thick Jewish accent, but he was so well liked that nobody dared do us any harm."

In addition to rescuing and concealing the Nissims and the Simantovs, Spiliakos provided for all of their material needs until the liberation made it possible for them to come out of hiding. After the war, as Albert Simantov confirms, he refused all attempts to repay him.

"My husband, my son, and I owe him our lives," Ida Covo states. "Needless to say, he was motivated by friendship and humanitarian feelings; he never asked anything from us in return, save our appreciation."

Albert Simantov says, "I owe him not only my life but also my professional development." This last statement refers to the fact that Spiliakos took Albert into his home after the war and helped him to make a fresh start. If not for Spiliakos, Albert says, he would never have attended the university and become an agricultural economist. (3566)

Dimitris Zannas and Stratos Paraskevaidis

Another rescue story from Salonika concerns the Florentin sisters, Maidy and Fanny. Maidy was twenty years old when, on April 6, 1943, her family received its deportation orders. "They spoke about work camps; none of us knew anything about extermination camps," Maidy recalls. The Jewish leaders, she continues, never dreamed that the community was slated for destruction, so "instead of spreading the word that *sauve qui peut* was the order of the day, they told us to trust in God."

Maidy and her family reported as ordered and lined up in the street with hundreds of others under the eyes of German guards. It was, she says, "a beautiful spring day, flowers in bloom everywhere, not a day to go to the slaughter." All of a sudden a man edged up and quietly told her to follow him.

The man was Dimitris Zannas, a young lawyer whose businessman father was the president of the local Red Cross and a member of the board of directors of the YMCA. Maidy knew him by sight, but they were not otherwise acquainted. As she later learned, Dimitris and a woman cousin had been watching the Jews line up. Noticing Maidy's doleful expression, the cousin had pointed her out to him: "Why are you standing there? Can't you do something for that poor girl?"

"I had to make the toughest decision of my life," Maidy recalls; "What was I going to do—stay with my parents and the thousands of others, or get away? I couldn't make up my mind alone. I whispered to my mother, who asked my father. He nodded that it was OK. I still didn't want to leave them. Finally, my mother pulled my knapsack from my back and pushed me off the line, then I put the yellow star in my pocket. I never saw my parents again." Ironically, it was the first day of the Passover holiday, which celebrates the Jewish exodus from ancient Egypt!

With Dimitris leading the way and Maidy following a few paces behind, the two young people slowly made their way through the crowd. Dimitris took Maidy to a farm about 45 kilometers from Salonika, where she was sheltered and cared for by Stratos Paraskevaidis for the duration of the war.

Maidy's elder sister, Fanny, had already escaped from the doomed ghetto. In March 1943, she and Leon, her husband of just a few days, left Salonika and headed for the mountains, where they joined the underground. Since Fanny was a nurse, she was assigned to a medical unit. Moving from place to place as the military situation warranted, she was, at various times, in Paikon, Vermion, Kaimaktsilan, Olympos, Perria, and other towns and villages.

In July 1944, Fanny was captured by the Germans. She was taken to a camp in Pavlou Mela and interrogated by S.S. officers, but fortunately they did not know she was Jewish. With the aid of other camp inmates Fanny was able to send a message to some family friends in Salonika, and this was passed on to Stratos Paraskevaidis.

Paraskevaidis and the father of Dimitris Zannas arranged for the International Red Cross representative in Salonika to intervene on Fanny's behalf with the claim that the partisans had captured her and forced her to work for them against her will. A hefty bribe to the S.S. clinched the deal, and Fanny was released. Outside the camp, Stratos was waiting for her with his motorcycle, and after a stopover at his mother's apartment he took her to his farm. "You can imagine my joy when I was reunited with my sister," Fanny relates.

Fanny and Maidy, the only members of the Florentin family to survive, remained on the Paraskevaidis farm until the liberation in October 1944. "I owe Stratos Paraskevaidis my life for saving me from the camp and hiding me," Fanny testifies. Maidy is equally grateful to Paraskevaidis but also praises Dimitris Zannas. "He saved me because of his love of liberty and of mankind, and he knew perfectly well that he was endangering himself. As long as I live I will never forget that I owe him my life."

Neither sister had known their two rescuers before the onset of the Nazi avalanche. Dimitris' sudden decision to intervene and save Maidy, and then, through his friend Stratos, her sister as well, made it possible for the two Jewish women to survive. (4465)

Epaminondas Morikis

In April 1943, Sam Nahmias, then a teenager, was drafted for forced labor and put to work, with about 900 other Salonikan Jews, in the stone quarries at Karyas Station, near Domokos. Severely injured when some boulders fell on him, he was taken to the hospital in nearby Lamia. While he was recovering there, the Germans sent the other quarry workers to Auschwitz. Fearful that they would soon return for him and not sure what to do, Sam confided in Iphigenia, his nurse. "This wonderful woman did everything she could to save me. She went from store to store in Lamia, telling the proprietors that there was an orphan boy at the hospital who needed work."

One of the places Iphigenia visited was the candy shop of Demetrios Bousios. He listened patiently, then politely said he could not help, but when Iphigenia left the shop, she was followed by a young man, Epaminondas Morikis, who had overheard her conversation with Bousios. "I ran after her," Morikis relates years later, "and caught up with her on the street; I told her who I was, and then she told me the truth about young Sam Nahmias." Morikis promised to help.

Rushing home, Morikis repeated the story to his parents and his seven brothers. After a brief conference they decided to do what they could to save the youth. The next day Morikis helped Sam get out of the hospital and gave him directions to the family's bakery. "Barefoot, and barely able to limp with the aid of a stick, I went to the bakery in Lamia," Sam says. He was warmly greeted by Epaminondas' father, Charalampos Morikis, who promised to put him up in the bakery's attic, turning to his wife and saying, "We must save him."

"From that day until the liberation of Salonika, I stayed there," Sam says. He was frightened at first, but felt more secure when Mrs. Morikis told her sons: "From now on you are eight brothers; don't ever forget it."

Treated as a member of the family, Sam slept in the attic with Epaminondas and earned his keep by working in the bakery. At first he was afraid to go outside, but in time he felt confident enough to stroll through the town, especially after he obtained a false identity card under the name Demosthenes Demetriadis. "The agony and fear, however, never left us," Epaminondas recalls, "especially when leaflets were distributed warning that any Christian hiding a Jew would be send to the well-known German camps. What can I say about those moments when Sam and I had to pass through German checkpoints? It was as if we were reborn every time."

When the war ended Sam returned home to discover that his parents and other kin were all dead. His pain was eased by the warm embrace of the Morikis family. "All of us have by now set up on our own," Epaminondas Morikis comments, "and we see ourselves, together with Sam, as a family of eight brothers, just as our mother urged us to be during the occupation." Thanks to "the excellent Sam," Morikis adds, they have had the pleasure of learning what Jews are like, "for we had known nothing about them before, as there had never been any in our town." (4057)

Angela Citterich and Sister Joseph

Albert and Eda Sciaky were at their wits' end. A girl had been born to them in April 1942. Now, a year later, with the deportations from Salonika in full swing, they were deeply troubled. Eda had Spanish papers and therefore was not in immediate danger, and Albert planned to join the partisans in the mountains, but what were they do do about little Rena?

On the advice of a relative who was an Italian national, they turned their daughter over to the Sisters of Charity of St. Vincent de Paul in Calamari. In order to explain the infant's presence in the convent in case the Germans made inquiries, Sister Rochette, the mother superior, persuaded Mrs. Angela ("Lena") Citterich, a local Italian national, to register her as her daughter under the name Gilberte and enroll her in the convent's nursery.

For the sake of plausibility Rena was frequently taken to visit the Citterichs. She and their young son Vittorio became fond of each other, and the Citterichs decided to adopt Rena if her parents failed to return after the war. "They treated me like their own child," Rena says, "with devotion and love, and at great risk to themselves."

Sister Joseph, who nursed Rena in the convent's hospital when she fell ill, also developed a strong attachment to her, and after her recovery doted on her at every opportunity. The convent was situated on the seashore, and whenever a German search was in the offing, Sister Joseph took Rena out in a boat until the danger was over.

In the meantime, Albert Sciaky escaped to Turkey by sea and then made his way to Palestine, arriving there in 1944, but Eda Sciaky, despite her Spanish papers, was apprehended and made to drink the bitter cup of the Bergen-Belsen camp . . . which she luckily survived.

In March 1947, learning that Albert and Eda were in Paris, Sister Rochette took Rena there by plane. Elise Acquarone, a schoolmate of Rena's, recalls their departure. "I still remember the day after the war when the news burst like a bomb in Calamari. Gilberte had found her mother, her true mother. Joy and relief! Sister Rochette, the mother superior, was leaving on a plane (at the time everyone traveled by train) for Paris to return Gilberte to her mother after her release from Bergen-Belsen. . . . Gilberte, who could have become another victim of the Holocaust, had been saved thanks to Sister Rochette and the Citterich family. She is now a happy woman, though certainly marked by personal memories—but she's alive."

In Rena's words: "In the period we are currently living in (1986), a period marked by wars, terror, antisemitism, and lack of faith in man, these people ought to serve as an example for all humankind." (3579)

Archbishop Damaskinos

The Jews of Athens, the capital of Greece, were spared the ravages of the Holocaust until the fall of Italy in September 1943. From then on they shared the travails of their brethren in other Nazi-occupied regions.

Even before this, however, many Athenians, including a prelate of the Greek Orthodox Church, were outraged by reports about the deportations in Salonika. On March 23, 1943, Archbishop Damaskinos and twenty-nine of the city's most prominent citizens submitted a letter to Prime Minister Logothetopoulos in which they strongly protested the government's apparent complicity in the planned annihilation of the Jewish population.

The document, which was drafted by the archbishop, began by declaring that the Jews of Greece were valuable and loyal citizens. It continued:

> Our holy religion does not recognize differences—superior or inferior—based on race and religion; it teaches that there is neither Jew nor Greek (Epistle to the Galatians 3:28) and therefore condemns all forms of racial and religious discrimination.

The letter ends with an admonition:

> It must not be forgotten that the nation will someday pass judgment on everything that happens during this difficult period, even things that are done against our will or not within our control, and all who were involved will be held responsible. This moral burden will weigh heavily on the nation's leaders on that Judgment Day if they fail to publicize the people's disapproval of such deeds as the deportation of Jews, recently begun.

While an official of the Jewish community waited nervously in his office, Archbishop Damaskinos personally delivered a copy of the petition to General Altenberg, the all-powerful German representative in Athens. When he returned, the archbishop told the Jewish leader to take immediate measures to save as many Jews as possible, adding that he would do whatever he could to help. "We are all children of the same Father," he said. "God created us all in His image and we are obligated to come to the aid of our fellow men and not allow Satan to rule over us." The archbishop then ordered all the priests and monks under his authority to open their churches and convents to Jews seeking shelter, adding that under no circumstances were they to exploit the situation as an opportunity for proselytizing. He also summoned the director-general of the Athens municipality, Panos Hazeldos, and told him: "I have taken up my cross . . . by resolving to save as many Jewish souls as I can, even if doing so endangers me. I will issue baptismal certificates for them, and you in turn will issue municipal documents allowing them to obtain identity cards as Christian Greeks."

With the collaboration of Angelos Evert, the police chief, hundreds of Athenian Jews were provided with new identities and thereby saved from extermination. Many others were given sanctuary in monasteries in compliance with the archbishop's instructions.

When the Germans demanded his resignation, Damaskinos replied: "Members of the Greek clergy never resign. They remain in the position God has appointed for them even if they are in danger of being put to death." The Germans, however, did not harm him. (547)

Ekaterina Sklavounos

Mathilde Bourla was studying pharmacology in Athens when the war broke out. Forced to abandon her studies, she found work as a nurse at the Elpis university hospital. One of her patients was Ekaterina Sklavounos, an old woman who eventually died from a fatal tumor.

In 1943 Mathilde's sister Bella and her husband escaped from German-occupied Salonika and found what appeared to be a safe refuge in Athens, which was then under Italian administration, but with Italy's surrender in September and the German takeover, the situation changed.

As a nurse, Mathilde was not in any immediate danger, but her sister and brother-in-law once again faced the threat of deportation with all that implied.

Trying to come up with some means of helping them, Mathilde decided to visit the family of Ekaterina Sklavounos in Megara, about 28 miles from Athens. "Not that I had much hope, but you never know," Mathilde explains. Perhaps, she reasoned, they would be sympathetic because she had taken care of their dying mother. In any case, it was worth a try.

Arriving unannounced, Mathilde found that the family was still in mourning. Ekaterina's daughters told her that their mother, on her deathbed, had made them promise to do anything they could for the young nurse. Mathilde was somewhat surprised. "I had cared for her with exemplary devotion, watching over her for many nights without being able to help," she says, "But I did the same for many other patients who were seriously ill."

The grieving family asked Mathilde how they could repay her. Mathilde was silent for a moment, then, regaining her composure, quietly asked them to help her sister and brother-in-law. She waited apprehensively, intently studying the faces of Ekaterina's daughters. They responded that they would have to discuss it with their father.

When the father returned home that evening, his daughters took him aside for a private conference. A few moments later he stepped forward and said: "For Mathilde we shall do whatever we can. Welcome to our house. May Jesus protect you, and us as well."

The next morning, Mathilde brought her sister and brother-in-law to the Sklavounos house. "Crossing their threshold, I felt enveloped by an infinite peace, as if no evil would ever strike me," Bella states. From that moment on, she and her husband were under the care of an extended family that provided for all their needs—not just food and lodging, but clothing as well, made by two daughters who were seamstresses. Depending on the situation, Bella and her husband were moved from one relative's house to another, with the help of the local underground. No one ever asked for payment of any kind.

Eventually, when Megara became too dangerous because of partisan activity in the area, Bella and her husband were moved to a hideout in Athens. There they witnessed the liberation on October 12, 1944. They had been saved from deportation and almost certain death by people who previously had been complete strangers, and who risked their own lives to save them in fulfillment of a vow made to their mother on her deathbed. (3087)

George Kaloyeromitros and George Peanas

In the mountainous Greek countryside, many people offered hospitality to fleeing Jews. The following two stories from Thessaly illustrate this.

Abraham Barouch was born in Trikala, Thessaly. Trained as an accountant, he worked in the loan department of the local agrarian bank. There he met George Peanas, and over the years the two became friends. "We often went to the villages together on bank business to talk to the farmers and help them," Abraham recalls. "We tried to help them become more productive and thus more prosperous."

In April 1941, Italy occupied Thessaly. Under Italian administration the local Jews felt secure, but in September 1943, when the Germans moved in, they knew they were now in for a hard time and many fled to isolated mountain villages. A few days after the Germans arrived in Trikala, an S.S. officer called the town's Jewish community board (of which Abraham Barouch was a member) to his office and told them: "Don't be afraid. Don't listen to what they say about the Jews in Salonika; there is nothing to worry about."

And so it was, at least for the first few months. By March 1944, nothing untoward had happened, and many Jews, their initial fears allayed, had returned to Trikala from their mountain hideouts. "At the time, I was working at my regular job in the bank in order to survive. This was a period of tranquillity and calm before the storm."

Abraham and his family (Alice, his wife, and Sarah, his four-year-old daughter) lived in the home of George Kaloyeromitros, who operated a wholesale grocery business. When the Germans suddenly struck on March 23, 1944, the Jews of Trikala were taken by surprise. At 4:30 a.m. Kaloyeromitros awakened Abraham with the bad tidings: "City hall just called and told me that at this very moment the Germans are arresting every Jew in town. Save yourself and your family." Abraham was beside himself with fear and uncertainty. "What were we to do?" he recalls. "Run? But how? There was a curfew in effect until 10:00 a.m. Our minds were confused and our bodies paralyzed." But Kaloyeromitros helped them to find at least a temporary respite, taking Alice and Sarah to a neighbor's house nearby.

As the day dawned, Abraham looked out the window and saw George Peanas on his way to the bank. Abraham approached him cautiously and asked for help. "Don't worry," Peanas replied; "I'll go to the bank to give the keys to the custodian and will be back in five minutes. Stay where you are."

Peanas returned as promised and took the Barouchs to a house outside the town. After resting there for a while, they went on to the village of Megala Kalevya, where Peanas left them with some members of the resistance. Then began a peregrination for Abraham, Alice, and the child through villages like Tsagale, Prodromos, Kore, and Gorgyoiri, moving ever higher in the mountains and from time to time meeting other Jews in hiding. Wherever they went the villagers, priests, and underground members helped them, and George Kaloyeromitros regularly supplied them with bread and cheese, which was in short supply in the mountains.

As the weeks turned into months, Abraham worked as a bookkeeper for the resistance in exchange for food and and other necessities.

When the ringing of church bells in the towns announced the German withdrawal in October 1944, the Barouchs returned home. "We came down to Trikala from the mountains and what we found was joy and sorrow. Joy because we were free at last, and sorrow for the loss of so many innocent loved ones." Abraham was especially thankful to George Kaloyeromitros and George Peanas for helping him to elude the Germans and avoid the fate of his forty relatives who were deported to the camps, of whom only four survived. (3699, 3700)

Stavros Diamantis

The village of Stomio is situated about 31 miles from Larisa, at the foot of Mount Kissavos. It is near the sea, about 8 miles from the main highway between Athens and Salonika.

During the German occupation four Jewish families, a total of twenty-five persons, discovered that Stomio was an ideal hiding place. The families of David Ezra Moissis, Isaac Eshkenazy, and Isaac Cohen from Larissa and of Isaac Shiaky from Salonika were brought to Stomio by Stavros Diamantis, a resistance leader. They remained there from September 1943 until March—April 1945, several months after the area was liberated.

"We were given a brotherly welcome by the inhabitants, who provided us with shelter, food, protection, and and every other kind of assistance necessary for our survival," says Ezra Moissis. "We used Christian names, even though everyone knew we were Jews and were persecuted."

Each of the Jewish families hiding in Stomio was given a small plot of land to cultivate; in addition, several became fishermen. Ezra Moissis served as secretary of the community in return for a nominal salary.

When the Germans issued a warning against offering shelter to Jews, the head of the village ordered them to leave, but Diamantis persuaded him to change his mind. On one occasion, when German troops came to the village, they were assured that there were no Jews in the area by a village spokeman who was himself a Jew. (3755)

* * *

On Rhodes, Corfu, and the other Greek islands, as on the mainland, there were many instances of humane and even heroic conduct on behalf of Jews threatened by the Nazis. In July 1944, for example, when the Germans began rounding up the Jews of Rhodes, the Turkish consul-general, Selahattin Ulkumen, interceded on behalf of those who were Turkish nationals. Thanks to his efforts, forty-five people were set free and thus spared the fate which the other 1,500 Rhodian Jews met at Auschwitz. (4128)

Selahattin Ulkumen, center, *receiving the Righteous Certificate of Honor from Mr. R. Dafni (1970). At* right, *Dr. M. Paldiel. Courtesy of Yad Vashem.*

Lucas Karreri and Bishop Chrysostomos

The following tale, perhaps the most beautiful of these humanitarian manifestations, makes a fitting close to the chapter.

The Jews of Zakinthos (Zante), in the Ionian Sea, and their Christian neighbors had lived on friendly terms for several centuries. During the early years of the war the island was garrisoned by Italians, but on September 9, 1943, German troops took over.

When the Germans demanded that the municipal government provide the names of the island's 275 Jews to facilitate rounding them up, Lucas Karreri, the mayor, refused to cooperate. He was accompanied to the office of the German commander by Bishop Chrysostomos, the island's prelate, who implored: "The Jews of Zakinthos are Greeks, peaceloving and industrious. They are totally harmless. I beg of you to rescind this criminal order." The German remained adamant. Undaunted, the bishop wrote his own name on an otherwise blank piece of paper, handed it to him, and said, "Here is a list of the Jews of Zakinthos. I am at your mercy. Arrest me, not them. If you still insist on arresting the Jews, then know that I will march to the concentration camp along with them." Taken aback by the bishop's bold stand, the German dismissed the two men, saying he would inform his superior officer and await further orders.

That evening every one of the island's 275 Jews was escorted into the hills, where the people of Zakinthos hid them and took care of them until the departure of the Germans on September 12, 1944, nearly a year later. As a result of this unprecedented act of humanity by virtually the entire populace of the island, the Jewish community of Zakinthos was the only one in Greece that had the same number of souls after the war as it did before. Not one Jew was lost. That this was so was due in the main to the courageous leadership of Mayor Karreri and Bishop Chrysostomos. (1257)

Archbiship Chrysostomos, who was instrumental in rescuing the Jewish community of Zakinthou, Greece. Courtesy of Yad Vashem.

Italy

By now the reader is familiar with Fascist Italy's refusal, in spite of its alliance with Nazi Germany, to lend a hand in the destruction of the Jewish people. He may therefore be led to conclude that no form of anti-Jewish persecution existed on the Italian mainland, and be surprised to learn that Italy initiated antisemitic legislation in 1938, before the onset of the war, an act which heralded the country's rapprochement with Nazi Germany. And yet, in spite of this ominous augury for Italy's Jews, the top military and diplomatic hierarchy strenuously exerted itself to uphold the rights of Jews in the Italian-occupied countries and territories. We witness the paradox of the top echelon of the Italian hierarchy almost furiously contending for the civic rights of Jews making questionable claims of Italian nationality, while at the same time disenfranchising its own centuries-old mainland Jews. Be that as it may, Fascist Italy, a staunch ally of Nazi Germany, remained obdurately opposed to the Final Solution of the Jewish Question in the form it took under Nazi auspices. Discriminatory measures, yes; inhumane treatment, let alone mass killings, certainly not.

Mussolini, a master opportunist when it came to propping up his tottering empire, vacillated on the question of how to treat the Jews, preferring his generals and administrators to act in a way which pleased them best. This led to a form of official antisemitism in Italy which, in the context of other Nazi-dominated countries, made it (and the Italian-conquered territories) a haven, a paradise indeed, for thousands of fleeing Jews.

Up to 1938, the Fascist government did nothing to jeopardize the social and legal equality enjoyed by the country's 47,000 Jews. Many Jews occupied important positions in the Fascist hierarchy, although the movement was not very popular among the rank and file of the highly

353

assimilated Jewish population. But Italy's alignment with Nazi Germany after the Ethiopian campaign (1936—39) forced the Fascist leadership to take at least one giant step in the direction of official antisemitism. The November 1938 legislation placed severe civil and economic restrictions on Jews in all spheres of public activity, reducing them to second-class citizens (and even lower). More painful was the provision stripping Italian citizenship from all Jews naturalized after January 1, 1919, who were henceforth to be considered as refugees.

With Italy's entry into the war in May 1940, foreign Jews were arrested and confined in various prisons and internment camps or forced to reside in specified localities. But here too the special Italian way prevailed. The sensibilities of those affected by these restrictions were generally taken into consideration and more humane methods used to lighten the burden of the victims of these measures. At the Ferramonti camp, for instance, one of fifteen such camps, prisoners were allowed to organize a nursery, library, school, theater, and synagogue. They held concerts and athletic events. They established baths, medical offices, and even a pharmacy. Other than localized antisemitic outbreaks, no further infringement on the rights of the 35,000 Jews (by then, some 12,000 Jews had emigrated elsewhere) occurred during the whole period up to the occupation of the country by Germany, following Italy's capitulation to the Allies on September 8, 1943. Up to then, not a single Jew was released to the Nazis for deportation, not even any of the German refugees on Italian soil. Quite on the contrary, while thousands were allowed freely to leave the country, other foreign Jews seeking refuge in Italy took their places (such as the 100 children, brought from Yugoslavia to the village of Nonantola, near Modena), in spite of prevailing anti-Jewish restrictions. This contrasts sharply with the behavior of Vichy France, which began delivering foreign Jews to the Nazis even before the occupation of that part of the country in November 1942.

In the occupied territories—Dalmatia and other regions of Croatia, Greece, and eight departments in southeastern France—the Italian army and diplomatic corps took exceptional measures, and resorted to every imaginable scheme and subterfuge, to resist repeated German demands for the deportation of Jews. Instructions from Rome were either ignored or rendered ineffective, to the annoyance of top German officials.

All this changed drastically with the occupation of Italy (more specifically, those parts from Rome north not yet liberated) by the Germans in September 1943. The Holocaust was set in full motion by a horde of German bureaucrats, aided by collaborating Fascist officials of the newly formed pro-Nazi regime (popularly known as the Salo Republic) headed by Mussolini, now only a German stooge with little power of his own.

A month later, the Germans struck in Rome. The target was the city's 8,000 Jews. In an "action" lasting two days, starting October 15, some 1,200 Jews were netted; most were dispatched to Auschwitz. The Germans were at first apprehensive because of the possible reaction of the pope and the Vatican hierarchy at this mass-scale operation literally under the walls of the pope's residence. These fears were allayed by the silence of the pope, although he is reported to have privately ordered that all religious houses be opened to fleeing Jews.

Local priests, monks, and nuns did not have to wait for such permission, but automatically admitted Jews to the security of their shrines and religious houses. The Germans were relieved. "The Pope," German ambassador Weizsacker wrote in a dispatch to Berin, "although reportedly beseeched by various sides, has not allowed himself to be drawn into any demonstrative statement against the deportation of the Jews of Rome. . . . He has done all he could in this delicate matter not to strain relations with the German Government and German circles in Rome," the German diplomat happily noted. Pius XII allowed German-born Bishop Hudal to urge the stoppage of the deportation "in the interests of the good relations which have existed until now between the Vatican and the German High Command." Unimpressed with these sanctimonious protestations by a lower church cleric, the Germans continued to press on with the deportation of the Jews.

In the following months, the Germans and their Fascist allies shifted their attention to other cities; Genoa, Florence, Milan, Venice, and Ferrara. What was advertised as a move to confine all Jews in local camps was a veritable deportation operation, with trains carrying their consignments of human cargo to the Auschwitz killing facility. All told, some 6,800 were deported, or 15 percent of the total 45,000 Jews in Italy in late 1943. The other 85 percent were saved.

Several reasons have been advanced to explain this relatively high rescue rate. It is suggested that the relatively late occupation period for Italy (Rome, for instance, was under direct German occupation for only nine months), coupled with the hatred of the Italians toward the Germans, combined to reduce the Holocaust casualty figure in Italy when compared with other occupied countries.

In addition, there can be little doubt that the rescue of 85 percent of Italy's Jews can be safely attributed to the massive support extended to fleeing Jews by the overwhelming majority of the Catholic clergy (without in most cases even waiting for clearance by their superiors) as well as of persons from all walks of life, even of officials and militiamen within the more intensely Fascist Salo regime.

Although there were not lacking pro-Nazi militiamen and denouncers to make life for Jews miserable and hazardous, there were by far more persons, of all professions, economic classes, and walks of life, prepared to undergo great risks to themselves and their families, by offering shelter to Jews in their homes or institutions (mainly religious), help in acquiring false credentials as well as guidance in escaping through hazardous and closely watched mountain passes to Switzerland, which at the time had moderated its previous anti-refugee admittance policy.

Some 6,000 Jews availed themselves of this opportunity and were allowed, sometimes begrudgingly, temporary asylum in Switzerland. However, the majority of Jews remained hidden on occupied Italian soil, out of reach of Nazi hands through the help of many segments of the Italian people. In this great humanitarian effort, the role of the clergy was of inestimable importance. In no other occupied Catholic country were monasteries, convents, shrines, and religious houses opened to fleeing Jews, and their needs attended to, without any overt intention to steer them away from their ancient faith, but solely to abide by the preeminent religious command of the sanctity of life. Through this, they epitomized the best and most elevated form of religious faith and human fidelity.

* * *

Italy is the seat of the Roman Catholic Church, and as the five following stories attest, many of the rescues that took place there were performed by members of the Catholic clergy.

Don Arrigo Beccari

In July 1942, a group of fifty Jewish children arrived in the village of Nonantola, near Bologna, from Dalmatia in the Italian zone of Yugoslavia. With the help of DELASEM, the Jewish communal welfare agency, they were housed in the Villa Emma together with fifty other children. Josef Itai, their leader, became friendly with Don Arrigo Beccari, a teacher at the Catholic seminary in the village.

Nonantola had seemed a safe place to sit out the war, but when Italy surrendered and the Germans overran the country, a reign of terror began for the Jews. In order to keep the children at the Villa Emma from falling into German hands, Beccari, without consulting his superiors in Modena, took as many as possible into the seminary and arranged for the others to be housed with friendly villagers. Food for all of them was provided by the seminary's kitchen.

Since the Nazis were methodically searching all schools and welfare institutions for hidden Jews, the children and their adult leaders, a total of 120 persons, had to be moved somewhere else. When a plan to sneak them through the German lines to the Allied forces in the south proved to be unworkable, it was decided to take them to Switzerland.

With the help of Dr. Giuseppe Moreali, Nonantola's physician, all 120 Jews were provided with documents identifying them as Italians. Then they boarded a train for the Swiss frontier, taking a terrible but unavoidable chance, for most of them could not speak Italian and even with impeccable papers would never have passed a police check. Luck was on their side, however, for no one bothered them, and on Yom Kippur eve of 1943 the group passed safely into Switzerland.

The Gestapo, discovering what had happened, seized Beccari and held him in the prison at Bologna. Despite the tortures inflicted upon him over the next few months, he refused to say who had helped him or to reveal the whereabouts of other Jews in hiding. Years later he wrote: "It would be difficult for me to erase the memory of the terror and suffering of those days or of my joy at doing the small good which was my duty and which had to be done." (35, 36)

Father Rufino Nicacci and Don Aldo Brunacci

About 150 miles south of Nonantola, in the Apennines range, stands the town of Assisi, with its many shrines, monasteries, and religious institutions devoted to the memory of St. Francis, the founder of the Franciscan order and principal patron of Italy.

Soon after the German occupation began in September 1943, Padre Rufino Nicacci, father-guardian of the San Damiano monastery, was given an unprecedented and dangerous assignment by Msgr. Giuseppe Placido Nicolini, the bishop of Assisi. A group of Jews from Trieste had just arrived in town. He wanted Father Nicacci to find places for them to stay until they could get out of the country.

Father Nicacci was a country friar who had never been far from his home village. He had never even met a Jew, and until this moment had led a quiet life with no need to make tough decisions. But now, tapping inner resources few would have suspected him of possessing, he arranged for 200 Jews to be provided with false credentials, hidden in private homes, and smuggled out of the country or given sanctuary in monasteries and convents. In one of the latter the nuns followed the dietary laws when preparing food for their Jewish guests, prompting a journalist to later comment that "Assisi could boast the only convent in the world with a kosher kitchen."

Also involved in the rescue operation was Don Aldo Brunacci, a professor canon at the San Rufino Cathedral. As titular head of the operation, which ultimately came to include far more than the original 200 Jews, he insisted that the Convent of the Stigmata and other cloisters open their gates to Jews. He also organized a clandestine school where Jewish children received religious instruction from Jewish teachers. In May 1944 he was arrested, but after the Vatican intervened was released on condition that he keep out of Assisi for the duration of the war.

Among the many Jews who sought refuge in Assisi were Miriam Viterbi, her parents, and her older sister. Born in 1933 in Padua, Miriam belonged to a family that had settled in Italy after the fifteen-century expulsion from Spain or, according to some accounts, in Roman times. Her father was a professor of photochemistry (experimenting with infrared processes) at the University of Padua, until his dismissal in 1938, and one of her grandfathers, a rabbi, had been the city's deputy mayor.

When the Germans took over Padua, the Viterbis fled southward. Miriam's father told her at the time that they were going to Assisi because legend said that St. Francis had been of Jewish ancestry and had composed a prayer modeled on the traditional priestly blessing. Now an adult, she realizes that the reputation of the city's mayor, Arnaldo Fontini, as a historian and a humanist was probably a more important factor.

The Viterbis arrived in Assisi on October 10, 1943. They stayed at the Il Sole Hotel for a month, then, with the help of two priests, Father Nicacci and Father Brunacci, found a place of their own at a reasonable price. After they moved the police visited the hotel a few times to find out where they were, but learned nothing from the owner, who had helped the priests relocate them.

Throughout their stay in Assisi, Mayor Fontini warned the Viterbis whenever a Nazi raid was in the offing. Miriam has many vivid memories of this period. She was in Father Brunacci's house when the Germans came to arrest him, but luckily for her they did not search the building. She also still recalls the break-the-fast meal prepared by the Sisters at one of the convents on Yom Kippur.

The Viterbis had originally been issued new papers under the name of Varelli, but these turned out to be defective and had to be replaced. Their new papers, provided by Brizzi, a local printer, changed their name to Vitelli and gave Lecce as their place of residence. Since this town was in the south, and thus in Allied hands, there was no way for anyone to check up on them.

The Viterbis were just one among many hundreds of Jewish families who found a refuge in Assisi. Remarkably, not one of them was betrayed, nor did any of the priests and nuns who helped them make even the slightest conversionary effort.

Before the war Jews had almost never gone to Assisi because of its many shrines and intensely Catholic atmosphere. During the war the townspeople stood together to help Jews, and the town's sanctity was called upon as an aid of sorts. It is said, for example, that when Bishop Nicolini had to conceal counterfeit papers while waiting for Jews to pick them up, he put them behind the portrait of the Madonna hanging over his desk, regarding it as both a secure hiding place and a source of blessing.

Father Brunacci wrote after the war: "In all, about 200 Jews were entrusted to us by Divine Providence. With God's help, and through the intercession of St. Francis, not one of them fell into the hands of their persecutors." (876, 1235, 1236)

Father Giovanni Simione and Father Angelo Della Torre

On September 8, 1943, the day the Nazis occupied northern Italy, Father Letto Casini, in Florence, gave sanctuary in his church to twelve Jewish women from France and Germany with their children. When he was arrested soon afterward, Father Giovanni Simione, then aged twenty-eight, took over from him as the group's protector.

Described by Mina Goldman, one of the twelve, as "our guardian angel, dedicated and prepared for the greatest self-sacrifice," Father Simione took the women to a convent. Only three of the nuns knew who they were, but when the Germans began searching religious houses, the convent became too dangerous, so they had to leave.

He moved them to a tunnel-like cellar that they nicknamed the "catacomb." The group stayed there for several weeks, but conditions were almost unbearable because of the dampness and lack of air, and Mrs. Goldman says, "I can still see him, his eyes wet with tears, sadly pacing back and forth, and struggling with his conscience. Suddenly coming to a stop, he said out loud: 'No, I cannot leave you here. You shall all come with me. I hope that merciful God will come to my aid.'"

Father Simione decided to take the women to his hometown of Treviso, near Venice, about 150 miles north of Florence. The journey was not without risks, for one of the women was in the last month of pregnancy and none of them spoke Italian well enough to pass a checkpoint. Footing the bill himself though his monthly stipend was quite modest, Father Simione had the pregnant woman admitted to a hospital, where she delivered a boy. Then, temporarily breaking the group up, he escorted the women to Treviso by twos and threes. Once there he was able to obtain help from two other priests, Father Angelo Della Torre and Father Giuseppe De Zotti.

Father Della Torre was especially devoted to the women, one of whom later wrote: "What didn't he do for us? As soon as we were assigned a room [in a convent], he brought us proper beds and kitchen utensils . . . even his mother's gas stove, as well as monthly allotments for various necessities, at a time of general scarcity for the population at large."

During the cold winter months Father Della Torre gave the women his monthly coal ration. When this was not enough, he "liberated" some more from the seminary's coal bin. And even though his allowance was as small as Father Simione's, he bought new leather shoes for the son of one of the women as a Passover gift.

In her deposition, Mina Goldman said: "We owe our lives to Don Giovanni Simione and Don Angelo Della Torre." Asked during the war why they were willing to take such risks for the sake of total strangers, Fathers Simione and Della Torre replied: "Why are we priests, if not to help the needy?" Father Simione, a man of strong faith, was the rescue operation's energizing force. "He gave us hope and taught us not to despair," says Ruth Mayer. (174)

Father Giulio Gradassi

Dr. Rubin Pick and his family, refugees from Poland, lived in Trieste until September 1943, but with the arrival of the Germans they set out for Rome, hoping to obtain protection from the Polish chargé d'affaires at the Vatican. On the way through Florence they asked a priest for road directions. Warning that traveling farther south would be too dangerous, he sent them to a brother priest at the Church of Santa Felicia.

The second priest took them in, but as the Nazis stepped up their searches for Jews hiding in the city, he became uneasy. Torn between fear if they stayed in the church and reluctance to betray the trust he had undertaken, he discussed the problem, one day at lunch, with a colleague, Don Giulio Gradassi. Father Gradassi, in response, took the Picks home with him to Castelione, boarding Dr. Pick in his own church and Dr. Pick's wife and daughter in a nearby convent.

Father Gradassi tended his three charges with love and courage. One night in December 1943, ill with bronchitis, he rode about on his bicycle in a freezing rain to find a new place for the women when a raid forced them to leave the convent. Returning late at night, coughing and with a high temperature, he happily informed them that he had found a host family. The following month, when the hosts changed their minds, he again biked through the countryside to find them a refuge. When Passover came in the spring of 1944, Father Gradassi surprised the Picks with a gift of matzot that he had secretly baked for them.

Don Giulio Gradassi was just one of the untold Italian priests who saved thousands of Jewish lives during the German occupation. (929)

Father Beniamino Schivo

In 1935 Paul and Johanna Korn, and their daughter Ursula, fled from Germany to the Italian Riviera and purchased a hotel in Alassia. When the war broke out in 1939 they were interned as aliens. Paul was taken to a camp in Salerno, Johanna and Ursula to several places in Umbria and finally to Collazzone, where they were befriended by the local priest. In 1941, on the eve of their transfer to Citta di Castello, where they were to be reunited with Paul, the priest told them to look up Father Beniamino Schivo when they got there. The Korn family's meeting with Father Schivo, who was the rector of the seminary in Citta di Castello, proved to be of momentous importance for them. In Ursula's words: "From that moment, Father Schivo became our protector, our one and only and best friend. . . . In every way, endangering his own life, he saved our lives, and he did so time and again, for he is the kindest man I have ever met." Father Schivo made sure that his newfound Jewish charges had adequate food and clothing, and arranged for Ursula to continue her schooling. Thanks to his assistance life was bearable despite the many restrictions on Jews in

Mussolini's Italy, but in September 1943, with the beginning of the German occupation, the situation changed. Now, for the first time, their lives were in danger. With Father Schivo's help, however, the Korns escaped. "He took off his habit and together with another young priest, in the dark of night, led us past the German patrols and up into the hills to a summer villa owned by the Salesian nuns. He broke in a side door, and we hid there for a month in the dark with all the windows closed, sleeping on the bare floor." Schivo arranged for a caretaker to bring the Korns some soup every midnight. When partisan activities in the area and Allied bombings made the villa unsafe, Father Schivo took them farther into the hills. On Christmas eve of 1943, he undertook a nine-hour nighttime hike through hilly terrain patrolled by the Germans to comfort his charges in their mountain hideaway. As advance units of the British Eighth Army moved in and fighting began in the surrounding countryside, Paul Korn joined an Italian partisan unit and Father Schivo took Ursula and her mother to a new hiding place outside the battle zone. Soon afterward he took them to the Convent of the Sacred Heart in Citta di Castello, where the mother superior provided them with nuns' habits and hid them in a locked room so that no one else would discover their presence. When the Germans searched the convent looking for partisans, Father Schivo slipped them out and hid them in an upstairs room of his seminary. Citta di Castello soon became the scene of bloody street fighting between British troops and the retreating Germans. Busy as he was with the many wounded, and always having to dodge the Germans because he was on their blacklist and they would have shot him on sight, Father Schivo visited the two women every night, bringing encouragement and food. The city was liberated on July 14, 1944. Three months later, when the Allies took over the area where his partisan unit was operating, Paul Korn rejoined his wife and daughter. Writing in 1985 from her home in the United States, Ursula said of Father Schivo: "I have never met a more wonderful, compassionate, and courageous man in my entire life. In his humility he does not for a moment feel that he did anything special by saving us. He says it is his duty to help those who are suffering. . . . My friendship with Monsignor (elevated to this rank after the war) Schivo will last as long as I live; he is my best friend." (3362)

* * *

The next two stories illustrate the role of Italian laymen in the rescue of Jews.

Ezio Giorgetti

On September 11, 1943, three days after Italy surrendered, a group of forty Jews from Asolo, province of Treviso, set out in three cars and made for the Allied lines in southern Italy. Mostly of Yugoslavian origin, they had come to Asolo from Dalmatia in 1941. Among them was Dr. Ziga Neumann, an attorney, who together with his wife had escaped from a concentration camp near Zagreb. When the group got to Bellaria, a town on the Adriatic coast near Rimini, Dr. Neumann, as their representative, went to see the Giorgettis, a prominent hotelier family, with a letter of introduction from a countess in Asolo. Asked by his father to find accommodations for the group, Ezio Giorgetti decided to reopen the Hotel Savoia, which had just closed down at the end of the summer vacation season. It was agreed that the group would pay a nominal fee for their board and would stay there until the liberation, which was expected momentarily. Soon after this, for military reasons, the Germans decided to clear all civilians out of the area where the Savoia was located. As a result, and with the unspoken connivance of the local gendarmerie commander, Osman Carguno, Ezio moved them to an empty hotel near Bellaria. When this too proved untenable, he moved them, with some furniture from the hotel, to an empty farmhouse and then to another empty hotel, the Pension Italia, telling the owner that Neumann and his companions were refugees from southern Italy. "The moment we put up at the Pension Italia, our financial relationship with Mr. Ezio Giorgetti came to an end," wrote Josef Konforti, one of the group's leaders. "Previously we might have thought that his actions had been motivated by an interest in prolonging the hotel season. But a close bond had formed between him and us through all our daily contacts, and for Mr. Ezio Giorgetti our destiny and his now somehow became linked." From then on, Ezio laid aside all considerations of profit and loss and made the group's survival his chief concern. His parents urged him to let them go, but he was adamant. In Konforti's words: "He did not falter for even a moment. He kept on advising and helping us, putting us in touch with the clergy, with the anti-fascist elements, and with the authorities in neighboring San Marino, and bringing medical help whenever required." All this was done without any remuneration; Ezio paid for everything out of his own pocket, sometimes neglecting the needs of his wife and children to do so. In the spring of 1944, with German and Italian Fascist officers frequently staying at the hotel, Ezio moved the group to the mountains behind San Marino and arranged for them to board with peasants in and around several local villages. After they were settled, despite the strict German controls that made it difficult to get around, he visited them regularly to see to their needs, and kept doing so until the liberation. At the conclusion of his testimony Dr. Neumann writes: "I am telling the unvarnished truth when I say that Ezio's help, personal sacrifice, and devotion saved the whole group, including my family and parents, from death at the hands of the Nazis." (51, 2763)

Lydia Cattaneo

We end with a story about an escape into Switzerland. In 1943 the seven members of the Weiss family were living in the resort town of Abbasia, near Fiume, in northeastern Italy. Irene Weiss had a friend who was an officer in the Italian army, and soon after Mussolini's fall he told her that his unit had decided to join the partisans. Before parting he gave Irene a letter addressed to his sister, Lydia Cattaneo, who lived in Bergamo, not far from the Swiss border, with instructions to contact her if she and her family ever needed help. The need arose when the Germans occupied northern Italy and launched a hunt for Jews. Hoping they would be protected by the anonymity of a big city, the Weiss family waited in Trieste while Irene went to Bergamo. Lydia and her family, Irene writes, "welcomed me with open arms, and embraced me as a token of protection. I was welcomed into her family. Lydia insisted that my whole family join me in her home, promising to hide us while making arrangements for our crossing into Switzerland." To show that she meant what she said, Lydia obtained new papers for the Weiss family and accompanied Irene to Trieste. When they were all safely back in Bergamo, Lydia set about finding some reliable smugglers. Since the Cattaneos were well off and money was no object, this did not prove difficult. In January 1944, several days before the appointed time, Irene broke her leg in an automobile accident. Insisting that the border crossing go ahead as planned, Irene stayed behind while Lydia accompanied the others to their late-night rendezvous with the smugglers. She joined them in Switzerland in May 1945 after the German surrender, but in the preceding months survived several close calls when Fascist militiamen searched the Cattaneo house after receiving tips that a stranger was hiding there. In a separate testimony, Irene's cousin Sarah Jakobowitz tells how she and ten other members of her family fled from Fiume to Bagnacavallo, an isolated village near Ravenna, in September 1943. Here they were taken in by Vincenze Tambini and several of his friends. Several weeks later some compassionate policemen warned that the authorities were planning to sweep the area for Jews. The night before the raid Mrs. Aurelia Tambini took Sarah and a few other members of the family to the home of another peasant, Antonio Dalla Valle. They stayed there for several more weeks, and every day the Tambinis visited with food for them. Several members of the Jakobowitz family were living elsewhere, and two of them were arrested. Under intensive interrogation they told everything. When Sarah and the others learned that their whereabouts were known, they fled to Lydia Cattaneo's house in Bergamo, having been given her name by Irene. Lydia arranged for them to go to Switzerland and accompanied them, on a train packed with German soldiers, to their meeting with the smugglers she had hired. The border crossing went off without a hitch except that elderly Leora Weiss sprained her ankle and was unable to go on. The smugglers hid her in the forest and got in touch with Lydia, who found her a place to stay until her ankle was healed and then had her taken into Switzerland. "I wish I were capable of describing Mrs. Cattaneo's dedication and courage in more moving terms," Sarah Jakobowitz writes, "but everything she did for me, my family, and other Jews placed her in great danger and was not done for monetary considerations but because of the highest ideals, involving the rescue of lives from the Nazi grasp." (871, 872)

Norway and Denmark

Nazi ideologues regarded the peoples of Scandinavia as Aryans and hence as natural partners in the creation of a new racial order in Europe. Germany conquered Norway and Denmark in 1940 and at first treated their inhabitants more or less considerately because of their Nordic blood. For the time being they also left the minuscule Jewish communities of the two countries alone. The goal of making Norway and Denmark *Judenrein* remained, however, and by the end of 1942 the Nazis were ready. They struck first at the Jews of Norway.

Norway

In April 1940, the Jewish populace of Norway numbered some 1,800 persons. Nearly 150 of them had managed to leave the country by October 1942, when the collaborationist government headed by Vidkung Quisling began arresting Jews for deportation to Germany, temporarily holding them in camps outside Oslo. Almost simultaneously the Norwegian underground undertook to help as many Jews as possible escape to neutral Sweden, while on November 10 the country's Lutheran Church officially condemned the persecution.

Between October 1942 and February 1943 about 800 Norwegian Jews were smuggled into Sweden. The remaining 760 were deported to Germany, 530 of them leaving for Stettin on the liner *Donau* on November 26, 1942. Except for 60 intermarried Jews who were held in a special camp until March 1945 and then allowed to go to Sweden, the country was completely *Judenrein*.

In saving what amounted to about half of Norway's Jewish population, the underground faced a daunting task. To begin with, a German decree of October 12, 1942 made death the penalty for helping a Jew to escape, and by the time the rescue operation was over, several participating resistance members had been executed and a number of others imprisoned.

Secondly, the logistics of a rescue operation were complicated. Prospective victims had to be warned of imminent raids, then be safely removed from their homes and provided with safe temporary hiding places. In some cases, new identity documents were needed, as were changes in physical appearance, such as dyeing "semitic" dark hair blonde. Where small children were involved, sleeping pills were sometimes necessary to keep them quiet.

Transportation to the Swedish border was also a problem. Generally trucks were used, but it was necessary to be on the lookout for patrols and frontier guards, and as the journey was a long one, overnight accommodations had to be provided for the passengers, and also for the drivers and guides. There were sometimes as many as fifteen or twenty underground members for each group of escapees.

The methods of crossing the Swedish border were quite diverse. Some escapees crossed into Sweden by the usual motor routes, hidden amid shipments of furniture, agricultural produce, hay, or bags of cement. Others were dropped off before reaching the frontier and then were rowed across the narrow Svinesund Fjord or boated from ports southwest of Oslo to the Swedish coastal town of Bohusiän. Still others crossed the border on foot, despite the intense winter cold.

One escape operation that attracted considerable attention involved fourteen children from the Jewish orphan home in Oslo. On November 25, 1942, the administrator of the home learned that the children were slated for deportation on the *Donau*, which was scheduled to depart Oslo harbor the next morning. She immediately informed the underground. Within a couple of hours the children had been removed from the orphanage and hidden in a village outside Oslo. Over the next few days they were taken to a point not far from the border and then guided across on foot.

Some refugees crossed the frontier on skis. One of them was Irene Klein, originally from Germany, who took skiing lessons expressly for the purpose of making the escape attempt. On the verge of arrest by the authorities, she and her four-year-old daughter were taken across some frozen lakes on a chair sled and embarked on a small passenger boat that took them to the other side of the Trondheim Fjord. A strenuous three-day trek through some hilly countryside followed, and then, accompanied by a guide and carrying her child in a rucksack, Irene began a long overland journey on skis, with occasional stops enroute at friendly farmsteads. Two months later she arrived safely in Sweden.

In addition to the 900-odd Jews who escaped from Norway to Sweden, a few made it to the Shetland Islands or Scotland, crossing the North Sea in small boats with other Norwegian refugees. Virtually all of the escapees from Norway were helped by non-Jews. A few typical stories follow.

Ingebjorg Sletten

Rabbi Julius Samuel and his wife, Henriette, had emigrated to Norway from Hitler's Germany and lived in Oslo. As the country's chief rabbi, Julius Samuel was arrested during the initial roundups and in October 1942 was returned to Germany. Several days later Ingebjorg Sletten, a neighbor of the Samuels' and also a member of the underground, phoned Henriette with a prearranged warning: "It's very cold tonight. Make sure that your children are covered."

Henrietta immediately got herself and her three children ready to leave. Less than an hour later Ingebjorg called for them and brought them to a house outside Oslo where several other people were already hiding. They remained there until the night of December 3–4, when they joined a group of about forty Jews who were being moved to a point near the Swedish border hidden in several trucks loaded with potatoes. After leaving the trucks they struck out on foot, in a temperature of 20 degrees below zero (Celsius), and made their way into Sweden. Rabbi Samuel was less fortunate than his wife and children; he perished in a German concentration camp.

Hans Christian Mamen

In early November 1942, the Germans launched a roundup of all able-bodied Jewish men in Oslo, but Felix Adler escaped because while at work he received a warning from his wife, Edith, not to return home. Through some friends, Edith Adler then got in touch with Hans-Christian Mamen, an underground agent, and later that night he took the Adlers to the home of the Eriksmoen family somewhere outside Oslo. "They welcomed us with open arms," Edith writes, and refused to accept any payment when the Adlers left a week later. From the Eriksmoen house the Adlers were taken to a farm, and after a week there they returned to Oslo by train. By then Mamen had made arrangements for the final stages of their escape. In accordance with Mamen's instructions, the Adlers boarded a bus heading for a town near the Norwegian-Swedish border. Mamen was on the same bus but took a separate seat and pretended not to know them. Everything went well at first, but when the bus reached the security zone near the frontier, two plainclothes policemen got on and began checking IDs. "To enter the zone you had to have a pass, which of course we didn't," says Edith.

There had been no time for the underground to obtain new papers for the Adlers, so they had no alternative but to produce their passports with the letter *J* stamped on them. To their surprise and relief, the two policemen "studied our passports for a long time without saying anything. Then they returned them to us and left."

The bus continued its journey and at a prearranged point Mamen and the Adlers got off and joined a group of eight other people who were waiting for them in the shadows. Underground guides led the group on foot to a small lake, rowed them across, and put them up at a nearby farmhouse. The next morning, after a hearty breakfast, Hans-Christian Mamen, the Adlers, and the other refugees hiked across some difficult terrain, aided by friendly woodcutters who had been alerted that they would be coming by.

Eventually the group crossed into Sweden. Once they were safely there, Hans-Christian Mamen returned to Norway to continue his underground work. Meanwhile, Swedish frontier guards took them to a military post. "We got coffee, milk, and white bread—things we hadn't had for a long time—and then a truck took us further into Sweden," where they remained until the end of the war, saved from the Nazis by Mamen's courage, and the compassion of two anonymous policemen.

Hans-Christian Mamen was involved in many other rescue operations. On one occasion, while he was taking three Jews to the Swedish frontier by bus, an incident occurred that was very much like what had happened to the Adlers.

A police car suddenly cut off the bus and forced it to stop. Two policemen got on. They began checking identity cards, and as they did so, one of the three Jews, sitting just behind the driver, turned toward Mamen with a terrified expression on his face.

Sitting in the rear of the bus, and pretending to read a theology book, Mamen watched out of the corner of his eye as the policeman asked for the man's papers. "He looked frightened and helpless," says Mamen. "My hands were damp. The man began fumbling for his identity card. He had typically Semitic features, and for that reason we had not provided him with a new card, for if he were caught it would only mean that many other people would end up in trouble."

The policeman studied the card, then said curtly, "I'll take care of you later." The other policeman came over, and the two of them whispered together for a few moments while Mamen and the Jew watched anxiously. Unexpectedly, one policeman said to the other, "Okay, let's go," and they left the bus without saying another word.

Sitting in the back with his book, Mamen heaved a sigh of relief. "I clasped my hands and gave thanks to God for the policeman who had performed his duty to mankind by sabotaging the tyranny."

During another rescue operation, Mamen, who became a minister after the war, carried the three-year-old son of a Jewish dentist in his arms during the long cross-country trek to Sweden. "I still remember how fiercely he gripped my hair," he says, "and how he bent his head and looked at me with his dark eyes. A son of Abraham and a good Norwegian boy he was."

Commenting on this incident, but also on his other efforts to save Jews, Hans-Christian Mamen later wrote: "The meaning was that this little boy and all of his race could have been killed. But he was saved from the gas chamber. Many people had contributed to this escape. . . . It was November 1942, and darkness ruled Europe. In Amsterdam, Anne Frank was hiding in an attic. In every country there were Jews in hiding. But more than six million people failed to escape. It was like a nightmare."

In 1977 Yad Vashem decided to honor all the members of the Norwegian underground who had aided Jews. In a special ceremony in Oslo that year, the Israeli ambassador presented the Righteous Among the Nations Medal to several representatives of the underground, to be put on display in the Home Front Museum in Oslo. After the presentation, former underground leader Ole Borge reponded: "It was a natural duty to save our countrymen." The following year, a delegation of former underground members planted a tree on behalf of the Norwegian underground in the Garden of the Righteous at Yad Vashem. (70, 616a, 1248)

Denmark

In Denmark, immediately to the north of Germany, the Jews enjoyed an unprecedented respite till late 1943. Upon their take-over of Denmark, in April 1940, the Germans announced that they would respect the country's independence, permit the parliament to function, and even allow the army to retain its weapons, thereby awarding a degree of autonomy unusual for a region under German domination. In keeping with Denmark's nominal independence, the ranking German representative in the country was a diplomat rather than a military officer. At this early stage, any interference in Danish internal affairs was considered out of the question, and as a result Denmark's 8,000 Jews felt safe.

All this changed radically during the summer of 1943 as a result of stepped-up resistance activities. A state of emergency was declared and the Danish army was disbanded. When Dr. Werner Best, the German plenipotentiary, suggested that the new situation could be exploited as an opportunity to strike at the country's Jews, and asked for additional security personnel for this purpose, his superiors in Berlin responded favorably. On September 18 Berlin ordered the deportation of Denmark's entire Jewish populace. Secret plans were made for a massive roundup to take place on the night of October 1-2.

Georg Duckwitz, a German shipping expert in Copenhagen, learned about the forthcoming operation and told a prominent Danish acquaintance, who in turn alerted the head of the Jewish community. On September 29, when the country's Jews assembled in their synagogues for Rosh Hashanah services, they were given the bad news.

The Danish underground immediately swung into action. People from all walks of life participated in the massive rescue operation. Within but a few hours, virtually all of the Jews of Copenhagen, the country's largest Jewish community, were spirited out of their homes, hidden, and then taken in small groups to fishing ports on the Sund, a body of water ranging from five to fifteen miles in width that separates Denmark from Sweden. The entire Danish fishing fleet was mobilized to ferry them to safety on the opposite shore.

On October 1, when the Germans began their planned roundup, moving from house to house with prepared lists of victims, their knocks went unanswered and in most places they found no one at home. They apprehended only 477 Jews, all of whom were sent to Theresienstadt. Meanwhile, well into the middle of October, boats laden with Jews left the Copenhagen area and the harbor town of Gilleleje almost daily. Not a single one was intercepted by the Germans or sunk, and all told some 7,200 Jews were saved.

The rescue of Denmark's Jewry was the only instance, throughout all of occupied Europe, of a Nazi liquidation operation meeting with failure. Because so many Danes, of all ages, classes, and backgrounds, participated in this unprecedented rescue effort, Yad Vashem, as a special gesture, awarded the title of Righteous Among the Nations to the entire Danish people.

Dr. Gideon Hausner presenting the Righteous medal to Georg F. Duckwitz (1971). Courtesy of Yad Vashem.

Concluding Words

Left out in this study are rescue stories emanating from Romania and Bulgaria proper. In both these countries, the repressive nature of the previous communist regimes made it difficult to gather sufficient information from rescuers and rescued alike. It must also be remembered that the Holocaust in Romania was not as rigorous and thorough as in other East European countries, for reasons which are connected with the internal politics of the Fascist regime of Marshal Antonescu, as well as the lack of direct German control of the country. Jews, nevertheless, suffered tremendously in the new lands conquered by the Romanians, when they joined their ally, Nazi Germany, in the war on Russia in June 1941. Witness the pogrom at Iassy, where thousands perished at the hands of rampaging Romanian soldiers. Some, though, were saved through the benevolent help of other Romanians.

The Holocaust affected the Jews in Bulgaria to an even lesser extent, when due to the intervention of officials in the political and religious hierarchy, such as Dimitur Peshev's public protest over the persecution of Jews, the deportation of the country's Jews was scuttled at the eleventh hour. This, however, did not prevent the Bulgarian regime from playing an active role in the wholesale deportation of thousands of Jews from the occupied regions of Greater Bulgaria (Thrace and Macedonia).

As this book goes to press, more information is flowing to Yad Vashem on rescue stories in countries just recently liberated from the yoke of totalitarian communism. Forty-seven years after the end of the Holocaust, the search for signs of goodness, care, and lovingkindness for fellow man goes on; a search spearheaded by those who witnessed and lived through the Nazi hell.

They and the generations after the Holocaust are committed to the same goal: that the final word not remain with the Nazis and their demented philosophy; that man need not be a destructive creature; that

371

the weak need not go under to leave the field clear for the rule of the strong; that life need not be predicated on force alone; that might does not mean right; that there is more to life than nature's tangibles. For the sake of future generations, the final word ought to be with those who asserted their humanity under the most difficult circumstances imaginable, and gave us encouragement that the search for a better humanity is not at all a vain hope.

Afterword
A Burden of Honor

I am a Holocaust survivor and I know how I survived.

I was not murdered—as so many children were—because someone risked her life to save mine.

In that time of terror, tyranny, and fear, it took a special kind of person to help Jews. For most people, it seemed easier to turn away, to ignore the pervasive persecution and perhaps even to profit as accessories to the mass murders.

Nevertheless, there were a few brave people who dared to help Jews even though doing so placed their lives in jeopardy. We who were rescued can never forget our rescuers, nor the great debt we own them. It is a debt of honor that we can never really repay. That is how my family and I feel about the woman who saved me and that is how we feel about every rescuer.

Who were the rescuers? They represented the diversity of humanity. They were in all the countries swallowed up by the Nazis—some even wore German uniforms—and they were from all walks of life: workers, farmers, doctors, lawyers, teachers. Whatever their background, they were a special breed, righteous gentiles.

Sadly, little is known about the rescuers and their heroic deeds. In the aftermath of the war, when the focus was on the reconstruction of shattered lives and the building of Israel, they were not a priority even though we did not forget them.

It is important that the world should know the rescuers' stories. That is why this book is so important and so welcome. It is the most comprehensive and detailed account to date of the rescuers and their accomplishments. Although many of the stories have much in common, each is unique in many details.

The story of my rescue is a good example. People find it difficult to believe that my rescuer was a nursemaid in our home. My parents turned to her in desperation. She had been in their employ for a long time, had become much more than a servant. They knew her, trusted her, and believed they could depend on her. And so, in what must have been a heart-wrenching moment, they asked her to take care of me when they fled, trying to escape the Nazis.

For me, it was an abrupt change. I was still a boy and did not really understand what was happening. The presence of a familiar figure was reassuring. We moved from my comfortable home in a Jewish neighborhood into a small apartment in a Catholic working-class area. I went to church. Instead of learning the *alephbet*, I was taught the catechism. And I was baptized. I assumed a new identity as the maid's son. We appeared to be a typical Catholic mother and child.

Finally, the war ended. Thankfully, my parents survived and were reunited. They came to claim me. Imagine their consternation when they found their beloved child had become, to all intents and purposes, a Catholic whom their former maid refused to relinquish.

It is a phenomenon, I believe, which affects many adoptive parents. After all that we had shared, she felt that she was my true mother. Moreover, I had been baptized and was now Catholic. Being a devout believer, she was not about to give me back to people who would rear me as a Jew.

My parents were determined not to abandon me. They were strengthened in their resolve by the memory of the 14 members of their family lost in the Holocaust. The maid was adamant. They felt that they had only one recourse: the courts.

Their suit became a famous case, the first of its kind in postwar Eastern Europe. Eventually, the court returned me to my parents, and that is why I am an observant Jew today and not a Catholic.

My experience, however, provided me with an insight into the plight of children who were hidden and raised as Catholics and today live a paradox—at one and the same time—Jew and Catholic, or perhaps neither.

Despite the maid's reluctance to return me, my parents remained grateful to her for saving my life. They voluntarily assumed the responsibility of ensuring that she would never be in want, considering it a matter of principle, a burden of honor.

What about other rescuers? How can we as a community repay them?

One particular group found the answer by establishing the Jewish Foundation for Christian Rescuers to search out these brave people and provide them with whatever help they need.

It is a mission that the Anti-Defamation League heartily endorses. In 1987, the League offered the infant organization a home with office space and ADL resources.

The Foundation has been growing ever since, providing individual rescuers with funds, medical supplies, and the knowledge that a grateful Jewish community had not forgotten them. Currently, the Foundation helps more than 1,000 rescuers.

The validity of each recipient's claim is thoroughly investigated by the Department of the Righteous Among the Nations at Israel's Yad Vashem.

The burden on the Foundation has substantially increased with the addition of newly discovered rescuers from the former Soviet Union. The insertion of one notice by JFCR/ADL in a popular Soviet magazine brought more than 700 replies with photographs and touching stories.

Recognizing that its efforts to help the growing number of rescuers depends upon an informed constituency, the Foundation has embarked upon a major program of education and interpretation that complements the ADL Braun Center for Holocaust Studies, the Hidden Child Foundation/ADL, and other ADL programs and activities in the overall fight against antisemitism.

Two successful national conferences on the rescuers and the Holocaust have been held, one at Princeton University and the other in Marin County, California. In their aftermath, six resource guides for educational purposes will be published.

Also being issued are several informative books and videos and a quarterly newsletter. The Foundation is looking forward to an international conference in Poland on rescuers.

To the Foundation and to ADL's leaders, the rescuers are not simply recipients of philanthropy but an important human resource of special significance and value to the Jewish people at this time of resurgent antisemitism and pseudo-scholarly revisionists who deny the very existence of the Holocaust. Like Holocaust survivors, rescuers are witnesses who can give personal testimony. They did more than see. They saved Jewish lives otherwise doomed to extinction. As non-Jews, their testimony is priceless as living refutation of the revisionists' denials.

It is almost a half-century since the killing stopped. In that span of time, the memory of the Holocaust has dimmed and a new generation of haters and bigots has emerged.

But we have not forgotten . . . and we have not forgotten those who stood beside us and risked their lives to save Jews. Now some of them need our help. Life had not necessarily been kind to them. Age had made them dependent. Many are needy, hungry, and ill.

They need our help as once we needed theirs.

They did not fail us.

To fail them would be unconscionable.

And so, with the help of Jews everywhere we will not fail.

It is a burden of honor.

Abraham H. Foxman
National Director,
Anti-Defamation League of B'nai Brith

Appendix
Some Reasons for Helping Jews

Religious Reasons

Once or twice in my life God has called me, and I have been there and responded to the call. . . . Across the horrors [of the Holocaust] I thank Providence for making it possible for me to obey the commandment in Deuteronomy to love one's neighbor, a precious heritage of the election of Israel.

Olga St. Blancat-Baumgartner, France

The law [under which the Jews are being imprisoned] is immoral, and one is not permitted to ignore such laws, but must actively resist them. There is no doubt in my mind that this is such a law, and such a time.

What I did for the Jewish people . . . was but an infinitesimal contribution to what ought to have been done in order to prevent this horrible slaughter, unprecedented and satanic, of more than six million Jews, which will undoubtedly remain the foulest stain in all of human history, a shame affecting all who participated or who allowed it to happen. They wanted to exterminate the Jewish people. But the Jewish people will not be exterminated. By divine decree, the Jewish people is determined to live and to fulfill its providential goals, for its own good, and finally for the good of all mankind.

Father Marie-Benoît, France

I was only a vessel through which the Lord's purpose was fulfilled. I know that when I stand before God on Judgment Day, I shall not be asked the question posed to Cain—where were you when your brother's blood was crying out to God?

Imre Bathory, Hungary

They were God's children, they were human beings. . . . I felt the hand of God leading me onward. Those countless refugees needed the help of a compassionate friend. They needed to see some sign of God's love amid the torment and terror of this awful war.

John H. Weidner, Netherlands

God gives us life as a precious loan. No one but God has the right to reclaim it. That's all I know. The rest is unimportant.

Eduard Fajks, Poland

We felt privileged to play a part in doing something to defy the powers of darkness. . . . As Christians we love all people, but the Jews, who are scripturally God's chosen people and are recognized by us as such, will always have a special place in our hearts and lives, as we were able to demonstrate during the German occupation of our country.

G. K. Van de Stadt, Netherlands

In the beginning we thought we were helping people in distress, and then we realized that it was they who were helping us, forcing us, through their presence . . . to abandon ourselves, our comforts and cowardice, our silence and complicity. Their   presence and suffering restored life's meaning for us, enabling us to discover the true meaning and basis of our selves; our encounter with the other saved us from the introverted egoism and callous isolation that constitute death in one of its worst forms. We thought we were going toward them, but in truth it was they who were coming toward us. They visited us, saved and liberated us . . . for they forced us to understand that 'the reasons for life are better than life itself.' . . . In every one of them, whoever he was, it was the Christ who came toward us, in the form of the rejected one, condemned and crucified. By loving them we received His love. When they invaded our homes and lives . . . , it was His mercy and joy that came into play. . . . On each occasion, as well, we knew afterwards that He had blessed us. All our defeats led us to the foot of the cross; all our victories, to the entrance of the empty tomb. Thus the presence of eternity, the expectation that the Kingdom will be inaugurated through His triumphal death, became our daily bread. In short, they expanded our horizons and gave our lives their true breadth.

Prof. Georges Casalis, France
(Les Clandestins du Dieu, pp. 203—204)

God gave me the spiritual strength to help a good many Jews by hiding them with farmers and later in city homes. I was very happy to have the privilege of doing something for God's people. . . . I am convinced that God has blessed us, and I apply to myself what the famous Artur Rubinstein said to an interviewer on Dutch radio, that he had met the world's happiest man and it was himself. I wrote him that I have the same feeling and consider myself no poorer than the richest man.

Gerrit Don, Netherlands

I did nothing but put into practice the values of Christianity and of love of one's fellow man.

Edouard Vigneron, France

The credit for what we did belongs to God, for it was He who filled our hearts with love for His persecuted people, making us see them as brothers and sisters, and protecting us from danger while we carried out the task He had entrusted to us. . . . By befriending these families we learned to love the Jewish people, the seed of Abraham, among whom our Christian roots originated, and also to love the State of Israel.

Pastor Charles Delizy, France

Actually, I should have written, "Do not use this story," because in the final reckoning, I was of no consequence in the affair. God wanted to save you, and neither you nor I knew it. Providence led you to us and then protected us so that no German could violate the boundaries of our domain, whereas the surrounding forests were relentlessly searched. . . . I was only an instrument of God's will. This required no merit, for we are all agents of the divine plan. We are all God's tenant farmers, and obeying His instructions is our primary duty. This is why the publicity about me is meaningless. . . . I believed in God's Providence and in heeding His voice. I obeyed Him. Unfortunately, times always erases the essential, and here the essential is the duty to appreciate God, who protected and saved us all.

Janusz Zwolakowski, France

Since I know that God arranged everything for us in advance, I don't like anyone to honor me. First and foremost, I thank God for making me what I am and granting me the privilege of helping the Jewish people—God's people.

Ludevit Kochol, Czechoslovakia

Performing One's Duty

It's like seeing someone drowning. You either stand on the side and don't do anything or you jump in and help. . . . It was something that had to be done.

Frederik Kabbes, Netherlands

I did nothing special and I don't consider myself a hero. I simply acted on my human obligation to the persecuted and suffering. I want to emphasize that it was not I who saved them. They alone saved themselves. I simply gave them a helping hand. . . . I sought no compensation for what I did . . . and in a way I am proud that while I was once rich, I am now destitute. To sum up, I should like to reiterate that I did no more than help forty-nine Jews to survive the Holocaust. That's all!

Wladyslaw Kowalski, Poland

My motivation for helping? Nothing in particular. Basically, I thought as follows: If my neighbor needs help and I can do something, then it is my duty and obligation [to do it]. If I discontinue my help, I fail to carry out the task which life—or perhaps God—requires of me. All people, I feel, constitute a single whole, and anyone who mistreats another person is slapping himself and everyone else in the face. This was my motivation.

Johanna Eck, Germany

She told me she had remembered the Bible. She had remembered that Abraham asked God whether He would spare Sodom if He found fifty good people there. And that God finally agreed to spare the city if He found only ten good people. She said it had looked so dark for all Europe that she felt it her duty to defend human dignity, to make sure that there would be a small opening left for life.

Interview with Leokadia Mikolajkov, Poland

We took this danger on ourselves because we felt it was our duty to help Jews in those difficult times.

Radovan and Rosa Djonovic,Yugoslavia

A Religious Duty

By helping Jews during the Second World War we were only doing our duty and putting into practice our Gospel and the teachings of the prophets, which are also ours. . . . The wonderful feeling that comes from having done something to rescue a family is our best reward.

Louisa Mercier, Belgium

I felt it was my duty. That's the way I was brought up. When someone is in need, you help them. . . . It was a Christian act done in Christian love. We felt it was our duty because they were God's people.

Henrietta Wiechertjes-Hartemink, Netherlands

I am someone who simply did her duty, nothing more. The duty of a human being toward fellow human beings condemned to agony and death by the murderous insanity of the Nazis. Seeing the martyrdom of your people made me honorably do my duty as a Frenchwoman and a Christian. . . . Seeing the suffering of a people whose civilization is so intimately bound up with ours encouraged me to actively pursue my duty as a Frenchwoman. . . . The duty of disobeying these inhuman laws was naturally accompanied by fear but also by a moral peace. Within the feeble limits of our means, we did everything we thought could be done in the interest and the respect of God's creatures.

Georgette Cheverry, France

A "Natural" Thing

What I did came naturally. It would have been unnatural not to do it.

Herta Muller-Kuhlenthal, Netherlands

We were doing what had to be done. . . . Things had to be done, that's all, and we happened to be there to do them. You must understand that helping these people was the most natural thing in the world. . . . Well, maybe it was unreasonable. But you know, I had to do it anyway.

Resident of Le Chambon, France

What my husband and I did in 1942 and 1943 to help and, where possible, to save Jews persecuted by the Nazis seems wholly natural to us. It would have been unthinkable to do anything else. That is why I am embarrassed about being given an award for doing what came naturally.

Gabrielle Remy, France

The Sanctity of Life

I was scared to death, like everyone else. But I made up my mind right then and there: If I can help, I will. . . . My mother always taught me that God made everyone the same; He doesn't care if they're Jews or not, because everyone has the right to live.

Mary Szul, Poland

No law in the world says that I should live and you die. The Nazis have decided that, but I am fighting against them and am not bound by their rules.

Stanislawa Ogrodzinska, Poland

Shame

We had to do it. Otherwise we would have been unable to show our faces.
Pastor Marc Donadille, France

We only did what was required of us as human beings. That was the least we could do if we were not to be ashamed of ourselves for the rest of our lives.
Pierre Mason, France

I ask you to remain with us for my sake, not yours. If you leave, I shall forever be ashamed to be a member of the human race.
Dr. Giovanni Pesante, Italy

When the Germans imprisoned the Jews of Vilna behind the walls of the ghetto I was unable to do my work [as a librarian]. I could not sit in my workroom, I could not eat; I was ashamed not to be Jewish. I felt I had to do something.
Ona Simaite, Lithuania

A Conscientious Act

I did what I did during the war because my conscience made me do it. It wasn't just to help the persecuted but because not doing anything would have diminished my spiritual freedom. I had to do it for myself in order to be free. Also, what I did took place with the cooperation of many others, and of course there were too many for all of them to be honored, and some of the bravest were killed during those years. So I cannot accept an award as an individual; I could not possibly have helped anyone on my own. For these reasons I cannot accept this high honor.
Elisabeth Nancy Van Steenhoven-Spaander , Netherlands

I have never asked for awards or medals for what I was able to do during the black night of the occupation. I only did my duty as my conscience dictated. My thinking was certainly that of a Righteous. The men and women I was able . . . to save from the concentration camp, death, and forced labor in Germany represented, for me, so many victories against an intolerable barbarism.
Georges Seurre, France

Suggestions for Further Reading

GENERAL WORKS ON THE HOLOCAUST

L. S. Dawidowciz, *The War Against the Jews 1933–1945* (New York, 1975).

A. Donat, *The Holocaust Kingdom* (New York, 1965).

M. Gilbert, *The Macmillan Atlas of the Holocaust* (New York, 1982).

Y. Gutman and L. Rothkirchen, eds, *The Catastrophe of European Jewry* (Jerusalem, 1976).

R. Hilberg, *The Destruction of the European Jews*, 3 vols. (New York, 1985).

N. Levin, *The Holocaust* (New York, 1973).

L. Poliakov, *Harvest of Hate* (New York, 1979).

E. Wiesel, *Night* (New York, 1960).

The short historical sketches at the beginning of each chapter are based on material from the preceding studies. For information on particular countries, the reader is advised to consult the relevant chapters in the *Encyclopedia of the Holocaust*, edited by Y. Gutman. The author has also found the following works to be quite useful.

FRANCE

M. R. Marrus and R. O. Paxton, *Vichy France and the Jews* (New York, 1981).

L. Poliakov, *L'Étoile Jaune* (Paris, 1949).

G. Wellers, *L'Étoile Jaune à l'Heure de Vichy* (Paris, 1973).

On the French Protestant churches:

E. M. Fabre, ed., *Les Clandestins de Dieu* (Paris, 1968).

P. Hallie, *Lest Innocent Blood be Shed* (New York, 1979), especially on Rev. André Trocme and the dramatic rescue of thousands of Jews in the Le Chambon area.

On the French Catholic Church:

P. Pierrard, *Juifs et Catholiques Français* (Paris, 1970), chap. 6.

On the rescue of children:
D. A. Lowrie, *The Hunted Children* (New York, 1963).
S. Zeitoun, *Ces Enfants Qu'il Fallait Sauver* (Paris, 1989).
Oeuvre de Secour aux Enfants. *L'OSE sous l'Occupation Allemande en France, 1940–1944* (Geneva, 1947).
On the Italian zone:
L. Poliakov and J. Sabille, *Jews Under the Italian Occupation* (New York, 1983).

BELGIUM

B. Garfinkels, *Les Belges face à la Persécution Raciale, 1940–1944* (Brussels, 1965).
L. Steinberg, *Le Comité de Défense des Juifs en Belgique, 1942–1944* (Brussels, 1973).

HOLLAND

On the German occupation:
L. De Jong and W. F. Stoppelman, *The Lion Rampant* (New York, 1943).
W. Warmbrunn, *The Dutch under German Occupation, 1940–45* (Stanford, Calif., 1963).
On the destruction of the Jewish community and life in hiding:
D. Barnouw and D. Van der Stroom, eds., *The Diary of Anne Frank: The Critical Edition* (New York, 1989).
J. Presser, *The Destruction of the Dutch Jews* (New York, 1969).
Leesha Rose, *The Tulips Are Red* (New York, 1978).
L. Yahil, "Methods of Persecution," *Studies in History* 23 (1972): 279–300.

GERMANY

On the Nazi state and the churches:
P. Friedman, "Was There an 'Other Germany' During the Nazi Period?" in *Roads to Extinction: Essays on the Holocaust* (New York, 1980).
L. Guenter, *The Catholic Church and Nazi Germany* (New York, 1964).
On help to Jews by individual non-Jews:
E. Boehm, *We Survived* (New Haven, 1949).
I. Deutschkron, *Ich Trug den Gelben Stern* (Cologne, 1978).
L. Gross, *The Last Jews in Berlin* (New York, 1982).
K. Grossman, *Die Unbesungenen Helden* (Berlin, 1961).
M. Krakauer, *Lichter im Dunkel* (Stuttgart, 1980).
H. Leuner, *When Compassion Was a Crime* (London, 1966).

POLAND

On Nazi plans for the dismemberment of Poland and its eventual incorporation into Greater Germany, the enslavement of its populace, and life for Poles under the occupation:
J. T. Gross, *Polish Society Under German Occupation* (Princeton, 1979), pp. 79, 83, 166.

J. Gumkowski and K. Leszczynski, *Poland Under Nazi Occupation* (Warsaw, 1961), pp. 12–15, 17, 20, 26, 28, 31.

I. Kamenetsky, *Secret Nazi Plans for East Europe* (New York, 1961), pp. 142–43, 135.

R. L. Koehl, *RKFDV: German Resettlement and Population Policy, 1939–1945* (Cambridge, Mass., 1957), pp. 65, 122, 142–45, 184, 199, 213.

C. Madajczyk, "Generalplan Ost," *Polish Western Affairs* 3, no. 2 (Poznan, 1962): 4, 6.

S. Piotrowski, *Hans Frank's Diary* (Warsaw, 1961), pp. 45–46, 87, 95–96.

On Jewish-Polish relations before the war:

C. S. Heller, *On the Edge of Destruction* (New York, 1977), p. 3.

On Jewish-Polish relations during the war:

J. Karski, *Story of a Secret State* (Boston, 1944), pp. 321–22 (on his dramatic encounter with leaders of Warsaw ghetto).

Z. Kubar, *Double Identity* (New York, 1989), pp. 14, 88, 23–25, 125, 131–32, 160–63, 172.

I. Gutman nd S. Krakowski, *Unequal Victims* (New York, 1989).

E. Ringelblum, *Polish-Jewish Relations* (Jerusalem, 1974), p. 6 (n. 13), 10, 11–12 (n. 2), 37, 123–28, 184–85, 217 (n. 32), 224–25, 303–4, 308, 310, 314–15.

N. Tec, *Dry Tears*. (Westport, Conn., 1982), pp. 72–73, 121–22, 129, 143–44, 214, 231.

For a contrasting opinion:

K. Iranek-Osmecki, *He Who Saves One Life* (New York, 1971), pp. 254–55, 260–61, 264–65, 269–77.

On Nazi threats against helping Jews:

W. Bartoszewski and Z. Lewin, *The Righteous Among the Nations* (London, 1969), pp. 632, 634, 639, 642–43. (This book represents a monumental effort to record every rescue that took place in Poland; not all of the Polish rescuers listed in it are on Yad Vashem's register of the Righteous Among the Nations.)

On the Polish underground:

S. Korbonski, *The Polish Underground State* (New York, 1978).

On Zegota:

J. Kermish, in *Rescue Attempts During the Holocaust* (New York, 1978), pp. 367–98.

UKRAINE

P. Friedman, "Ukrainian-Jewish Relations During the Nazi Occupation," in *Roads to Extinction* (New York, 1980), pp. 176–208.

LITHUANIA

Y. Arad, *Ghetto in Flames* (Jerusalem, 1980) (on the destruction of the Vilna ghetto).

S. Neshamit, "Rescue in Lithuania During the Nazi Occupation," in *Rescue Attempts During the Holocaust* (New York, 1978), pp. 289–331.

HUNGARY

P. Anger, *With Raoul Wallenberg in Budapest* (New York, 1981).

J. R. L. Braham, *The Politics of Genocide: The Holocaust in Hungary*, 2 vols. (New York, 1981).

E. Levai, *Black Book on the Martyrdom of Hungarian Jewry* (Zurich, 1948).

ITALY

The most authoritative English-language study on the Holocaust in Italy is:

S. Zuccotti, *The Italians and the Holocaust* (New York, 1987).

On help by Italians outside Italy:

D. Carpi, "The Rescue of Jews in the Italian Zone of Occupied Croatia," in *Rescue Attempts During the Holocaust* (New York, 1978), pp. 465–525.

I. Herzer, "How Italians Rescued Jews," *Midstream*, June–July 1983, pp. 35–38.

L. Poliakov and J. Sabille, *Jews Under the Italian Occupation* (New York, 1983).

See also:

M. Briskin, "Rescue Italian Style," *Jewish Monthly* 100, no. 9 (May 1986), pp. 20–25

DENMARK

L. Yahil, *The Rescue of Danish Jewry* (Philadelphia, 1969).

* * *

Two important studies on the motives of those who rescued Jews are:

S. Oliner and P. Oliner, *The Altruistic Personality* (New York, 1988).

N. Tec, *When Light Pierced the Darkness* (New York, 1986).

* * *

See the Bibliography for a more complete listing of works relevant to the subject of this book.

Selected Bibliography

Ancel, J. "Plans for Deportation of the Rumanian Jews." *Yad Vashem Studies*16 (1984): 381-420.

Anger, P. *With Raoul Wallenberg in Budapest: Memories of the War Years in Hungary.* Translated by D. M. Paul and M. Paul. New York: Holocaust Library, 1981.

Arad, Y. *Ghetto in Flames.* Jerusalem: Yad Vashem, 1980.

Arad, Y., Y. Gutman, and A. Margaliot, eds. *Documents on the Holocaust.* Jerusalem: Yad Vashem, 1981.

Barnouw, D., and G. Van der Stroom. *The Diary of Anne Frank: The Critical Edition.* New York: Doubleday, 1969.

Bartoszewski, W., and Z. Lewin. *The Righteous Among the Nations: How Poles Saved Jews.* London: Earls Court, 1969.

Bauminger, A. *The Righteous.* Jerusalem: Yad Vashem, 1983.

Bejski, M. "The 'Righteous Among the Nations' and Their Part in the Rescue of Jews." In *Rescue Attempts During the Holocaust: Proceedings of the Second Yad Vashem International Historical Conference, Jerusalem, 8-11 April, 1974,* pp. 627-647. New York: Ktav Publishing House, 1978.

Berenstein, T., and A. Rutkowski. *Assistance to the Jews in Poland (1939-1945).* Warsaw: Polonia Foreign Languages Publishing House, 1963.

Berman, A. "The Fate of the Children in the Warsaw Ghetto." In *The Catastrophe of European Jewry,* edited by Y. Gutman and L. Rothkirchen, pp. 400-421. Jerusalem: Yad Vashem, 1976.

Bierman, J. *Righteous Gentile: The Story of Raoul Wallenberg.* New York: Viking, 1981.

Block, G. and Drucker, M. *Rescuers: Portrait of Moral Courage in the Holocaust.* New York: Holmes & Meier, 1992.

Blond, S. *The Righteous Gentiles.* Tel Aviv: S. Blond, 1983.

Boehm, E. H. *We Survived: The Stories of Fourteen of the Hidden and the Hunted of Nazi Germany.* New Haven: Yale University Press, 1949.

Borwicz, M. *Les Vies Interdites* [Forbidden lives]. Paris: Casterman, 1969.

Braham, R. L. *The Politics of Genocide: The Holocaust in Hungary.* 2 vols. New York: Columbia University Press, 1981.

Carpi, D. "The Rescue of Jews in the Italian Zone of Occupied Croatia." In *Rescue Attempts During the Holocaust: Proceedings of the Second Yad Vashem International Historical Conference, Jerusalem, 8-11 April, 1974,* pp. 465-525. New York: Ktav Publishing House, 1978.

Chary, F. B. *Bulgarian Jewry and the Final Solution, 1940-1944.* Pittsburgh: University of Pittsburgh Press, 1972.

Dawidowicz, L. S. *The War Against the Jews, 1933-1945.* New York: Holt, Rinehart & Winston, 1975.

De Jong, L. "Help to People in Hiding." *Delta: A Review of Arts, Life and Thought in the Netherlands* 8, no. 19 (Spring 1965): 37-79.

———. "The Netherlands and Auschwitz: Why Were the Reports of Mass Killings So Widely Disbelieved?" In *Imposed Jewish Governing Bodies Under Nazi Rule,* pp. 11-30. YIVO Colloquium, December 1967.

Deutschkron, I. *Ich Trug den gelben Stern* [I wore the yellow star]. Cologne: Wissenshcaft und Politik, 1978.

Donat, A. *The Holocaust Kingdom: A Memoir.* New York: Holt, Rinehart & Winston. 1965.

Ehrenburg, I., and V. Grossman, eds. *The Black Book of Soviet Jewry.* New York: Holocaust Library, 1980.

Fabre, E. *Les Clandestins de Dieu: CIMADE 1939-1945.* Paris: Fayard, 1968.

Feingold, H. *The Politics of Rescue: The Roosevelt Administration and the Holocaust, 1938-1945.* New York: Holocaust Library, 1981.

Fleischner, E., ed. *Auschwitz: Beginning of a New Era?* New York: Ktav Publishing House, 1977.

Fogelman, E., and V. L. Wiener. "The Few, the Brave, the Noble."*Psychology Today* 19, no. 8 (August 1985): 60-65.

Ford, H. *Flee the Captor.* Nashville: Southern Publishing Association, 1966.

Frank, A. *The Diary of a Young Girl.* Garden City, N.Y.: Doubleday, 1967.

Friedman, A. J., ed. *Roads to Extinction: Essays on the Holocaust.* Philadelphia: Jewish Publication Society, 1980.

Friedman, P. "Righteous Gentiles in the Nazi Era." In *Roads to Extinction: Essays on the Holocaust,* edited by A. J. Friedman, pp. 409-421. Philadelphia: Jewish Publication Society, 1980.

———. Their Brothers' Keepers. New York: Holocaust Library, 1978.

———. "Ukrainian-Jewish Relations During the Nazi Occupation."*YIVO Annual of Jewish Social Science* 7 (1958-59): 259-296.

Garfinkels, B. *Les Belges Face à la Persécution Raciale, 1940-1944.* Brussels: Université Libre, 1965.

Gilbert, M. *Auschwitz and the Allies: A Devastating Account of How the Allies,Responded to the News of Hitler's Mass Murder*. New York: Holt, Rinehart & Winston, 1981.

——. *The Macmillan Atlas of the Holocaust*. New York: Macmillan, 1982.

Goldstein, B. *Five Years in the Warsaw Ghetto*. Garden City, N.Y.: Doubleday, 1961.

Gross, L. *The Last Jews in Berlin*. New York: Simon & Schuster, 1982.

Grossman, K. *Die unbesungenen Helden* [The unsung heroes]. Berlin-Grunewald: Arani Verlag, 1961.

Guenter, L. *The Catholic Church and Nazi Germany*. New York: McGraw-Hill, 1964.

Gutman, Y. *The Jews of Warsaw, 1939-1943: Ghetto, Underground, Revolt*. Translated by I. Friedman. Bloomington: Indiana University Press, 1982.

——, ed. *Encyclopedia of the Holocaust*. 4 vols. New York: Macmillan, 1990.

—— and S. Krakowski. *Unequal Victims: Poles and Jews During World II*. New York: Holocaust Library, 1986.

—— and L. Rothkirchen, eds. *The Catastrophe of European Jewry*. Jerusalem: Yad Vashem, 1976.

—— and E. Zuroff, eds. *Rescue Attempts During the Holocaust: Proceedings of the Second Yad Vashem International Historical Conference, Jerusalem, 8-11 April 1974*. New York: Ktav Publishing House, 1974.

Hackel, S. *Pearl of Great Price: The Life of Mother Maria Skobtsova, 1891-1945*. London: Darton, Longman & Todd, 1981.

Haesler, A. *The Lifeboat Is Full: Switzerland and the Refugees, 1933-1945*. New York: Funk & Wagnalls, 1969.

Hallie, P. *Lest Innocent Blood Be Shed: The Story of Le Chambon and How Goodness Happened There*. New York: Harper & Row, 1979.

Heller, C. S. *On the Edge of Destruction: Jews of Poland Between the Two World Wars*. New York: Schocken Books, 1980.

Hellman, P. *Avenue of the Righteous*. New York: Bantam Books, 1981.

Herzer, I. "How Italians Rescued Jews." *Midstream*, June-July 1983, pp. 35-38.

Hilberg, R. *The Destruction of the European Jews*. 3 vols. New York: Holmes & Meier, 1985.

Horbach, M. *Out of the Night*. New York: Frederick Fell, 1967.

Huneke, D. *The Moses of Rovno*. New York: Dodd, Mead, 1985.

——. "A Study of Christians Who Rescued Jews During the Nazi Era." *Humboldt Journal of Social Relations* 9, no. 1 (1981-82): 144-150.

Im Hof-Piguet, A.-M. *La Filiere: En France Occupée, 1942-1944* [The network: In occupied France]. Yverdon-les-Bains, Switzerland: Edition de la Thiele, 1985.

Joutard, C., C. Poujol, and P. Cabanel. *Cévennes: Terre de Refuge (1940-1944)* [Cévennes: Land of refuge]. Club Cévenol: Presses du Languedoc, 1987.

Kamenetsky, I. *Secret Nazi Plans for Eastern Europe: A Study of Lebensraum Policies*. New Haven: College and University Press, 1961.

Karski, J. *Story of a Secret State*. Boston: Houghton Mifflin, 1944.

Keim, A. M. *Yad Vashem: Die Judenretter aus Deutschland*. Mainz: Matthias-Grunerwald Verlag, 1983.

Keneally, T. *Schindler's List*. New York: Simon & Schuster, 1982.

Kermish, J. "The Activities of the Council of Aid to Jews ('Zegota') in Occupied Poland." In *Rescue Attempts During the Holocaust: Proceedings of the Second Yad Vashem International Historical Conference, 8-11 April 1974*, pp. 367-398. New York: Ktav Publishing House, 1978.

Klarsfeld, S. *Memorial to the Jews Deported from France, 1942-1944*. New York: Beate Klarsfeld Foundation, 1983.

Krakauer, M. *Lichter im Dunkel*. Stuttgart: Quellverlag, 1980.

Krantz, M. *Hitler's Death March: A Survivor's Story*. New York: Zebra Books, 1978.

Krausnick, H., and M. Broszat. *Anatomy of the SS-State*. New York: Walter & Co., 1968.

Kubar, Z. *Double Identity: A Memoir*. New York: Hill & Wang, 1989.

Kugler, V. "The Reminiscences of Victor Kugler, the 'Mr. Kraler' of Anne Frank's Diary." *Yad Vashem Studies* 13 (1979): 353-385.

Kulka, O. D., and P. R. Mendes-Flohr, eds. *Judaism and Christianity Under the Impact of National Socialism*. Jerusalem: Historical Society amd Zalman Shazar Center for Jewish History, 1987.

Kunze. P. *Dorothea Neff: Mut zum Leben* [Courage to live]. Vienna: ORAC / Pietsch, 1983.

Laqueur W., and R. Breitman. *Breaking the Silence: The Secret Mission of Eduard Schulte, Who Brought the World News of the Final Solution*. London: Bodley Head, 1986.

Latour, A. *The Jewish Resistance in France, 1940-1944*. Translated by I. R. Ilton. New York: Holocaust Library, 1981.

Lazare, L. *La Résistance Juive en France*. Paris: Stock, 1987.

Leboucher, F. *The Incredible Mission of Father Benoît*. Translated by J. F. Bernard. Garden City, N.Y.: Doubleday, 1969.

Leuner, H. D. *When Compassion Was a Crime: Germany's Silent Heroes, 1933-1945*. London: Oswald Wolf, 1966.

Levin, N. *The Holocaust: The Destruction of European Jewry, 1933-1945*. New York: Schocken Books, 1973.

Littell, F. H. *The Crucifixion of the Jews*. New York: Harper & Row, 1974.

—— and H. G. Locke, eds. *The German Church Struggle and the Holocaust*. Detroit: Wayne State University Press, 1974.

London, P. "The Rescuers: Motivational Hypotheses About Christians Who Saved Jews from the Nazis." In *Altruism and Helping Behavior*, edited by J. R. Macaulay and L. Berkowitz, pp. 241-250. New York: Academic Press, 1970.

Lowrie, D. A. *The Hunted Children: The Dramatic Story of the Heroic Men and Women Who Outwitted the Nazis to Save Thousands of Helpless Refugees in Southern France During World War II.* New York: Norton, 1963.

Marrus, M. R., and R. O. Paxton. *Vichy France and the Jews.* New York: Schocken Books, 1981.

Michaelis, M. *Mussolini and the Jews: German-Italian Relations and the Jewish Question in Italy, 1922-1945.* New York: Oxford University Press, 1978.

Midlarsky, M. I. "Helping During the Holocaust: The Role of Political, Theological and Socioeconomic Identifications."*Humboldt Journal of Social Relations* 13, nos. 1-2 (1985-86): 285-305.

Midlarsky, E., and L. Baron, eds. *Altruism and Prosocial Behavior.* Special issue of *Humboldt Journal of Social Relations* 13, nos. 1-2 (1985-86). Atara, Calif.: 1986.

Morley, J. F. *Vatican Diplomacy and the Jews During the Holocaust, 1933-1943.* New York: Ktav Publishing House, 1980.

Morse, A. D. *While Six Million Died: A Chronicle of American Apathy.* New York: Random House, 1967.

Neshamit, S. "Rescue in Lithuania During the Nazi Occupation." In *Rescue Attempts During the Holocaust: Proceedings of the Second International Yad Vashem International Historical Conference*, 8-11 April 1974, pp. 289-331. New York: Ktav Publishing House, 1978.

Oliner, S. P., and P. M. Oliner. *The Altruistic Personality: Rescuers of Jews in Nazi Europe.* New York: Free Press, 1988.

Paldiel, M. "Hesed and the Holocaust." *Journal of Ecumenical Studies* 23, no. 1 (Winter 1986): 90-106.

———. "Radical Altruism: Three Case Studies." *Midstream* 33 (April 1987): 35-39.

———. "Sparks of Light." *In Faith & Freedom: A Tribute to Franklin H. Littell*, edited Libowitz, pp. 45-69. Oxford: Pergamon Press, 1987.

———. "The Altruism of the Righteous Gentiles."*Holocaust & Genocide Studies* 3, no. 2 (1988): 187-196.

———. "To the Righteous Among the Nations Who Risked Their Lives to Rescue Jews." *Yad Vashem Studies* 19 (1968): 403-425.

———. Articles in *Encyclopedia of the Holocaust*, edited by Y. Gutman. 4 vols. New York: Macmillan, 1990 (s.v. Abegg, E.; Andre, J.; Baublys, P.; Beccari, A.; Benoit, M.; Binkiene, S.; Bogaard, F.; Borkowska, A.; Choms, W.; Deffaugt, J.; Douwes, A.; Evert, A.; Getter, M.; Gruninger, P.; Hautval, A.; Helmrich, E.; Kowalski, W.; Le Chambon sur Lignon; Lipke, J.; Lutz, C.; N.V. Group; Nevejean, Y.; Nicolini, G.; Overduijn, L.; Schindler, O.; Schmid, A.; Sendler, I.; Simaite, O.; Skobtsova, E.; Sousa Mendes, A.; Sugihara, S.; Sztehlo, G.; Van der Voort, H.; Zabinski, J.).

Petrow, R. *The Bitter Years: The Invasion and Occupation of Denmark and Norway, April 1940-May 1945*. New York: Morrow, 1974.

Pinkus. O. *The House of Ashes*. Cleveland: World Publishing Co., 1964.

Poliakov, L. *Harvest of Hate*. New York: Holocaust Library, 1979.

—— and J. Sabille. *Jews Under the Italian Occupation*. New York: Howard Fertig, 1983.

Prekerowa, T. *Konspiracyjna Rada Pomocy Zydom w Warszawie, 1942-45* [Clandestine aid to Jews by Zegota in Warsaw]. Warsaw: Panstwowy Instytut Wydawniczy, 1982.

Presser, J. *The Destruction of the Dutch Jews*. New York: Dutton, 1969.

Ramati, A. *The Assisi Underground: The Priests Who Rescued Jews*. New York: Stein & Day, 1978.

Reiss, J. *The Upstairs Room*. New York: Thomas Y. Crowell, 1972.

Ringelblum, E. *Polish-Jewish Relations During the Second World War*. Edited by J. Kermish and S. Krakowski. New York: Howard Fertig, 1976.

Rittner, C., and S. Myers, eds. *The Courage to Care*. New York: New York University Press, 1986.

Rorty, J. "Father Benoit." *Commentary* 2, no. 6 (December 1946): 507-513.

Rose, L. *The Tulips Are Red*. New York: A. S. Barnes, 1978.

Rosen, D. *The Forest My Friend*. Translated by M. S. Chertoff. New York: World Federation of Bergen-Belsen Associations, 1971.

Rothkirchen, L. "Czech Attitudes Towards the Jews During the Nazi Regime." *Yad Vashem Studies* 13 (1979): 287-320.

Sauvage, P. "Ten Things I Would Like to Know About Righteous Conduct in Le Chambon and Elsewhere During the Holocaust."*Humboldt Journal of Social Relations* 13, nos. 1-2 (1985-86): 252-259.

Shirer, W. L. *The Rise and Fall of the Third Reich*. New York: Simon & Schuster, 1960.

Silver, E. *The Book of the Just*. New York: Weidenfeld & Nicolson, 1992.

Steinberg, L. *Le Comité de Défense des Juifs en Belgique, 1942-1944* [The Jewish Defense Committee in Belgium]. Brussels 1973.

Szonyi, D. M. *The Holocaust: An Annotated Bibliography and Resource Guide*. New York: National Jewish Resource Center, 1985.

Tec, N. *Dry Tears: The Story of a Lost Childhood*. New York: Oxford University Press, 1984.

——. *When Light Pierced the Darkness: Christian Rescue of Jews in Nazi-Occupied Poland*. New York: Oxford University Press, 1986.

Ten Boom, C. *The Hiding Place*. London: Hodder & Stoughton, 1971.

Thomas, G., and M. Witts. *Voyage of the Damned*. New York: Stein & Day, 1974.

Warhaftig, Z. *Refugee and Survivor: Rescue Efforts During the Holocaust*. Translated by A. Tomaschoff. Jerusalem: Yad Vashem, 1988.

Warmbrunn, W. *The Dutch Under German Occupation, 1940-1945*. Stanford, Calif.: Stanford University Press, 1979.

Wells, L. *The Janowska Road*. New York: Macmillan, 1963.

Wiesel, E. *Night*. New York: Hill & Wang, 1960.

Wundheiler, L. N. "Oskar Schindler's Moral Development During the Holocaust." *Humboldt Journal of Social Relations* 13, nos. 1-2 (1985-86): 333-356.

Yahil, L. *The Rescue of Danish Jewry: Test of a Democracy*. Translated by M. Gradel. Philadelphia: Jewish Publication Society, 1969.

Zeitoun, S. *Ces Enfants Qu'il Fallait Sauver*. Paris: Albin Michel, 1989.

Zuccotti, S. *The Italians and the Holocaust: Persecution, Rescue, and Survival*. New York: Basic Books, 1987.

Zuker-Bujanowska, L. *Liliana's Journal: Warsaw 1939-1945*. London: J. Piatkus, 1981.

Index

DATE DUE

JUN 0 9 1994		
DEC 1 2 1994		
MAR 1 2 1997		
MAR 2 9 2000		
OCT 2 7 2000		
NOV 2 8 2007		